Hunger 1992

Second Annual Report on the State of World Hunger

Ideas That Work

Bread for the World
INSTITUTE
On Hunger &
Development

802 Rhode Island Avenue, N.E.
Washington, DC 20018, USA

Bread for the World Institute on Hunger & Development

President
David Beckmann

President Emeritus
Arthur Simon

Director
Don Reeves

Editors

Marc J. Cohen
Director of Research

Richard A. Hoehn
Senior Research Associate

Copy Editor
Carole Zimmerman

Art Director
Timothy Achor-Hoch

Publicity Director
Kraig Klaudt

Tables by LaDonna Mason

Printer: Art Litho, Baltimore, Md.
Cover photo: NASA
Manufactured in the United States of America

First edition published October 1991

ISBN 0-9628058-3-1

Table of Contents

Tables and Graphs..4
Preface 5
Acknowledgements...6
Introduction. 7

Ideas That Work

Food Bank Networks Respond
    to U.S. Hunger Crisis by Barbara Murock............12
    The Hartford Food Experience
    by Richard A. Hoehn...16
    Federal Domestic Assistance Programs................18
Food Aid That Is Not a Band Aid
    by Marc J. Cohen 22
    How Not to Use Food Aid: The Case of Egypt........28
    Changes in U.S. Food Aid Legislation. 30
Saving Trees Without Sacrificing People
    by Patricia L. Kutzner 32
    The World Bank and the Environment
    by Marc J. Cohen 38
Green Revolution Reduces Hunger in India
    by John W. Mellor...42
    Equity, Ecology, and Alternative
    Agricultural Technologies
    by Don Reeves & Marc J. Cohen 44
Demilitarization Fosters Justice
    by Richard A. Hoehn
    Part One: Costa Rica 50
    Part Two: Global Demilitarization 58
Economic Policies Diminish Hunger in Indonesia
    by David Beckmann..64
    Adjustment in Africa 68
    by Patience Elabor-Idemudia
    Economic Crisis in Nigeria 70
    by Patience Elabor-Idemudia
Refugees Rebuild Their Villages in El Salvador
    by Ana E. Avilés...74
People Organize for Water and Jobs in
    Tanzania and Saint Louis by Maria Simon..........82
    Jobs for Your Community
    by Kathleen Crowley, CSJ 84
    Grassroots Partnerships 91
IAF Builds Political Clout in Texas
    by Richard A. Hoehn...92

The Power of Confrontation
    by Richard A. Hoehn...94
Citizen Advocacy Changes National Hunger Policies
    by Marc J. Cohen 100
    WIC at a Glance 101
    Who's Who: Hunger Advocacy Groups...............102
    Arthur Simon: Twenty years in the Movement.....106

Regional Updates

Africa by Gayle Smith 110
Asia and the Pacific by Marc J. Cohen 118
    Laos: Wrestling with Change
    by Marc J. Cohen 120
    Hunger, Inequality, and Conflict in Sri Lanka
    by Rapti Goonesekere 124
Latin America
    by Ana E. Avilés and Maria Simon 128
    North American Free Trade Agreement
    by Barbara Segal 130
    Peru 'Hambre' by Maria Simon 137
Middle East
    by Rapti Goonesekere 142
    Upholding the Right to Food in a
    "New World Order" by Marc J. Cohen.................144
North America
    Canada by Jennifer Kennedy.............................152
    Native Peoples by Jennifer Kennedy....................155
    United States by Richard A. Hoehn 157
    Hunger Bytes by Richard A. Hoehn....................162
Soviet Union and Eastern Europe
    by Remy Jurenas 166

Appendix

Tables...178
Sources for Tables...194
Abbreviations and Glossary 196
Sources and Bibliography 198
Index 210
About the Writers..215
Sponsors..216
Publications Order Form

Tables and Graphs

Text

Food Bank Networks..14

    Number of Food Banks

    Millions of Pounds of Food Distributed

    Number of Agencies

Total U.S. Population in Poverty...15

Arms and Food, United States...18

World Food Aid...23

    World Food Aid by Category of Use

    Sources of World Cereal Food Aid

    Recipients of World Cereal Food Aid

PL 480 Assistance to Egypt...29

Three Neighbors: Costa Rica, Nicaragua, Panama 56

Economic Factors: Costa Rica, Nicaragua, Panama..........................57

Military Expenditures for Armed Forces 59

Military Expenditures: United States and Soviet Union 59

Military Expenditures: Ten Highest Countries...................................60

Arms Transfer Deliveries 61

Ten Top Quality of Life Countries 62

Indonesia: Declining Poverty 65

Indonesia: Declining Infant Mortality 66

Iraq's Food Imports..143

Human Effects of the Gulf Crisis...148

Education Levels of Toronto Food Bank Recipients.........................154

Public Policy vs. Private Voluntary Solutions to Hunger.................155

Food Security Among Native Americans 157

America's Children 159

U.S. Median Income, 1989..160

Changes in Family Income and Tax Rates (U.S.)..............................161

Appendix

Table 1: Demographic Indicators..178

Table 2: Health and Nutrition 1980-89 180

Table 3: Human Welfare Indicators – Urban/Rural 182

Table 4: Economic Indicators..184

Table 5: Demographic Indicators – Small Countries 186

Table 6: Health and Nutrition – Small Countries 187

Table 7: Economic Indicators – Small Countries 188

Table 8: Income Distribution...189

Table 9: Change in Real Minimum Wages 190

Table 10: United States – Trends in Poverty 191

Table 11: United States – Conditions of Poverty..............................192

Preface

*H*unger 1992 details the alarming growth of hunger in the United States and throughout the world. The essays on "ideas that work" provide hope and help for next steps to mitigate hunger.

During my years with Lutheran World Relief and the World Bank, I have observed the struggles of people in the developing world. Here in Washington, D.C., I see the faces of poor and hungry people on my way to work every day.

But far and wide I have also witnessed the efforts of people of conscience who are called to join the movement to end hunger. In particular, I am grateful to Arthur Simon, President Emeritus of Bread for the World and the Institute.

Hunger 1992 describes projects in which people have risen up to solve local hunger problems – food banks, food pantries, soup kitchens, water projects, repopulation efforts, job creation, political organizing. *Hunger 1992* also shows the need for governmental policies that are humane and just. The combination of individual, private, and collective public efforts is the way we must work together to solve world hunger.

The wars in the Persian Gulf, Ethiopia, Mozambique, Angola, and Cambodia reminded us this past year of the effects of militarization and arms sales on poor people; confronted us with vivid images of the desperate needs of refugees; and showed us what can happen when food is used as a weapon. Essays in the report detail things we have learned about the relationships between the environment, economic policies, the uses of technology, food aid, and hunger.

There is hope. We can make a difference. Our combined moral vision and practical action can eliminate mass hunger in our lifetime. I pledge the resources of Bread for the World and the Institute toward this end.

– David Beckmann
Washington, D.C.
October 16, 1991

Acknowledgements

We are deeply grateful to everyone who has so graciously assisted in the creation of this report. The following people reviewed the full manuscript: Nancy Aadland, David Beckmann, Marie Bledsoe, Betsy Bumgarner, David Fouse, Tom Getman, Chuck Hassebrook, Patricia L. Kutzner, Hershey Leaman, Martin McLaughlin, Maria Otero, Arthur Simon, William Whitaker, Jayne Wood.

These individuals reviewed parts of the manuscript: Stephen Acree, George B.N. Ayittey, Emily Bauermeister, Carolyn Bay, Kim Bobo, Bill Bolling, John Burstein, Claudia Camp, Eliza Carney, John Clark, Peggy Comfrey, Kathleen Crowley, Cindy Darcy, Barry Davidson, Alan Durning, Beatrice Edwards, Rick Emrich, Hannan Ezekiel, Ruth Flower, V. Kimble Forrister, Karen Funk, Marito Garcia, Robert Goodland, Ken Gray, Diane M. de Guzman, Gretchen Hall, Ann Hardison, Sam Harris, Pharis J. Harvey, Stefan Harvey, Doug Hellinger, Martha Honey, Barbara Howell, Patricia James, Dr. L.W. Kennedy, Michael Klein, Peter L. Koffsky, Subh Kumar, Mike Kurtzig, Jason Lamb, Maurice Landes, Charles Leight, Mark Lemeke, John Lewis, Andy Loving, Carl Mabbs-Zeno, Nancy Bushwick Malloy, Alexandre Marc, Cheryl Morden, elmira Nazombe, John Parker, Sharon Pauling, Tom Peterson, David Pimentel, Kathy Pomroy, Jeffrey Pulis, Eileen Purcell, Kumar K. Ramanathan, Helena Ribe, Cecile Richards, Roger Rumpf, David Sa'adah, Tim Schouls, Gretta Tovar-Siebentritt, Larry Sly, Valerie Strauss, David Super, Charles Sykes, Ed Synder, Charles Teller, Luther Tweeten, E. Lane Vanderslice, Mark Winne, Ben Wisner.

We also received invaluable assistance from Ken Gray, Mike Kurtzig, and Masao Matsumoto at the U.S. Department of Agriculture; Newman Fair, Marsha McGee, Christine Matthews, Randall Salm, Patricia Theiler, and Glenn White at Bread for the World; Howard Hjort and others at the North American Liaison Office of the Food and Agriculture Organization of the U.N.; Steve Vosti at the International Food Policy Research Institute; Susannah Name at the U.N. Information Center, Washington, D.C.; and Bill Frelick at the U.S. Committee for Refugees.

Introduction

The finding of this report on hunger in 1990-1991 is stark: there are more hungry people in the world than ever before. But, there are ideas that do work to overcome hunger. The principal barrier to ending world hunger is neither lack of resources nor insufficient knowledge. It is the failure to put ideas that work into practice on a broad scale.

A Year of Increasing Hunger

In 1991, more than half a billion adults and children experience continuous hunger. Even more people are vulnerable to hunger. Over a billion face nutritional deficiencies, particularly lack of iodine (goiter), iron (anemia), and Vitamin A (vision problems). The Alan Shawn Feinstein World Hunger Program at Brown University estimates that, in 1990, 1.05 billion people, 20 percent of the world's population, lived in households too poor to obtain the calories needed for an active work life.[1]

Between September 1990 and August 1991, hunger was frequently in the news. Chronic hunger was newsworthy when it became famine. Continuing civil wars in the Horn of Africa, coupled with drought, brought more than 20 million people to the brink of starvation. Relief aid is arriving, but too little, too late. The deadly combination of war and poor weather also led to increasing hunger in Angola, Mozambique, Afghanistan, the Philippines, and Cambodia. War alone caused hunger-related deaths and illness in Liberia. Another cyclone hit Bangladesh, killing tens of thousands and leaving 10 million people homeless and at risk of cholera.

Some reports concern newly hungry people. The aftermath of the Persian Gulf war continues to threaten the lives of Iraqi children. Many of the Kurds who fled from Iraq to hastily erected refugee camps along the Turkish and Iranian borders were middle-class professionals, hungry for the first time in their lives. More than a million foreign workers fled from the Persian Gulf during the early months of the crisis. Many were the sole supporters of their families in Egypt, Yemen, Bangladesh, Pakistan, the Philippines, India, Sri Lanka, or the dozen other countries from which they came. The breakdown of economies in the USSR and several Eastern European countries has led to dramatically higher food prices and shortages. The disarray fueled the failed coup attempt in Moscow in August 1991.

A weak world economy and reduced government commitment to social services had a severe impact on the developed countries as well. UNICEF reports that between 1981 and 1990, the proportion of children living in poverty, and therefore vulnerable to hunger, increased substantially in several of the world's wealthiest nations: the United Kingdom, Canada, and the former West Germany.[2] According to the Food Research and Action Center, one child in eight under the age of twelve is vulnerable to hunger in the United States.[3] The number of people in the United States receiving food stamps reached an all-time high in 1991.

But most causes of hunger are not news. Tens of millions of families in rural South Asia remain landless. Shanty towns continue to spring up in Latin America. Per capita incomes and food production continue to decline in most of sub-Saharan Africa. In many nations, rich and poor alike, the bottom 40 percent of the population receives less than 15 percent of the national income. Poor and hungry people lack the political power to change their circumstance or obtain government benefits, and often face outright hostility from their governments. World military expenditures exceed the total income of the poorest half the world's population. One third of all children under the age of five in developing nations, 177 million in all, are so poorly nourished that their development is permanently impaired.[4]

Ideas that Work

Hunger 1992 presents examples of successful and promising approaches to reducing hunger and attacking the poverty and powerlessness which cause hunger. Although the number of people who are hungry is higher than ever, the proportion of the world's population that lives in hunger is slowly declining. Dennis Avery reports, "More people enjoyed adequate nutrition during 1990 than ever before in the world's history."[5] In the populous nations of South and Southeast Asia, where the majority of the world's hungry people reside, steady economic growth and supportive public policies are reducing hunger and poverty. With notable exceptions, not only the proportion, but the absolute number of hungry people in Asia is slowly declining. In much of Latin America and Africa, where hunger is increasing, citizens are planning and carrying out community projects and programs that improve their lives.

Hunger 1992 examines a wide range of fruitful ideas for ending hunger, including food aid, sustainable agricultural development, national policies, grassroots community development, and organizing for political change. The point is not to suggest panaceas, but to attempt to learn from practical experiences.

Food Aid

Immediate food aid is a necessary response to famine or personal emergencies. But long-term food aid and, in many cases, even emergency food aid, raises questions about dignity, dependency, and self-reliance. Careless use of food aid can make hunger worse in the long-term.

Barbara Murock salutes the people who have created and sustained food banks, food pantries, and soup kitchens in the United States over the past decade. She notes the increasing emphasis on helping food aid recipients to take charge of their own lives and on involvement in public policy advocacy. She also examines the devastating impact of the reduced federal government commitment to public food assistance programs.

Marc Cohen describes Integrated Child Development Services in India, a cooperative venture among the Indian government, state governments, the residents of 240,000 villages, the U.N. World Food Programme, and the U.S. private voluntary organization CARE. He details how the program improves the well-being of Indian children and their mothers, but raises questions of dependency and the impact of food aid on local agriculture. In a sidebar, he argues that food aid has undermined development in Egypt.

The Green Revolution, Rural Communities, and the Environment

Thoughtful people disagree about the social and environmental trade-offs inherent in technologies which increase food production to match population growth. John Mellor reviews the "green revolution" – the use of high-yielding seeds, chemical fertilizers, and artificial pesticides. He looks at four states in India where this technology, combined with appropriate public policies, raised farm productivity and reduced poverty. In the Philippines, new technology likewise increased productivity, but rural incomes declined.

Patricia Kutzner explores the potential of alternative farm technologies which require less cash, use more labor, and are less risky to the environment. She details instances, mainly in Africa, in which local community organizations have helped these alternatives gain widespread acceptance. A sidebar by Marc Cohen describes citizens' efforts to get the World Bank to look more carefully at how its development loans affect the environment and poor people.

National Policies

David Beckmann underscores the importance of constructive national economic policies in reducing poverty. He points to Indonesia's policies, which have contributed to economic growth and poverty reduction through the 1980s. Sidebars by Patience Elabor-Idemudia, drawing on Nigerian experience, highlight the pain which the economic traumas of the 1980s have brought to many developing countries, and the necessity of involving poor people in crafting solutions to the global debt crisis.

Richard Hoehn reviews Costa Rica's forty-year experiment with deliberate demilitarization. He notes that it is both a consequence of, and a contributor to, a different national ethos. He then explores correlations between military expenditures and hunger and social well-being in other nations, rich and poor, including the United States. He challenges conventional wisdom on how to define and achieve national and world security.

Grassroots Community Development

Three studies center on communities in which people have decided the direction their lives and communities should take. With varying amounts of outside assistance, they have developed and carried out their own plans.

Ana Avilés describes resettlement/repopulation efforts in El Salvador. In the face of active opposition from the government, whole communities have returned from exile to rebuild their villages. They have devised new ways of making community decisions about allocation of food, land, resources, and energy. In taking power for themselves, they have created a model that is promising to poor communities everywhere, but threatening to old orders of power and privilege.

Maria Simon and Kathleen Crowley describe projects of grassroots development with substantial outside partnerships in very different settings. A Tanzanian community organized, then sought assistance to build a water pipeline, freeing women and children from the daily chore of fetching water from a spring. In St. Louis, Mo., a coalition of community organizations convinced the mayor to issue an order assuring a share of federally funded jobs for city residents and minority and female workers.

Organizing for Political Change

Richard Hoehn reviews the efforts of the Texas Industrial Areas Foundation (IAF) Network to solve social and economic problems by empowering poor and middle-class people. IAF groups have achieved improvements in community services, but their confrontational style has drawn criticism.

Marc Cohen presents a contrasting style of organizing for political change. He examines how Bread for the World members have won funding increases for WIC, the U.S. government program providing supplementary food to women, infants, and children who are at nutritional risk.

The section of *Hunger 1992* on ideas that work concludes with an interview with Arthur Simon, founder and president-emeritus of Bread for the World and Bread for the World Institute.

Other Ideas Also Work

Dozens of other ideas that work might have been chosen for this collection, such as the creation by the Food and Agriculture Organization of the U.N. of a Global Information and Early Warning System that has helped improve the world community's response to famine; the raising of incomes through export manufacturing, which has reduced poverty and hunger while generating many problems; and investments in developing human resources, from ensuring the health of infants through their training as research scientists and artists.

Some General Propositions

Hunger is many-faceted and complex. It is a premise of this report that hunger in a particular instance probably has no single cause, and almost certainly no "miracle cure." Each case is unique, and reducing or eliminating hunger will require responses shaped to fit. And each "cure" has its pitfalls.

The essays on ideas that work and the reality of increasing hunger at home and abroad point toward several general propositions:

1. *Popular participation, the involvement of hungry people in devising policies and in planning, implementing, and evaluating projects, is essential to long-term efforts to overcome hunger.* If efforts to reduce hunger are to succeed, people must feel a sense of "ownership," whether the need is to overcome powerlessness, change a public policy, create a child survival program, adapt a particular technology, or seek ways for people to grow food without harming the environment.

2. *National governments must foster a climate in which participatory efforts to end hunger are encouraged.* Without some measure of national government support, most of the efforts included in this volume would not have succeeded. Those which face continuing government hostility, as in El Salvador, are greatly constrained by continuing repression.

3. *Outside assistance often plays a critical role in the success of hunger alleviation efforts.* Material or technical assistance for carrying out locally planned programs may come from national or foreign governments, from international institutions, or from local or international

Introduction

private voluntary groups, including those created by poor people through their own efforts.

4. *National and international economic decisions can create hunger, relieve hunger, or overwhelm other programs and policies.* Some developing nations have taxed agriculture, discouraging food production. Artificially high foreign exchange rates or large budget deficits often lead to inflation, driving food prices out of reach of poor families. Other developing country governments have enacted policies which foster growth in food production while also guaranteeing access to food and social services for the most vulnerable people. Many industrial nations' trade policies discriminate against imports from developing countries.

5. *Demilitarization could release resources and foster a more hospitable climate for people-centered and sustainable development.* Using financial and human resources for military purposes typically reduces monies available for schools, health care, environmental protection, and food supplement programs. Perhaps more serious, excessive military spending can discourage attitudes of cooperation and accommodation and lead to the postponement of needed social and economic reforms.

Our Hope For *Hunger 1992* . . . and Your Response

As Bread for the World Institute on Hunger & Development has prepared this report on the state of world hunger, the first goal has been to inform. We welcome feedback from readers on whether the studies, updates, tables, and references have increased your knowledge and understanding of the causes of, and possible solutions to, hunger.

A second goal is to motivate people to action. Knowledge about hunger is of little consequence unless acted upon. For the world to have the resources and the knowledge to overcome hunger, yet not to effect the end of hunger, is a catastrophe for millions of people. For many of us, it is sin. For all of us, it is a failure of moral vision, political will, and collective action.

The sponsors of *Hunger 1992* (see pages 215 – 216) are involved in efforts to reduce hunger and poverty. They provide emergency assistance and work for long-term community development, both in the United States and abroad. Nearly all are concerned with policies that affect hunger. Some devote substantial resources to changing policies through advocacy or education.

Hunger 1992 is an invitation and a challenge. The sponsors invite you, the readers – concerned citizens, community leaders, teachers and students, activists, opinion-shapers, policymakers – to join us, in partnership with poor and hungry people everywhere, in building a movement strong enough to overcome hunger.■ – Don Reeves and Marc J. Cohen

About the Structure of the Report

I. Ideas That Work

The range of case studies suggests the range of problems inherent in overcoming hunger. Several criteria were used in their selection: geography, the conclusions of *Hunger 1990* (see box above), the agencies involved, and most of all, the variety of circumstances in which hungry people live. In each study, it is our intent not only to present ideas and programs that work or show promise, but to examine the premises and problems of each approach. A four-session study aid may be helpful for use with study groups (see order form, page 217).

II. Regional Updates

The six regional updates are intended primarily to note the major hunger-related events between September 1990 and August 1991. In most instances the material supplements the forty-five country profiles in *Hunger 1990,* but should not require readers to have that volume at hand. Events dictate the addition of some profiles not included last year, most notably the sections on Eastern Europe and the Soviet Union. Space precludes repeating comments for countries where little has changed since last year. In a few instances, e.g. India, one or more of the "ideas" essays help fill that gap.

The updates examine the hunger impact of such diverse subjects as the relationship between the central government and the republics in the USSR (page 166 ff.); trade negotiations among Mexico, Canada, and the United States (page 130 ff.); war and natural disasters in Africa, Asia, and the Middle East (pages 110 ff.,118 ff., 142 ff.); drugs, disease, and death squads in Peru (page 137 ff.); and unemployment on American Indian reservations (page 155 ff.).

Hunger 1992 also notes the emerging worldwide consensus that every person on earth has a right to enough food for a decent life. Fulfilling this promise may require the international community occasionally to intervene on behalf of beleaguered people. In April 1991, Gulf War allies, with United Nations backing, ignored Iraq's sovereignty to aid Kurdish refugees. No one, however, intervened in such concerted fashion on behalf of millions in the Horn of Africa.

III. Tables; Supplemental Features

Hunger 1992 also includes updated bibliography, glossary, and tables, with added data for life expectancy, GNP per capita, growth in GNP, and change in the mortality rates for children under five years. The index (page 210 ff.) has references to both this report and *Hunger 1990.*

IV. Numbering the Series

Having selected an annual release date in October, we have skipped to "1992" in the title of this report to reflect the period of dissemination and use. There is no *Hunger 1991.*

V. Hunger 1993

Bread for the World Institute has begun work on *Hunger 1993,* scheduled for release on World Food Day, 1992. It will look at hunger among a growing global population of displaced persons and refugees.

Notes

1. Millman, p. 8.
2. UNICEF, *The State of the World's Children 1991,* p. 29.
3. FRAC, *Community Childhood Hunger Identification Project.*
4. *The State of the World's Children 1991,* p. 29.
5. Avery, p. 10.

Food Bank Networks Respond to U.S. Hunger Crisis

by Barbara Murock

Photo: Harvesters, Kansas City, Mo.

Increased hunger has driven people to new depths of despair.

Overview

While working for a hunger coalition in Pittsburgh in the early 1980s, I delivered food to an older woman who had called our emergency food hotline. Wringing her hands, the woman showed me her bills, which she had spread out across her kitchen table. I could see the impossible situation she was in – her income did not cover housing, utilities, health care, taxes, and food.

Since 1981, growing numbers of people have found themselves in a similar situation – inadequate income from employment or assistance programs to meet their basic needs. Hunger decreased during the 1960s and 1970s but increased during the 1980s. The country underwent the worst economic downturn since the 1930s. The gap between rich and poor widened.

Fewer well-paid industrial jobs were available; many new jobs offered poverty level wages. The minimum wage remained at $3.35 per hour throughout the decade, losing 20-25 percent of its purchasing power. Meanwhile, costs for housing, health care, quality education, transportation, and child care, as well as food, often rose faster than inflation. The mentally ill were released from institutions without adequate community services; this added to the ranks of homeless and hungry people.

In the midst of all this, the government sharply cut federal food programs and other social spending. By 1987, federal food assistance programs provided $12 billion less in benefits than under 1980 rules.[1] The Food Stamp Program enrolled fewer families and contributed less to their food purchasing power than in the past. The cuts also undermined school nutrition programs, which are effective in reducing hunger and malnutrition, and provide some poor children with the only meals they eat. By the end of the 1980s, 32 million Americans lived on incomes below the official poverty line ($13,400 for a family of four in 1990); 12.5 million of them lived on incomes of less than half of the poverty line.

Poor Americans need longer-term solutions to poverty – beginning with increased opportunities for jobs with adequate wages and benefits, affordable housing, and child-care. However, restoring sufficient funding for federal food assistance programs would eliminate much of the hunger in the United States today.

In response to the growing need, local communities began organizing charitable food programs, helping millions of desperate people who have nowhere else to turn, and making a life-sustaining difference for many. These private emergency food efforts grew at a staggering rate across the country as hunger and poverty increased. Thousands of concerned citizens became involved as service providers, fund-raisers, or contributors in these private emergency food efforts. This led the Maryland Food Committee to comment, "During the last decade, the war on poverty moved from the halls of government to the church basement."[2]

Private Charitable Food Assistance

Most of the private food assistance in the United States is carried out through a grassroots system of food banks, food pantries, and soup kitchens. Food banks as we know them today did not exist before 1975. Prior to 1980 there were only a few soup kitchens and food pantries; there are currently more than 180 food banks, 23,000 food pantries, and 3,300 soup kitchens across the country. They have become a growth industry (see graphs on page 14). *Food pantries*, generally run by church and community groups, provide needy households with several days of groceries. They vary widely in eligibility criteria, amount of help provided, and geographic area served.

Soup kitchens are hot meal programs, usually located in poor urban areas. They are typically sponsored by religious organizations, and generally do not have a screening process to determine need. Many homeless people, senior citizens on fixed incomes, and increasing numbers of families with children rely on soup kitchens as their main source of food.

Food banks are community-based warehouses that receive, store, and distribute large quantities of food. Many nonprofit food banks (though not all) obtain a portion of their food from a national network called Second Harvest. Local food processors, growers, retailers, and wholesalers also supply food banks, which in turn distribute food to agencies like food pantries and soup kitchens. Members of the Second Harvest network usually charge a small handling fee. Many of the independent food banks do not. Food banks typically supply only a part of what these agencies distribute. Emergency food agencies in the Kansas City area, for example, obtain 38 percent of their food from Harvesters, the local food bank.

Second Harvest began with a federal grant in 1979 as a channel for donations from the food industry to charitable organizations providing food to low-income people. Prior to that, as much as 20 percent of the food produced in the United States (140 million tons) was wasted. Much of the food, unsalable because of labeling or packaging mistakes, warehouse damage, or production overruns, was still safe to consume.

The country underwent the worst economic downturn since the 1930s. The gap between rich and poor widened.

Number of Food Banks

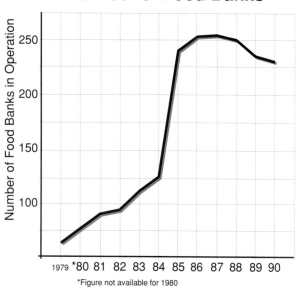

*Figure not available for 1980

Millions of Pounds of Food Distributed

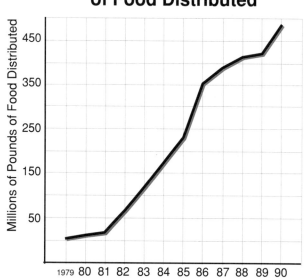

Number of Agencies

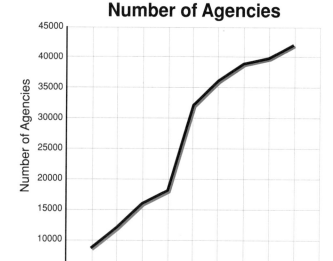

Food Banks (first graph) – community warehouses for salvaged and other donated food – receive food from a variety of sources and distribute (second graph) to food pantries, soup kitchens, senior citizen and day care centers, and homeless shelters (third graph). There were few private feeding agencies before 1980, and food banks did not exist in the United States before 1975.

Source: Second Harvest

By 1990, Second Harvest had grown to 180 food banks around the country, which distributed 476.4 million pounds of food (up 18 percent from 1989), worth $755 million, to over 42,000 member agencies. These included pantries and soup kitchens, as well as shelters for the homeless and abused spouses, senior citizen centers, and day-care centers.

Despite the rapid growth of food banks and food pantries, the need for food assistance is growing even faster. A 1988 survey by the U.S. Conference of Mayors found that 62 percent of emergency food assistance programs had to turn people away because of insufficient resources. The number of first-time users of food assistance programs is increasing, while the need for other people has become chronic.

Harvesters, in Kansas City, Mo., is one of the largest Second Harvest food banks. Started in 1979, it serves 577 agencies, including 294 pantries in twelve Kansas and Missouri counties. Like many food banks, Harvesters has also instituted a program to recover and distribute surplus prepared food from restaurants directly to agencies serving on-site meals. In two years, this effort recovered over one million pounds of food from 100 donor establishments that the food bank warehouse could not handle. Harvesters is also one of many food banks distributing surplus U.S. government commodities made available for poor people. In addition to distributing donated food, Harvesters, like most food banks, has developed a wholesale cooperative buying program where agencies can purchase staples such as tuna, macaroni, and peanut butter.

Food Banks like Harvesters benefit from the Value Added Program (VAP), begun by Second Harvest in 1990 to process large volume, perishable donations into family-sized canned or frozen portions. Various

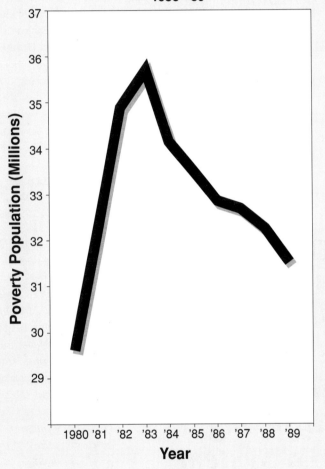

Total U.S. Population in Poverty (Millions)

1980 - 89

Source: U.S. Census Bureau

By the end of the 1980s, 32 million Americans lived on incomes below the official poverty line ($13,400 for a family of four in 1990); 12.5 million of them lived on incomes of less than half of the poverty line.

corporations donate labels, cans, and food processing services.

Religious, community, and civic organizations around the country, youth groups like the Boy Scouts, local businesses, and celebrities help collect food for food banks. In Texas, Hunters for the Hungry brings together deer hunters, processing plants, several state agencies, the End Hunger Network-Houston, and the state's Second Harvest food banks. Hunters bring deer to a specified packing plant and pay a $15 processing fee, receiving a tax deduction for the value of the meat. The food banks are then able to distribute processed venison.

Second Harvest works to increase donations of meat, an expensive and sought after commodity. Nevertheless, donations

of protein-rich foods remain scarce. Meat made up 2.3 percent of 1990 donations to the Second Harvest network. Member agencies cannot run their programs solely on the "reharvested" food which food banks have available. Food banks have been criticized for having large supplies of condiments, sauces, and sugary foods, but few staples. It is often impossible to provide a nutritionally balanced diet with available donations.

Arguably, food banks were not established to provide for all of the community's food assistance needs, though at times that is the public's perception. Food bank inventories vary depending on the items and quantities donated by the food industry. The growing consolidation of the food industry has caused donations to fluctuate

The Hartford Food Experience: *From Suffering to a System That Works*

by Richard A. Hoehn

The mission of the Hartford Food System is to increase the access of lower income and elderly Hartford residents to high quality, affordable food. We believe that all people should be able to obtain food through normal channels and not have to rely on emergency food programs. This mission is achieved through the long-term development of a more equitable and sustainable food system capable of addressing the underlying causes of hunger and poor nutrition. In this regard, programs have been oriented toward food production, agricultural marketing, local food retailing, nutrition education/information, and community economic development.

The Hartford Food System (HFS)

feeds people. But it is not a federal program, a food bank, a grocery store, or a restaurant. It is a system for putting together people who have fresh food with people who need fresh food. Believing that people should not have to rely on food banks and soup kitchens, HFS works to rebuild the links between farms and families, especially poor families.

Although Connecticut is a wealthy state, a quarter of the people (40 percent of the children) in Hartford, the capital, live at or below the poverty line, making it the fourth poorest city in the nation. Since 1968, any food, let alone fresh food, has become increasingly hard to find, as supermarkets have fled the city. Since World War II, 83 percent of the farms in the state have folded.

People in Hartford decided that there had to be a commonsense

considerably. Through experience, food banks have also learned that the cost of handling donated food can sometimes exceed its value.

To help agencies and their clients make the best use of available foods, Harvesters, the Kansas City food bank, formed a nutrition advisory committee in 1987 to develop materials and programs for its member agencies. Harvest-Ed furnishes videos, recipes, lesson plans, and training to help food pantries teach clients how to shop, avoid marketing gimmicks, stretch food dollars, and prepare economical and nutritious meals.

Networks have developed in Kansas City and other metropolitan areas to coordinate food and other assistance programs.

Hotline information and referral services direct people to the closest pantry. Those in need of housing or utility help are referred to appropriate agencies. For example, a family in Kansas City, Kansas may be referred to the Mount Carmel Church of God In Christ, the food bank member agency that is closest to their residence. There, the family is interviewed and required to provide verification of income, family size, and address. Along with providing for their immediate need for food, Mount Carmel provides budget and crisis counseling, and job and housing referrals, as well as advocacy and intervention when needed. This holistic approach is in keeping with the agency's policy of treating people in need with respect and dignity.

Spending time on the front lines increases awareness that a few grocery bags of donated food cannot pull people out of poverty.

way to help farmers stay in business and at the same time help consumers get fresh, healthful produce. So they started a downtown farmer's market, community farm stands in neighborhoods, a grocery delivery service to homebound seniors, a small store in a residence for senior citizens, and a coupon system for recipients of the Special Supplemental Food Program for Women, Infants, and Children (WIC). It took a dozen years, but HFS put together a successful farm-to-family food program that works with existing economic resources to help assure the availability of fresh food for people in poor neighborhoods. A food bank is connected to the system as well.

HFS, working in coalition with other groups, convinced the Connecticut legislature to allocate funds for vouchers for WIC participants and low-income seniors, good only at farmers' markets. HFS helped start farmers' markets in neighborhoods where people who received vouchers could easily get to them. In 1987, the WIC/Farmers' Market Coupon Program was launched, providing more than 4,000 Hartford women and children with 80,000 pounds of fresh produce.

By 1991, the program issued coupons to 42,000 people and enrolled 150 farmers. The year before, participating farmers had redeemed coupons worth $225,000. Farmers' markets have doubled since the mid 1980s, as have the farmers who bring their produce to these markets. Using games and printed materials to demonstrate the benefits of organic and local produce, HFS has developed an education campaign through the farm stands.

Neighborhood mom and pop stores had higher food prices because they could not purchase at the same high-volume low rate available to supermarket chains; thus people dependent on these stores had to pay more than people in wealthier suburban neighborhoods. HFS worked with small store owners to start a grocers' association that helped them consolidate buying to get cheaper prices.

HFS tries to find ways to work with ongoing resources, collaborate with other organizations, and stitch together programs that are self-supporting.

For further information, write HFS at 509 Wethersfield Avenue, Hartford, CT 06114. ∎

$300 Billion

Military Budget

$200 Billion

$100 Billion

Value of Food Distributed Through Second Harvest Network

Cost of Federal Food Programs

0

Arms and Food
United States
1990

Sources: Second Harvest, USDA, and Office of
Management and Budget

Cafe 458 in Atlanta also provides needy people food while maintaining dignity. People order food from a printed menu, as in a restaurant. The program also offers a legal clinic, job counseling and placement, and drug rehabilitation. These efforts are coordinated with homeless shelters.

Initially, Second Harvest worked with hunger activists to initiate food banks. Other sectors of the community joined in responding to hunger. By now, food industry representatives, but few food recipients, are found on food bank boards. Some operations are dominated by business and media interests. This occasionally raises questions about whose needs are ultimately being served.

Next Steps:
Ending the Cycle
of Poverty and Hunger

Hundreds of thousands of citizens across America give countless hours of time and raise millions of dollars to feed hungry people. These volunteers are on the front lines, they hand out bags of groceries or serve hot meals. They are face to face with those in need.

Spending time on the front lines increases awareness that a few grocery bags of donated food cannot pull people out of poverty. Increasingly, as in Kansas City and Atlanta, those engaged in private food assistance have linked their work with efforts to build self-reliance and change public policies.

The Maryland Food Committee (MFC), a

Federal Domestic Food Assistance Programs

In fiscal 1990, the U.S. Department of Agriculture (USDA) spent $24 billion – equal to about a month of military spending – on domestic food assistance programs, which included:

Food Stamp Program. Provides low-income households with coupons to purchase food in grocery stores. Benefits are based on income, household size, and the Thrifty Food Plan, USDA's lowest-cost suggested food plan for providing a nutritious diet in emergency situations. Few families receive an adequate diet under this plan. An average of 20 million people received food stamps each month, with average monthly benefits per person of $58.50 between July and September; the total annual cost was $15.5 billion. A

twenty-one-year-old state-wide advocacy group based in Baltimore, became increasingly involved in raising money for direct assistance in the 1980s, as the pantries and soup kitchens in Maryland grew from fifty to over 600. In an effort to reverse the growing dependency on food assistance, the committee helped convince donors, who contributed over a quarter of a million dollars in 1990 for direct assistance, to allocate some of their funds for self-sufficiency efforts.

MFC awarded grants to innovative programs administered by ongoing emergency food and shelter programs. These programs reached a small number of the estimated 714,000 people in Maryland who are at risk of going without food at some point every month. But preliminary findings show tangible results with the people they did reach. Grant recipients include:

Super Pantry, located in West Baltimore, provides participants with emergency food along with classes in nutrition and cooking, budgeting, meal planning, and other skills. The program also includes education about domestic and substance abuse, voter registration, goal setting, and self-esteem. Graduates are encouraged to continue their education and to seek job training. Out of thirty-two women participating in initial classes, twenty-eight no longer require emergency food assistance. Three women have jobs, one is in college, three have found permanent homes, and one left an abusive relationship. Ten women moved on to Project Independence, Maryland's welfare-to-work program. MFC has replicated the Super Pantry model in other parts of the state with

separate nutrition assistance program for Puerto Rico cost $937 million.

School Lunch Program. Provides students with about a third of the recommended daily diet. Eligibility for free or reduced price lunches is based on family income and size. USDA provides schools with commodities and cash; the program cost $4 billion, and fed an average of 24 million students each month.

School Breakfast Program. Provided subsidized breakfasts to an average of 3.8 million poor children each month of the school year at an annual cost of $594 million.

Child and Adult Care Food Programs. Provides day care homes, child care centers, and adult care facilities with food.

Served an average of 1.6 million meals a day to children and 18,800 a day to adults, at an annual cost of $812 million.

Special Milk Program. Provided 183 million half pints of milk worth $19 million.

Special Supplemental Food Program for Women, Infants, and Children (WIC). Provided coupons for supplemental foods to a million poor pregnant and nursing women, 1.4 million infants and 2.1 million children who were "at nutritional risk." Also provided nutrition education, health referrals, and other services at a total cost of $2.1 billion.

Commodity Supplemental Food Program (CSFP). Distributes monthly food parcels to low-income pregnant and nursing mothers, in-

fants, children, and senior citizens. Participants cannot enroll in WIC. An average of 274,000 people participated each month at an annual cost of $69 million.

Food Distribution Programs. USDA provided food assistance to a monthly average of 138,000 families who live on or near Indian reservations and in U.S. Trust Territories at an annual cost of $58 million. USDA also provided food and cash to the Nutrition Program for the Elderly, benefiting a daily average of 928,000 people at an annual cost of $139 million.

The Emergency Food Assistance Program (TEFAP). Formerly the Temporary Emergency Food Assistance Program, distributed surplus government food to poor people at a cost of $257 million. ■

similar success.

Mid-Town Churches Community Association in Baltimore helps homeless mothers and their children by offering shelter, guidance in education and job seeking, and classes on health, nutrition, parenting, and computer skills. Several participants moved out of shelters and into their own homes; most report significant changes in cooking, shopping, and eating habits.

Clients Helping Clients is an all-volunteer program near Washington, D.C., run by current and former clients of public assistance programs, who offer guidance to other clients. Members have become advocates both in public assistance offices and with legislators. This group won a Harry Chapin Food Self-Reliance Award from World Hunger Year in 1989. The Maryland Department of Social Services recently asked Clients Helping Clients to run its client relations program.

MFC has supported two other projects which work with poor women. **The Community Leadership and Education Organization** develops leadership abilities among public assistance clients. Participants have testified before both state and federal legislatures.

The Self-Help Empowerment and Development Program is a computer-based program that teaches participants about gardening, cooperative food buying, and nutrition as well as reading, writing, and other self-sufficiency skills. Group support enables participants to make changes in their lives and is key to the success of these programs.

Food pantries, soup kitchens, and community self-help efforts cannot substitute for the billions of dollars cut from federal food assistance programs. As Ray Pletz, manager of a soup kitchen in St. Petersburg, Fla., puts it, "We're just here because the government's refusing to do its job."[3]

As a network, Second Harvest's advocacy work focuses primarily on seeking the extension of federal surplus food distribution programs and pressing for legislation offering incentives for donations to food banks. But at local and regional levels, strong links are being forged between emergency food assistance providers and hunger advocates. One example is Just Harvest, a Pittsburgh-based hunger advocacy group that organizes food assistance providers to lobby for increased funds for food programs. Recently, in two area school districts, food pantry providers have joined Just Harvest in supporting school breakfast programs.

Concern about hunger has also led to the formation of city or state-wide hunger advisory bodies bringing together government, business, philanthropic, and community leaders with hunger organizations. One example is the Oregon State Legislature's Task Force on Hunger. Emergency food providers in Oregon have helped to document and profile assistance needs.

Like food providers across the country, they also testify at public hearings, appear in documentaries, and share their experiences with people in their churches, synagogues, and the broader community. Many direct service providers also belong to national organizations such as Bread for the World and the Food Research and Action Center (FRAC). The Association of Arizona Food Banks has worked with FRAC on its End Childhood Hunger campaign, and has urged food companies to get involved in this effort.

To expand its advocacy work, Harvesters in Kansas City has restructured its board of directors to include a public information and awareness committee with a speakers bureau. Harvesters is also involved with the Missouri Association for

Social Welfare and the Reorganization of Welfare, which seeks to make state welfare legislation more just and compassionate. The Association helps give those in need a voice by connecting them with legislators. Harvesters has selected ending childhood hunger as its 1991 advocacy focus. The food bank asked pantries, employees, volunteers, and clients to write letters encouraging their legislators to act on hunger issues. These letters were written on empty paper plates.

Conclusion

Food banks, food pantries, and soup kitchens are the legacy of a decade of rising poverty, cutbacks in federal assistance, and declining job opportunities. The countless hours of volunteer time and thousands of tons of donated food testify to a groundswell of concern for poor and hungry people in the absence of adequate policies to reduce poverty and hunger in the United States.

But private charitable food assistance, despite tremendous increases year after year, cannot compensate for billions of dollars cut from federal food programs nor jobs paying only poverty level wages. These efforts are not adequate for hungry people to meet their daily food needs. As Joyce Rothermel, director of the Greater Pittsburgh Community Food Bank puts it,

The network of soup kitchens, food pantries and food banks is only one immediate response to the massive, inexcusable problem of food insecurity that is a frequent occurrence in the lives of millions in the U.S., a land of plenty.

Particularly when combined with programs which encourage self-reliance, food assistance programs can bring people and communities dignity, hope, and positive change. When they are joined with advocacy efforts aimed at ending poverty and hunger, they can foster more humane and just policies. ∎

Notes

1. *Christian Science Monitor.*
2. *Maryland Food Committee, "Not By," p. 1.*
3. *St. Petersburg Times.*

Food Aid That Is Not a Band Aid

The Indian government is providing supplementary food to poor, nutritionally at-risk children with the help of CARE, an American private voluntary organization.

by Marc J. Cohen

Can international food aid help support equitable and sustainable development? Scholars, policymakers, development practitioners, and citizens of developing countries have debated this question for decades. During short-term food emergencies – shortages caused by natural disasters or war – food aid saves lives. However, emergency food is just a small portion of the millions of tons of food aid which governments and international organizations donate or sell at discounted prices each year (see graphs, page 23).

Food aid can also help promote long-term development in nonemergency situations in a variety of ways, such as helping to reduce undernutrition among poor mothers and their young children. As Hans Singer and his colleagues at the University of Sussex Institute of Development Studies have pointed out,

> *Lack of proper nourishment at an early age can cause lasting mental and/or physical handicap and thus hinder the proper development of the human resources available to a nation.*[1]

Poverty and undernutrition are closely related. Poor people tend to be hungry because they lack the resources to grow sufficient food and the income to buy it. Chronically undernourished people have a reduced capacity to earn income and contribute to development. Broad-based, environmentally sustainable development offers the best long-term way to break this poverty-hunger link, but in the short-run, food aid programs can help.

Food Aid and Child Survival in India

Pregnant and nursing mothers and children from birth to age five have greater nutritional needs than the rest of the population, but they are the least well-nourished people within low-income households in developing countries. Males tend to receive more and better food than females, and as poverty leads women to work outside the home, they have less time to take care of their children or themselves. The Alan Shawn Feinstein World Hunger Program at Brown University estimates that in 1990, there were 204 million undernourished children in developing countries.[2]

According to a recent study by the National Council for International Health,

The cost-effective way to prevent malnutrition is to target underweight small children and their mothers for feeding programs, and combine this with other health services, such as immunization against childhood diseases like measles. Malnutrition and disease are closely interrelated, with the interactions tending to result in a downward spiral of health. Malnutrition reduces the body's defenses against disease, and illness and disease can increase malnutrition. This vicious circle takes its highest toll on children.

Approximately 14 million children die each year in developing countries, approximately half from causes that could be prevented at low cost.[3]

The U.S. private voluntary organization (PVO) CARE and the U.N. World Food Programme (WFP) are providing food aid to support one such comprehensive child survival program, the Integrated Child De-velopment Services (ICDS) in India. CARE manages food aid commodities provided through the U.S. government's Food for Peace program, which is also WFP's largest source of food.

India's ICDS program, established in 1975, provides nutrition, health, and pre-school educational services for poor children from birth to age six, along with pregnant and nursing mothers. The program is targeted to benefit poor and nutritionally vulnerable people, mostly in rural areas. ICDS has grown rapidly, and now covers about half the country's "blocks" (administrative units of 100,000-150,000 people); the Indian government hopes to cover the entire nation by the year 2000.

Most of the staff involved in ICDS are women. Indian women are discriminated against in both the workplace, where they receive lower pay than men, and in the home. Eighty percent of the girls aged thirteen to eighteen and 70 percent of adult women consume less than the recommended level of calories each day. ICDS workers, especially at the community level, often serve as role models, showing that women can run a program that makes a difference in people's lives. Also, ICDS health and nutrition education allows village mothers to play an increasingly important role at home in managing their families' well-being.

An evaluation conducted for the U.S. Agency for International Development (AID), which oversees PVOs' involvement in Food for Peace, calls ICDS a model for maternal and child health feeding programs worldwide. ICDS includes rigorous needs assessment and good targeting of

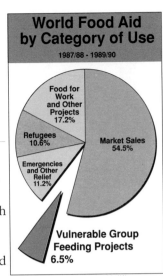

World Food Aid by Category of Use
1987/88 - 1989/90

Food for Work and Other Projects 17.2%
Refugees 10.6%
Emergencies and Other Relief 11.2%
Market Sales 54.5%
Vulnerable Group Feeding Projects 6.5%

Source: Food and Agriculture Organization of the U.N.

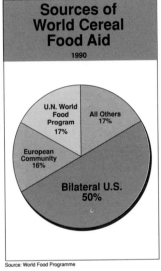

Sources of World Cereal Food Aid
1990

U.N. World Food Program 17%
All Others 17%
European Community 16%
Bilateral U.S. 50%

Source: World Food Programme

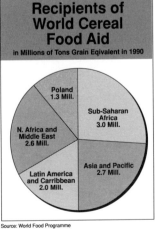

Recipients of World Cereal Food Aid
in Millions of Tons Grain Eqivalent in 1990

Poland 1.3 Mill.
Sub-Saharan Africa 3.0 Mill.
N. Africa and Middle East 2.6 Mill.
Asia and Pacific 2.7 Mill.
Latin America and Carribean 2.0 Mill.

Source: World Food Programme

services to poor, malnourished children; good management; good monitoring of logistics; a good evaluation system that leads to program improvements; and effective integration of supplementary feeding with health and education.[4]

India has made progress in child survival since the creation of ICDS, although there are still an estimated 74 million undernourished children in the country. Independent evaluations by Indian and foreign experts have concluded that ICDS has played a significant role in raising birth weights by improving maternal health and nutrition and in reducing the incidence of severe malnutrition among children. ICDS has also increased the immunization rate of poor children, and has helped India lower its infant mortality rate from 125 per thousand children born in 1979 to ninety-five in 1991 (still high compared to neighboring Sri Lanka's twenty-eight or forty in the Philippines). Between 1980 and 1989, the mortality rate of Indian children under five declined by 2.4 percent annually. According to UNICEF, this was the third best performance among the thirty-eight countries with "very high under five mortality rates." ICDS has done all this in a cost-effective manner.[5]

The program provides supplementary food to nutritionally at-risk participants 300 days per year. The food includes a cereal-based hot meal or snack, as well vitamin and mineral supplements. Families are encouraged to add their own vegetables and condiments. After staff salaries, food is the major recurring cost item in the ICDS budget. Under India's federal system, the purchase, transportation, and monitoring of the food is the responsibility of the thirty-two state and territorial governments. These governments vary widely both in their ability to pay and their commitment to social welfare programs.

During 1991-1992, ten states turned to CARE to obtain all or part of their ICDS food. CARE programmed nearly a quarter of a million metric tons of food for 7 million children and 1.7 million pregnant and nursing mothers. This was 40 percent of the ICDS food; WFP provided another 20 percent, while state governments purchased the remainder of the food from national government stocks and India's private sector.

In the states which receive food from CARE, the organization has a considerable level of involvement, managing, coordinating, and monitoring logistics as well as providing the food. In some states, CARE carries out additional development activities involving ICDS families. In order to finance this work, CARE sells a small portion of the Food for Peace commodities it receives on the open market. The U.S. government absorbs the cost of the commodities – a blend of U.S.-grown corn and soy flour fortified with vitamins and minerals, along with a small quantity of cooking oil – and ocean freight, while the Indian state governments pay for transportation within India and for CARE's program management services. An independent evaluation of CARE's participation in ICDS, conducted for AID in 1986, had high praise for CARE's managerial and logistical role.[6]

Despite substantial CARE involvement in many states, according to Charles Sykes, CARE's chief Washington representative and a former director of the agency's program in India, ICDS is driven by the Indian government's policy decisions, budget allocations, and development plans. "The country itself has thought through its own problems," he says, and adds that CARE's role is largely defined by these Indian decisions. The 1986 evaluation of CARE's participation in ICDS seems to bear this out, noting the organization's good working relationships with the national and state governments and ICDS workers on the ground.[7] These good relationships stem in part from CARE's reliance on Indian staff.

While evaluators have given high marks to ICDS and CARE's participation in the program, they have also made some criticisms. Economist Per Pinstrup-Andersen has noted, "Supplementary feeding treats the symptoms, not the causes" of undernutrition.[8] Given the close relationship between undernutrition and poverty, measures which effectively reduce poverty are the most effective and lasting way to improve nutrition. Yet many of the children who survive, thanks to ICDS, face economic insecurity: tens of millions of Indian children between the ages of six and fourteen are working in low-paying jobs instead of going to school. As S. Guhan has pointed out, India's social welfare policies are sincerely aimed at improving the lives poor people, but seek to do this within the existing distribution of wealth:

> **[M]ajor structural changes have been ruled out.** *The redistribution of assets (especially land), or incomes, or consumption to the poor have been de-emphasized as policy objectives.*[9]

Evaluators have also criticized specific aspects of ICDS. The extent of community participation varies considerably, even though the Indian government theoretically requires community involvement in program planning and implementation. Because hunger results from a complex set of factors related to poverty and powerlessness, successful efforts to reduce hunger must involve the intended beneficiaries in making decisions. This participation is especially critical in maternal and child feeding programs, which often try to change family food consumption patterns.

Also, the community has a critical role in making sure the program reaches everyone who can benefit.

According to CARE's Sykes, a great deal depends not only on the interest of the community, but on the training and commitment of ICDS staff. Other ICDS observers note that the heavy workload imposed on ICDS community workers, whose levels of education and training vary considerably, can affect the quality of programs, especially nutrition education. ICDS is also constrained by traditional prejudices against women and "untouchables" (low-status people who account for a high proportion of the program participants), which remain strong in India.

The 1986 evaluation of CARE's role in ICDS found that the participation of children aged three to six is generally better than that of younger children and pregnant and nursing mothers; community needs surveys are often of uneven quality; and supplementary feeding is often used in a more curative than preventive way, that is, children receive supplemental food not to prevent severe malnutrition, but rather after it begins.[10]

CARE staff say that a number of steps have been taken to overcome these weaknesses. ICDS nutrition education has improved, while a new policy of allowing working mothers to come to ICDS community centers after work has increased their participation. Stepped-up community outreach activities by ICDS workers have improved coverage of younger children and mothers, who generally are the most difficult groups for supplemental feeding programs to reach. CARE has helped train ICDS workers to conduct surveys and to monitor the growth of children enrolled in ICDS; this helps make feeding efforts more preventive.

Food Dependence

A major issue is whether external food aid distributed by CARE and WFP might create dependence. The 1986 evaluation called the blended and fortified cereals that CARE provides an "outstanding supplementary food" for the nutritional circumstances of ICDS participants, and also noted that the commodities are readily acceptable to participants.[11] However, this opinion is not universally shared. A number of analysts have expressed concern about maternal and child feeding programs which use specialized foods not available locally, and that may only be obtained through food aid programs. This can undermine nutrition education, which emphasizes greater self-reliance.[12]

CARE officials disagree with these criticisms. Sykes notes that whether ICDS feeds participants with U.S. food aid commodities or local cereals, the food prepared "is usually a bland porridge which tastes like local gruels once condiments are added; there is nothing 'exotic' about bland porridge." Also, CARE officials point out, in the early 1970s, CARE and the Indian government had experimented with blending U.S. food aid cereal with Indian peanut flour, but this effort failed because Indian private contractors had difficulty in providing adequate quantities of high quality flour.

Food aid analysts recommend that programs such as CARE's support for ICDS include a plan for phasing out external food or turning the program over to the host country; American PVOs have phased-out" or "phased-over" food aid programs elsewhere. Both CARE and the Indian government consider PVO and WFP involvement in ICDS to be "interim support," with total use of Indian food the ultimate goal. However, evaluators of CARE's input into ICDS acknowledge that foreign assistance will be necessary for some time due to the financial weaknesses of many Indian state governments.[13]

Food Aid vs. Financial Aid

Some food aid critics argue that donors ought to provide their aid in the form of cash. In India, this would allow state governments to buy more Indian food for ICDS and promote rural development as well as child survival. Yet food aid enjoys a much stronger constituency than other kinds of foreign aid in donor countries, especially the United States. Farmers anxious to move surpluses off the market, food processors, and shippers, along with the PVOs which distribute food aid, form an impressive support group. Advocates of food aid point out that it is rather simplistic to assume that cash can readily substitute for food aid and the community-based services that ICDS provides, and that India's harvests are subject to year-to-year variations in the weather. Finally, according to CARE's Sykes, the voluntary agencies which distribute food aid have themselves pressed hard for authority to sell or barter Food for Peace commodities so as to be able to purchase more local food.

A recent evaluation of AID's worldwide participation in maternal and child health feeding programs contends that the question is not whether the food comes from the host country or abroad, but whether the supply is reliable.[14] In the past, the U.S. government has often given extremely low priority to targeted feeding programs aimed at chronically undernourished populations, such as CARE's participation in ICDS. In times of short supply, U.S. policymakers have often withdrawn resources from these programs in order to assure the availability of food for emergency relief (an objective with which it is hard to quarrel) and programs which advance foreign policy objectives (e.g. food aid to Egypt, which does little to advance humanitarian and development goals (see sidebar, page 28).

Not only is food usually easier to get from abroad than cash, but CARE staff in India argue that people simply would not participate in ICDS programs in the absence of supplemental feeding. It is a major device for getting people to make use of the other ICDS services. According to a UNICEF evaluation of supplementary feeding in child survival programs, this incentive effect is the major positive feature of such feeding. Other analysts believe that well-run programs which make a difference in people's lives should not have to use food to get them to participate, but proponents of maternal and child health feeding point out that these programs conserve the time, energy, and health of poor pregnant and nursing mothers.

In any event, evaluations of Indian supplemental feeding programs suggest that they are effective precisely because they are tied into a package of services which have tangibly improved the lives of Indian women and children.[15]

Using Food Aid to Support Self-Reliant and Sustainable Development

CARE's support of ICDS is just one example of food aid supporting humanitarian and development objectives. In other instances, both in India and elsewhere, temporary food aid programs can help people achieve long-term food self-reliance. Also, some food aid programs use local rather than imported food, thereby potentially boosting local farm income. Finally, creative "food-for-work" programs, where workers receive part of their wages in food, can help create long-term employment opportunities, stimulate environmental protection, expand infrastructure, and further education. For example:

- In southern India, the Kottar Social Service Society successfully used Food for Peace commodities distributed by Catholic Relief Services to promote a variety of community development activities, ranging from fishing and potter cooperatives to health education, soil and water conservation, and resettlement schemes. According to an evaluation of the program, "the food served as the starting point for a process of developing a sense that people could exercise control over their lives."[16]

- Church World Service (CWS) and the Mennonite Central Committee have raised private American dollars to purchase Indian wheat. Working in partnership with the Indian Churches' Auxiliary for Social Action, the U.S. church groups use the food to supplement the wages of rural development workers who build roads, water and sanitation systems, and other rural development infrastructure.

- In a small town in India's Maharashtra state, a group of untouchables left their jobs as household servants in Bombay to become largely self-sufficient farmers. They market surplus grain and dairy products. A modest amount of donated U.S. food aid, provided through U.S. and Indian PVOs, helped tide them over until their first crop came in.

- Similarly, in the eastern jungles of Peru, unemployed petroleum workers organized a new agricultural colony. Food aid enabled them to survive until their first rice harvest.

- Food aid has also helped urban poor people achieve self-sufficiency in Peru. Food distributed by the Catholic charity Caritas helped women in Lima start cooperative kitchens, which save fuel, allow them to purchase additional food in bulk (thereby eliminating the need for further food aid), and save time in food preparation so that they can look for employment.

- On the Indonesian island of Sulawesi, CWS is working in partnership with the Indonesian Communion of Churches to help resettled people become farmers. The partnership seeks to provide communities with material and technical assistance in meeting what they identify as their needs. CWS distributes a small quantity of Food for Peace commodities prior

to the first harvest.

- In Haiti, CWS has used food aid to supplement the low salaries of school teachers, so that they can continue to work in the education field.

Project vs. Program Food Aid

Unfortunately, the use of food aid to support projects which directly benefit poor people is the exception rather than the rule, especially in the case of the U.S. Food for Peace program. Between 1987 and 1990, according to the Food and Agriculture Organization of the U.N., governments of countries receiving food aid sold 54.5 percent of the commodities in local markets (see graph, page 23). While the governments may use funds from these sales for a variety of development purposes, they generally do not account precisely for the money.

This type of food aid, where the com-

How Not to Use Food Aid: The Case of Egypt

Since 1974, the United States has provided Egypt with massive shipments of U.S. food, through both concessional and commercial channels. As Egypt becomes more urbanized, political stability depends heavily upon secure access to food for city dwellers. About a third of

the Egyptian government budget pays for urban food subsidies. The U.S. commitment to provide Egypt with food aid – mainly wheat and wheat flour – escalated after the Camp David Accords during the Carter administration. Between Fiscal years 1974 and 1983, Egypt received more than $2 billion in Food for Peace assistance, mostly in the form of program food aid credits. Egypt also received $2.8 billion in commodity grants under a U.S. program aimed at strategic allies, and much of this was additional wheat and flour. Food for Peace and the commodity grants account-

ed for 57 percent of all U.S. assistance to Egypt during these years. Altogether, Egypt has received nearly $3.5 billion under Food for Peace since 1960 (see graph, next page).

U.S. food aid has directly undermined Egyptian food security. A 1987 AID evaluation of U.S. food aid to Egypt found that low-priced food aid commodities and subsidized food distribution have discouraged Egyptian farmers from growing wheat. Increasing meat consumption among affluent Egyptians has stimulated demand for local feed production, however. By the early 1980s, Egypt was import-

modities are not used in specific development projects, is called "program food aid." Its major impact is to provide the recipient government with extra budget resources. Only if the government is committed to equitable and sustainable development will these resources benefit poor and hungry people. Recent studies conclude that program food aid is unlikely to have an immediate direct impact on poor people because it does not generally increase their access to food and rarely provides them with extra income.[17]

The United States provides most of its food aid resources as program food aid, and unlike most donors, its program food aid has been in the form of low-interest loans tied to the purchase of U.S. food rather than donations. This has contributed to developing countries' debt problems. Since World War II, the United States has been the largest supplier of international food aid, although its share of the total has declined from 90 percent per year in the 1950s to 50 percent in 1990 (see graph, page 23).

In fiscal 1989, the United States provided $750 million dollars worth of program food aid worldwide, accounting for 61.5 percent of the $1.2 billion Food for Peace budget. Another 17.9 percent went to refugee feeding and emergencies. Just 5.9 percent supported nonemergency food-for-work projects, and the share devoted to maternal and child health feeding projects like ICDS was only 8.2 percent ($99 million). According to economist Lane Vanderslice, most Food for Peace maternal and child health projects are not well integrated with AID's $200 million health-oriented child survival program; in the case of ICDS, integration was an Indian initiative.

Food for Peace (PL 480) Assistance to Egypt

ing some 75 percent of its wheat (the major staple), with 20 percent coming in under Food for Peace. Egypt is now the leading market for U.S. milled flour, and the number three market for wheat and wheat products of all kinds. Because of Egypt's support for U.S. policies in the Middle East, successive administrations have assured it a steady supply of food aid, but if U.S. policy should change, Egypt would have to pay for commercial imports.

Since the 1970s, U.S. law has required that program food aid commodities or the proceeds from

their sale contribute directly to improving the lives of poor people in the recipient country. There is no evidence that this has occurred in Egypt. Virtually all of the Food for Peace commodities go into subsidized bread consumption for city residents. The subsidies are not targeted to poor city dwellers; rather, they mainly benefit the middle class. While AID has a major agriculture and rural development program in Egypt, there is little effort to use the proceeds from the sale of program food aid to help finance this effort. Instead, the funds mostly provide the Egyptian

government with general budget support.

Meanwhile, undernutrition persists among poor Egyptians, although the country has made progress in reducing the proportion of both the urban and the rural population with inadequate diets and in lowering the infant mortality rate. Still, in impoverished rural areas of southern Egypt, the rate is 187 per 1,000 live births, compared to the national rate of sixty-seven. In affluent Cairo, 80 percent of children under two and 90 percent of adult women suffer from anemia. ■

fice of Food for Peace does not have even one full-time nutritionist on its staff.[18]

Program food aid has attractions as a tool to support foreign policy initiatives, but it can have serious negative consequences in the recipient country. Development experts have long worried that food aid can undermine recipient country agriculture by depressing prices on local markets and hurting local farmers. Program food aid has had this effect in El Salvador. Careful management of food aid can prevent such an impact, but food aid can also create a false sense of security within the receiving country's government, discouraging the implementation of measures which promote rural development (see sidebar on Egypt, page 28).

Program food can promote development. In 1986, the U.S. government agreed to ship wheat to Zimbabwe and allowed that country to pay for the imports by shipping some surplus corn to neighboring Mozambique. This "triangular" food aid bolsters agricultural development in the food donor developing country, encourages regional trading links and food security, and saves on ocean freight expenses. However, the United States seldom agrees to such arrangements, because disposing of

Changes in U.S. Food Aid Legislation

In 1990, Congress made sweeping changes in the Food for Peace program. The key change in the law is the removal of the U.S. Department of State from a direct role in food aid decision-making. Previously, the department had dominated the inter-agency committee which set policy and determined country allocations, causing diplomatic and strategic concerns to figure heavily in U.S. food aid.

Now, the purpose of Food for Peace is to enhance "the food security of the developing world" and to "promote broad-based, equitable, and sustainable development, including agricultural development." The U.S. Department of Agriculture will manage Title I of the program, which provides credits tied to the purchase of U.S. agricultural products, with an eye to developing new export markets. AID will oversee food aid grants under Title II and directly administer Title III grants. Title II provides commodities programmed by private voluntary agencies (PVOs) and the World Food Programme, while Title III is an improved form of program food aid. The new law provides Title II programs with increased guaranteed minimum tonnage, makes cash grants to PVOs for project design and implementation, and gives PVOs a greater role in policy-making.

AID is directed to target Title III resources according to need and commitment to equitable development, factors which tended to play a minor role in past program food aid allocations. The recipient government may use the commodities in feeding programs or to establish food reserves. If the government sells the commodities, it must use the proceeds to carry out programs which benefit poor people, such as child survival activities, measures to enhance food security, environmental protection efforts, and programs which generate income and employment. At least 10 percent of the funds must go to indigenous non-government organizations which work directly with poor people.

Other provisions require AID to improve the integration of food aid with other forms of development assistance, particularly child survival

U.S. surpluses and promoting agricultural exports have historically been major Food for Peace objectives. In contrast, WFP and the European Community frequently provide triangular food aid.

In 1990, Congress passed legislation making significant changes in Food for Peace which would enhance the use of U.S. food aid as a tool for combating malnutrition and promoting development. The new law also seeks to reduce the use of food aid to support foreign policy initiatives and promote exports (see sidebar, page 30). ■

Notes

1. Singer, p. 175.
2. Millman, p. 11.
3. Vanderslice, p. 1.
4. Mora, pp. iii, 16, 21, 36, 38, 43-45, 57.
5. *Ibid.*, p. 21; *ICDS—Integrated Child Development Services in India*, pp. 21, 27.
6. King, pp. v, 20.
7. *Ibid.*, p. 20.
8. P. 251.
9. P. 191, emphasis in original.
10. King, pp. vi, 3-4, 18-19, 30-31.
11. *Ibid.*, pp. 28-29.
12. Jackson, pp. 45-51, 72; Stevens, pp. 148-149.
13. King, pp. v, 26, 61.
14. Mora, p. iii.
15. *Ibid.*, pp. 16, 18, 21, 30; Kennedy, p. 155; Singer, pp. 174-175.
16. Quoted in Jackson, p. 36.
17. Bremer-Fox, p. viii; *Prospects for Food Aid*, pp. 18, 20-21.
18. Vanderslice, pp. 1, 6-8.

and nutrition programs. Countries will normally receive Title II and III food aid on a multi-year basis.

A wide variety of humanitarian, development, health, agricultural export, and food processing organizations worked to support the changes in the legislation, including Bread for the World, Interfaith Action for Economic Justice, Church World Service, Lutheran World Relief, the U.S. Catholic Conference, the National Council for International Health, CARE, Interaction (a coalition of PVOs and development education organizations), Protein Grain Products International, the National Cooperative Business Association, and the North American Export Grain Association. Not surprisingly, the State Department vociferously objected to efforts to limit the use of food aid as a foreign policy tool.

This is not the first piece of legislation which has sought to assure that food aid supports equitable and sustainable development in the countries which receive it, but previous changes served mainly to add good intentions to the law, while administrations of both parties continued to use Food for Peace primarily as a political instrument, and, secondarily, to promote food exports. This time, though, four factors make it more likely that the legislation will actually change the nature of U.S. food aid:

- Previous amendments simply added new requirements to the program without changing its fundamental design, but the 1990 revisions are much more sweeping, notably in reducing the influence of the State Department and creating clear lines of administrative authority and accountability;
- The changes have the strong support of key actors on Capitol Hill who are willing to subject Food for Peace to careful oversight;
- Related to this, the law now requires the General Accounting Office, a Congressional investigations agency, to conduct regular program audits;
- And finally, the end of the Cold War has generated pressure for making foreign assistance more effective, rather than just providing rewards to "friendly governments." There is debate over what is really effective, but in this new climate, growing numbers of members of Congress recognize that meeting basic human needs is in the long-term U.S. interest. ■

Saving Trees Without Sacrificing People

Photo: WFP

Reforestation workers in Ghana help develop sustainable sources of fuelwood with assistance from the U.N. World Food Programme.

by Patricia L. Kutzner

Overview

Environmental deterioration in developing countries greatly increases vulnerability to hunger. Deforestation, exhaustion of soil fertility, soil erosion, and other types of desertification hurt the rural poor most. In Asia and Africa, 80 to 90 percent of those living below the poverty line of their countries are found in rural areas. In Latin America, the figure is 60 percent. Directly or indirectly, their livelihood depends to a large extent on agriculture; whatever reduces the land's fertility and productivity makes that livelihood even more marginal. Poor people also depend on the free fuelwood, medicinal herbs, construction materials, and wild foods they can gather or hunt in their natural environment. Hardship grows when nature's bounty shrinks.

Farmers and pastoralists see the declining conditions of the environment around them. Women – the chief gatherers of fuelwood and fodder, the providers of household water, and the producers of at least 50 percent of the food eaten by rural families – experience acutely the harmful consequences of environmental destruction. But to many who clear forests in order to plant crops or raise cattle, who strip the hills of fuelwood in order to cook otherwise inedible food, who crop marginal land better left in wild grasses, or who wear out the soil, there seems to be no choice. The circumstances of their lives offer no alternative to the downward spiral of destruction. Changing the circumstances and developing alternatives for poor people is the twin challenge for sustainable development.

The United Nations Environment Program warns that at least 11.3 billion acres, 35 percent of the earth's land surface, are in various stages of desertification. More than 850 million people live in these areas. The problem is almost universal, but the most extensive damage is occurring in the regions of greatest hunger – Africa, Asia, and Latin America. Farmers moving from degraded land cut half of the new forest area cleared each year.

Millions of urban and rural households in developing countries depend on fuelwood to cook and heat their homes. Wood is the main energy source for nine out of ten Africans and provides more than 58 percent of total energy consumption in Africa. In much of the continent, women and children have to walk more than five miles and spend five to eight hours every four to seven days searching for fuelwood. This leaves women with less time for agricultural work, food preparation, and child care; in this exchange, children's health and nutrition pay dearly. When dead wood is gone, live trees and bushes are cut. Even the dried stalks of harvested crops are burned, depriving soils of mulch and compost that could increase yields.

In the semi-arid west African nation of Burkina Faso, older people remember thick forests around their villages filled with wild animals. Farmers today find bedrock only a few inches down where soils a generation or two ago were abundant and deep. And each year for weeks on end, clouds of unprotected soil blow away in the fierce "harmattan" wind, darkening the sky and turning the noonday sun red. Households more destitute with each passing season abandon once-productive farms.

Commercial lumbering, sanctioned and encouraged by government policy in the pursuit of economic development, competes with fuelwood as another major cause of deforestation. In the Himalayas for example, large-scale timbering begun under the British continues under the Indian government. Himalayan deforestation is the primary cause of the frequent floods that devastate Bangladesh, especially poor people who live in the most flood-prone areas. In India, the area subject to severe annual flooding has more than tripled since 1960. Deforestation by timber companies is occurring more rapidly across Asia, Africa, and Latin America. Southeast Asia's logging industry currently accounts for nearly 90 percent of the world's $7 billion annual trade in tropical timber products.

Deforestation costs India 30 to 50 million tons of foodgrains each year because of land lost to erosion. Soil eroding from denuded hills quickly silts up new dams in India, Central America, and elsewhere.

The connection between hunger and environment is especially obvious in Africa. Africa today faces twin crises: a hunger crisis, in which population growth has outpaced food production, and an environmental crisis. Each is a cause and an effect of the other: people desperate for food seek to produce on marginal lands and strip away forests to get fuel for cooking. At the same time, the degraded environment is less able to sustain basic human needs. Meanwhile, dangerous infestation by disease-bearing insects makes large areas of potentially fertile land uninhabitable.

Colonial policies set the stage for environmental degradation in Africa. On the best land, export monocropping for European markets replaced traditional mixed cropping, agroforestry, and fallow systems. Poor peasants not absorbed into the European-style agriculture were forced to resettle onto less arable land to try to produce subsistence crops. Independent African governments, following advice from western experts and donor agencies, have gen-

Wood is the main energy source for nine out of ten Africans and provides more than 58 percent of total energy consumption in Africa. In much of the continent, women and children have to walk more than five miles and spend five to eight hours every four to seven days searching for fuelwood. This leaves women with less time for agricultural work, food preparation, and child care; in this exchange, children's health and nutrition pay dearly.

erally continued these policies. Modern agricultural science now recognizes that indigenous patterns of food production often were better adapted to Africa's particular ecology. Agricultural technology transferred from quite different environments and social systems has done much harm to African soils, the African food system, and the millions of peasant households that are the backbone of African societies.

Africa's population in the post-colonial era has grown at a faster rate (currently 3 percent per year) than any continent at any time in history. This adds to the pressure on the environment. Food production per person declined by 28 percent between 1967 and 1990, and more new families are seeking ever more land to farm. In the absence of greater access to more education and higher status for girls and women, early marriage and frequent child-bearing will continue. And while security in old age for both men and women wholly depends on their surviving children, most Africans will continue to want large families.

All of the world's tropical forests lie within the borders of developing countries. According to most estimates, between 25 percent and 40 percent of the original forests have now disappeared and an area roughly four times the size of Massachusetts is being lost to nonforest uses annually. The humid tropics cover only about 6 percent of the earth's surface, but contain an estimated 50 percent of all living species.

Tropical forest soils quickly become unproductive when they lose a protective canopy of dense foliage, are exposed to the relentless sun and pounding rain, and are no longer fed by the complex symbiosis of forest species. Within a few years, the new settlers' crop harvests drop sharply and cattle ranchers take over the cleared land. Soon, however, the ranchers find it hard to feed their cattle – overgrazing is common. Finally, the soils compact to a hardness rain scarcely penetrates, and few plants of any kind can grow. This pattern is spreading throughout the tropical forests of South and Central America. Once cleared, tropical forests do not regenerate; they are gone forever.

The search is on for a third option for economic development in such forests, an option where settlers earn income by extracting renewable products from the forest in ways that leave the forest unharmed.

Brazil's 500,000 rubber tappers and tribal societies in the Amazon Basin like the Kayapo Indians illustrate such a third option, although at a very low level of income. Their livelihoods depend on what is called a "vernacular economy": a combination of traditional self-provisioning subsistence activities and cash-earning activities based on native forest resources such as wild animals, medicinal plants, nuts, and wild rubber trees. The Kayapo apply intimate knowledge of the forest's ecology to grow food in a complex twenty-year cycle of intercropping and fallow that leaves the soil more fertile than it was at the beginning. Rubber tappers have been continuously extracting and selling latex from wild rubber trees for more than a century without damaging the forest. Before development planners are convinced that a third option – sustainable extractive development – is the right policy choice, however, the economic gains to forest settlers will probably have to permit much higher levels of material consumption than the rubber tappers and the Kayapo now enjoy (or seem to want).

Sustainable Development: Turning the Tide

Sustainable development was not yet in the lexicon when the first United Nations

Conference on the Environment met in Stockholm in 1972. Delegates from developing nations argued that environmental issues were unimportant compared with the need for economic development, while those from industrialized nations were slow to see that a lack of alternatives could force poor people to harm the environment. Deforestation, for example, bothered them greatly, but not the shortage of fuelwood; desertification was not even on the agenda in Stockholm.

Within a year or two, however, the terrible drought of 1968-1974 in Ethiopia and the Sahel produced pictures of skeletal figures walking gauntly out of African moonscapes, dead cattle lying in the sand, and hollow-eyed children too weak to eat. These scenes made desertification a household word, and even the most conservative conservationist came to realize that Sahelian people had to gather fuelwood, regardless of the environmental cost.

By contrast, when the United Nations Conference on Environment and Development meets in Rio de Janeiro in June 1992, environment and sustainable development will be prominent on the agendas of both South and North. Nevertheless, it is as difficult now as it was then to persuade national policymakers to give the needs of poor people high priority. The fuelwood shortage affecting the daily lives of nearly 2 billion people in sixty-three countries has to compete with planners' greater interest in energy issues affecting industry and automobiles, while Northern people with full stomachs generally get more excited about acid rain, the ozone layer, and the possibility of polar icecaps melting than about the environmental aspects of rural poverty.

Outside Rio's conference halls, though, people from all over the developing world are offering models of sustainable development. Their success stories involve not merely the marriage of development with environmental protection, but the active participation of the affected people in managing and carrying out programs.

Reclaiming the Desert in Burkina Faso

One example of sustainable development comes from Burkina Faso. A traditional village-level association of young unmarried men and women, called Naam, has become a moving force for locally initiated, community-controlled development. The Naam movement has adopted ingeniously effective low-cost technologies for reversing desertification and is inspiring similar action among villagers in other countries of the Sahel, the semi-arid region stretching across sub-Saharan Africa from the Atlantic to the Red Sea. Food security in this zone is an enormous challenge for hundreds of thousands of poor people whose livelihoods depend on agriculture, and humans must work very carefully to maintain the productivity of a fragile ecosystem.

Large-scale irrigation is not a viable option, due to unfavorable geology, easily salinated soils (which stop supporting crops as irrigation water increases the soil's salt content), limited underground water sources, few rivers with year-round flow, high evaporation in the intense heat, and inadequate gravity flow, so expensive pumping has to distribute collected water. Where large-scale irrigation has been attempted, as in Nigeria and Senegal, for example, it tends to benefit a minority of farmers while undermining traditional downstream production systems, such as fisheries and floodwater farming, upon which poorer households depend.

Instead, throughout northern Burkina Faso, the most arid part of the country, hundreds of Naam groups are spreading a self-help technique of rainwater management. This technique makes it possible to produce crops within a year on land so degraded that it has been abandoned to the encroaching desert for as long as twenty years. Long rows of little dikes ("diguettes" to the local people) are built across fields by piling loose stones six to eight inches high along level contour lines. The diguettes check the downhill flow of scarce rainwater long enough to moisten a few feet of earth behind each diguette before it seeps past the stones to pause again behind the next lower diguette, and on to the bottom of the field.

Only diguettes that cross a field on level contour lines collect water long enough to be effective. To locate level points of a field with the unaided eye, however, is generally impossible. That is why a low-cost method for surveying the correct lines for diguettes was essential, a method that any Burkinabe (as the local people are called) farmer could learn and apply easily. After much experimentation, the method taken up by the Naam movement was developed by a dryland water management specialist who had been a Peace Corps volunteer there, Peter Wright, a consultant in Burkina Faso for Oxfam-UK, a voluntary development assistance organization.

In any container, water will try to rise to the same level in all parts of the container. "Water seeks its own level." That is the key to Wright's two-person technique for placing the diguettes correctly. The survey tool consists of a transparent plastic tube containing water and fastened for an equal length at each end to two tall sticks marked identically as measuring sticks. One person stands one of the measuring sticks upright on the ground to mark a starting point along a contour line, while the other person stands the second measuring stick on the ground at various points

nearby until, by trial and error, the water in the tube rises to the same place on each stick. The surveyors know then that their sticks mark two points of ground that are on a level with each other. Rocks are placed in a line between those two points, and the whole process is repeated to find a third point of ground at the same level, and then a fourth, and so on, over and over, to build as long a diguette as the survey team chooses.

The process is slow and laborious, but in the dry season there is time for extra labor; the cash expense is little or nothing and the eventual reward is great. Crop yields have increased in some places by a ton or more per hectare (two-and-a-half acres) where the diguettes are used. When it rains, the moisture retained in the soil behind the diguettes gives millet and sorghum a better chance to sprout and grow. Loose sandy soil carried along in the rainwater or blown by the "harmattan" also collects behind the diguettes, along with the seeds of wild plants that take root and help hold the soil in place during the dry season. Slowly but surely, topsoil begins to accumulate and desertification recedes.

Soon after Oxfam began teaching the technique for diguettes in 1982, members of the Naam movement discovered its benefits for themselves. Promoted by Naam groups, diguettes spread rapidly from village to village. Now hundreds of hectares of degraded land are being reclaimed by this process.

The Naam movement as it operates today started in 1967, but it is rooted in the ancient Naam tradition where young unmarried men and women formed into groups of workers to assist with the grain harvest. A Burkinabe teacher and community development worker, Bernard Ouedraogo, realized that an underutilized reserve of energy, enthusiasm, and talent was lying dormant here. If, with approval of village elders, the Naam tradition could be adapted also to cooperative projects during the dry season when less labor was needed for the crops, a new dynamism could be unleashed to address the development needs of local communities from within their own culture.

Ouedraogo's idea worked. Now there are more than 1,300 Naam groups that select and carry out their own projects for the dry season, seeking hands-on technical training from outside the village as needed – projects in reforestation and agroforestry, woodlots, land reclamation, wells, composting, construction, primary health care, and other village improvements. The national government is generally supportive. Since 1976, European donors have provided simple hand tools and a revolving loan fund to the Naam movement through an intermediary organization, also initiated by Ouedraogo, "Se Servir de la Saison Seche en Savanne et au Sahel" (making use of the dry season in the Sudano-Sahel), or the 6-S Society. Several donor agencies are assisting Naam members to introduce the movement's spirit and methods to villagers in other Sahelian countries.

Agroforestry in Africa

Leaders of the Naam movement first urged everyone to plant trees, but farmers knew trees had to wait: growing more food came first. After diguettes, composting, mulching, and other improved farming methods increase harvests and household food security, time and labor are available to plant and tend trees for fuelwood and to prevent erosion. Thorn trees make living fences to keep livestock away from growing crops and in enclosures where manure can be collected as fertilizer. Whole farm systems become more productive.

Agroforestry is the planned integration of multipurpose trees with agriculture. Planting a nitrogen-fixing tree like the acacia provides a natural source of fertilizer. The variety "acacia albida" loses its leaves during the rainy season, allowing farmers to grow other crops underneath without shading them. In the hot dry season, its shade is a boon for livestock and homesteads. Tree leaves and branches provide valuable mulch to check wind erosion and weed growth while conserving moisture in the soil. Leaves and young branches can also provide fodder for livestock and reduce the need for grazing. Many fast-growing trees can be lopped or pruned repeatedly to provide fuelwood and construction poles; the growth that has been harvested regenerates within a year. Fruit trees add important nourishment to family diets and produce a cash crop. Alley-cropping, highly developed for the low-land tropics of West and Central Africa by scientists at the International Institute of Tropical Agriculture (IITA), is a particular form of agroforestry in which food crops are grown between rows of trees that enhance their growth.

Kenya Takes Trees Seriously

If all of Africa's 35 million smallholders were to become avid tree planters, African reforestation could be accomplished rapidly. Something like that is happening in Kenya.

The Kenya Forestry Department and the Soil Conservation Program both had tree extension programs when, in 1977, the National Council of Women of Kenya started the Green Belt Movement, with the aim of getting each community to establish "green belts" with at least 1,000 trees on open spaces, in school grounds and along roads. Under leadership of Wangari Maathai, a professor at the University of Nairobi, tree planting became a national passion shared by the news media, political leaders, voluntary organizations, schools, and Kenya's 6,000 women's groups. Now all of the women's groups and many schools plant trees. Operating a tree nursery is a popular group income project. The government's 1,300 tree nurseries provide free seedlings.

Women's groups, trained by well-prepared agricultural extension agents, are also the most active soil conservationists in Kenya, using their relatively lighter work load in the dry season as a time to help each other dig drainage ditches, build ter-races, and plant trees, shrubs, and grasses strategically to check erosion and retain rainwater. Kenya's soil conservation program was initiated in 1974 with the aid of the Swedish International Development Authority. It started with the best traditional practices found in the country, adding only improvements that smallholder farmers can apply easily with their own labor and resources. By 1985, at least 365,000 Kenyan farms – two out of every five – had been terraced.

Kenya's Ministry of Energy operates six agroforestry research centers, the most

The World Bank and the Environment

by Marc J. Cohen

The World Bank is the largest public source of development financing. It currently disburses $16 billion a year in loans and credits, which is 60 percent of the funding provided by all multilateral organizations. The World Bank is affiliated with the United Nations system and owned by 152 member governments. The Bank has historically sought to promote economic growth and poverty alleviation by supporting specific investment projects. In the 1980s, it has redirected a substantial share of its lending to support broad changes in economic policy ("structural adjustment") intended to help hard-pressed developing countries recover from financial crisis (see chapter on "Economic Policies").

In the early 1980s, a group of U.S. environmental organizations launched a campaign to get the World Bank to pay more attention to the environmental aspects of development. They were provoked by World Bank support for Brazil's Polonoroeste Project. This project included a highway across much of the Amazon state of Rondonia. The project was supposed to include measures to protect the tropical forest and indigenous people, and to direct land-hungry settlers to areas of Rondonia where soils are suitable for agriculture. The Brazilian government moved ahead quickly with the highway, however, and much more slowly with the environmental and social aspects of the Polonoroeste Project.

Logging companies rapidly expanded their operations in Rondonia. Poor settlers followed close behind, clearing the remaining forest by fire. In much of Rondonia, the soil can support only a few years of agriculture. Settlers soon move on to clear more forest, with cattle ranchers often buying up the worn-out land for grazing. Environmental groups were dismayed that a huge World Bank project was contributing to the destruction of the Amazon forest. Eventually, the Bank withdrew its support of the Polonoroeste Project, and it is now financing Brazil's national environmental program.

As environmentalists studied the Bank's operations, they identified other projects with serious problems. The Bank initially resisted pressure for change, pleading it needed to respond to the priorities of developing-country governments. So U.S. environmental organizations began to build a worldwide coalition of concerned citizens, including nongovernmental organizations in developing countries. Partly at the urging of these organizations, the coalition increasingly raised questions about the impact of World Bank operations on poor people as well as on nature.

This international coalition has

highly developed agroforestry research network in Africa. Fuelwood replaced hydroelectric power in the Ministry's national energy planning almost from its beginning in 1979, assisted by the U.S. Agency for International Development (AID). AID also sponsored a Kenyan inventor's 1983 development of a more fuel-efficient model of Kenya's traditional charcoal stove, the "jiko." Produced and sold by Kenyan artisans, the improved "jiko" has gained wide consumer acceptance in the country, saving an estimated 1.5 million tons of fuelwood annually.

Poor People's Agroforestry in Haiti

Haiti, the poorest country of the Western Hemisphere, has lost 90 percent of its trees since 1950. Little soil of good quality remains and none at all on the denuded hills where the poor majority are forced to eke out their livelihoods. Many erosion control projects attempted with foreign assistance ended in failure until it was realized that trees must become economically profitable very quickly. Otherwise, poor people will not give trees the space needed for food crops or divert labor from other livelihood activities to plant and care for them.

demonstrated its effectiveness in the ongoing controversy over the proposed Sardar Sarovar dam in India. The World Bank agreed to help finance this dam because it will provide irrigation and electricity for millions of people. Yet, the dam will also flood vast areas of forests and farmlands, displacing up to 100,000 people, mainly extremely poor, low-status "tribal" Indians. The World Bank's original appraisal of this project failed fully to assess environmental and social factors.

Local private agencies that work among the threatened tribal people have become active in organizing protests, in collaboration with environmental advocacy groups in Washington, London, Bonn, and Tokyo. On many occasions, these people-to-people networks have provided industrial-country governments better, more vivid information than the World Bank has been able to obtain through its governmental channels.

Partly in response to pressure

from this environmental coalition, the Bank has, over the last few years, established an Environment Department and revamped controversial projects. The Bank is urging many developing-country governments to pay greater attention to environmental problems, and environmental components feature in half its new loans. In 1992, the Bank's *World Development Report* will be devoted to the environment.

The Bank's actual practice has lagged behind stated changes in its policies. The Bank sometimes succumbs to other pressures, notably the pressure to get on with lending, at the expense of social and environmental concerns. Some argue that social and environmental problems call for a major revamping of the model of economic development which the Bank supports – with much less emphasis on growth in exports and production and much more on poverty reduction, environmental protection, and grassroots democracy. Environmentalists charge that the Bank has no

coherent vision of sustainability. In current research, Bank economists are seeking new ways to analyze environmental costs and benefits in order to make them more obvious as economic factors in making loans.

The Bank's policies now require borrowing governments to consult with affected communities and local nongovernmental organizations about all new projects with significant environmental implications. Such consultation with poor communities and citizen activists has been rare in the developing world, and implementation of this far-reaching World Bank policy has been limited.

But a worldwide coalition of environmental groups has shown that popular pressure can improve the environmental and social impact of large-scale development projects. ■

In 1981, AID's Haiti Agroforestry Outreach Project began to promote trees as a cash crop for hillside households, providing funds for technical assistance and tree seedlings. An intermediary nongovernmental organization was AID's link to 170 smaller Haitian and expatriate organizations working directly with poor rural households. Five years later there were thirty-nine tree nurseries producing 5 million seedlings a year, and 110,000 farmers had planted more than 25 million nitrogen-fixing trees with a 50 percent survival rate. Farm income increased from the sale of wood and other tree products. Crop yields increased, too, as soils became more fertile and soaked up rainwater better, while reduced erosion improved the usefulness of marginal land.

Improving Incomes and Land in Ecuador

On the Andean slopes of Ecuador, where almost all of the country's domestic food supply is produced and 40 percent of its agricultural population lives, farms are losing soil at a rate twenty times greater than the maximum soil loss considered acceptable by the U.S. Soil Conservation Service. In 1985, the Ecuadoran Ministry of Agriculture and CARE together started the Community Land Use Management Project to spread soil conservation and regenerative agriculture techniques throughout forty communities. As in Honduras, the techniques are easy to learn and teach, and inexpensive for farmers to use. The Ecuador project added agroforestry to produce fruit and wood for household use and income.

Within two years, 2,300 farm families became involved. Harvests of traditional crops – barley, potatoes, fava beans, onions, quinoa, corn, wheat, and cassava – increased by an average of 49 percent and deeper soils were permitting new crops to be grown. Household income from farming had increased by 56 percent. Highly encouraged by these successes on poor plots, some of the men began to give up off-farm jobs, purchasing and reclaiming badly eroded land that had been abandoned. In this part of Ecuador, women's labor on family crops typically exceeds that of men, who often have to seek additional employment off the farm to augment the family's meager farm earnings. With patient persistence, the project's specially trained extensionists, whose language and socio-economic background must fit the local culture, persuaded the men of each community to allow women also to receive training in the new agricultural methods (by female extension agents in classes near their homes).

CARE and the Ministry of Agriculture knew that the project would fail unless the local communities invested themselves in its success. Therefore, a well-established local credit union serving the forty communities was selected as the project's third sponsor. Committees chosen by each community manage all aspects of the project locally: planning and promoting training courses taught by project extensionists; organizing work groups to improve terraces, irrigation channels, and other infrastructure; managing seed banks; and screening loan applications before they are submitted to the credit union. To qualify for credit, a landowner must comply with soil conservation and cropping plans jointly prepared by the loan applicant, the Community Credit Committee, and the project extension agent.

Conclusion

Examples of success in reducing hunger and poverty while protecting the environment are still more the exception than the rule, but these successes demonstrate that it can be done. Several lessons seem clear.

The deep poverty of many rural people in developing countries leaves them with few choices and no margin for error. Therefore, whatever poor people are asked to do in order to protect the environment must not reduce their food security and should improve it almost immediately.

The methods used must harmonize with the social ecology as well as the natural ecology of the local situation. Unless they are understood by the people affected and are accommodated to their satisfaction, they will not accomplish their intended purpose. Indeed, unless this accommodation occurs, new technology may worsen hunger and inequality, as happened with large-scale irrigation in Nigeria. In contrast, Ouedraogo's enlisting the Naam movement in sustainable development efforts in Burkina Faso nicely meshed technology with local resources and culture.

Beyond accepting innovations that protect the environment, local people must want them to work badly enough to apply their own time, thought, labor, and land or other resources to make it happen. People asked to support change must feel some "ownership" in the processes and fruits of that change.

Changes undertaken by local communities succeed in the long run only when the policies, priorities, and actions of the national government support these new initiatives. In the success stories examined here, national governments played a positive role either with active programs or tacit encouragement. The immediate economic gains apparent in each instance were doubtless as significant to government policymakers as to the poor people themselves.

Governments faced with economic crisis, like poor people, often find themselves driven to maximize immediate gains from the resources at hand, regardless of the environmental cost. In 1989, developing countries owed a foreign debt of $1.2 trillion, 44 percent of their collective GNP. For the most heavily indebted countries, progress toward equitable and sustainable development may be impossible without debt relief. International trade patterns and the assistance policies of multilateral and bilateral donors also greatly affect the ability and inclination of national governments to pursue development strategies that protect the environment.

Rural communities in developing countries want desperately to reverse environmental deterioration, but their first priority, of necessity, is to meet present need. Sustainable development accomplished by and for poor people will reduce hunger and protect the environment at the same time if the policy environment – nationally and internationally – is right. ■

Green Revolution Reduces Hunger in India

Photo: WFP/FAO

New agricultural technology and supportive government policies have boosted food production and reduced poverty in four Indian states.

by John W. Mellor

Since the 1960s, the "green revolution" has spread rapidly in Asia. Many farmers have adopted scientifically bred varieties of food crops that mature rapidly and produce more. These varieties depend on irrigation and chemical fertilizers and pesticides. In some Indian states and Asian countries, a sharp drop in rural poverty has accompanied widespread cultivation of green revolution crop varieties. In the Philippines, many farmers planted green revolution rice, but poverty worsened. A comparison of India's green revolution states with the Philippines shows the importance of government policies in determining the impact of agricultural technology on hunger, poverty, and the environment.

Poverty Reduction in India

Between 1963 and 1983, the proportion of the rural population living below the poverty line dropped by half in five Indian states: Punjab, Haryana, Gujarat, Andhra Pradesh, and Kerala. That is a startling achievement for states with such low incomes. Four states had the highest agricultural growth rates in India during this period; these are the green revolution states. Punjab is a small state in India, with a population of 16 million. The other states range up to three times as large and each is equivalent to the major countries of Europe in population.

Income in poor, primarily agricultural countries varies from year to year with the weather. Year to year comparisons can be distorted by selecting dry years versus wet years or vice versa. But India had normal weather in both 1963 and 1983, with 1963 somewhat better. Thus, comparing these two years understates the decline in poverty.

Farmers in Punjab and Haryana, in the northwest, increased cultivation of short, stiff-stemmed wheat varieties and double cropping of high-yielding varieties of rice. Well irrigation and chemical fertilizer use likewise increased rapidly.

Andhra Pradesh is a large rice producing state in southern India, with vast, fertile plains along the coast, with similarly widespread irrigation and rapidly increasing use of fertilizer on the new rice varieties. Unlike the northwest, though, Andhra's higher rainfall and humidity held back the rice revolution until plant breeders developed varieties more resistant to pests and diseases.

Gujarat is a different story. It has little irrigated area, hence the green revolution had to come through much more complex and difficult processes associated with the development of new, high-yielding, hybrid varieties of corn and sorghum. Fertilizer use also grew rapidly, but from a very low base, with less intensity of use, a lower rate of return, and consequently a less spectacular effect on net income. Sophisticated government extension and fertilizer distribution services played an important role. States with less well-developed systems of public administration are not likely to succeed with agricultural improvements under the complex conditions of dry-land agriculture. Gujarat's experience does show, however, that success is possible with adequate public support.

Gujarat has also taken advantage of India's rapidly growing market for milk. Farmers with extremely small plots of land – mainly poor women – account for most of the increased milk production, and poverty has declined considerably as a result. This contribution of increased milk production to poverty reduction (the "white revolution") stems in large part from an extraordinarily effective milk marketing cooperative which has brought fame to Kaira district and to Dr. Verghese Kurien, its prize-winning, charismatic leader.

In India's four green revolution states, farmers spent much of the income they gained from the new technology on goods and services produced by local nonagricultural industries. These new businesses generated many off-farm jobs, which played a key role in reducing poverty.

The rapid reduction in poverty in states that have done well in agriculture should not be surprising. Agriculture was similarly the leading edge in Taiwan's rapid economic growth. That country has virtually eliminated absolute poverty and has increased its per capita income ten-fold since the mid-1950s. Then, Taiwan's income per person was significantly lower than that of Sri Lanka and the Philippines.

Thailand and Indonesia have also experienced rapid agricultural growth and have cut in half the proportion of the rural population in poverty. Thailand did this without the rates of growth in fertilizer use which characterized the other countries, because it has had little population pressure on its abundant land resources. Instead, Thailand rapidly expanded its rural road network, initially in connection with the war in Vietnam, which allowed intensive annual crop cultivation in an expanded land area. Recently, agricultural growth associated with reduced rural poverty has occurred in some parts of Bangladesh as well.

Some Indian states, like Bihar, have had an abysmal record on poverty reduction. Indeed, in some cases, the proportion of the population in poverty has increased. These states have experienced little agricultural growth, either because of inadequate agricultural research for their conditions or lack of government support for rural development. In these states, dynamic population growth and stagnant agricultural technology have proved to be a lethal combination for rural poor people, leaving them worse off economically and more vulnerable to exploitation by landowners.

The south Indian state of Kerala also reduced poverty by more than half between 1963 and 1983, even though it had a poor agricultural growth record. Agricultural progress is not the only way to reduce rural poverty. The Kerala state government has consistently invested heavily in social welfare programs and public education. This has paid off in many ways. Since the 1970s, Keralans have migrated in large numbers to the Persian Gulf region and sent about half their high Gulf incomes back home. These remittances raised incomes in Kerala radically, but the Gulf war reduced this income source sharply.

Agricultural Success Does Not Always Reduce Poverty

The Philippines, like the successful agricultural states in India, increased agricultural production as a result of the green revolution. It is the home of the International Rice Research Institute, which pioneered the crossbreeding of Taiwanese rice with the Indica varieties of South and Southeast Asia. Yields increased radically due to greater response to high levels of fertilizer.

Nevertheless, in the Philippines, the green revolution did not translate into less poverty. Small farmers benefited markedly from increased productivity and employment, but real wages declined gradually and absolute poverty increased. What went wrong?

Most important, rural employment in small- and medium-scale nonagricultural

Equity, Ecology, and Alternative Agricultural Technologies

by Don Reeves and Marc J. Cohen

The spread of the green revolution has increased supplies of staple foods and lowered prices, especially in parts of Asia and Latin America. Questions remain, however, about its effects on the distribution of land and income, as well as its long-term sustainability. The challenge for the future is to develop farming systems which increase productivity and fit the resources of small farmers and poor people, enhancing environmental quality, and offering resilience in the face of likely future resource constraints.

The green revolution has benefited consumers and reduced hunger in India and elsewhere. Despite production gains, Indian yields remain below those of Japan, China, Indonesia, and Bangladesh. As major food importing nations like India and Indonesia attained food grain self-sufficiency, they had foreign exchange savings available to invest in development. Yet the revolution, as carried out, brought with it socioeconomic and environmental problems. Its technologies were not suited to the production and climatic conditions of much of the world's farming regions, especially in Africa. In addition, population growth and poor weather have offset some of the gains.

Hundreds of millions of people depend on subsistence agriculture for their food. Many of them work poor soils and face erratic rainfall with no access to irrigation. Subsistence farmers often have little cash income and no access to affordable credit or stable markets. They cannot afford to buy fossil fuel-based chemical inputs, which are a critical part of green revolution technology. In Latin America, the debt crisis has put the technology out of the

enterprises did not expand rapidly. In part, that was because the government promoted the development of capital-intensive, large-scale industry, concentrated in the area around the capital city. This soaked up the country's limited capital while creating little employment and draining resources from the small industries which rising agricultural incomes might have stimulated.

Lack of investment in rural infrastructure compounded the problems. The Philippines reached independence with better than average rural infrastructure by East and Southeast Asian standards. Rather than adding to these facilities, the Marcos administration (1965-1986) pursued a policy of neglect. An overvalued foreign exchange rate and a system of subsidies reinforced this unfortunate tendency. Rapid population growth meant an expanding labor force, and slow growth in employment caused real wages to decline. The Philip-

pines' experience contrasts sharply with that of Taiwan, Thailand, and India's green revolution states.

An inequitable system of land holding also helped prevent the green revolution from reducing poverty in the Philippines. A reasonably effective land reform in rice growing areas set land rentals at rates which favored tenants. Thus tenants received a larger share of income increases from improved technology. Unfortunately, the Philippines did not institute land reform in its sugar or coconut producing areas, which account for half of its farm production. Those areas gained less from the green revolution, and even where other technological gains were made, they did not favorably affect employment.

In India's green revolution states, land tenure systems are far from perfect. Land distribution is quite unequal, and many rural people are landless. Still, the more well-to-do people in these states form a

reach of most farmers. Research on how to expand yields of Africa's staples – millet, sorghum, and cassava – has just begun. Altogether, the green revolution has spread to only about a third of the grain acreage in the developing world.

There are other equity questions. Development experts disagree whether the green revolution increased rural inequality in Asia. In many instances, small farmers have adopted the new technologies at about the same rate as larger farmers. But if new methods are more accessible to larger and more well-to-do farmers, smaller farmers may not be able to compete for higher land rents and purchase prices and lose access to land. As

landless laborers dependent on cash wages, they are more vulnerable to poverty and hunger in economic downturns or bad weather. The evidence is clear that Asian farmers without access to irrigation did not generally adopt high-yielding rice varieties, and were hurt to the extent that overall production gains reduced prices.

In India's green revolution areas, farmers tend not to rotate crops, but plant most of their land in a single commodity, year after year. This contributes to increased soil erosion rates, which for all of India are thirty times greater than the rate of soil formation. On erosion-prone soils and on a national basis, the loss of soil nutrients through ero-

sion exceeds those added by commercial fertilizers. This means that farmers must use ever greater amounts of costly fertilizer. In India and elsewhere, soil sediment hampers irrigation, and poor irrigation management has made some soils too salty or too waterlogged to support agriculture.

Careless fertilizer use pollutes surface and groundwater, killing fish that provide a vital source of protein and raising a variety of health risks. Careless pesticide use creates similar problems, requiring new pesticides or new approaches, such as biological control. Some communities in the United States have responded to chemically-induced health risks with multi-

farming class whose consumption patterns have stimulated rapid growth in nonfarm rural employment.

The Theory of the Agriculture-Poverty Relationship

A green revolution cannot solve the problems of poor people directly or by itself, as the case of the Philippines demonstrates. Increased farm output will bring down food prices, which benefits poor people, but rising agricultural labor productivity does not solve employment problems. Rather, tapping the vast potential for developing rural small enterprises is the key. The higher incomes that farmers enjoy as a result of their higher yields can provide the stimulus for creating such businesses. Where the green revolution has been associated with a reduced poverty rate, farmers spend 40 percent of their increased income on goods and services produced in local labor-intensive nonfarm enterprises, and 20 percent on labor-intensive agricultural commodities, such as fruits, vegetables, and livestock products. These new employment opportunities depend on a good rural infrastructure and

a high level of rural education. Credit availability is also important and helpful.

Highly concentrated land ownership, as in Ethiopia before 1974 or in much of Central America, puts green revolution incomes into the hands of people who spend most of it abroad or on the products of highly capital-intensive domestic industry. Thus, they transfer little or no purchasing power to poor people.

Turning the argument around, successful programs which increase the incomes of rural poor people by helping them produce goods and services usually depend on relatively higher-income rural people purchasing the products. Without people who can afford to buy these products, there will not be an expanding market. Therefore, efforts to create jobs for unemployed rural dwellers seem to work only when aggregate income in the region is increasing. Small-scale programs – such as providing small loans – to help very poor rural people may improve their incomes. But if these programs are reproduced on a larger scale for a whole region, they will not generate sufficient economic growth to improve the incomes of poor people.

For poor agrarian countries, more jobs

million dollar investments in new water systems and water treatment that most developing nations cannot afford. This makes pollution prevention vital.

Improved management of green revolution technologies and better ecological practices could overcome some of these problems. Smaller amounts of chemical fertilizer used in conjunction with compost or crop residues, for example, can boost productivity at less risk to the environment. Private

research centers like the Rodale Institute in Pennsylvania, along with the public Consultative Group on International Agricultural Research (which includes the International Rice Research Institute and the International Institute of Tropical Agriculture) have begun to look at technologies which are ecologically sound and appropriate to the conditions of poor farmers.

Some of this research is quite innovative, focusing on the development of perennial food crops,

for example. Much of the work on sustainable agriculture, however, involves research on traditional agricultural practices which improve productivity through more careful management and work in concert with nature to reduce pests, supply and preserve nutrients, and conserve soil and water. Such practices include intercropping grain with nitrogen-fixing plants, crop rotation and fallowing (see previous chapter).

Many of these techniques re-

and higher incomes can result from accelerated agricultural growth or from export production. In manufacturing goods for export, problems such as quality control and lack of capital or markets may plague beginning industries. The four Indian states that have reduced poverty directed their available resources to increased agricultural productivity. In turn, farmers with more income bought more goods and services, providing rapid growth in employment.

The green revolution can have different impacts on poverty, depending on government policies, the social structure, and how farmers spend the added income. Similarly, technology has varied effects on the environment.

Environmental Impact

Farmers' adoption of green revolution technology can enhance the environment. In Gujarat, for example, technological improvements appear to have discouraged farmers from clearing perennial grasslands for cultivation. Agriculture on such poor land in such areas is not sustainable, and leads to increased soil erosion. Some evidence indicates that as technology has permitted Gujarati farmers to intensify grain and milk production on existing farmland, pressure to plant the lowest rainfall areas has eased.

Intensifying agriculture brings its own problems. Indian rates of fertilizer use, even in the green revolution areas, remain far below the levels of the Netherlands or even the Corn Belt of the United States. However, lack of agricultural education and relatively poor technical support services result in much less capacity to use inputs at high levels of productivity. Often, relatively more fertilizer runs off, polluting the soil and water. Less crop is harvested for each unit of fertilizer than in North America or Western Europe. Farm surveys in the Indian Punjab show many practices that result in inefficient use of fertilizer, waste, and pollution.

Farmers want any fertilizer they apply to go into the plant, not into the ground water table. At higher levels of use, though, farmers must do scientific soil testing to ensure the correct mix of nutrients, apply fertilizer at the appropriate time, and place it near the plants' roots. The level of support services and education in the rural United States facilitates such careful use, although it does not ensure it. It will take

quire even more intensive management than the green revolution. Most require more labor but lower cash outlays. The increased management and labor requirements can enhance economic opportunities if those requirements are designed to fit the experience, skills, and capabilities of small farmers and enable them to increase their incomes by reducing expenditures on fossil fuel-based products. This is likely to become more important in years to come as oil supplies dwindle and the price of petroleum-based products increase.

Well-managed alternative technologies appear to have the potential for productivity gains roughly comparable to the green revolution's with less costly inputs, while avoiding some of the social and environmental risks. The research and educational tasks of discovering and/or adapting these techniques to local conditions and gaining their adoption by small farmers are probably comparable to those required for best management and further development of green revolution technologies. Gains from risk-reducing alternatives may be slower to appear; their immediate adoption would probably carry a higher risk of failure. The potential social and environmental gains, however, require that the research agenda be broadened, and that a larger share of resources be devoted to exploring these alternative technologies. ■

vigorous development of government institutions and broadening of education before it becomes possible in Punjab.

The same point can be made about chemical pesticides. Integrated pest management, which relies on biologically-oriented pest control and minimal use of chemicals, offers great potential for improved crop protection. The returns to such techniques are higher in the humid, high rainfall areas of the tropics and semi-tropics, where chemicals quickly wash away and where pests multiply rapidly, than in the United States. Integrated pest management is a highly sophisticated applied science, however. Its successful use requires strong government support mechanisms and effective agricultural education. It is easier to teach a poorly educated farmer to throw on vast quantities of pesticides than to demonstrate the scientific means of measuring pest populations as the basis for minimal, timely applications.

We are learning and applying low input solutions in the United States and making slow, steady progress. But to do likewise in poor countries will take time. It will require an immensely expanded effort to educate farmers and build governmental institutions to support them.

The Requisites of Technological Progress in Agriculture

What did Punjab, Haryana, Gujarat, and Andhra Pradesh do to encourage the agricultural growth that translated into rapid growth in rural employment and radically reduced poverty? A complex series of activities can be simplified into three categories. These states provided institutions which fomented improved technology in agriculture; each vigorously expanded rural infrastructure, particularly all-weather roads; each expanded rural education. States like

Bihar did poorly in each of these areas and saw their poverty levels increase.

The agricultural technology institutions start with research, to adapt work done elsewhere to local conditions. Then an effective extension system must be developed to spread the technological knowledge. Systems for distributing inputs must be developed, and rarely does the private sector initiate such systems, even though it may be effective in moving in once there is a system. In rain-fed states like Gujarat, it takes considerable effort to develop such systems. Rural credit is needed to finance not only farming, but input and marketing systems as well.

The need for roads is obvious, but the most important aspect is perhaps less so. How can educated people, who are essential to effective rural institutions, be induced to live in rural areas if they cannot move freely back and forth to urban areas? Rural areas must become decent places to live if doctors and school teachers will be content to live there and help create the environment necessary to attract accountants and business managers. All-weather roads, not muddy tracks, are the first requirement, but electricity and telephones, taken for granted in urban areas, are just as important to rural businesses and hence to rural employment creation.

New nonfarm business ventures, as well as changing agricultural technologies, require new skills and understandings. Both formal and informal educational efforts are required.

In addition to the above three changes, there is the need for broad distribution of land, so that consumption patterns of farmers with growing incomes will stimulate local nonfarm activity. That does not require equality of holdings. Moderate inequality may favor savings, investment, and consumption patterns which create employment, but inequality must not be so great that consumption patterns favor imported goods and the products of capital-intensive urban industry.

Conclusion

Four states in India epitomize poverty reduction based on yield increasing technological advances in agriculture. They also demonstrate the complexity of the process and the critical role of a partnership between public institutions and actions on the one hand and the private activities of small farmers and small business people on the other.

A myriad of small entrepreneurs cannot provide critical technological and other public services on their own. Government is essential. At the same time, small private operatives cannot be precisely regulated by central planners; markets and market processes are also essential. Above all, government needs a strategy to diagnose what is needed to energize its own rural sectors. This will assure that accelerated growth takes place in ways which rapidly reduce poverty. ■

Demilitarization Fosters Justice

by Richard A. Hoehn

The horrors of militarization, in the midst of an otherwise peaceful farming village, are evident in this drawing. The artist, Jose _____ , 13, lives in a village in Guatemala.

The Regular Army of Costa Rica. . . surrenders the key to this barracks to the schools, for which to be converted into a center of culture. The Junta of the Second Republic officially declares the dissolution of the national army.[1]

— Oscar Arias, quoting José Figueres[1]

The Demilitarization Hammer

When Costa Rican President Oscar Arias won the 1987 Nobel Peace Prize, it was fitting that the award go to the leader of a country with a long history of peace, democracy, and concern for social justice. In 1949, José Figueres took "a hammer to the tower of San Jose's main fort," symbolizing the disbanding of the army and substitution of a Civil Guard as police force.[2] Arias and Figueres are no accident. Both were deeply rooted in the values of Costa Rican culture.

Costa Rica is nestled between two neighbors, Panama and Nicaragua. In the 1980s, that meant living between the pressures generated by Panama's strongman Manuel Noriega and Nicaragua's Sandinista President Daniel Ortega. Drugs, the war in Nicaragua, and control of the Panama Canal captured more media attention than the quiet struggles for peace and justice in Costa Rica.

Costa Rica, named "rich coast" because the native people were wearing gold pendants when Columbus arrived in 1502, was actually one of the poorest regions in Latin America. The greediest European explorers took a quick look and kept on going.

The native population was thinly spread, mobile, decimated by European diseases, and resisted enslavement. Because of the scarcity of minerals and cheap labor, the country did not develop the large estates typical in Latin America. Instead, by the nineteenth century, Costa Rica was a society of small landholdings worked by their owners, even the Spanish colonial governor. The culture is described by historians as that of independent farmers – industrious, peaceful, and egalitarian; a place where people would band together to help their neighbors; a society rich in humane values, if not gold. This, it is said, explains Costa Rica's "exceptionalism."

Other historians claim that though the degree of inequality was less than in other Latin American countries, Costa Rica was not the idyllic pastoral paradise sometimes portrayed. The introduction of coffee and banana plantations led to the rise of a wealthy elite that dominated political life from the 1840s to 1940. Inequality rose sharply. By the twentieth century, there was a large class of landless laborers and squatters.

Costa Rica also had its share of violence and turmoil. There were several rounds of military coups between 1838 and 1870. Between 1824 and 1889, the average term of a president was 2.4 years. More than one-third resigned before the end of their term and one-fifth were removed by coups. Of course, things were not peaceful in the rest of the Americas either. The United States fought a civil war, annexed one-third of Mexico, and conducted military campaigns against Native Americans. Between 1865 and 1981, four United States presidents were assassinated and five survived assassination attempts.

Figueres, known to Costa Ricans as Don Pepe, said that war got his blood pumping.

He participated in schemes to assassinate Anastasio Somoza García of Nicaragua, and Somoza supported efforts to overthrow him, including a 1955 personal challenge to a duel. Costa Rican society is not pacifist.

Figueres' disbanding of the army following a bloody civil conflict had the dual effect of keeping the defeated army from mobilizing against the victorious junta and freeing up money for social justice. It was perhaps an exercise in practical morality – do the right thing, but make sure your bases are covered.

There was historical precedent for suspicion of the dangers of armies. The first president of Costa Rica, 120 years earlier, had warned that armies are often "an ominous instrument of tyranny, a dark source of anarchy and disorder, or a plague that has devoured men and their properties."[3]

President Juan Rafael Mora's reaction to a 1855 invasion was: "Attention Costa Ricans. Don't interrupt what you are doing, but get your weapons ready."[4] They did, and won. However, they also had help from Salvadoran, Honduran, and Nicaraguan volunteers and were armed by the British. In times of military crisis, Costa Rica has sought outside negotiators to mediate the problem. In the twentieth century, Costa Rica has looked to the Organization of American States to mediate some conflicts and to the United States as a military back up.

Costa Rica has had a strong civilian bias, and has not developed a powerful military clique. Most of the nineteenth century presidents were civilians and many military coups had grassroots support. Several military regimes legitimized their coups by quickly installing civilian presidents. After the 1949 abolition of the army, presidents had the power to fire members of the Civil Guard and appoint their own partisans, thus undercutting the military's ability to accumulate power.

Figueres held the "yeoman farmer" view of an army. He believed that the Civil Guard could, if necessary, take up arms to defend the country from attack:

> *When your child is sick, it is crucially important that the doctor make a house call. But that doesn't mean he has to live with you all your life.*[5]

The Costa Rican peace record is based on fear of despotism, a cultural tradition that favors compromise and discussion over conflict, and a belief in the efficacy of the citizen soldier. Their peace record is also grounded in a respect for civilian rule, elections, and the values of liberal and social democracy.

Progressive Social Policies

Slavery was abolished prior to Costa Rica's independence from Spain. Education has been highly valued; the country opened its first university in 1843, and established free and compulsory education in 1869. A "Law on Individual Rights," which guarantees the inviolability of life, freedom of religion, and due process, was promulgated in 1877. Capital punishment was abolished in 1882.

Late nineteenth and early twentieth century Costa Rican political culture, under sway of the "coffee barons," emphasized private property, protection from government, secular education, a free trade orientation, and an open society. Though most Costa Ricans are nominally Catholic, a local saying goes, "We are good Catholics, but not fanatics." The Catholic Church has played a background role in Costa Rican life, culture-forming but not as politically activist as in some other Latin American countries.

In the early twentieth century, a reform party espoused some of the principles in Pope Leo XIII's encyclical *Rerum Novarum,* such as tax reforms and the legalization of labor unions. It lost the presidential election, but left a mark on the country's moral life. The founder of that party became advisor to the president who preceded Figueres, Rafael Angel Calderón Guardia.

Calderón, a person of wealthy origins, surprised those who had elected him by initiating a program of social reform. His Social Guarantees of 1942 included "social security, minimum wage, eight-hour work day, child labor laws."[6] He sought support for his reforms in the social principles and hierarchy of the Catholic Church, which was alarmed by the growing number of communists and protestants. But Calderón also turned for support to the communists, who had been organizing plantation workers. In opposing Calderón, Figueres saw himself as resisting communism. Calderón's supporters saw Figueres as engaging in "red scare" tactics in support of the social elite.

Even though Figueres came to power in a coup that overturned an election, he won the respect of his people and the applause of other nations when, after eighteen months, he returned the government to the duly elected president. Figueres was later twice elected president, partly on the strength of his surrender of power the first time around. His act symbolized a strong commitment to elections as the legitimate process for the transfer of power.

The nation has had a tradition of regular elections since 1824, though a literacy requirement kept participation low until the twentieth century. In 1949, the Supreme Electoral Tribunal (*Tribunal Supremo de Elecciones* – TSE), which calls and supervises elections, became virtually a fourth branch of government. TSE is a permanent body with members selected by the Supreme Court. It can ban inflammatory or irresponsible propaganda and call upon the police for enforcement. TSE has earned a reputation of making Costa Rican elections "among the most efficient and honest in the world."[7]

During Figueres' eighteen months as de facto head of the junta, women were granted full voting rights, the banks were nationalized, low-cost health care and child support were instituted, and a 10 percent tax surcharge was levied on the wealthiest citizens. A curious and telling fact is that Figueres, and later Arias, were middle-of-the-road, sometimes even conservative voices in the political spectrum.

In spite of the differences between Costa Rica's liberals and conservatives, it can broadly be said that both were committed to constitutional democracy, peaceful development, land reform, and social welfare. Figueres' abolition of the army, though meeting some practical needs, was connected to a moral vision shared among many Costa Ricans.

In 1961, a constitutional guarantee promised social security, including maternity, health, disability, old age, and death expense benefits, within ten years. The constitution not only makes it illegal to restart an army, but also to station other nations' military forces on Costa Rican soil. It affirms individual rights of citizens and establishes a policy of asylum for political refugees. However, Indians only achieved citizenship within the past year.

Values and Culture

The image of the independent farmer had a strong hold on Costa Rican imagination. Its importance lay in its ability to affect the national psyche and behavior rather than whether or not it accurately reflected nineteenth century developments.

Images, stories, and sayings that a people repeat about themselves as taken-for-granted parts of their culture – the "of course it's that way" beliefs – shape the way they create and recreate society in millions of small and large decisions.

Oscar Arias summarized the cultural identity of many Costa Ricans when he received the Peace Prize. His 1987 comments parallel local sayings recorded in

Costa Rican Sayings: 1944	Oscar Arias Sánchez: 1987 President, Costa Rica
• We have more teachers than soldiers. • When a neighbor is sick, we all run to help. • Our soil is so fertile a stick will grow; nobody starves to death here. • Our presidents stay in for four years. Right now we have four living ex-presidents; sometimes we have had as many as seven or eight. • In Costa Rica we don't have classes – there are rich and poor but the rich are not so rich as in some countries, and the poor are not so poor. No one feels inferior to anyone else. • We have a better democracy than many other countries.[8]	*My land is a land of teachers. For that reason, it is a land of peace. We discuss our successes and failures with complete openness.* *Because mine is a land of teachers, we closed the army barracks and our children march with books under their arms, not with rifles on their shoulders.* *We believe in dialogue, in negotiation, in looking for a consensus. We repudiate violence.* *Because mine is a land of teachers, we believe in convincing, not vanquishing our adversary. We prefer to raise the fallen, not oppress him, because we believe that no one has absolute truth.* *Because mine is a land of teachers, we look for an economy [which affirms cooperation, not competition] to annihilation.* *For the past 118 years in my land, education has been obligatory and free. Today medical care protects all citizens, and public housing is a fundamental tenet of my government.*[9]

1944 by John and Mavis Biesanz. The two show remarkable similarities, revealing dominant cultural values and perceptions affirmed by Costa Ricans over time.

One way of judging how these values have taken the shape of social well-being is to compare Costa Rica with two countries which adjoin it – Nicaragua and Panama (see **Tables 1 and 2**, pages 56 and 57). Costa Rica's disbanding of the army permitted relatively large social expenditures.

Costa Ricans refer to themselves as "Ticos," from *hermaniticos* "little brothers." The English language newspaper is the *Tico Times*. This sense of connectedness is played out in several ways. Costa Rican culture emphasizes consensual decision-making processes, believing that every effort should be put into resolving problems by negotiated compromises. A description of a banana plantation strike in 1934 says that in spite of "all the lies and the provocations" and "four long weeks of a hard struggle":

> *We came to the capital and negotiated for many hours and at last a solution pretty favorable to the workers was signed, that the government promised would be respected.*[10]

Sharp inequality exists, but many observers have reported that "haves" and "have nots" mutually recognize each other's common humanity. The ethos which pervades economic life includes a belief that while some people may have much, no one should go without food and basic needs for survival. When peasants have a grievance, they not only express their needs, but their perception that they are being treated unfairly, their sense of injustice:

> *A strong sense of moral motivation is clear. . . They are working to defend and enforce their shared vision of social justice. . . [They evidence] a sense of dignity, pride and self-assertion. . . often undermined among this class.*[11]

There are, of course, conflicts between poor and rich people. Peasants bring collective pressure on owners for improved conditions. Unions call strikes. In the early 1980s, frustration with government austerity measures led peasants to block urban highways, causing food shortages in the city. For a time, strikes and civil turmoil were common.

Overall, the same value commitments – to education, consensus, neighborliness, peace, democracy, and social justice – account for why Costa Rica demilitarized, remained nonmilitarized, and used its resources instead to reduce hunger and poverty.

Economic Challenges

The constitution of 1949 established a number of "parastatals," or quasi-autonomous government companies to oversee transportation, education and health, social insurance, land reform, and public works. These agencies implement social goals independent of the regular legislative process. Since they develop autonomous budgets, services and costs grow without regard to how the bill will be paid.

Between 1950 and 1979, Costa Rica had the fastest economic growth rate in Central America. Rural credit banks had grown from four in 1937 to fifty-five by 1973. Agricultural extension offices expanded from two in 1947 to forty-five in 1973. In 1973, the government started a rural health program. The infant death rate plummeted. Costa Rica developed the highest rating in

Central America, comparable to wealthier nations, on the Physical Quality of Life Index developed by the Overseas Development Council. In the 1980s, per capita calorie availability was 124 percent of minimum daily requirements. By the late 1970s, Costa Rica ranked alongside the world's best in health care, education, and social services.

The 1980s brought economic difficulties. Oil prices and interest rates rose sharply. The international market for agricultural products crashed. Having become dependent on food exports to industrialized nations, falling demand was devastating.

Costa Rica's total debt service as a share of exports rose from 23.1 percent in 1975 to 56.8 percent in 1983. Net losses in export earnings from changes in export prices from 1980 to 1986 were US$400 million, compared with $139 million for Panama and $307 million for Nicaragua (which was under a U.S.-imposed embargo for much of this period). The government of Costa Rica tried to cover its fiscal crisis by printing more money.

In 1982, the inflation rate rose to 100 percent and unemployment to almost 10 percent. Per capita GNP dropped 30 percent in the early 1980s. The government borrowed heavily to sustain its social safety net. In 1977, government debt was $8.3 million, by 1980 $1.8 billion, and by 1986 $4.4 billion. Costa Rica suspended debt payments. The Central American economies were brought to their knees:

Costa Rica's democracy should have come apart in the collapse of 1981-82. But the strength of Costa Rica, with its stress on education and openness, lay precisely in long-cherished democratic institutions and civil traditions, which withstood near depression and a government whose approval rate in the polls hovered slightly above 3 percent. In 1982, Costa Ricans changed governments, as usual, in honest, peaceful elections.[12]

Interpretations about the economic crisis depend largely on the ideological lens of the interpreter. From one perspective, the social welfare side of government with its uncontrolled parastatals resulted in escalating costs at a time when income had fallen drastically. The nationally owned and operated banking system was as inefficient and wasteful as the government.

Another perspective says that Costa Rica had been talked into a development model that was inappropriate to a small developing nation. With trade depending largely on the ability to compete in the international agricultural market, Costa Rica was intensely vulnerable to larger market forces. All, however, would agree that the steep rise in oil prices had the same negative effect on Costa Rica's economy that it had on other non-oil producing countries during the period.

In 1982, the administration of President Monge hammered out deals with the International Monetary Fund (IMF) that called for harsh austerity measures. Social services, food subsidies, and agricultural credit for small farms were cut; wage controls were enacted, cutting into lower class incomes, and taxation became more regressive, i.e. attuned to the interests of upper class people. By 1986, the highest 20 percent of households received a 54.5 percent share of total household income; the highest 10 percent 38.8 percent.

The burden of austerity fell heavily on poor people, who had the least ability to weather a time of crisis. Limitations were placed on parastatals. Private banking was expanded. Less emphasis was placed on rural credit for local food production and

Table 1: Three Neighbors

	Costa Rica	Nicaragua	Panama
Population (000's)	3,015	3,871	2,418
Infant mortality rate			
1960	84	140	69
1990	17	57	22
Under 5 mortality rate			
1960	121	209	105
1989	22	92	33
Adult literacy rate (f.)			
1970	87	57	81
1985	92	na	86
Life expectancy (f.)			
1965	66	52	65
1989	77	66	75
ME % of GNP			
1978	0.7	3.4	1.2
1988	0.5	(17.2)'85	2.4
ME % of CGE			
1972	2.6	12.3	0
1989	1.7	(26.2)	7.9
ME per capita			
1978	12	19	20
1988	7	(61)	45

ME % GNP = Military Expenditures as a % of Gross National Product.

ME % CGE = Military Expenditures as a % of Central Government Expenditures.

ME per capita = Military Expenditures per person in constant 1998 US$.

na = not available.

more on agro-export crops. Costa Rica wound up importing food.

Though the austerity measures worked a hardship on Costa Ricans, the economy stabilized and there was renewed hope for improvement in economic life for at least some of the people – a hope not yet realized among poor people. However, through all the changes, Costa Rica was able to maintain the basic progressive social trends indicated by **Table 1** (above) and remain high in social indicators in Latin America and the Caribbean.

Challenges to Peace

In 1955, Costa Rica's commitment to peace was put to the test when it was invaded by Nicaragua. Figueres asked the Organization of American States to mediate the conflict. The United States provided aid: "Eisenhower sold the Costa Ricans four P-51 fighters for a dollar apiece."[13] Nicaragua did not pursue the intrusion. Costa Ricans say the country has three seasons: a dry season, a wet season, and a season of conflict with Nicaragua.

The other major and more extended challenge to the Costa Rican commitment to peace came from the Sandinista-"contra" (anti-Sandinista guerrillas) war in neighboring Nicaragua. By 1979, the northern border of Costa Rica was an armed camp, ready to support a Sandinista invasion of Nicaragua. Costa Ricans generally favored the Sandinista cause in its early years; most opposed the Sandinistas later because the democracy and open political system they had hoped for did not develop. In 1979, Costa Rica's Minister of Public Security permitted United States helicopters to land at an air strip in northern Costa Rica as a show of force. When the legislative assembly heard about this unconstitutional act, they demanded the removal of the helicopters. The helicopters were there three days.

This incident symbolizes on a small scale the repeated and intensive efforts by the U.S. Central Intelligence Agency (CIA) and the "contras " to use Costa Rican soil as a base of operations. The Costa Ricans resisted, even, as former U.S. Ambassador to Costa Rica Frank McNeil put it, after "a clumsy U.S. request to bring in 1,600 combat engineers for road building." Costa Ricans feared becoming "meat in a left-right sandwich."[14] They did grant asylum to political refugees on both the political left and the right.

Many of the Costa Rican Civil Guard received U.S. military training. Costa Rica became a major transshipment point for arms. And, several "contra" groups operated from CIA or privately owned land in Costa Rica. The border was notoriously difficult for the Costa Ricans to police. As recently as the summer of 1991, small groups of renegade "contras" victimized and plundered households.

The U.S. government, concerned about what it called the brewing communist menace in Nicaragua and economic instability in Costa Rica, began pouring money into the Costa Rican treasury, much of it for military purposes. The U.S. Agency for International Development (AID) insisted on funneling these funds into private banks and enterprises. The presence of U.S. money and AID personnel strengthened the U.S.-oriented contingent in Costa Rican society and moved Costa Rica marginally closer toward U.S. goals for the region.

In spite of immense pressures generated by the war in Nicaragua, Costa Rica continued to work for peace and justice. In 1983, Costa Rica convened a conference in which the United States actively participated. The gathering adopted the San Jose principles for peace in Central America:

- negotiations within and among countries,
- reduction of armaments and military establishments,
- elimination of military and security advisors,
- cessation of support for insurgents, and
- democratization.[15]

These principles laid the groundwork for the (Contadora) process that eventually led to peace in Nicaragua and won Oscar Arias the Nobel Peace Prize. He symbolized

Table 2: Economic Factors

	Costa Rica	Nicaragua	Panama
Cereal imports, metric tons			
1974	110,000	44,000	63,000
1989	357,000	140,000	109,000
Food aid in cereals, metric tons			
1974/75	1,000	3,000	3,000
1988/89	84,000	32,000	na
Total external debt as a % of GNP			
1980	59.5	104.9	92.3
1989	91.2	na	142.5
Total debt service as a % of exports of goods and services			
1980	29.0	21.5	11.5
1989	19.2	8.6	0.1
Official development assistance receipts, $ per capita			
1989	81.9	60.8	7.2

Costa Rican commitments to peaceful justice when he donated the Nobel Prize money to a foundation that built a day-care center, its first project, in a working class neighborhood.

Even though Costa Rica increased military spending in recent years, it has remained essentially nonmilitarized. It has earned a positive reputation which it now seeks to preserve. Courageous political decisions made years ago have become part of Costa Rican national character. The nation continues to provide leadership toward world peace, typically calling on international bodies to strengthen their peace programs. In 1989, Costa Rica brought an Education for Disarmament resolution to the United Nations that expresses the values described above:

As education and communication were essential factors in the process of combating the psychological and cultural causes of war, the arms mentality and violence . . . only by making use of the formal and informal means which these two social institutions provided was it possible to find solutions to the underlying problems of global and regional disarmament.

The resolution, adopted by a vote of 149 to none with five abstentions, says:

> *a peace that could secure the unanimous, lasting and sincere support of the world must be founded, if it is not to fail, upon the intellectual and moral solidarity of mankind.*[16]

The values that flourish among Costa Ricans are not unique. Perhaps their historical configuration is unusual. And perhaps Costa Ricans work harder than some others to express those values in political life. But the same values exist around the globe. In that there is hope for us all. ■

PART TWO: GLOBAL DEMILITARIZATION

World Military Expenditures

"During the 1980's, militarism was king."[17] Militarism is a spirit, policy, and practice that aggressively exalts the military. A militarist country predicates its international relations on military power or threats, aggressively builds its military preparedness, and has domestic policies that emphasize military over civilian priorities. The spirit inherent in militarism can pervade a whole social order down to individual personal relationships.

"Militarization" and demilitarization describe the relative processes of moving toward or away from a militarist posture. Demilitarization can occur slowly or quickly. It can be so minimal that a country remains highly militarized, or it can continue until the ethos of demilitarization shows not only in the absence of a military force but in daily social relationships.

Militant preparation for war, both offensive and defensive, gripped developed and developing countries alike over the past decade. The depth of war-anxiety and national hostilities is seen in the 1 trillion dollars a year (2 million dollars a minute) the world spends on militarization. That is much more than the total income of the low-income developing countries, which together represent more than half of the world's population. More than a billion people in the world survive on less than the equivalent of one dollar a day.[18]

If governments had instead spent a major portion of the money used for militarization on reducing poverty and hunger, millions of lives would have been saved, and our streets, homes, and nations would be more secure.

Some discussions of demilitarization focus only on the trade-offs between military and social spending. But a nation might: (1) demilitarize so slightly that little money becomes available, (2) accumulate such a large deficit while militarizing that deficit reduction takes priority over social spending, (3) enact tax policies that channel savings to the wealthier segments of society, and/or (4) spend the money in other ways. Though the subject of militarization is more complex than statistical tables suggest, statistics provide helpful background information and paint a picture of the relationship between militarization and hunger, as well as demilitarization and the potential for improved quality of life.

Table 3 measures militarization in four different ways. Each index gives a partial picture, but used alone could be mislead-ing. Thus, military expenditures can de-crease as a percentage of other expendi-tures yet show an actual dollar increase. Thailand's military budget rose $600 million dollars between 1978 and 1988, but military expenditures (ME) as a percent of gross national product (GNP) dropped from 3.6 to 3.1 because the GNP grew faster than the defense budget (unless otherwise noted, all dollar amounts are constant 1988 United States dollars – US$). The absolute expenditure rose, but the relative amount (the percent) fell slightly.

World military expenditures began a modest decline before the Berlin Wall was dismantled in 1989. The drop was initiated by developing countries in 1984 and fol-lowed by developed countries in 1988. Third World countries had to make cuts because they faced harsh economic con-straints with large debt payments, up to a third of which were due to arms imports. In 1988, Colombia's external debt service plus military expenditures was 71 percent of its current government revenues. In Indonesia the figure was 64 percent; in Jordan 119 percent; in Pakistan 62 percent; in the Philippines 58 percent; and in Zim-babwe 41 percent. Another reason for the decline in Third World military spending may be the spread of democracy and a concomitant shift from weapons to im-proved living circumstances.

The United States and the Soviet Union

In 1988, the United States and the Soviet Union were spending the most money on militarizing (70 percent of the world's mili-tary expenditures) and providing most of the arms to other countries (73 percent of the world's military arms transfers). **Table 4** shows their expenditures over an eleven-year period.

Table 3
Military Expenditures for Armed Forces 1978-1988[19]

		ME % GNP	ME % CGE	Soldiers per 1,000 people	ME per capita US$
World	1978	5.4 ↓	19.8 ↓	6.1 ↓	198 ↑
	1988	5.0	18.3	5.5	202
Developed	1978	5.0 ↑	18.9 ↓	9.4 ↓	617 ↑
	1988	5.2	18.2	9.0	754
Developing	1978	6.9 ↓	23.1 ↓	5.1 ↓	60 ↓
	1988	4.3	18.6	4.6	42
U.S.A.	1978	4.9 ↑	23.0 ↑	9.3 ↓	824 ↑
	1988	6.3	27.5	9.1	1,250
U.S.S.R.	1978	12.5 ↓	58.5 ↓	14.9 ↓	1,023 ↑
	1988	11.9	43.2	13.6	1,047

See Table 1 for an explanation of ME % GNP, ME % CGEs, and ME per capita US$.

↓ = decrease 1978 to 1988   ↑ = increase 1978 to 1988

The Soviets outspent the United States an average of ten cents per person per year. But they were spending a much higher percent of their gross national prod-uct and central government expenditures than the United States, a situation that be-came increasingly untenable. Whether or

Table 4
Military Expenditures for Armed Forces United States and the Soviet Union
(average per year, 1978-1988)[20]

	ME % GNP	ME % CGE	ME per capita US$	GNP per capita US$
U.S.A.	5.96	25.35	1,063.45	17,785.45
Soviet Union	12.69	50.42	1,063.55	8,381.82

See Table 1 for an explanation of ME % GNP, ME % CGEs, and ME per capita US$.

Table 5
Military Expenditures and Armed Forces[21]
Ten Highest Countries, 1988 (unless noted)

ME % GNP	ME % CGE	Soldiers per 1,000 people	ME per capita US$
Iraq 30.7 '85	Yugoslavia 67.5	Jordan 57.9	Qatar 3,707 '80
N. Yemen 22.0 '86	Afghanistan 64.4 '84	Iraq 56.9	Israel 1,396
Jordan 21.0	Iraq 50.8 '82	Israel 44.4	Iraq 1,312 '85
N. Korea 20.0	Chad 45.1	N. Korea 38.3	U.S.A. 1,250
Vietnam 19.4 '86	Poland 44.1	N. Yemen 36.1	Oman 1,083
Oman 19.1	Soviet Union 43.2	Syria 34.6	Soviet Union 1,047
Nicaragua 17.2 '85	United Arab Em. 41.1	Cuba 28.7	Saudi Arabia 878
Saudi Arabia 16.5	Vietnam 40.7 '86	Libya 21.7	E. Germany 863
Guyana 14.6	N. Korea 40.7	Nicaragua 21.7	United Arab Em. 801
Israel 13.8	Libya 40.0 '84	Un. Arab Em. 21.7	Libya 781 '87

See Table 1 for an explanation of ME % GNP, ME % CGE, and ME per capita US$.

not it was a deliberate Reagan strategy to spend so much money on the military that the Soviet Union would bankrupt itself trying to keep up, the combination of the militarization money war and the inefficiencies of the Soviets' economic system triggered their economic crisis.

Many people believe that the United States' spending prevented a nuclear war. Others believe that military parity could have been reached at lower levels and the world would be a safer place with fewer destructive weapons. The nuclear, chemical, and biological weapons and their wastes will remain for decades. In 1991, "the Pentagon and the Department of Energy's nuclear weapon's branch will spend more than $6 billion in environmental cleanup and compliance."[22]

The six (U.S.) and twelve (U.S.S.R.) percent of GNP spent on armed forces sound small enough that they may obscure the actual cash amounts. The sum from 1978 through 1988 for the United States was $2,346,700,000,000, for the Soviet Union $2,674,200 000,000 or a total of $5,020,900,000,000 – more than $5 trillion (in "current dollars," i.e. not adjusted for inflation). This does not include interest on debt from prior years' military expenditures.

In 1988, the direct cost (not including interest, veterans benefits, etc.) to the average United States' family was $4,724.18. The military build up drained money from other uses and contributed toward the weakening of the American industrial sector, crumbling public infrastructure, diminishing public services, rapidly cumulating public debt, and increasing hunger and homelessness.

Militarization and Global Security

Table 5 lists the ten highest military spenders and most soldiers per capita. It is virtually a list of wars – recent, current, or imminent.

Iraq is near the top in all four measures. Iraq's GNP per capita fell from $7,123 in 1978 to $3,742 in 1988 as the nation fought Iran and continued its military build up. Iraq's sacrifices came to naught when faced with U.S.-led U.N. forces during the Persian Gulf crisis. Iraq's militarization did not enhance either national or global security. The money could have been used to decrease Iraq's infant mortality (69 per thousand live births) and improve literacy (41 percent for females, 75 percent for males). Instead, an estimated 100,000 Iraqi children may die of disease and malnutrition as a result of the Persian Gulf War in 1991.

Few of the countries in **Table 5** have open political systems. It usually takes a strong central government and/or the immediate threat of war to lead people to forego not only luxuries, but basic necessities. Countries with extremely high military spending do not generally rank high on quality of life indexes.

It is possible for a wealthy nation to dedicate substantial resources to military purposes and still support education, health care, and food security. The United States sustained a high standard of living for most people while spending huge sums on its military. Part of the cost was passed forward as public debt for future generations to pay. Some OPEC countries with oil-rich economies have been able to improve the quality of life for their citizens while arming.

Ruth Leger Sivard ranks the five worst countries in economic-social standing in 1987 as: Ethiopia, Somalia, Chad, Mozambique, and Burkina Faso. All were involved in military conflicts. Wars kill directly with bombs and bullets; indirectly by further impoverishing economies and depriving people of the food, clothing, and shelter they need.

Unfortunately, even some of the poorest of poor people are forced to make tremendous sacrifices to cover military spending. From 1978 to 1988, the GNP of Chad fell in constant dollars and per capita, but military expenditures as a percent of central government expenditures rose from 25.8 to 45.1. The 1988 GNP per capita for Chad was $189 compared with a world average of $4,028. Ethiopia's GNP per capita rose $1 from $113 to $114 from 1978 to 1988, but military expenditures rose by more than $1 billion to $5.5 billion. That, plus a drought led to the suffering children whose pictures were seen on the front pages of newspapers.

Television images of Kurdish refugees fighting for frozen chickens, Soviets pushing and shoving in food lines, and Ethiopians struggling for survival vividly illustrate how militarization and war contribute to hunger. The end of the Cold War will

Table 6
Arms Transfer Deliveries 1978-1988[23]
Selected Areas & World Totals
(in billions of 1988 US$)

Recipient	Supplier Communist	Supplier Noncommunist	World total
Middle East	85.2	91.4	177.0
Europe	47.8	47.3	95.4
Africa	50.8	18.0	69.2
World total	256.1	227.1	483.1
Developing	216.2	169.6	385.9
Developed	39.4	57.1	97.4

allow even further reductions in spending in the U.S. and Soviet blocs. But arms sales to Third World countries may boom. Arms companies will turn their attention more to the Third World, and, without Cold War rigidities, civil wars may proliferate (e.g. Yugoslavia).

The responsibility for militarization lies not only with the governments that arm, but with those nations that supply the arms. Political alignments shift and nations find themselves fighting their own or their allies' technologies in unanticipated wars. Short-term profits from the arms trade can be wiped out if the arms are used. The cost of war and of economic recovery (not to mention human life) following war can far exceed income from sales.

Demilitarization and the Quality of Life

Some countries have successfully used demilitarization to improve the quality of life. Costa Rica abolished its army and used the money for social programs. **Table 7** (next page), lists ten countries which the U.N. Development Programme's *Human Development Report 1991* ranks as having the highest quality of life. Sivard, using somewhat different criteria, also ranks most of them among the top ten in economic-social standing.

All but the United States spend less than the world average for military as a percent of central government expenditures and as

Table 7
Top Ten Quality of Life Countries

Human Development 1991	Sivard Ec.Soc. 1987	Life expect. yrs.	Infant mortality	ME % CGE	ME % GNP	ME per capita US$	GNP per capita 1988
1 Japan	7	78.6	5	6.0	0.9	235	23,290
2 Canada	4	77.0	7	9.0	2.1	384	18,090
3 Iceland	4	77.8	6	0.	0	0	23,140
4 Sweden	7	77.4	6	6.9	2.8	593	20,880
5 Switzerland	13	77.4	7	(10.8)	2.1	590	28,660
6 Norway	2	77.1	8	6.9	3.2	691	21,620
7 U.S.A.	9	75.9	10	27.5	6.3	1,250	19,840
8 Netherlands	12	77.2	8	5.4	3.0	457	15,320
9 Australia	14	76.5	9	10.0	2.7	379	14,120
10 France	10	76.4	8	8.8	3.9	644	16,490
World ave.		65	71	18.3	5.0	202	4,028
Developed		74	15	18.2	5.2	754	14,610
Developing		62	79	18.6	4.3	42	976

Infant mortality = deaths under 1 year of age per 1,000 live births
See Table 1 for an explanation of ME % GNP, ME % CGEs, and ME per capita US$.

a percent of GNP. In so doing, they have freed up funds for human needs. Some of them do not need a military force because they exist under the umbrella of other powers, e.g. Iceland. Others, such as the Scandinavian countries, have faced security risks while continuing to maintain a high quality of life.

By world standards, U.S. quality of life ratings are high. However, when viewed as a comparison of resources available and how they are used, there is ample room for the United States dramatically to improve the quality of life. This change would need to become a first priority not only to the elected but to those who do the electing.

Trends and Possibilities

Militarization and demilitarization cannot finally be treated solely in quantitative terms or merely as trade-offs in domestic economic policy. Militarization is more than a number of forces or the amount of dollars spent on them. It is predicated on a view of reality and on values and practices which, unchecked, lead to exalting the military rather than seeing it as a necessary evil in a world too often at war.

The U.S. economy has come to depend upon the current state of militarization. A degree of demilitarization is possible without abandoning preparedness. But, demilitarization does not come easily. Large, entrenched economic and political interests lobby for military spending. Local communities raise a hue and cry when a base or defense plant is to be closed.

Given the recent changes in U.S.-Soviet relations, the trend toward demilitarization is likely to continue at a modest pace. The United States demilitarized rapidly after World War II: "At the peak of World War II, defense spending represented 39.1 percent of total U.S. economic output. By 1948 that had dropped to 3.7 percent."[24] A major difference now is that whereas people in the late 1940s were returning to a pre-war "normal" condition, U.S. citizens now accept militarization as normal.

The presence of large military forces and the expectation they will have a global function is part of the everyday thinking of many, if not most, Americans. General Colin Powell, reflecting on the role of the U.S. military in the post Cold War era, said:

We no longer have the luxury of having a threat to plan for. What we plan for is that we're a superpower. We are the major player on the world stage with responsibilities around the world, with interests around the world.[25]

A U.S. citizen living in Costa Rica commented how different life is in a place where children consider the absence of a military force normal.

The old expression "guns or butter" seems hardly adequate to today's technological reality. Perhaps a more apt contrast would be "bombs or babies," i.e. increasing weapons spending or using that money to save the lives of children here and abroad. The twentieth century is the first in human history in which eliminating hunger has been possible. Often viewed as the most progressive century, it has also been the most violent – Hiroshima, the Holocaust, the Khmer Rouge – wars too numerous to count and too bloody to imagine. Technology and economic progress that are not guided by humane values are of little benefit to humankind.

Demilitarization will not of itself lead to improvement in social and economic well-being any more than a high GNP guarantees the elimination of hunger. A country could reduce the size of its military without substantially changing its values or structures to insure that monies saved would help the people in greatest need. Only

when the values that underlie peace, justice, and ecological concerns become part of a culture's self-understanding will a peace dividend become a meaningful justice dividend. These values affirm the well-being of nature and humanity, with particular focus on the needs of those who are most vulnerable.

The solution to hunger will not be achieved solely by technologies, modest reductions in military spending, or even more prosperous economies. The cause and effect equation does not go: demilitarization + social spending = social-well being and the elimination of hunger. The process is neither that simple nor that automatic. Instead, the equation goes: humane values = a commitment to seek peace + social well-being, including the elimination of hunger. ∎

The only weapons we know are the shared values of democracy, tolerance, peace, liberty, and solidarity.
    – Oscar Arias Sánchez

Notes

1. Rolbein, p. 11.
2. Edelman and Kenen, p. 87.
3. Juan Mora Fernández, quoted in Edelman and Kenen, p. 6.
4. Rolbein, p. 29.
5. Rolbein, p. 103.
6. Rolbein, p. 92.
7. Nelson, p. 206.
8. Biesanz, pp. 16-17.
9. Rolbein, p., 230.
10. Fallas in Edelman and Kenan, p. 82.
11. Anderson, pp. 89-113.
12. McNeil, pp. 23-24.
13. The planes were "piloted by, among others, Captains Victory and Guerra (war), their real names." McNeil, p. 77.
14. McNeil, p. 169.
15. McNeil, p. 168.
16. U.N., *Disarmament Yearbook*, pp. 390-392.
17. Sivard, p. 7.
18. Calculated from figures in World Bank, *World Development Report*, used in speeches by A.W. Clausen.
19. U.S. ACDA, pp. 31, 65, 68. Experts disagree about how to determine equivalent values across national lines. The ACDA says "It should be recognized by users of the statistical tables that the military expenditure data are of uneven accuracy and completeness," p. 134. The reader is advised to consult "Statistical Notes," pp. 133-140.
20. Calculations based on U.S. ACDA data.
21. U.S. ACDA, Table 1.
22. Pearlstein, p. H1.
23. U.S. ACDA, Table 4.
24. Simon, p. 70.
25. Quoted by Oberdorfer, p. A14.
26. Rolbein, pp. 12-13.

Economic Policies Diminish Hunger in Indonesia

Photo: FAO

The Indonesian government's economic policies have reduced poverty and raised farm incomes.

by David Beckmann

Throughout the world, poor people tend to think of government as remote, allied with privileged groups, and sometimes hostile – with good reason. Governmental economic policies are responsive to many interests, and helping hungry people is seldom a high priority.

Still, there are many examples of government economic policies helping to reduce hunger. When the southern African nation of Zimbabwe gained independence in 1980, a small number of large-scale, white-owned commercial farms dominated food production, while most indigenous Africans produced subsistence crops on marginal land. The government allowed the prices small farmers received for producing food crops to increase above and beyond the rate of inflation. It helped poor peasants to acquire better land, made seeds and fertilizer available, and maintained a favorable climate for small farmer cooperatives. As a result, the small farmers' share of the national market for corn, the staple food, increased from 8 to 45 percent by 1986.

In contrast, in much of Africa, governments have generally depressed the prices paid to farmers and in other ways biased economic policies in favor of the urban sector. The result has been a severe decline in agriculture, especially food production for local consumption, and in rural incomes.

Indonesia is another developing country where national economic policies have helped reduce hunger. Its experience shows how appropriate policies can help a country dependent on exports weather economic recession without jeopardizing the well-being of low-income people. The 1980s are considered the "lost decade" for most developing countries in terms of progress against hunger and poverty, but Indonesia's poverty rate declined even faster in the 1980s than in the "oil-boom" decade of the 1970s (see graph below).

Declining Poverty in Indonesia

Indonesia is the world's fifth most populous country, with 184 million people living on 13,000 islands. In 1970, it was one of the poorest countries in the world: 70 million people, 60 percent of the population, lived below the official poverty line. In Indonesia, that line is defined as the income needed for households to provide their members 2,100 calories per person per day. When people make do with less food, they typically have too little energy to live fully alert and productive lives.

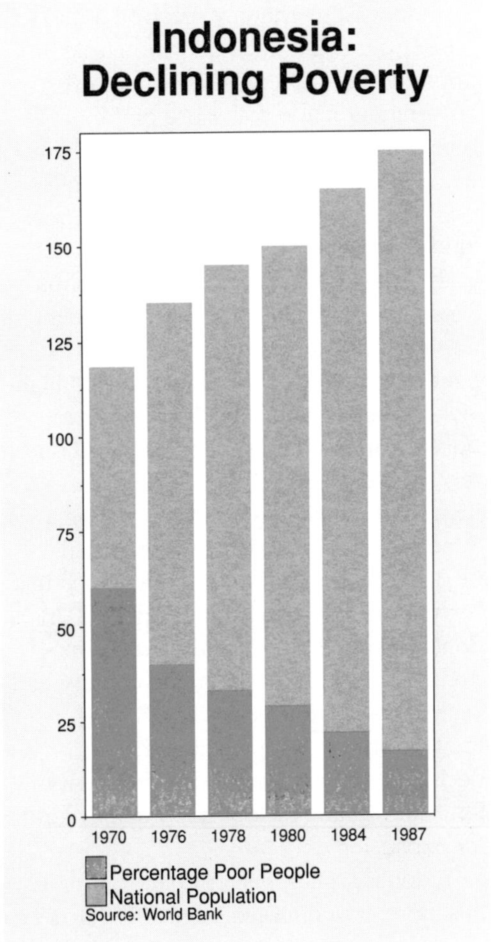

In 1987, the average Indonesian's income was $450, and the country was still considered "low-income." However, the poverty rate had fallen to 17 percent, or about 30 million people.

Most of the reduction in poverty occurred on Java, where 100 million of Indonesia's people live. Most of the people who remain below the poverty line are also on Java, although the proportion of people in poverty is now much higher on Indonesia's other islands.

Infant mortality declined 45 percent between 1971 and 1989 (see graph, page 66). However, Indonesia's rate is still higher than that of any other Southeast Asian country except poverty-stricken Laos and war-torn Cambodia.

Hunger has declined as well, although undernutrition continues to be a serious problem in the country. According to the Food and Agriculture Organization (FAO) of the U.N., 28 percent of the population was undernourished in 1969-1971, compared to 13 percent in 1979-1981 and 11 percent in 1983-1985. Anemia and iodine deficiency remain widespread. The incidence of Vitamin A deficiency among Indonesian children is one of the highest in the world. Surveys in the mid-1980s found that 53 percent of the children under age five were moderately-to-severely underweight. The rates of severely underweight preschool children dropped somewhat between 1979 and 1986, from 6 to 4 percent in a twenty-seven-province survey. The decline was greater in urban than in rural areas, and there is considerable variation among provinces. FAO attributes high

Indonesia: Declining Poverty

Percentage Poor People
National Population
Source: World Bank

rates of preschool undernutrition to poor maternal nutrition, which contributes to low birthweights; limited food availability at the household level; poor nutritional practices; and poor consumption patterns.

According to anthropological studies cited by the World Bank, the experience of one Indonesian village, Belearjo, in East Java, shows how improvements in agriculture and income have helped at the local level. Belearjo is about eight kilometers from the nearest town, connected to the outside world by bumpy dirt roads. In 1985 farmers were producing three times as much rice per hectare as in 1953. Rice was available throughout the year. In 1953, rice was available only four months a year; villagers would then eat corn and, when that ran out, cassava.

Much of the hunger in Indonesia is among landless or near-landless laborers, so the wage rate for agricultural labor is a key indicator of hunger. In Belearjo, the daily wage went from two kilograms of rice in 1953 to four kilograms in 1985.

Background

General Suharto took power in 1966, after several months of chaos in which the armed forces and vigilante groups massacred up to a million supposed subversives. Suharto has ruled the country ever since. His regime has been characterized by suppression of dissent, rigid controls on political activity, and widespread official corruption.

Early on, Suharto brought a group of Western-trained economic "technocrats" into the government. They have exerted considerable influence over economic policy, although the armed forces retain ultimate decision-making power. Since the mid-1970s, the government has maintained balanced budgets and a realistic exchange

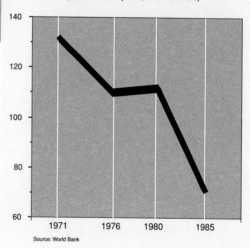

Declining Infant Mortality
(infant deaths per 1,000 live births)

Source: World Bank

rate. The country has also benefited from substantial foreign aid, with the regime's anti-communism and openness to foreign investment helping to attract financial support from donors.

Indonesia's economy received a major boost from rising international petroleum prices during the 1970s. The Indonesian government made better use of the oil bonanza than many other oil-blessed governments did. The Indonesian authorities used oil money to finance the "green revolution" on Java. Partly in response to riots in the capital city, Jakarta, over rice shortages, they gave high priority to achieving rice self-sufficiency. The government expanded irrigation systems, introduced high-yielding seeds, and subsidized fertilizer prices. Improvements in agriculture did not rely on "the magic of the marketplace." Instead, the military-dominated National Supply Agency ("Badan Urusan Logistik," or BULOG) controlled the price of rice for both farmers and consumers. In 1978, Indonesia was still the world's largest importer of rice, but by 1984, the country had achieved self-sufficiency. Since then, though, production per capita has declined, due to diminishing returns from fertilizer use and lack of good quality land for expansion.

Indonesian farmers' income from rice has more than doubled since 1970. However, inequality and landlessness remain serious problems. By 1988, 69 percent of farming households owned less than 2.5 acres of land, while just 6 percent owned more than 7.5 acres.

The government also used oil revenues to invest in non-food export crops, generally neglecting cassava and corn, the main foods of poor people. It improved transportation (a major problem for this archipelago nation) and financed a massive program of school expansion. Primary school enrollment jumped from 37 percent of school-aged children in 1973 to 92 percent in the early 1980s.

Spending on health was more modest. Yet, Indonesia developed a fairly effective nationwide system to identify and provide supplemental food to undernourished children, and expanded family planning efforts.

These were all top-down programs. However, the central government did pass much of the money on to lower levels of government, which managed the construction of roads, schools, and other infrastructure. The central government also systematized a nationwide network of village headmen and village councils. These consolidated the government's political control, but also effectively connected government programs to local needs and activated local self-help efforts. The women's groups associated with village councils have mobilized hundreds of thousands of volunteers and most of the nation's mothers to help government health staff monitor nutrition among children and to provide immunizations, supplemental food, and nutrition education.

Adjustment and More Progress Against Poverty

Beginning in 1983, falling oil prices dramatically worsened Indonesia's economic circumstances, costing the country 10 percent of its national income, equivalent to the direct impact of the debt crisis on Latin America. But while most Latin American economies were knocked into a downward spiral, Indonesia's economy only slowed down. Incomes continued to rise, and low-income groups continued to benefit from growth. This was partly because many of the public investments from the oil boom period were paying off. Also, the "technocrats" managed a relatively quick and sophisticated shift in economic policies to cope with declining oil revenues.

The government's adjustment policies worked in favor of the poor in two ways. First, the government devalued Indonesia's currency to make the country's exports more competitive internationally, and Indonesia's main exports, aside from oil, are farm products. Moreover, key agricultural exports, such as rubber, coffee, and tobacco, are often grown by small farmers under labor-intensive conditions. In other countries, where exports are produced by a small number of capital-intensive enterprises, devaluation would help rural poor people less.

Second, as the government cut its spending, it protected expenditures for agriculture, local government, health, and education. The U.N. Children's Fund (UNICEF) considers Indonesia's National Family Nutritional Improvement Project to be a model of "adjustment with a human face," i.e. measures aimed at making fundamental changes in the economy to achieve long-term growth while maintaining social services for the poorest people, especially women and children.

Drawing the Right Lessons

Indonesia's experience does not support the idea that curtailment of the public sector and more reliance on markets is a "miracle cure" for development problems. The public sector continues to play a large role in Indonesia's economic and social progress.

Also, the lesson from Indonesia is not that authoritarian government is good for economic development or reducing hunger. Many developing countries had authoritarian governments in the 1970s, and many of these accumulated debts and failed to invest the money well. The economic failures of the authoritarian governments of the 1970s help explain why people overthrew dictators in so many countries during the 1980s.

There are other countries that have successfully carried out "adjustment with a human face" in the context of democratic politics. Examples come from nations as diverse as Botswana and Zimbabwe in southern Africa and Venezuela, Costa Rica, and Jamaica in the western hemisphere.

The Indonesian government has been encouraging some participatory decision-making at the local level. Some officials recognize that in many sectors they have reached the limits of what can be done by top-down development projects. The government built massive irrigation systems, for example, but these systems cannot be efficiently operated and maintained unless

The Debate on Adjustment in Africa

by Patience Elabor-Idemudia

In 1980, African heads of state issued the Lagos Plan of Action, the first attempt to devise an African plan to address the continent's economic crisis. It stressed self-reliance, food self-sufficiency, industrialization, and regional economic integration.

The following year, the World Bank issued its "Berg Commission Report," which attributed Sub-Saharan problems to failed domestic policies – over-valued exchange rates, inappropriate pricing policies and excessive state intervention in economies. The report said that Africa's dependence on imports for production and consumption was

excessive. It also proposed greater emphasis on production for export; reducing government's role in the economy; encouraging private enterprise; cutting wages; and charging fees for state services such as health, education, transportation, electricity, and water.

Many Africans criticized the report for down-playing the role of external factors in the crisis. The Bank later conducted a second study, *Toward Accelerated Development in Sub-Saharan Africa,* which addressed food problems and recognized the severe political constraints within which African economies functioned. However, during the 1980s, the World Bank tended to condition new loans to developing country governments on their implementing Structural Adjustment Programs (SAPs) along the lines suggested in the Berg Report.

Former U.S. State Department official Carol Lancaster says that

SAPs in Africa have led to deregulation, reduced subsidies, privatization, layoffs, external borrowing, high debt servicing to export ratios, imposition of user fees on social services, and suppression of dissent. But the plans have not encouraged the inflow of foreign investment, reduced debt, or promoted growth, stability, respect for human rights, or social and political harmony, as intended. The World Bank's own evaluation of SAPs said: "Sub-Saharan Africa as a whole has now witnessed almost a decade of falling per capita incomes, increasing hunger, and accelerating ecological degradation."

In 1989, the U.N. Economic Commission for Africa (ECA) proposed "structural transformation" in place of structural adjustment. This African Alternative Framework (AAF) relies on a human-centered strategy of economic recovery, with emphasis on the full participation

the farmers themselves have a say in their management.

An important positive lesson from Indonesia's experience since the mid-1970s is that *government economic policies are tremendously important to poor people –* often for ill, but sometimes for good.

Adjustment and Increasing Poverty in the Developing World

The world economy has been harsh for most developing countries since the early 1980s. In most hard-hit countries, poverty and hunger have worsened. Nearly all of Africa continues the relentless economic decay which began in the mid-1970s. Latin America carries an impossible debt burden, and incomes have still not quite risen back to the levels from which they dropped when the debt crisis first hit. East Asia is the only region of the world where most countries have managed to adjust to serious shocks from the world economy and recover economic and social progress.

Nearly all regions of the developing world experienced growth in average income per capita between 1965 and 1980. Economic growth was slowest in the poorest regions – Africa and South Asia. Social indicators, such as school enrollment and life expectancy, improved throughout the

of the general population in the formulation, implementation, and monitoring of adjustment programs. The ECA recommended an end to subsidies, except for social programs and key industries; reduced military spending; reduced spending on the nonproductive public sector; guaranteed minimum prices for food crops and higher investment in agriculture; separate exchange rates for essential and nonessential imports; allocating credit and foreign exchange to priority economic sectors; liberalization of trade; and land reform.

In 1989, the World Bank's *From Crisis to Sustainable Growth* set out proposals aimed at empowering ordinary people and marginalized groups to take greater responsibility for improving their lives. The report says that SAPs should continue, but with "broadened and deepened special measures. . . to alleviate poverty and protect the vulnerable."[1] The report stresses the need for an enabling environment for the productive use of resources and development strategies that are "human-centered," in line with concerns expressed by the ECA and UNICEF. The Bank also recommends better governance, health, education and food security, the involvement of women in the process of change, a stable economic and political environment in order to attract investors, environmental protection, and population control. The report calls for policy changes to promote democracy, accountability, and political stability, as well as an attack on corruption.

In a similar vein, in 1990, the ECA, in collaboration with African nongovernmental organizations (NGOs), published *The African Charter for Popular Participation in Development*. The charter seeks to operationalize the AAF's recommendations for transformations that are not just narrow, economic, and mechanical, but which mobilize the participation of popular forces – workers, peasants, women, professionals, students, trade unions, and intellectuals, in organizations and as individuals. The charter calls on the international community to support indigenous efforts which promote a democratic environment and people's effective participation and empowerment in the political life of their countries.

Only when African people's voices are heard can they take action to improve their living conditions. Then, if people have to make sacrifices, at least the decisions will be theirs rather than imposed on them. ■

Notes

1. African Alternative Framework, p. 4.

developing world, including Africa and South Asia.

In the 1980s, economic growth slowed down markedly in all regions of the developing world except Asia. In Africa and Latin America, incomes per capita declined and hunger increased.

Much of the debate about how to turn this depressing situation around has focused on the policies which developing countries in crisis should pursue. In the early stages of the international debt crisis, the IMF extended emergency credit to many developing countries, stressing immediate cut-backs in consumption which would bring countries' imports into line

Grappling with Economic Crisis in Nigeria

by Patience Elabor-Idemudia

During British rule (1884-1960), Nigeria became an exporter of primary goods, with large farms producing cash crops for export at the expense of food for domestic consumption. The colonial administration took land away from peasant farmers and created export crop plantations. Men moved to these plantations and to cities seeking employment, leaving women behind to run households and grow subsistence crops on left-over, low–quality land.

After independence, the Nigerian government continued to neglect small-scale, mostly female farmers. During the "oil boom" (1973-1980), the federal and state governments channeled oil revenues into construction, transportation and communication, housing, and social services, rather than agriculture and industry. Increases

in public spending, combined with a drop in agricultural prices, led many rural people to migrate to the cities. Domestic food production declined and dependence on imported food increased.

Nigeria borrowed large sums of money from foreign commercial banks and official creditors. Corruption increased dramatically. Contractors became the brokers of large transactions, sometimes inflating costs as much as 300 percent, then never completing the projects. These malpractices, combined with the fall in oil prices after 1980, rising interest rates, and falling income from sales of agricultural products, culminated in the government's inability to pay its debt. Government austerity measures between 1982 and 1985 failed to arrest deterioration of the economy, and the populace began to experience hardship.

In 1986, the government turned to the World Bank for help, and agreed to implement a Structural Adjustment Program (SAP). This sought to diversify the domestic resource base, especially through non-oil exports; service existing debt to open up new lines of credit; privatize public corporations; deregulate interest rates; and re-

move subsidies.

Some reforms resulted in successes. They brought to light the depth of Nigeria's economic and social crisis and exposed the myth of the oil boom. Nigerians now know that oil is vulnerable to the vagaries of the international system and internal mismanagement.

Local industries now increasingly rely on local raw materials rather than on imports. Bakeries, breweries, publishing, and pharmaceutical industries have increased their use of local resources from 10 to 15 percent to 40 to 70 percent. This has stimulated some agricultural production and marginally increased wealth in rural areas. The textile mills in Nigeria now produce cotton fabrics for Nigerians.

In spite of these gains, the SAP has combined with structural imbalances in Nigeria's economy to create severe hardships for Nigerians. Cutbacks in social services and the introduction of user-fees have hurt poor people. Reduction of government subsidies resulted in increases in the price of farm inputs, petroleum products, and natural gas. Public transportation became costly, so people trekked long distances to work and resorted to using wood for cooking, accelerat-

with their reduced ability to pay. An alternative is to increase exports or expand national income through improvements in economic efficiency. The World Bank has focused on growth-oriented adjustments of this kind.

Meanwhile, most countries in economic crisis have vacillated, delayed, and to some extent floundered in the face of adversity. Nigeria provides a sharp contrast to Indonesia (see sidebar, page 70).

UNICEF and other critics have urged the IMF and World Bank to support adjustment policies which do more to protect poor and vulnerable groups. Still other critics, notably Africa's political leaders, have ar-

ing deforestation. Currency devaluation by over 500 percent reduced buying power and inflated prices of essential commodities, foodstuffs and farming inputs. Wealthy farmers (mostly men) received more for their crops, but small farmers (mostly women) found themselves increasingly marginalized. Poor people who could not afford high-priced food eliminated essential food groups such as meat, poultry, milk and fish, leading to malnutrition and poor health. Similarly, elimination of imports of some essential food items and commodities without a parallel increase in local production resulted in food shortages, escalating prices and increasing hunger.

My 1989 study of the impact of the SAP on rural women found that:

- Women's access to credit, farming inputs, extension services and the market has not improved. In some cases, it has grown worse, possibly because few extension agents are female and male extension agents do not regard women as farmers or heads of households;
- The limited training programs made available to women tend to focus mainly on food processing;
- Women still tend to earn less income than men, making it harder for female-headed households to live adequately;
- The standard of living in many rural households deteriorated during the SAP implementation (1986-1989). People cut back to one or two meals a day to stretch limited family budgets.

Women have been unable to get the resources needed to improve agricultural production. Many rural women have, in addition to farming, set up small retail businesses, but cannot expand them because of lack of credit. These businesses generate barely enough income for subsistence and children's school expenses. Even if women could get improved access to the market, their ability to earn enough income is constrained by lack of affordable child care; limited access to land, income, credit, and capital for investment; and declining soil fertility and labor shortages in the mainly female subsistence farming sector. Women need public services – water supply, electricity, health care, education, transportation, and appropriate technology – that re-

duce the burden of manual labor. They also need help from their husbands with housework.

In recent years, Nigerian women's organizations have moved to provide support systems in some of these areas, including health care, family planning programs, income-generating projects, and literacy and education services. These organizations have become increasingly important because they are typically community-based, providing members access to information and resources.

The Nigerian government, for its part, has begun to revitalize the mainly female, small-scale rural sector. The government has established a Directorate of Food, Roads, and Rural Infrastructure to provide infrastructural services to rural areas; it launched the People's Bank in 1990 to provide credit facilities and stimulate agricultural research and seed multiplication; and it set up the Raw Materials Research Council in 1988 to give marketing advice to farmers and small-scale industrial processors. These small steps are significant because they indicate a new willingness on the part of the government to support poor people's own initiatives. ∎

gued for a less export- and market-oriented model of adjustment (see sidebar, page 68).

Some developing countries are in such deep trouble that their governments really cannot do much to protect poor people from the crisis. Moreover, better-off groups usually defend themselves politically. A socially-oriented adjustment program would cut military spending, but dissatisfaction among the military is politically risky. A socially-oriented adjustment program might cut subsidies for hospital care to expand funding for rural clinics and preventive care. But urban middle-class families – many of whose incomes have already fallen drastically – understandably insist on keeping hospitals open and affordable.

The United States and other industrial countries dominate the global economy. Their policies determine the conditions with which developing countries have to cope. In the late 1970s and early 1980s, the industrial countries' budget and monetary policies set off the longest world recession since the 1930s, with the highest real interest rates in 200 years. In the process, the industrial countries triggered the international debt crisis.

The U.S. government has taken some action on domestic debt problems, such as farm debt and the savings and loan crisis. But the United States has consistently been less willing than most other industrial country governments to reduce the debt burdens of developing countries. International responses to the debt crisis are difficult to organize without U.S. government support, and commercial lenders frequently take their lead from "official lenders" in restructuring or relieving developing country governments' debt.

At the same time, the United States and other industrial countries have been slowly increasing their barriers against developing country exports. Without export income, developing countries cannot possibly hope to make a dent in their debt obligations.

The public interest groups that lobby the U.S. government on global poverty issues can sometimes influence foreign aid programs, but have seldom had much impact on U.S. international finance and trade policies. U.S. policies regarding banks, interest rates, tariffs, and trade affect poor people around the world much more than aid, but these policies also have more impact on U.S. business interests and the pocketbooks of U.S. voters. It will take a broader and deeper movement of U.S. citizens concerned about hunger to make U.S. economic policies more favorable to poor people around the world. ∎

Refugees Rebuild Their Villages in El Salvador

Photo: John Grant

Villagers in the repopulated Salvadoran community of Guarjila share a shipment of coffee.

by Ana E. Avilés

The growing of their own food is the hallmark of self-sufficiency and empowerment for which each repopulated community aspires.[1]

Between 1980 and 1986, El Salvador's civil war forced an estimated 1 million people to flee the country. It displaced another 500,000, leaving them economically vulnerable and subject to military attacks. The vast majority of these civilians were uprooted from their rural homes by the Salvadoran armed forces' counterinsurgency campaigns against the armed opposition force, the Farabundo Marti National Liberation Front (FMLN).

Beginning in 1985, many refugee and displaced families returned to their homes, in spite of continuing conflict. This repopulation movement has brought people a greater sense of stability and security, and offered a model of sustainable development for the rural population of El Salvador. Although the war continues to make life dangerous and difficult for those who have repopulated their villages, many have successfully created new forms of self-government, are growing their own food, have set up community enterprises, and established basic social services.

The Salvadoran government has also carried out resettlement programs since the mid-1980s. Because these programs are part of the government's counterinsurgency policy, they have not empowered the resettled persons in the same way as the independent repopulation efforts.

Between 1985 and 1986, internally displaced Salvadorans began returning to their homes in Tenancingo and El Barillo, in the department (province) of Cuscatlan, and San José las Flores, in the department of

Chalatenango. This set the stage for the repatriation efforts of thousands of refugees who had lived in camps in Honduras for as long as eight years. These early repopulations inspired other refugees and displaced families because the people who carried them out had designed their own plans for self-reliant community development.

Between October 1987 and March 1991, nearly 10,000 Salvadoran refugees left the barbed wire confines of the Mesa Grande refugee camp in Honduras and returned to their home towns in El Salvador. An additional 10,000 refugees from two other camps in Honduras, San Antonio and Colomoncagua, have also joined this movement (see map, page 76). These refugees, together with recent returnees from Nicaragua and Panama and the internally displaced, make up an estimated 40,000 Salvadorans who have repopulated at least sixty rural communities.

The Central America Peace Plan of 1987, commonly called the Esquipulas II Agreement, provided an opportunity for collective repatriation of Salvadoran refugees living in camps in Honduras. The Esquipulas plan provided a comprehensive settlement of Central America's conflicts and included provisions on the repatriation of the region's dispersed Salvadoran refugee population. It legitimized the refugees' right to resettle in their places of origin; it was signed by five Central American presidents, including Jose Napoleon Duarte of El Salvador, in August 1987.

In January 1987, refugees in the Mesa Grande camp appealed to the United Nations High Commissioner for Refugees (UNHCR) and the governments of Honduras and El Salvador for the right to move back to their homes. The Honduran government supported their appeal. UNHCR resisted during the negotiating period, at least partly because it was unprepared to deal with massive repatriation.

Both during and after the negotiations, Salvadoran authorities made many attempts to prevent the refugees' return. They tried to deny them entry into their home towns, citing security concerns. The Salvadoran armed forces subjected the refugees to bombing and strafing in areas chosen for repatriation. Nevertheless, the refugees began to return in October 1987, having decided that they would accept the risks involved in re-establishing their communities.

Draining the Sea

El Salvador's civil war, begun in 1979, is rooted in the country's unequal distribution of wealth, land, and power. During the 1980s, government forces engaged in a deliberate policy of depopulation, in an effort to deprive the FMLN of civilian supporters and resources. Known as "draining the sea," this policy drove hundreds of families to seek refuge in church sanctuaries sponsored by the Catholic Archdiocese of San Salvador. Hundreds of thousands more fled to neighboring Central American countries, Mexico, and the United States.

Throughout the early 1980s, entire villages were deserted due to aerial bombardments, strafing, mortar shelling, and army ground sweeps aimed at civilians in FMLN-controlled areas. In one intensive military campaign, Operation Phoenix, launched in 1986, more than 5,000 elite army troops with air support destroyed large areas of farmland and drove hundreds of peasants from their homes. Government forces acted without regard to the 1977 Additional Protocol II of the Geneva Conventions on the conduct of war, which prohibits deliberate attacks on civilians and their means of subsistence. The Salvadoran military designed and executed the operation with the

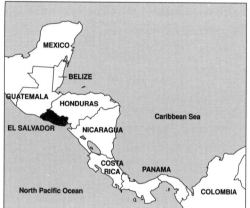

Repopulations ◆
1. San Jose las Flores
2. El Barrillo
3. Tenancingo
4. Arcatao

Repatriations ✖
5. Guarjila

Government Resettlement sites ✻
6. Canton Ichanqueso

Refugee Camps ⬗
7. Mesa Grande
8. San Antonio
9. Colomoncagua

10. San Salvador ★

He added that civilians had fled the free-fire zones in Chalatenango and taken refuge in camps in Honduras or were among the displaced people living in the capital, San Salvador. Relief officials in San Salvador, however, confirmed that civilians remained in the free-fire zones. One such civilian in Chalatenango said:

> We had to look for our defense in places that the army had not yet reached. We often had to live in caves or holes in the ground in order to protect ourselves from the military operations. . . women were forced to suffocate their own children so they would not cry and expose the entire community.[3]

Another civilian recounts the struggle to seek refuge in Honduras:

> The army moved in with the intention of killing all life – women, children, farm animals, anything. . . .We were on the run to cross the border into Honduras where the Honduran military was shooting at us from the other side. . . .[4]

Meanwhile, the government made several attempts since 1983 to resettle internally displaced people, such as Proyecto Mil (Project One Thousand), which attempted to establish 1,000 villages for 500,000 civilians. Another such project was the National Plan, funded by the U.S. Agency for International Development (AID). In 1986, the government launched United to Reconstruct (UPR), a three-phase counterinsurgency campaign associated with Operation Phoenix.

Government resettlement schemes sought to wean the peasants away from the FMLN and achieve stable government con-

explicit purpose of depriving rural communities in the conflict zone of the basic necessities of life: food, shelter, and medicine.

The armed forces' policy was to force all civilians from contested areas. According to Sigfredo Ochoa, former commander of the First Military Detachment in Chalatenango:

> In these [conflict] zones, there are no civilians. There are only concentrations of guerrillas, so we keep these areas under heavy fire . . . . Our first goal is to clean up the province militarily. This means we cannot permit civilian contact with the rebel army. . . . The civilians can return when we have searched the area. Without civilians, the rebels have no food and cannot maintain their army.[2]

trol of the rural areas through the establishment of strategic settlements. The government's efforts to relocate displaced people into secured areas have failed, due to inadequate funding, mismanagement, the armed forces' inability to hold the targeted relocation areas for extended periods of time, and the government's policies to prevent resettled people from achieving self-government or economically viable communities.

A number of analysts have compared UPR to the coercive strategic hamlets established by the United States during the Viet Nam war and to the equally repressive Model Villages project in Guatemala.[5]

Canton Ichanqueso, a town in the jurisdiction of Suchitoto, department of Cuscatlan, was a UPR resettlement site. Its people shared the social and political characteristics of most of the displaced. They were mainly landless farmers, and some had skills such as bricklaying, tailoring, and commercial cooking. Salvadoran government agencies and the armed forces sponsored the Ichanqueso project, along with AID. The National Commission for Assistance to the Displaced of El Salvador (CONADES) and other relief organizations implemented the project, under the direction of the military. CONADES reported that the project had the following objectives:

1. To promote. . . voluntary participation of the population in the productive process of the nation.

2. To advise, orient, and implement productive projects. . . which will permit these populations to become self-sufficient.[6]

By March 1987, approximately seventy-four families had returned to Ichanqueso. However, the community's distrust of the military grew, and the residents resisted the establishment of civilian security patrols. The village relied heavily on government assistance and did not develop the political and economic self-reliance seen in independently repopulated communities. Furthermore, the elected community council did not receive organizational or leadership training, and lacked initiative and decision-making authority.

The mayor of Suchitoto, who was well informed about the social and political problems at Ichanqueso as well as at other UPR projects, said:

At Ichanqueso, the people aren't organized; they have their community council only to ask for help. So far, there has been nothing done about land tenancy in these projects [Ichanqueso]. Instead, people get 6 colones a day for work, which isn't even enough to buy food.[7]

Although the government described its resettlement projects using development-oriented language, their basic purpose remained counterinsurgency. This overrode other concerns and left little scope for cooperative ownership, particularly land ownership, or active participation in development activities. The Ichanqueso project is now defunct, and many of its participants moved to surrounding areas after losing hope. Others remain in this conflict area, surviving without any government assistance and not much hope to improve their lives.[8] Complete external control, coupled with corruption and military domination of civilian affairs, seriously undermined these projects from the start.

The Repopulation Movement

As El Salvador's civil war dragged on, many peasants who had fled to urban squatter settlements and shanty towns, mainly in San Salvador, became increasingly dissatisfied with their conditions of dependency, overcrowding, and unemployment. Dissatisfaction motivated them to begin the repopulation movement during the mid-1980s. Similarly, refugees who lived in camps in Honduras stated that their decision to return to their home towns was based on the poor living conditions of the camps, the lack of security, and a strong desire to re-establish their original communities.

Thousands of refugees and displaced people have returned to their home towns since 1986. They received some assistance from self-help groups like the Christian Committee for the Displaced of El Salvador and the National Coordination for Repopulation, Salvadoran churches, and some international humanitarian groups. Today, these communities are undertaking projects aimed at creating sustainable access to land, food production, employment, preventive health care, housing, and education.

Many of the former refugees and displaced persons, especially those who repatriated from Honduras, brought back organizational and technical skills which have allowed them to design and implement community development efforts. For example, since returning, most communities have made decisions through elected community councils and have set up vocational skills training programs, clinics, and schools. They acquired these skills through training provided by relief agencies administering the camps. These included the United Nations High Commissioner for Refugees, CARITAS, Catholic Relief Services, CEDEN (a coalition of Central American evangelical groups), the Mennonite Central Committee, and Doctors without Borders.

Civil war and military hostility continue to threaten most of the repopulated communities. In some cases, government troops have stolen or burned crops, slaughtered livestock, destroyed homes, and even killed villagers, just as in the early 1980s. The military has also prevented food and medicine from entering the villages and restricted relief agencies' access. In violation of the Esquipulas agreement, the government has refused to issue national identification documents ("cédulas") to many resettled civilians. This has been a major problem in areas where the ruling Republican Nationalist Alliance (ARENA) controls the local government.

Without a "cédula," a person cannot gain access to public services, register to vote, or engage in any legal transaction, including marriage and registration of a child's birth. The Mayor of Arcatao, a repopulated community in Chalatenango, who was elected by ARENA supporters in an election which excluded repatriates, said to a church worker, "If I give the people their "cédulas," they'll go get election registration cards. And if they can vote, they'll vote me out of office."[9]

The Salvadoran human rights organization Tutela Legal blames the army for the vast majority of human rights violations, but both Tutela and the U.S.-based Americas Watch have denounced the FMLN for causing civilian casualties by laying land mines and other explosives in populated areas during the ongoing warfare. Despite these violations of their civil and political rights, residents of the repopulated communities continue to demand that the authorities permit them to rebuild their communities in peace.

Guarjila – A Model of Rural Development[10]

In October 1987, Salvadorans returning from the Mesa Grande refugee camp re-populated four villages, among them Guarjila, located in the northeastern part of the war-torn department of Chalatenango. These refugees had fled the war and lived in camps in Honduras since 1979. Once the community cleared Guarjila of weeds and debris left behind by the war, the villagers collectively built provisional housing for each family, starting with widows, the elderly, and disabled persons. Since their return, they have planted hundreds of acres in basic staples such as corn, beans, and rice. They have also built grain storage facilities, houses, two schools, a health clinic, and a chapel. They carried out these tasks under the leadership of the community council, a governing body elected by the villagers. This community of 2,000 people, half of whom are children, cooperatively manages all housing and land.

During the initial year of repopulation, before the first harvest, Guarjila needed start-up funds to secure food. The community received money for food and construction materials from Salvadoran churches and local and international nongovernmental humanitarian aid organizations. However, during this time the villagers mostly relied on their own initiative and creative instinct to survive.

The people of Guarjila work about half the land cooperatively. The remaining area is divided into small plots for each family's private use. Community members work three days on cooperative projects and the rest of the week on family plots. The community also organized a food distribution system after its first harvest. In addition to housing and crop production projects, the community runs a poultry and cattle cooperative, providing additional protein, draft animals, and fertilizer.

Since resettling, the community has established an emergency food project to store surplus grain which the community council purchases. The council decides whether to keep this grain as a reserve for free distribution in case of an emergency or sell it in local markets for profit. In the latter case, proceeds are used to purchase other items that the village cannot manufacture, such as sugar and salt.

Guarjila trades items such as milk and eggs within the village and with other communities. Neighboring repopulated communities often lack these items. Guarjila's cooperative ownership and management enables the community to buy supplies, such as seeds and fertilizer for everyone's use from the proceeds of the crops, eggs, clothing, and shoes which they sell in local markets.

Guarjila has established services to benefit all members of the community. In addition to the education and primary health care systems, these services include a dental clinic, facilities for producing herbal medicines and enterprises, such as shoe-making, carpentry, and sewing. A day care center provides children with supervision and well-balanced meals.

Residents of Guarjila played an instrumental role in helping to build a bridge across the Sumpul River. They are also involved in a road project intended to connect several of the most isolated rural communities in the region with each other and with the major market in the provincial capital of Chalatenango City. The construction of the bridge and the road will advance the local economy and help the repopulated communities enter more fully into the economic life of the nation.

Villages in Chalatenango, including Guarjila, plan to establish an agricultural training school. This is a three-year project which cooperatives will implement in four areas: training, research and experimentation, crop and livestock production, and administration.

Many repopulated communities have developed projects to prevent soil erosion, and have employed various new planting techniques. Guarjila plans to undertake a reforestation project in coordination with two Salvadoran universities.

Like other repopulated communities, Guarjila is hoping to help establish a regional nonprofit credit union or rotating fund which will make loans available for long-term development projects.

The Archdiocese of San Salvador has sponsored a project to empower poor women living in rural areas, including Guarjila, and help them find solutions to their problems through education and training programs, workshops, retreats, and conferences. Guarjila and other repopulated communities have established projects focusing on women, enabling them to assume less traditional roles, such as community council members, cooperative leaders, health promoters, and teachers. Historically, Salvadoran peasant women's social and economic tasks have consisted of cooking, gathering firewood, carrying water, caring for their children, and providing agricultural labor for their families.

A 1991-1992 plan developed by CORDES, a Salvadoran nongovernmental organization serving dozens of repopulated communities, including Guarjila, focuses on various future development projects, including expanded production of grain, dairy products, vegetables, and vegetable oil.

War and repression hang over Guarjila's efforts to achieve rural development. The village had the highest number of reported explosives-related accidents among repopulated communities during 1988. Seventeen villagers were detained and wounded or "disappeared" during the first months of repatriation. Many are subject to military harassment, detention, and torture. On March 19, 1991, government troops shot and killed a nine-year-old girl in the village.

Nevertheless, Guarjila's people continue to struggle to survive as a community and meet their basic needs. Once a ghost town, today it is both a vibrant village and an exciting model for Salvadorans and others. However, like many other repopulated communities, Guarjila has striven to overcome obstacles and failures since the villagers' return, especially given the lack of support from the Salvadoran government in providing their basic needs. The residents have made remarkable progress in securing access to housing, food, health, and education in spite of the problems they faced during the re-establishment of their community. Each community aspires to rely primarily on its efforts, however, some communities still receive limited outside assistance today.

Guarjila and other repopulated communities are taking important steps toward rural development in the midst of an eleven-year-old war. In an effort to improve living conditions, foster security, and provide for fatherless families of the rural population, these villagers have chosen to live communally and self-reliantly. They are developing a long-term solution to the problem of displacement and an alternative to the traditionally class-divided economic, political, and social structures of El Salvador. Massive numbers of returning refugees, who had lived in the camps in Honduras, strengthened the repopulation movement and attracted both national and international support. While the Salvadoran government has continued to violate civil and political rights in repopulated communities, it has not succeeded in suppressing this movement.

Rural Development as Part of the Solution

El Salvador is the smallest, most densely populated country in Central America. According to Ruth Leger Sivard, the ongoing civil war has claimed about 75,000 lives.[11] More than 4 billion dollars of United States military and economic aid has fueled the war. Meanwhile, 70 percent of the rural population lives in absolute poverty. The combination of war and poverty makes the rural population unable to purchase enough food to meet minimum nutritional requirements. The government spent only $28 per capita for sanitation, health care, food, and nutrition in 1990, while nearby Costa Rica spent $95 per person.

The repopulation movement has helped foster a new social and economic structure for rural communities on a regional level. This alternative model of development has transformed bombed-out villages into dynamic and productive civilian communities. These communities' design of cooperative ownership, collective cultivation, and management, along with models of health care, education, and cultural development, has improved the quality of life. In contrast to the government-sponsored resettlement projects, where communities lacked organizational and leadership skills to improve their standard of living, the independently repopulated communities are conducive to empowerment and acquiring the skills and raw materials to attain, step by step, a society that provides for all its people. Because of the war, the future of the repopulation movement remains uncertain. But in spite of the war, the repopulation movement offers hope for El Salvador's rural population.

The movement's potential for achieving sustainable rural development has inspired refugees in neighboring countries, such as Guatemala. El Salvador's repopulation experience may someday offer lessons for restarting the development process in other Third World zones of conflict with large refugee populations.

As Monsignor Ricardo Urioste, the Vicar of the Archdiocese of San Salvador, says about the repopulated communities:

The greatest hope is offered by the people themselves: their courage, their valor, their efforts, their decision, their clear vision of what they want – to work, to live in peace. . . . This is what gives the repopulations a potential for great advance.[12]

A peace settlement would allow the communities to move into new and more profound development programs. The recent United Nations-monitored negotiations between the Salvadoran government and the FMLN may lead to constitutional reforms, monitoring of human rights violations, and a permanent cease-fire. These changes can pave the way to new democratic politics and a stable economy. Meanwhile, the repopulated communities are making important contributions toward achieving those same goals. ∎

Notes

1. Cited in Compher and Morgan, p. 109.
2. Schrading, p. 17.
3. *Ibid.*, pp. 18-19.
4. *Ibid.*
5. Edwards and Siebentritt, pp. 61-67; Popkin, p. 6.
6. Cited in Edwards and Siebentritt, p. 70.
7. Cited in *Ibid.*, p. 80.
8. Interview with Gretta Tovar-Siebentritt, July 26, 1991.
9. Church World Service.
10. The information contained in this section is based on a number of published and unpublished sources, including interviews with representatives of humanitarian aid organizations and a religious leader from the Guarjila community. Published sources: Compher and Morgan; Schrading, pp. 104, 106; Foundation Cordes; "Human Rights and Humanitarian Aid," pp. 6, 11, Annex II, Annex III, pp. 1-2.
11. Sivard, p. 22; *Hunger 1990*, p. 77.
12. Cited in Schrading, p. 113.

People Organize for Water and Jobs in Tanzania and Saint Louis

Credit: FAO

Piped water means improved health and nutrition, and that Tanzanian women no longer have to spend time and energy fetching water from springs.

by Maria Simon

Grassroots development involves a bottom-up approach, where poor people initiate local, small-scale projects which meet urgent and pressing needs. The people who benefit from the projects are also the principal conceivers, organizers, implementers, and managers. A participatory process, where people take control of their lives and struggle to improve their situation, has consequences beyond the immediate achievement of a project's goals. Grassroots development helps them gain more control over resources and power.

Poor people face significant obstacles to participation in development. They are often undernourished, inadequately sheltered, underemployed, uneducated, and lack material resources. Yet, through collective action, they can change their lives, improve health care, increase their income or crop yields, or obtain a basic necessity such as water.

Some international development agencies are becoming increasingly involved with grassroots projects. These agencies do not conceive of development primarily in terms of growth in a nation's economy. Instead, they judge projects by concrete improvements in the quality of life of the poorest people. They recognize that large-scale, top-down development projects and efforts to change national policies often fail to improve the lives of poor individuals. They see that equity, environmental sustainability, and democratic decision-making are as important as economic growth in the development process.

However, these agencies provide only a fraction of the total aid to developing countries. For example, the African Development Foundation (ADF), a U.S. government international development agency which stresses the grassroots approach, received only $13 million in fiscal 1991. That was less than 0.1 percent of the U.S. foreign aid budget of $15 billion. The main security assistance programs (Economic Support Funds and Foreign Military Financing) received $7.8 billion (nearly 50 percent).

Nonetheless, there is growing recognition of the importance of people's participation in development. Instead of implementing a pre-conceived plan designed to benefit poor people, a partner relationship calls for the development agency to act in response to the needs that people articulate. Ideally, the agency helps people accomplish their own goals by providing funding, technology, and/or training, without imposing the donor agency's own agenda. The donor serves as a facilitator and poor people as leaders. A recent example of this approach to development comes from Tanzania, in East Africa.

The Partnership Between the Villagers of North Rombo and the ADF

The average American uses approximately twenty gallons of water each morning for showering, brushing teeth, flushing the toilet, making breakfast, and washing dishes. Most Americans take their access to water for granted. People in developing countries live under different circumstances. According to Worldwatch Institute, 1.9 billion people do not have access to safe drinking water. The United Nations Children's Fund (UNICEF) reports that unclean water, coupled with inadequate sanitation, causes 75 percent of all disease in developing countries. Five million children a year die of diarrhea, mainly due to water-borne germs. Clean water is essential to improved health and nutrition.

The reality of scarce water shapes the everyday lives of the villagers in Usseri and Takakea, two northern divisions of the Rombo District, located on the slopes of Mount Kilimanjaro in northeastern Tanzania. In these divisions, annual family incomes averaged $200 in 1988, the lowest in the Kilimanjaro area. Child mortality was higher than the national average. Both children and adults frequently suffered from preventable illnesses like intestinal worms and diarrhea, which in turn often lead to undernutrition. A study found that 45 percent of the villagers had traces of parasitic disease in their stools.[1] The nearest springs lay four kilometers (two-and-a half miles) from this village. Women and children daily engaged in the exhausting chore of fetching water from a spring or river. Women lost time from household and agricultural tasks, and children missed school.

The villagers in Usseri and Takakea sought outside resources in order to bring water to their communities. Today, a gravity-fed pipeline from the springs brings water to the communities, thanks to collaboration between the villagers, a Tanzanian development organization, and the African Development Foundation.

The U.S. Congress created ADF in 1980; its purpose is to "enable the poor to participate in the process of development."[2] ADF funds projects based on participation, sustainability, replicability, and results. Participation refers to people's involvement in project activities and decision-making. Sustainability implies the continuation of the project over time. Replicability suggests the possibility of duplicating the project in other locations. Results refers to specific project outcomes, such as fostering social and economic development.

When villagers in North Rombo raised a "public outcry" for water, ADF responded with a $100,000 grant to fund the pipeline.[3] ADF project grants range from $700 to $250,000, averaging approximately $90,000. Villagers from Usseri and Takakea participated substantially in initiating and implementing the project. By requiring grassroots groups to formulate projects, ADF hopes to insure that these groups will continue to feel a sense of ownership. Village leaders explained to ADF that water was a top priority. They had no reliable water supply during the dry season, about six months each year, due to unreliable rains and a lack of permanent rivers.

The villagers committed themselves to paying one-third of project costs and pro-

viding the necessary labor:

[They] volunteered to dig and bury 14 kilometers of trenches for the new piping; they dug up, cleared and buried a lot more old pipes to which the new ones were connected, they cleared up old water tanks, cut trees, bushes and rocks, carried construction materials such as pipes, fittings, sand, chippings, and cement on their heads through narrow and steep foot paths in the Kilimanjaro forest area.[4]

Community residents played a smaller part in project management. They had

Jobs for Your Community

by Kathleen Crowley, CSJ

Red, white, and blue "JOBS FOR YOUR COMMUNITY" signs at urban redevelopment projects proudly display the mayor's name, the relevant city agency, and the federal funding source. In St. Louis, Mo., in the middle 1980s, the St. Louis Association for Community Organizations (SLACO) inquired whether these "community jobs" were going to people who lived in the city. SLACO, a coalition of ten community associations in predominantly African-American neighborhoods, had previously convinced the city government to board up vacant buildings, mow city-owned lots, and penalize gouging slum landlords – typical concerns that groups organize around to build a

community power base. SLACO turned to employment issues to stabilize neighborhoods and get federal funds directed to local needs.

Background

Major redevelopment was taking place in St. Louis during the 1980s, especially downtown. SLACO was interested in duplicating Boston's resident job policy, which reserved a percentage of government-funded construction jobs for city residents, with a percentage of these reserved jobs guaranteed to members of minority groups and women. St. Louis had received $1.75 billion in government construction funds between 1975 and 1984, mostly from federal Urban Development Action Grants and Community Development Block Grants. Residents of SLACO neighborhoods were surprised to learn that these programs are targeted to cities with high rates of poverty and unem-

ployment. SLACO estimated that the construction projects in question created the equivalent of 14,000 full-time, one-year jobs in St. Louis, but the question was, "for whom?"

In 1983, according to a study by the Missouri Association for Social Welfare, 30 percent of St. Louis residents lived below the poverty line, double the statewide rate. Forty-six percent of all city children and a similar proportion of all African-American residents (who made up 46 percent of the populace) lived in poverty. The rate was 63 percent for African-American children. St. Louis unemployment rates also exceeded those for the state during the mid-1980s: in 1985, the city rate was 8.7 percent, compared to 6.7 percent for the state.

The same study found widespread hunger in the city. In 1983, 38 percent of the residents were eligible for the Food Stamp Program, although only 58 percent of

found an ally in the Padre Alois Shauritanga Memorial Fund (SMF), a Tanzanian nongovernmental development organization composed of professionals originally from North Rombo. SMF had helped villagers look for a funding agency, and now agreed to administer the grant and serve as the liaison between ADF and the villagers. The Rombo district government trained villagers in maintenance and repair. Village leaders, along with the elected district council, took responsibility for implementing the project.

Sustainability refers to people's ability to maintain a project independently. This involves the use of local, low-cost building materials and simple, easily maintained technology. The design of the North Rombo water project utilized local inputs and the technology of a gravity-fed line. Construction, carried out with hand tools, relied on local labor and avoided the expense of heavy equipment, as well as environmental damage such equipment might have caused.

Project sustainability may also require anticipating the on-going need for financial resources. Poor African governments are often unable to pick up where development agencies leave off. ADF required the establishment of a revenue collection system, to assure resources for replacement

---

those eligible actually participated. In 1984, the city infant mortality rate was 14.7 per 1,000 live births, compared to the state rate of 10.0 and the national rate of 10.8. A March 1984 survey found that during one week, 26,000 people received emergency food assistance – nearly 20 percent of 1983 poor people and 6 percent of all city residents.

Organizing Strategy

Local construction union representatives admitted that the construction jobs were not going to St. Louis residents, as no more than 15 percent of their members lived in the city. SLACO considered 7 to 8 percent a more realistic figure.

SLACO set out to organize citywide support for an ordinance or a mayoral executive order to set aside jobs for residents. As a largely African-American organization, SLACO needed assistance in reaching predominantly white Southside

St. Louis. It approached the Roman Catholic Archdiocesan Human Rights Office (HRO) for assistance in setting up meetings in Southside churches. HRO, a long-time supporter of SLACO, also had good connections to the labor unions from earlier collaboration on defeating proposed state legislation to ban contracts requiring workers to join unions (a "right to work" law). With the assistance of HRO, SLACO gained support from fourteen Southside Catholic parishes and seventeen Protestant churches.

Fairness Issue

Mayor Vincent Schoemehl initially opposed a resident job policy, but recognized that this issue could unite racially disparate neighborhoods by appealing to people's basic sense of fairness. If the federal government provided funds based on unemployment and poverty levels, then it made sense to reserve some of the jobs to help

eradicate the problems which made the city eligible for the money. For six months, SLACO held neighborhood meetings and testified at city government hearings.

The mayor then called a meeting of SLACO and its allies, representatives of the building trade unions, and the contractors' association. He stated that he would issue an executive order mandating a St. Louis resident job policy if these three parties could agree on one. The unions insisted on reserving 15 to 20 percent of their apprenticeships for city residents, while SLACO wanted to set aside 30 to 35 percent of the apprenticeships and 25 to 30 percent of other positions. Construction firms opposed any resident job policy, claiming that a bureaucratic nightmare would result. Though SLACO maintained a strong stance, it also made every attempt to convince the unions that it wanted African-American city residents to join in

parts and repairs. SMF implemented a payment system that involved an initial fee equivalent to eight dollars for individual household connection and substantially smaller monthly payments. Poor households can gain free access via "domestic water points" placed 500 meters apart throughout both villages.[5]

A fair, affordable, and equitable payment system need not be burdensome if it represents people's choice to participate. Although SMF, rather than the villagers, designed the payment system, the local people voted to accept it.

The water project required a large initial investment; ADF's grant financed pipes, materials, transportation, and technical assistance. The probability of replication depends on the availability of a similar sum of money for other projects.

In a future evaluation, ADF staff will look critically at the effect the project has had on the empowerment of the villagers through their decision-making and joint action. This evaluation will focus on social and economic, as well as physical improvements.[6] The goal of bringing water to the village was accomplished in this pro-

the labor movement, which has enabled other low- and middle-income Americans to achieve economic self-sufficiency. In short, the policy offered an opportunity to reduce poverty, income insecurity, and hunger in St. Louis.

Policy Victory

The three sides eventually reached a compromise. The mayor's order requires any contractor who works on a city-assisted project to fill at least 30 percent of all apprenticeships in his/her total workforce with city residents. Fifty percent of these residents must come from minority groups and 10 percent must be women. Contractors on a city-assisted project must also fill 25 percent of all other construction jobs in their total workforce with city residents; again, 50 percent of the residents must be members of minority groups and 10 percent must be women. The parties agreed to achieve these goals in specific steps between 1986 and 1989. The order barred

contractors who failed to comply or at least "show good faith" from future participation in city projects.

The contractors had raised valid concerns about shifting workers to particular projects solely on the basis of their residence. For this reason, the order covered each contractor's total workforce rather than specific projects. Of course, this offered contractors considerable leeway on any given project's workforce, while also allowing them to factor relatively small projects into the calculations of their workforce. It also meant that city residents would not necessarily see the executive order's impact when they looked at particular construction sites.

Despite these limitations, SLACO had opened new employment opportunities to city residents, minorities, and women.

Outcome

It is one thing to win a victory and quite another to achieve the desired results. It took the city of

St. Louis almost a full year with continued prodding by SLACO to establish a Compliance Committee of community people and industry representatives, hire staff, and draw up implementation guidelines for contractors and unions.

Implementing the policy was more complex than it at first had seemed. Skilled people had to be recruited to meet the goals. In order to enroll in the apprenticeship program, people had to know how to work the system so they could get a "letter of intent" from the contractor. People also had to assess the validity of testing procedures used by various construction schools.

Project organizers have generally been pleased with the results because they were able to make an impact on the system as a whole, not just on one contractor at a time. The executive order is a vehicle that secures well-paid union jobs with health and pension benefits, in contrast to the low wages paid by many of the new jobs created in

ject; however, the development of local institutions and self-reliance within the community remains unevaluated and unclear. Evaluations, particularly of longer-term social and community goals, are occasionally hampered by a development agency's need to show legislators and taxpayers successfully completed projects.

The water project only addresses a part of people's needs. ADF has not played a role in any follow-up health care or educational activities. Health training could better inform the villagers of the connection between clean water and health. This would involve recurring costs, making it difficult to design a self-sustaining program. The on-going presence of SMF and similar intermediate organizations offers the potential to continue community development beyond the water project.

Also left uncertain, pending formal evaluation of the project, is whether SMF effectively taught the villagers management skills. As they face the continuing challenge of distributing the water fairly, managing the revenue collection system, and maintaining the pipeline, their ability to run the system for themselves is a key component

the 1980s. SLACO sees securing apprenticeships as particularly important, as these allow people to enter the construction industry and learn long-term skills.

Number of Jobs Actually Secured

The executive order secured city residents, members of minority groups, and women – fewer apprenticeships than its goals required. While the Construction Industry Compliance Committee called for 15 percent of the apprentices to reside in the city in 1986, only 10 percent did. Only 34 percent of these resident apprentices were members of minority groups, compared to the goal of 44 percent. The failure to meet minority resident apprenticeship goals continued through 1990. However, during the first half of 1988, 9 percent of the resident apprentices were women; this slightly exceeded the goal of 8 percent.

In 1989, hiring fell far short of the goals, with city residents filling an average of 19 percent of the apprenticeship positions instead of the target of 30 percent. Minority residents were supposed to fill 50 percent of these reserved apprenticeship slots, but actually received 25 percent. Women filled 4 percent of these positions, instead of the target rate of 10 percent.

To address the shortfall, city officials, the construction industry, and community people formed the St. Louis Construction Orientation Intake Center to act as an "honest broker" between individuals and the system, helping each party better meet its own needs.

Establishing a Support System

The Intake Center may have turned out to be the most beneficial spin-off effect of the job policy. It was established to facilitate communication among the unions (which cover twenty-six separate trades), contractors, and people needing employment. The center received grants from the Compliance Committee and the contractors' association, private contributions from the community, and funding from the city Economic Development Corporation. Center staff screen job applicants, assist them in getting necessary tutoring in order to get into a construction training school, and help them through the system.

The current director of the program, Armand Paulet, has been a staunch Southside supporter of the organizing strategy connected with the executive order. He had represented the community in negotiating meetings and has a long history of working in employment programs for low-income people. Having him in such a vital position enables SLACO to refer qualified persons to the center with confidence that they will receive the assistance they need.

A September 1990 report shows that in the short time since the establishment of the Intake Center, a major contractor hired four candidates referred by the center to work on expansion of the local convention center. All four were

of the project's sustainability. Developing management capacity among the villagers would also allow them to carry out future projects.

Women's Participation in Grassroots Development

The village women of Usseri and Takakea benefit from easier access to clean water. Moreover, they have more time for food and cash crop cultivation, other income-generating activities, and child care. Women participated actively in project implementation; they dug trenches, laid pipes, and carried sand and stones. ADF presently has not assessed their role in project decision-making, however. An evaluation of earlier ADF projects by the Congressional Office of Technology Assessment found that women "rarely participated in management." ADF staff note that their mandate requires them to respond to proposals initiated by communities in

Africa. These proposals invariably reflect the cultural attitudes of those communities, including attitudes toward women.[7]

Yet women have a vital role to play in development in Africa. They are responsible for an estimated 80 percent of subsistence food production, as well as for child-rearing. Pierre Pradervand, an Africa expert, writes, "If asked what is currently Africa's most precious and valuable human resource, I would not hesitate to reply: its women."[8] Tanzanian women are insisting on a more prominent role in development, as Maria Shada, of the Tanzanian Women's Media Association, notes: "There has been a kind of awakening of women. They have always belonged to groups, but they are becoming more and more organized."[9]

For example, in another Kilimanjaro village, Nronga, women organized alternative income earning activities following a coffee blight in 1984. They began a dairy cooperative to upgrade the herd and acquired a vehicle to transport fresh milk to

from a minority group; two were women. This project also hired a minority plumber apprentice referred by the Intake Center. Thirteen contractors have contacted the center regarding employment referrals for the school system's capital projects. Following a pre-award meeting for a $2 million street project with the St. Louis Development Corporation, a city agency which currently oversees the implementation of the job policy, another major contractor agreed to use the Intake Center as the primary resource for fulfilling its city resident employment requirements. The Center is also helping recruit workers for a light-rail system contract.

Room for Improvement

Since the mayor issued the resident job executive order, supporters of the policy have recognized the need for additional changes, such as:

Increased federal funding.

Urban America needs more federal funds to meet a variety of needs, including housing, emergency food assistance, employment, and redevelopment. During the 1980s, the federal government cut urban development spending drastically. Thus, a great deal of St. Louis' redevelopment took place prior to and during the time of organizing for a resident job policy. Since the implementation of the

policy, employment in city construction projects has fallen, due to declining federal funds and recession. If the federal government targeted a percentage of the jobs created by increased urban development funds to those most in need, local community organizations could insist on compliance by local governments, as they did in St. Louis.

Developing skills.

Partly because of deficiencies in the public school system, many people in inner cities are unable to complete basic math tests and other requirements for entering an apprenticeship program. The St. Louis Intake Center is seeking

the city.

In 1989, the women approached Technoserve, a private voluntary organization, seeking help to limit milk losses due to poor refrigeration facilities and impassable roads. In consultation with the villagers, Technoserve recommended a simple cultured dairy process to preserve milk for subsequent sale. Cultured milk can be stored for ten days without refrigeration and without losing its nutritional value. Readily available milk can improve health and nutrition, as well as producing income.

Villagers in Naisinyai, also in the Kilimanjaro region, improved their nutrition and income by upgrading their cattle herd. When asked about their problems by the Maasai Health Services Project (MHSP), a local organization, the villagers identified the loss of cattle to tick-borne fever. Women suggested building a cattle dip to prevent disease in the herd. Through MHSP the village contacted the local Oxfam office, which agreed to fund the construction of the dip. The women continue to manage the dip, which earns income from user fees.

Dynamics of the Partner Relationship

In a grassroots project that involves outside assistance, the development agency's behavior plays as large a role in the outcome as local people themselves. ADF chose a low-profile role in North Rombo. It limited its involvement to performing an independent feasibility assessment, providing funds to cover input costs and technical assistance, requiring quarterly reports on activities and finances, and the pending evaluation. Tanzanian ADF staff had all the contact with the villagers and SMF.

Keeping the presence of foreign development agents at a minimum generally allows greater room for flexibility, improvisation, and adjustment by participants during implementation. It also furthers self-

funds for a job readiness program that will provide hands-on training and math instruction to twenty-four minority students during two four-week sessions to ready them for construction training school. The center plans to assist in the recruitment of prospective students for this program and provide job placement services for them.

Effective monitoring and enforcement.

While the Intake Center staff currently have a good working relationship with many of the unions and contractors, they recognize that vigorous city government enforcement is needed to back up their efforts. Otherwise, contractors will be tempted to ignore the order.

Conclusion

This case study suggests that five basic elements made the St. Louis resident job policy work as well as it has:

• A committed group of well-organized citizens who are secure in the power which comes from banding together out of self-interest to get city officials to respond to their needs;

• A legal vehicle which pries open the system and mandates a job policy for city residents, women, and minorities, making employment opportunities available;

• Skills training, so that people can meet the minimum requirements to fill the jobs;

• An institution to assist candidates through the entire process from application to apprenticeship and journeyman certification, as well as relating to the unions, contractors, and city officials for employment possibilities; and

• Unionized employment, which clearly offers a means for assuring that jobs pay decent salaries and guarantee health and pension benefits.

The study also highlights the need for more government action – investment in urban development and schools, and enforcement of rules enacted to assist low-income minorities.■

reliance. ADF was able to limit its involvement because SMF provided the managerial skills often lacking at the grassroots level.

Other development organizations take a different approach. While some hire local people to staff their overseas offices, others send their own foreign personnel. Some organizations send their staff into the villages to live and work; others maintain staff in the city, often removed from the projects. Technoserve maintains field offices, and its staff provides management training in projects for two to five years. A large amount of time is dedicated to the transfer of technical skills early in the project and then gradually scaling down involvement. Oxfam maintains regional offices and limits its role to feasibility studies and funding community initiatives.

The best approach depends on the personalities involved and the goals the organization is trying to achieve. Too much contact may foster dependence on outside "experts." However, a donor organization would be negligent to send money and resources without monitoring their use. Above all, donors must base contact on participation and mutual respect.

The Importance of National Commitment

National policies also impact heavily on grassroots efforts. A government may foster grassroots initiatives through supportive policies, or it may directly or indirectly undercut such efforts. Tanzanian government rhetoric supports grassroots efforts. *A Proposed Programme for Child Survival and Development in Rombo District,* for example, outlines a three-part, continuous decision-making process for communities, aimed at reducing child mortality rates. This "Triple A" approach calls for: *assessment* of the magnitude and characteristics of the problem, *analysis* of the cause of the problem, and appropriate *action.*[10] Villagers in Tanzania's Iringa District have won international recognition for effectively employing this approach to child survival.

While Tanzania's national self-help policy is partly driven by the government's desperate lack of resources, it does create a supportive framework for grassroots efforts. The government's attempt to decentralize and its successful literacy campaign (literacy now stands at 90 percent) show a commitment that moves beyond rhetoric.

Unfortunately, the government creates many plans at a centralized level with little popular input. For instance, the child survival plan for Rombo was produced in the capital, Dar es Salaam, yet it depends on local people for implementation. Such top-down planning is at odds with encouraging villagers to evaluate and act on their own needs. Effective local leadership might coordinate government plans with local interests, but the pervasiveness of Tanzania's one-party system adds an additional hurdle to democratic local decision-making.

The state's long-term ability to channel resources to villages is also crucial to development. The Tanzanian government has long had financial difficulties, compounded in recent years by austerity measures undertaken in conjunction with International Monetary Fund loans. Governments around the continent face similar problems.

There is growing recognition of the importance of popular participation in development. In February 1990, nongovernmental organizations and the United Nations convened a conference in Arusha, Tanzania. The resulting *African Charter for Popular Participation in Development and Transformation* declared:

> . . .[P]opular participation provides the driving force for collective commit-

ment for the determination of people-based development processes and willingness by the people to undertake sacrifices and expend their social energies for its execution. As an end in itself, popular participation is the fundamental right of the people to fully and effectively participate in the determination of the decisions which affect their lives at all levels and at all times.[11]

However, many poor people in Africa and elsewhere do not have the level of government support present in Tanzania. In addition to the crippling limitations of poverty, poor people are often confronted with hostile governments that view grassroots initiatives as a threat to their hold on power. As Alan Durning has observed, "[L]ike all development, self-help is inherently political: it is the struggle to control the future."[12] All over Africa, people continue this struggle. Even in the Horn of Africa, there are many grassroots development efforts, despite war, drought, and government repression.

For example, in Eritrea, a territory torn by recurring famine and a bloody independence struggle, people are involved in a myriad of grassroots activities. The National Union of Eritrean Women (NUEWmn) has organized literacy, health care, and craft production programs, and supports local efforts to improve women's lives and position in their communities. In partnership with Grassroots International, NUEWmn trained 250 women as tailors in 1986 and 1987, thereby increasing local self-reliance.

Elsewhere in the Horn, Sudanaid, the relief and development arm of the Sudan Catholic Bishops' Conference, has supported both development and relief projects proposed by local grassroots organizations. The civil war in Sudan has forced the organization to devote more resources to relief activities, but not to the complete exclusion of development projects. It conducts nutrition monitoring and distributes food, blankets, medicine, vehicles, and spare parts. Sudanaid also provides child and adult education centers for people who have fled the fighting in southern Sudan for the capital city, Khartoum.

Conclusion

Grassroots development can improve the lives of people faced with powerlessness, poverty, and hunger. Development agencies which wish to support this approach to development must pay close attention to who is making decisions and who is benefiting, in order to insure a participatory and sustainable process. People-motivated change in the context of overwhelming poverty is complicated and difficult. Grassroots initiatives offer a hopeful avenue, but at best they can have limited effects without collaborative efforts on the national and international levels. ■

Notes

1. ADF, "Project Appraisal," pp. 2-3.
2. U.S. Congress, OTA Report, p. 1.
3. ADF, "Grant Application," p. 3.
4. Maskini.
5. ADF fax.
6. U.S. Congress, Grassroots, p. 7.
7. *Ibid.,* p. 5; written comment by ADF staff, June 10, 1991.
8. Pradervand, p. 12.
9. Telephone conversation, April 26, 1991.
10. District Executive Director, p. 3.
11. United Nations Economic Commission for Africa, p.19.
12. Durning, *Action at the Grassroots,* p. 53.

Agencies Involved in Grassroots Partnerships

Besides the groups mentioned in the text, U.S.-based private voluntary organizations involved in grassroots partnerships in the developing world include Catholic Relief Services, World Vision, Unitarian Universalist Service Committee, Mennonite Central Committee, CARE, Church World Service, Lutheran World Relief, Mercy Corps International, Africare, Adventist Development and Relief Agency International, Overseas Education Fund, Trickle Up Program, Inc., World Concern, Americares, Food for the Hungry, and World Neighbors. ■

IAF Builds Political Clout in Texas

by Richard A. Hoehn

*A peasant came to me.
"Father, I have sinned."
"What have you done?"
"I have not organized."
I was perplexed.
"Why is that a sin?"
"It means that I do not care
about women, children, and my
nation. I do not have love."*

– Fr. Jose Alas of El Salvador

pow·er (pou′er), *n*. **1. the ability to ACT.**

*(logo from the organizing convention of ACT
- Allied Communities of Tarrant
County, Fort Worth, Texas)*

A week before the 1990 congressional elections, 10,000 Hispanic, Anglo, African-American, and Asian Texans converged on the Hemisfair Arena in San Antonio as part of an organization that is, arguably, the most notable expression of grassroots democracy in the United States today. They traveled hundreds of miles to meet for two hours with Ann Richards (now governor) and other political candidates. But it took seventeen years of organization-building to arrive at this event. The meeting brought together ten Industrial Areas Foundation (IAF) groups from cities across Texas to participate as one political entity – the Texas IAF Network.

IAF, often noted for the confrontational tactics of founder Saul Alinksy, began work in Texas in the early 1970s. Alinsky had scared some people and inspired others with books like *Rules for Radicals* and assertions like "Better to die on your feet than live on your knees,"[1] and "The means -and-end moralists or non-doers always wind up on their ends without any means."[2]

Alinsky had given years of thought to questions of power and politics. What sort of power do ordinary, especially poor, people have? How can they discover and use their power to attain legitimate goals in a system where established organizations have massive, controlling power?

Whereas most policy and development efforts define hunger as an economic problem, IAF analysis defines powerlessness as a major cause of hunger and other social problems. The typical answer to why people are hungry is poverty – they lack jobs, education, or child care because they are poor. IAF analysis pushes the question back one step. Why are they poor? There are historical reasons, e.g. racial, ethnic, age, and gender discrimination, and socio-geographic reasons like place of birth and the happenstance of parentage. Yet there are people within those subgroups who are not poor or hungry.

People are poor because they lack power. When Allied Communities of Tarrant (ACT), the county-wide Fort Worth IAF group, held its first convention, posters used a pun to express a central insight of IAF groups: "*pow.er (pou'er), n. 1. the ability to ACT." People who feel a sense of personal power have a sense of "can do" that enables them to solve problems in their personal lives. People who have learned how "the system" works are able to make it work for them. People who have been successful in changing the system have a wider knowledge and larger sense of power that enables them to shape their communities.

IAF views economic realities through a political lens. Hunger is first and foremost a problem of power and powerlessness – a political problem. IAF believes the long-term solution to hunger lies not just with feeding people or helping them get jobs, but in helping them gain the personal power to affect their daily lives (jobs, family, church, neighborhood) and the political power to affect larger institutional structures. IAF groups strive to change people

and structures. The way they do it, however, often evokes anger.

In the 1970s, when Chicago Mayor Richard J. Daley's administration delayed promised urban improvements, The Woodlawn Organization (TWO), an IAF project, devised a strategy to occupy, for one day, all toilets at O'Hare Airport. TWO figured out how many toilets there were and how many people it would take to keep them tied up – sitting in the stalls reading a paper, standing five deep in front of urinals. When word of their plans reached the administration, the city suddenly lived up to its promises.

A group of college students complained that they were powerless, that gum chewing was about the only thing they were allowed to do. Alinsky told them that maybe gum chewing was their leverage to get the administration's attention. Imagine sticky gum on the marble floors, walls, refectory tables. A Chicago columnist wrote, "The epitaph for Saul Alinsky should read: 'Here lies the man who antagonized more people than any contemporary American.'"[3]

When Alinsky died in 1972, IAF was looking for a model for organizing people that would draw on its traditional strengths – grassroots organizing, realistic political assessment – and yet be applicable to changes in American culture. The new IAF builds long-term, effective organizational power by bringing poor and middle-class people together to organize for action around issues that affect their interests and values, including religious values.

While it might seem peculiar to blend self-interest and basic values, people's basic self-interests lie in access to nutritious food, clean water, secure housing, health care, quality education, and meaningful employment. Alinsky argued that it is in

IAF analysis defines powerlessness as a major cause of hunger.

the self-interest of people who have bread to see that other people also have bread. Otherwise those who are well-fed will have to worry that hungry people may kill them to get the bread.

Self-interest is important to involvement, because the person who has a self-interest at stake is willing to make sacrifices, to stay with a project when the going gets tough. He or she is more highly invested in the outcome than the person who is doing good deeds for other people.

One criticism of Alinsky's early organizing efforts was that he organized people around their self-interests, whatever they were. Thus, some years after he organized the Back of the Yards organization in Chicago, they used their organization to keep blacks out of the community. The new IAF balances interests with religious values and bases its operations within the context of Christian and Jewish organizations. This ethical center provides a counterbalance to self-interest, narrowly exercised.

Religious organizations provide an operational base where there are people and financial resources committed to humane values. Cecile Richards, a labor union organizer, comments:

> In our labor organizing in Texas, the majority of our strongest union leadership in low-wage industries came from women who were already active in their church. There was an immediate identification with both issues of social justice and the benefit of organizing together.

Many religious organizations find IAF to be a useful avenue to express concern for poverty and powerlessness. However, other churches disagree with IAF-proposed policies, are alienated by IAF tactics, or reject political involvement in principle.

Getting Started

A community interested in forming an IAF organization first creates a sponsoring committee from churches and religious organizations, e.g. charities. The sponsoring committee shows its seriousness by raising enough money (sometimes "borrowing" part of the funds from IAF) to guarantee two years of salary

The Power of Confrontation: A Personal Note

by Richard A. Hoehn

In the early 1980s, during the coffee break of an evening class, I wandered downstairs to the room where IAF organizer Ernie Cortes was holding his first major public meeting in Fort Worth. I had taught a course on community organizations and participated in meetings of Alinsky groups in Chicago in the late 1960s, so was interested in IAF's new strategy. With only a ten-minute break, I lingered in the open doorway.

Cortes saw me, paused in his presentation, and commanded, "Come in or get out. You can't stay there half-in and half-out."

I had to return to class, so I got out. But, I was embarrassed in front of activist friends and angry that this stranger from out of town could order me around in my own building. Yet I had complied!

The class ended about the same time as their meeting. So, I went back downstairs and made sure he saw me shaking hands, greeting, and laughing with friends. I was the local activist; he was the outsider.

I thought about the confrontation many times. I remained annoyed, and decided that I would never again let anyone order me around like that; that if I wanted to

and expenses for an organizer. When this guarantee is in place, IAF sends a professional organizer.

IAF organizers receive formal instruction and spend time as apprentices to senior organizers. Even after becoming fully qualified, a "lead organizer" continues to be supervised by senior, national staff.

Once on site, the organizer holds individual meetings with hundreds of persons. IAF organizer and MacArthur Foundation "genius award" winner Ernesto Cortes, Jr. claims that he did "one-on-one meetings with a thousand persons" for his first organizing project in San Antonio.[4] Each person suggests other people who might be interested, especially potential leaders. During these meetings, the organizer discerns people's interests, values, and hopes for themselves, their families, churches, and communities.

People hold small group meetings to share their concerns and form personal relationships. These relationships bond members to one another, enabling them to act in concert and survive stressful disagreements. People with divergent life styles and from sharply contrasting parts of the city often become friends. The founding convention of ACT in Fort Worth brought together one of the most racially and ethnically mixed gatherings residents had seen.

The organizer seeks out "natural leaders" who have constituencies they can mobilize, or who have strong leadership potential. Class sessions help people learn the realities of power politics, and begin to see themselves as actors in, rather than passive victims of, the system:

> *The center of such an effort is the training and development of people. It is successful when it is connected to people's real values, anxieties, and concerns, enabling them to make important and sophisticated choices.[5]*

Successful Organizing Projects

In San Antonio, Communities Organized for Public Services' (COPS) first major victory occurred when they convinced the city to agree to, and people to vote for, a $46 million bond election to correct an unsafe and unsanitary water system that caused extensive neighborhood flooding during

---

stand where I had a right to stand, he or she would have to move me physically.

Mary Beth Rogers recounts a training event in which Ed Chambers, the executive director of IAF, sequentially orders a pastor, a social worker, a school teacher, and a lawyer out of the room. They all obeyed, just as I had. But then the minister got angry. Why was he having to stand outside the door, trying to hear the lecture while others were allowed to remain inside?

Why did he, an ordained minister, automatically accept Chambers' command to leave the room?. . . And who the hell is Ed Chambers anyway! An enraging click of awareness propels the minister back into the classroom, and Ed Chambers, with a smile breaking across his face, stops his lecture. . . . 'Congratulations, Pastor Sinnott. . . . What you (all) have seen is someone taking charge of his life; you have seen courage, even a revolutionary action. Pastor Sinnott is chang-

ing history by taking action. He is changing what is happening to us here and now. . . . That took courage, and courage is the beginning of power.'[6]

Ernie Cortes was not just being rude. He was teaching me something about personal power, inviting me to become more powerful; and at the same time suggesting to the audience that the organizing project would not be a half-in and half-out activity for the lukewarm. ■

heavy rains. Immediately after winning, they proposed an additional $100 million in neighborhood improvements. The city balked.

Invoking classic Alinsky tactics, hundreds of COPS members descended on a downtown department store and tried on every piece of clothing in sight without making a purchase. Another group formed lines at a local bank and changed dollar bills into coins and then back into dollar bills, tying up business for the day. "It was gutsy stuff for priests and nuns, housewives, federal civil service employees, and the dozen or so grandmothers who stood their ground with the city fathers."[7]

The bank decided it could indeed grant a loan for local improvements. Downtown merchants, worried about business, complained to the Chamber of Commerce, which brought the city into the discussion. Eventually, the city agreed to $100 million in improvements.

The poorest counties in the United States are south of San Antonio in "the Valley," along the Rio Grande River (known in Mexico as the Rio Bravo) on the Texas-Mexico border. Third World people from Latin America, Africa, and Asia wade or swim across the river in search of political asylum or better lives. They arrive with little clothing or money and perhaps a day's worth of food. This puts enormous stress on direct service agencies to respond to hunger and other basic human needs.

Many long-term U.S. residents in the Valley also live close to the economic edge. They compete with illegal immigrants for low paying jobs. Until recently, crop dusters sprayed pesticides on farmworkers as they worked in the fields. Severe freezes have damaged thousands of citrus trees, eliminating jobs until new trees can mature. Though the Valley has fertile farmland, unemployment and hunger are

common. Poor people take to the road, and become migrant laborers, with families jammed into station wagons traversing the midwest in search of crops to pick.

For cultural reasons, and because of the instability of their lifestyle, farmworkers and migrants will make almost any sacrifice to have a place they can call home. Unscrupulous developers sell tiny plots of land, sometimes with cheap houses and outhouses, to people of Spanish and Indian descent. Communities of these homes, called "colonias," are established outside city jurisdiction, not subject to building and sanitation codes. Roads are typically unpaved; sewers and household water, nonexistent:

> The Valley has the highest incidence of parasitic intestinal diseases outside of the Third World. . . . After heavy rains, people in the "colonias" literally drink their own sewage.[8]

Water barrels and tanks on trailers dot front yards. Residents pull the tanks to spigots where they pay to fill them.

Valley Interfaith, an IAF-affiliated organization, amassed power to get water lines extended to the "colonias," providing safe water to cook, wash food, and drink. Sanitary water is a primary requisite for good nutrition and health.

Issues and Leadership

IAF groups choose issues that are visible and winnable, issues that "give the people a picture of what they can do."[9] The problem chosen might not be the largest or most urgent. If a group tackles too big an issue and loses, it dissipates power, and members become frustrated or depoliticized. IAF organizations do not always win; however, it is important in organization-building to win at the outset. Members feel

Today's neighborhood success builds power for tomorrow's city-wide victory, which builds power that can shape a state's political agenda.

empowered and the organization gains credibility.

A primary criterion for the selection of an issue is that it builds the power of the organization for the long haul. Today's neighborhood success builds power for tomorrow's city-wide victory, which builds power that can shape a state's political agenda. Whereas other groups might try to bring world peace, a newly forming IAF organization might start with a local public service. Local participants carefully research facts relevant to the issue and gather information about the political structures that they will have to affect in order to win. In the process of researching the issue, mobilizing their constituencies, and dealing with city government, grassroots activists acquire research skills, learn organizing techniques, and become personally empowered to act in winning ways.

IAF activists learn how to stand toe-to-toe with city officials and politicians with facts in hand and arguments well rehearsed. Immediately after a public meeting, they hold evaluation sessions, the political equivalent of tough love, in which they critique one another's performance. Unlike many organizations that depend chiefly on staff to do the actual lobbying, IAF's professional organizer fades into the background so that members can more easily acquire the lobbying skills and confidence. Cortes says the Iron Rule of Organizing is "Never, ever, do for people what they can do for themselves."[10]

Sophisticated organizers know that they are never going to be the builders. What they're going to do is find the leaders who will come together and build the organization. Your role as an organizer is to teach people how to organize. . . you're always looking for people whom you can

spark, whom you can challenge, whom you can agitate. You want to tap their energy, tap their vision, tap their imagination and their curiosity. . . get them to see beyond themselves and their situations.[11]

Success consists not only in short-term issue victories, but in building long-term effective leadership in the organization. IAF tells potential participants that the skills they learn can benefit them in all their activities. It tells churches that IAF-trained people will become more effective parish leaders.

Pros and Cons

IAF is quick to point out that its organizing techniques are different from those found in single-issue interest groups or most development models. Groups that manage to get one or two self-help projects going or win a single victory from city hall often later discover that the gains have been wiped out by larger political or economic processes. For people to gain control of their economic circumstances, they must have political clout to address a wide range of issues – social services, education, housing, employment, community safety, nutrition – over a long period of time. This requires a patient, labor-intensive effort that builds slowly from the bottom up. It requires an organization that has demonstrated its power over time.

Economic self-sufficiency grassroots development models are neither sufficient nor secure until people have the political power to reduce their vulnerability and attain a measure of control over long-term events. The goal is not merely to win one issue victory or build one co-op, but to create an organization that will influence many issues. Though political parties and a few highly organized interest groups have

Grassroots political power is necessary to offset the ability of elites and special interests to shape public policy toward their own ends.

traditionally played this role, there is accumulating evidence that Americans feel alienated from formal political structures. Politicians are seen to be influenced primarily by their own self-interests or powerful interest groups. Problems seem too large, individual efforts seem not to matter, other people are perceived to be the "real movers and shakers," and the pace of change is slow.

There are few institutions in American society which bridge the gap between people and government, organizations that enable people to have a sense of control over their lives and communities. Grassroots political power is necessary to offset the ability of elites and special interests to shape public policy toward their own ends.

IAF trains and involves people more extensively than is common in most social justice groups. Members hold public "accountability" sessions to get public candidate commitments to IAF community goals. After the election, IAF stays in conversation with and tracks the record of officials to be sure they deliver on their promises.

IAF's critics question whether accountability meetings that look like party nominating conventions – with slogans, balloons and signs, precisely timed speeches (you can tell the players by who is monitoring their watches), and choreographed cheering – are really grassroots participation, or an exercise in which masses mechanically follow the cues of ego-tripping leaders.

Other critics question how IAF can claim to do grassroots organizing built around the interests of local people and still have a state-wide agenda. It strains credulity to believe that all ten IAF groups and thousands of individual members in Texas spontaneously and independently come to the conclusion that one piece of legislation, out of hundreds, is their highest priority. It appears to be central, organizer-dominated planning rather than a truly grassroots initiative.

IAF's critics argue that other public interest and social movement groups with different political styles have also been able to affect public policies. IAF is not flustered by its critics. It retains confidence in strategies developed over years of patient grassroots organizing. Besides, they say, "It works."

Conclusion

The IAF organizing style, like any other, has its limitations. After twenty years of IAF work in Texas, crime, poverty, hunger, and homelessness still exist in San Antonio, the Valley, Houston, El Paso, and Fort Worth. While IAF is having an effect on one bill, hundreds of other decisions with a potential impact on hunger and poverty are being made at local, state, and national levels. Established structures of power continue to prevail – sometimes for good, sometimes for ill – on most issues, most of the time.

It is difficult to mobilize a mass-based organization around more than one major issue at a given moment. Union organizer Cecile Richards points out,

To maintain their political clout, they must insure that the local groups continue to prosper while the organization is spending more time and energy on statewide issues.

It may prove impossible to extend the IAF strategy to the national level. The larger the mass of people needed to affect an issue, the more difficult it is to mobilize them.

IAF has developed a highly articulate and carefully considered political strategy. IAF-trained people know how the system works, have gained the courage that comes to those who confront and win, and the satisfaction of having improved their communities. There is no way to document fully the benefits that occur at all levels of peoples' lives and in their communities once they define themselves as actors and initiators, rather than as cogs of a mass society. IAF-trained activists spread out and use their skills in a variety of organizations.

IAF claims 400,000 members in Texas; 1 million nationwide, with organizations in New York, Maryland, Arizona, Tennessee, New Jersey, Pennsylvania, and California. If their techniques work at state and national levels as they work at the local level, IAF is likely to become a major force in American political life.

Hunger 1990 says, "Progress against hunger and poverty depends mainly on the initiative of poor people and others in the developing countries." Progress against poverty and hunger in this country also depends mainly on the political initiatives of poor and middle class people. ■

Notes

1. Sanders, p. 61.
2. Alinsky, Rules, p. 25.
3. Horwitt, p. 540.
4. Rocawich, pp. 9-10.
5. Cortes, p. 20.
6. Rogers, pp. 48-49.
7. *Ibid.*, p. 15.
8. *Ibid.*, p. 21.
9. Rocawich, p. 10.
10. Rogers, p. 15.
11. *Ibid.*, p. 10.
12. *Ibid.*, pp. 48-49.

Citizen Advocacy Changes
National Hunger Policies

Top: *Bread for the World staff plan advocacy strategy.*
Bottom: *Bread for the World activists meet with Rep. Norman Dicks (left).*

by Marc J. Cohen

Public opinion surveys show a growing political cynicism among American citizens, due in part to corruption scandals and a sense that vested interests are too powerful for ordinary people to change anything. Yet citizens concerned about hunger and poverty, at home and abroad, have discovered that they *can* make a difference.

For example, Bread for the World (BFW), a 45,000 member Christian citizens' lobby against hunger in the United States and around the world, has worked with other advocacy organizations to obtain steady funding increases for the Special Supplemental Food Program for Women, Infants, and Children (WIC). WIC helps improve the nutrition of poor pregnant and nursing mothers and their children (see "WIC at a Glance," page 101).

1989 WIC Campaign Background

According to Barbara Howell, BFW's director of issues, hunger and poverty advocacy organizations spent much of the 1980s trying to stave off efforts to cut domestic social programs. "There was no possibility for increases" in funding of most programs for low-income people or major new initiatives in such a political context. In 1982, Bread for the World's main legislative campaign – its "Offering of Letters" – successfully sought to prevent further cuts in food stamps and child nutrition programs. Congress rejected the Reagan administration's efforts to make deep cuts in WIC funding for fiscal years (FY) 1982 and 1983. Nevertheless, Congress failed to increase funding adequately, and by 1987, the program reached less than half of the eligible mothers and children.

BFW's 1987 Offering of Letters campaign, "Entitled to Life," sought a major increase in the WIC budget. That was a good year to work on WIC. The program was celebrating its 15th birthday, and recently published studies had confirmed its cost-effectiveness. Also, the congressional balance of power had shifted back toward human needs advocates.

Twelve hundred churches generated 90,000 letters to legislators. Congress appropriated $73 million for WIC above the current services level (the previous year's budget plus inflation), allowing an additional 150,000 women and children to participate. In 1988, Congress approved a $55 million increase over current services, enough to add an additional 100,000 participants to the rolls. A bi-partisan group of

200 House members and sixty senators signed letters favoring the increases.

The momentum from this success "set the context" for a more ambitious WIC campaign in 1989, Howell says. In 1987 and 1988, the congressionally-appointed National Commission to Prevent Infant Mortality, the National Governors' Association, former Presidents Ford and Carter, and business-oriented groups like the Committee for Economic Development and the Council on Competitiveness called for major expansion of WIC. The business groups argued that America's economic future depends on the health and education of today's children. Meanwhile, 75,000 citizens signed a petition calling for funding WIC at a level which would allow all

WIC at A Glance

The Special Supplemental Food Program for Women, Infants, and Children (WIC), established in 1972, provides federal funds for programs administered by state and local public health agencies. Some states and the District of Columbia supplement the federal funding from their own resources. The program targets mothers and children under five who are "at nutritional risk" and have incomes which do not exceed 185 percent of the federal poverty line (an annual income of $24,790 for a family of four in 1990). WIC beneficiaries receive coupons that they can use in grocery stores to purchase foods rich in key nutrients such as iron, calcium, and vitamin C. These foods

include milk, cheese, eggs, juice, cereal, infant formula, peas, beans, and peanut butter. Participants also receive nutritional assessments, nutrition education (which stresses the importance of breastfeeding during infancy), health screening, and medical referrals.

WIC enjoys bi-partisan support because studies have shown that it is cost-effective. Studies by the U.S. Department of Agriculture and the Harvard School of Public Health have estimated that every dollar spent on the prenatal component of WIC saves up to three dollars in public health expenditures for the care of low birthweight babies. Poor children enrolled in WIC are much less likely to suffer from anemia than those who are not. And low-income children whose mothers enrolled in WIC during pregnancy tend to do better in school.

According to Djamillah Samad, a former New York state WIC recipient who works as an outreach coordinator for the program:

WIC clinics do not send a woman home with just WIC checks in her hand. At the WIC site, a woman receives nutrition education with her checks. She and her child receive screening for common diseases and potentially damaging illnesses. She receives health related information on AIDS, drug and alcohol abuse, and referrals to other local and federally funded services. She has access to recipes, parenting classes, car-seat loaner programs, and job and school referrals. She also has the opportunity to go to a place where she can take her child and feel good about seeking help. ∎

eligible people to participate; the program still reached just 51 percent of the potential beneficiaries.

"No Child Should Go to Bed Hungry"

WIC supporters set out to put WIC on the same footing as "entitlement programs." These include Social Security, Medicare, Medicaid, and the Food Stamp Program, which serve all those who meet the eligibility criteria, and are not limited to annual appropriations.

Bread for the World; the Center on Budget and Policy Priorities, which Howell calls "our basic think tank on domestic issues;" the Food Research and Action Center (FRAC); and WIC supporters in Congress came up with the concept of "mandated funding increases." The idea was that Congress would agree to annual increases of $150 million over current services levels for five years. This would make WIC a "capped entitlement," with funds still limited to appropriated amounts, but

Who's Who: Hunger Advocacy Groups [1]

Bread for the World (BFW) and BFW Institute on Hunger & Development

Founded by Arthur Simon and others who wanted Christians to engage in public policy advocacy on hunger as well as in direct service, Bread for the World began organizing nationally in 1974. Today it has active members in every state and congressional district. Members come from all segments of the Christian community – Protestant, Catholic, Evangelical, and Orthodox. The organization has an outreach program to racial minority churches, and encourages whole congregations to affiliate as "Covenant Churches."

Bread for the World has devised an innovative lobbying technique called the "Offering of Letters" (OL), in which church members write letters to their legislators during a worship service, Sunday School, or fellowship meeting. Each year, Bread for the World's board of directors selects an OL topic, based on recommendations from members and staff. That topic becomes the centerpiece of the organization's lobbying agenda. Bread for the World tries to pick an issue on which it is likely to achieve legislative victories which will make a substantial difference in the lives of hungry people, and around which it can generate member enthusiasm and active participation.

In addition, in many congressional districts, BFW members have organized telephone networks known as "quicklines." These can generate thousands of telephone calls to congressional offices just prior to key votes. Bread for the World also has a network of "local media coordinators" and "media activists" who use the editorial pages of their local newspapers to educate their communities and encourage their members of Congress to support anti-hunger legislation. BFW members regularly visit their representatives and senators when they are home in their districts. Both local BFW members and national staff participate in coalitions with other activist groups on hunger-related issues.

Bread for the World Institute on Hunger & Development, the publisher of this report, is a separate but related organization which engages in policy research and educational activities to seek justice for hungry people. Bread for the World and the Institute have a combined annual budget of $3 million, supporting a staff of fifty.

Interfaith Impact for Justice and Peace (I/I)

Interfaith Impact was established in 1990 through a merger of Interfaith Action for Economic Justice and National IMPACT.

Interfaith Action, (founded in 1974 as the Interreligious Taskforce on U.S. Food Policy), was a coalition of the Washington offices of

with increases coming automatically. WIC supporters believed that these increases were high enough that at the end of the period, the funding level would permit full participation (rising commodity costs and increasing need have since meant that more funds will be necessary).

A group of Washington-based hunger advocates pressed members of Congress to support "mandated funding." This group included Howell; the Center on Budget's director, Robert Greenstein and its WIC expert, Stefan Harvey; and Ed Cooney of FRAC. Other key players included the National Association of WIC Directors; Bill Ayres, director of World Hunger Year, and the hunger lobby RESULTS (see "Who's Who," p. 102, for more detail on some of these groups).

Support from key legislators also proved crucial. Rep. Matthew McHugh, a member of the Appropriations Agriculture Subcommittee, which controls WIC funds, played a pivotal role. Rep. George Miller, chairman of the Select Committee on Children, Youth, and Families, and the late Rep.

major Protestant, Catholic, and Jewish denominations and agencies, originally established to coordinate the religious community's response to the global food crisis. Agency representatives, assisted by a small staff, conducted research, coordinated lobbying activities, and issued publications, with a focus on foreign aid, food and agricultural policy, and domestic human needs.

National IMPACT was established in the late 1960s. It was composed of religious organizations and 15,000 individual members (many of them leading voices within member denominations). IMPACT worked on a broad range of national issues – civil rights, the environment, foreign and military policy, and domestic human needs. It also established lobbying offices in several state capitals. Interfaith Action and IMPACT worked closely together for most of the 1980s before merging in 1990.

RESULTS

In 1980, hunger activist Sam Harris began RESULTS to create the "political will" which President Carter's Commission on World Hunger had identified as the key to eliminating hunger.

Four years later, RESULTS had forty membership groups in twenty-seven states, and Harris became its first paid staff member. The groups are built around four or more key volunteers known as "partners," who each month participate in three meetings: a nationwide telephone conference with experts to learn about an issue; a "delivery" meeting at which they practice speaking on issues; and an "education and action" meeting at which the partners and other group members write letters to editors, legislators, and policymakers.

Today, RESULTS has 100 groups around the United States, eleven in Australia, seven in Canada, five each in Germany and Japan, fifteen in the United Kingdom, and two in the USSR, with a total membership of about 4,000 activists. A budget of $800,000 supports a staff of 10 in three countries. According to Harris, in 1989, RESULTS groups gener-

ated some 1,573 print media articles (1,027 in the United States).[2]

RESULTS works on "long-term solutions to hunger and poverty" through efforts to "improve food production and incomes among the rural poor and to promote people's participation...."[3] RESULTS groups in the United States have focused mainly on international hunger issues, such as increasing U.S. support for microenterprise loans and funds for child survival and basic education. The organization has also worked on domestic affordable housing legislation. RESULTS groups have urged legislators to press the World Bank for greater attention to poverty reduction in its lending programs.

In 1990, RESULTS took the lead in organizing candlelight vigils in seventy-five countries in support of the World Summit for Children. More than a million people participated in these gatherings. In 1991, the group is leading a broad coalition in the Vigils '91 – Keeping the Promise Campaign. Harris calls this an effort "to insure that the promis-

Mickey Leland, chairman of the Select Committee on Hunger, helped forge congressional consensus in favor of WIC increases. Major Senate allies included Agriculture Chairman Patrick J. Leahy; Dennis DeConcini, a member of the Appropriations Committee; and Rudy Boschwitz, a leading Republican voice in favor of child nutrition programs.

For its part, Bread for the World again made WIC its Offering of Letters. As part of the "No Child Should Go to Bed Hungry" campaign, local BFW groups conducted surveys of hunger and WIC participation in their communities and visited WIC clinics. Many BFW groups developed close working relationships with WIC recipients as well as state and local WIC administrators, encouraging them to speak in churches and write to members of Congress. Bread for the World mobilized a large cross-section of "ordinary people in the pews" who knew what to tell their members of Congress and when to contact them, bringing a critical mass to the campaign. BFW director of organizing Kathy Pomroy says this grassroots activism pushed more conservative legislators, such as Rep. Henry J.

Hyde and Boschwitz, to support WIC increases.

BFW media director Kraig Klaudt adds that BFW members sent 100,000 birthday candles to their congressional representatives, along with messages urging them to support more money for WIC. The candles underscored the need to "Keep WIC Lit."

Thirteen hundred congregations around the country conducted Offerings of Letters on WIC, and 120 BFW members from thirty-six states visited Capitol Hill during the organization's June 1989 national membership gathering. When BFW members came to Washington that summer, they left three-pound packets of newspaper articles supporting WIC at their representatives' offices. Just prior to key congressional votes, BFW's "quickline" telephone network generated hundreds of telephone calls to legislators.

In addition, BFW members wrote 300 letters to the editor about increased WIC funding. The publications ranged in size from the mass circulation *Star and Tribune* in Minneapolis to the weekly *Press and Post*, read by about 4,500 families in Cambridge, N.Y. The campaign also generated

es made by world leaders at the World Summit for Children are kept."[4]

Center on Budget and Policy Priorities

The Center on Budget and Policy Priorities was established in 1981 with financial assistance from foundations and religious organizations. It has become a leading research center on how federal budget policy affects hunger and poverty in America. The director, Robert Greenstein, is a quintessential Washington "insider," well regard-

ed by Democrats and Republicans alike. He frequently testifies at congressional hearings. During the Carter administration, Greenstein served as administrator of the domestic food and nutrition programs at the Department of Agriculture.

Because the Center does not have a popular constituency it can mobilize, it works closely with grassroots lobbies like Bread for the World, and participates in umbrella groups like the Coalition on Human Needs.

Food Research and Action Center (FRAC)

FRAC is a public interest law firm established in 1970 to assist low-income people and community organizations in dealing with the maze of bureaucracy and regulation that often surrounds federal food programs (especially food stamps). It also conducts research, provides technical assistance and training in advocacy, and has become increasingly involved in grassroots lobbying in collaboration with local anti-hunger advocacy groups and low-income organiza-

sixty-four editorials, forty-two opinion columns, and 300 radio segments. Daily and weekly papers, along with religious, women's, and African-American publications, printed 1,000 feature stories about the WIC funding gap.

Press attention focused not only on BFW's birthday candle messages to Congress, but on the research and advocacy work of other groups, such as FRAC, the Center on Budget and Policy Priorities, and the Children's Defense Fund.

Thirty-eight prominent Protestant, Catholic, and Jewish leaders endorsed increased WIC funding, along with 100 national hunger, welfare rights, religious, child welfare, senior citizen, labor, public health, civic, food and social service, local government, women's, civil rights, and farm organizations.

The legislative result was impressive. In May, seventy-three senators signed a letter to Senate Agriculture Appropriations Subcommittee Chairman Quentin Burdick, asking for a substantial increase in WIC funding. A month later, 225 House members – a majority – sent a similar letter to Burdick's counterpart, Rep. Jamie Whitten.

In the House, signers came from both sides of the aisle, every region of the country, and across the ideological spectrum. Congress appropriated $118 million above current services. This was the largest funding increase in five years, enabling 5 percent more pregnant and nursing mothers, infants, and children (tens of thousands of participants) to benefit from WIC.

The campaign did not achieve all its objectives. Congress did not agree to multi-year, mandatory funding increases, due to growing budgetary pressures, and the single year increase fell below the $150 million target. Nevertheless, Howell calls the actual achievements "significant": the campaign led to substantially more funds in a time of growing austerity. Furthermore, the campaigns of 1987 and 1989 built momentum for continued increases. In 1990, when rapidly rising food costs led many states to run out of WIC funds well before the end of the year, Congress quickly passed legislation allowing states to borrow against their FY 1991 allotments. Also, the FY 1991 WIC appropriation included $130 million more than the current services level. President Bush proposed $129 million over

tions such as the National Anti-Hunger Coalition and local welfare rights associations. FRAC's Campaign to End Childhood Hunger is active in forty-seven states, and its Community Childhood Hunger Identification Project has broken new ground in assessing hunger among U.S. children (see U.S. Update). FRAC's director, Robert Fersh, ran the Food Stamp Program during the Carter administration.

Children's Defense Fund (CDF)

Since 1968, CDF has served as a leading advocate on behalf of American children. In recent years, CDF has offered alternative budget proposals to enhance the well-being of children, especially poor and minority children. It has also analyzed the impact of national, state, and local policies on children. Increasingly, CDF seeks to mobilize grassroots supports for its initiatives through local churches. CDF's president, Marian Wright Edelman, was a long-time civil rights lawyer and, like the Center on Budget's Greenstein, is a well-known Washington "insider" as well as a popular lecturer around the country.

World Hunger Year (WHY)

The late singer Harry Chapin was the driving force behind WHY, which he and current Executive Director Bill Ayres established in 1975. The organization publishes *WHY* magazine (formerly *Food Monitor*) and engages in advocacy work on domestic and international hunger. WHY annually confers Hunger Media Awards for exceptional coverage of hunger issues. ■

current services for FY 1992, and as this report went to press, members of Congress seemed ready to increase that amount.

In 1991, Tony Hall, chairman of the House Select Committee on Hunger, introduced legislation providing full funding of WIC over a five-year period as part of a larger omnibus anti-hunger bill. BFW's Howell says that persistent lobbying and broad support for the program have brought "mandated funding" and full participation much closer to reality, although in 1991 WIC served only about 54 percent of those eligible.

The efforts of the advocacy community expanded WIC's coverage, making it possible for more poor mothers and their children to improve their well-being. It allowed advocacy groups to close out the otherwise depressing 1980s on a hopeful note. It also empowered the citizens who became involved in the campaign. Sam Harris, executive director of RESULTS, says that advocacy organizations serve as "an acknowledgement of the dignity and courage in ordinary individuals to organize for extraordinary action."[5] A survey of BFW members "found that for a majority of them, BFW membership was their first entrance into the political system, outside of voting."[6] Thus, advocacy groups like Bread for the World and RESULTS provide avenues for people to become effective and active participants in democracy.

Public policy advocacy also has its limitations. Groups seldom achieve all their objectives immediately. Sometimes, the annual results of a BFW Offering of Letters are fairly small, e.g. the inclusion of BFW-favored language in congressional resolutions and committee reports.

Efforts to address the fundamental causes of hunger, e.g. domestic employment legislation and proposals for a more just international trading system, are particularly difficult and rarely won. These are "long-haul" undertakings, involving substantial resources and raising controversial questions.

Bread for the World is more successful in influencing important but more narrowly focused issues, such as WIC, international child survival programs, or increased emergency food aid. Both the large "structural" initiatives and the narrower programs are critical steps toward the elimination of hunger and the poverty which causes hunger. Both require the sustained, active involvement of concerned citizens. Bread for the World and other advocacy groups' long-term education efforts on the issues and how to impact on public policy lay a foundation for advances in overcoming hunger. ∎

20 Years in the Movement Against Hunger

An Interview with

Arthur Simon

In 1991, almost two decades after founding Bread for the World, Arthur Simon retired as president of Bread for the World and Bread for the World Institute on Hunger & Development. Simon, who received the 1990 End Hunger Lifetime Achievement Award from President Bush, is an ordained minister of the Lutheran

Church – Missouri Synod, and the author of seven books and numerous articles about hunger and poverty at home and abroad. Simon became concerned about hunger in America while serving as pastor of a church on New York's impoverished lower east side.

Q Why has Bread for the World tended to focus more energy and attention on international than domestic hunger?

A Hunger is much more widespread and acute in the Third World than in the United States. However, poverty and hunger in a wealthy nation is even less justifiable than in a poor country.

Q Looking back over the last twenty years or so, what do you see as the main accomplishments of the anti-hunger movement?

A The movement has accomplished a great deal. Some of the achievements are tangible, some harder to measure. I am particularly pleased with growing public awareness of hunger and its roots in poverty and militarization. This has created stronger public support for action. At the same time, Bread for the World and similar organizations have succeeded in fostering some understanding of the critical role of public policy in overcoming hunger, enabling many citizens to become effective advocates for anti-hunger measures. Still, people typically equate hunger with famine and miss the deeper problem of chronic malnutrition.

Q But hasn't hunger actually increased since Bread for the World began?

A The 1980s were discouraging, but things would have been much worse without citizens' groups organized against hunger.

Q What do you see as some of Bread for the World's specific accomplishments?

A Establishment of the international Child Survival Fund, reforms in various domestic and international programs, increased emergency aid in response to famines, tax reform for working poor people, and the establishment of grain reserves. Equally important, we had less tangible achievements like the first Offering of Letters, which resulted in Congress passing the Right to Food Resolutions in 1976. By mobilizing citizens, Bread for the World helped create the climate and the support for later legislative gains.

Q Doesn't a middle-class movement which claims to work for hungry people have a certain air of "noblesse oblige"?

A Bread for the World stresses the universal right to food. Upholding a right is different from giving people handouts: the right to food combines charity and justice. It recognizes poor and hungry people as subjects, people with dignity, not mere objects of pity. All people deserve the opportunity to feed themselves and their families adequately. When they cannot, through no fault of their own, then others who are more fortunate have the responsibility to assure them access to a "safety net."

Q Is it fair to say that Bread for the World spends most of its time working on ways to treat the symptoms, rather than the causes of hunger?

A It is true that Bread for the World tends to work on relatively simple, noncontroversial, and nonideological approaches to reducing hunger. These attract bipartisan support and allow the organization to make some significant headway. The single most important step toward ending hunger in America would be full employment. But obtaining such a program involves a complex, long-term effort, which Bread for the World is not well-placed to lead. Until there is such a scheme (and probably even then), "safety net" programs like WIC and food stamps remain crucial to limiting the impact of hunger.

Q Are you saying that there are limits to what an advocacy group like Bread for the World can accomplish working within the system?

A The difficulty in achieving structural changes like full-employment can lead to disillusionment, whereas smaller, incremental achievements can empower people. There are no quick fixes for complex problems. Bread for the World is about ordinary people doing what they can to make changes that will benefit hungry people. This involves working within the existing

political system to make it function better. While voices which challenge the fundamental assumptions of that system are needed, BFW's role is to make changes within the system and make the system more responsive to human needs.

Q What do you think of the present size and scope of the anti-hunger movement?

A I take some satisfaction with the growth of Bread for the World and other hunger organizations, but we have only attracted the tip of the iceberg in terms of the potential. A key task for the future is enlisting individuals and organizations involved in direct services (food banks, famine relief, and international development work) in advocacy. As I've often said, the struggle to overcome hunger walks on two legs, private assistance and public policy.

Q But don't service providers operate to a fair degree on the basis of self-interest?

A Service providers, it is true, have an interest in maintaining and expanding their programs and budgets. So does Bread for the World. Many private service agencies consciously put a time limit on specific projects, and these groups do absolutely essential work. They are also a major source of information on human needs. And private international relief agencies have played an important role in conflict situations by making sure that aid goes to all people in need, regardless of who controls the territory they are in.

Private agencies are increasingly working for long-term development, as well as immediate relief, and more are testifying to the need for public policy changes, too.

Q What do you think about in-fighting among groups that work on hunger issues?

A I don't see much of this, but when it happens it is a barrier to our efforts. The main problem is that hunger groups are overworked, so we do not have enough time for strategic planning and coalition building. Developing a common agenda among like-minded groups is one of the important tasks for the future.

Q Bread for the World is a Christian organization, but the Christian community is deeply divided on matters of public policy.

A There are long-standing disagreements on matters of theology and public policy between mainline Protestants and conservative fundamentalists, for example, although Bread for the World tries to draw its members from the broadest possible cross-section of Christians. The Bible offers clear guidance – but not legislative prescriptions – to Christians on their responsibility to feed hungry people and pursue peace and justice. I've argued that there are "no grounds for divorce" between Christian faith and public policy advocacy.[7] There's a need for institutional separation, but functional interaction between church and state. Christians can and should get involved in the policy-making process. At the same time, there is no straight line from revelation to legislation. The Bible gives directions, not directives. Therefore, people of faith should be humble and civil when they draw different conclusions regarding particular programs and policies. Still, Christians share core values, and that should help them find common ground on major issues.

Q If you could go back twenty years, would you choose the same path, spending half your adult life building a Christian citizens' movement against hunger?

A Absolutely! ∎

Notes

1. The discussion is limited to U.S. advocacy groups. It excludes groups that are active in public education on hunger issues like the Institute for Food and Development Policy (Food First), the Hunger Project, World Hunger Education Service, and the Community Nutrition Institute, which generally do not take the lead in lobbying efforts, but are often major sources of information for those who do lobby. Nor are hunger lobbies in other countries discussed in detail.
2. Harris, pp. 313-314.
3. *Ibid.*, p. 315.
4. Personal communication.
5. Harris, p. 318.
6. Hertzke, p. 157.
7. See Simon.

Africa Update

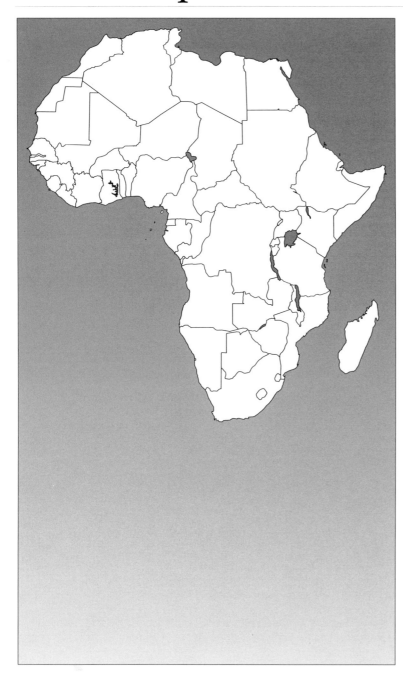

by Gayle Smith

One quarter of Africa's population continued to face chronic food insecurity or outright hunger in 1990. According to the U.N. Development Programme, 400 million Africans will live in absolute poverty by 1995 unless the continent's downward economic trend is reversed. Participants in UNICEF's World Summit for Children, convened in New York in September 1990, stated that Africa's child mortality rate will likely increase and the continent's share of infant and child deaths will reach 40 percent by the end of the century.

Food Production

Overall food production in Africa increased by approximately 5 percent in 1990, but the U.N.'s Economic Commission for Africa estimates that the overall food self-sufficiency ratio was just over 80 percent, down from 85 percent five years ago. Food imports decreased 12.5 percent from 1989 to 15.9 million metric tons, but food import needs for 1990-1991 are expected to increase, in large part due to famine in the Horn and Southern Africa. Experts predict that Africa will remain a food deficit region for the next decade.

It is ironic that though there were more people hungry in Africa in 1990 than in previous years, Africa as a whole recorded an economic growth rate of 3 percent and, as a result of adequate rainfall, saw a 3.4 percent growth rate in the food sector. However, many other factors continue to impact upon Africa's struggle against hunger. Chief among these is civil strife.

Hunger and Militarization

The U.N. World Food Programme estimates that despite a record cereal harvest worldwide, food aid needs for Africa in 1991 will approach or even exceed those of 1984-1986, when Africa experienced its worst famine in living memory. The continent will need approximately 4 million tons of emergency food aid to meet the needs of some 27 million people, most of whom reside in Ethiopia, Mozambique, and Sudan, countries which have been at war for decades.

There are more civil conflicts being fought in Africa today than in any other region of the world. The militarization of the continent has decreased somewhat with the easing of tensions between the United States and the Soviet Union, but military spending in Angola, Chad, Ethiopia (through the end of 1990), Uganda, and Zaire remained double the combined total of health and education outlays.

Famine is still the order of the day in countries where armed conflict is chronic. War turns farmlands into battle zones, removes able-bodied producers from the agricultural sector, disrupts transport and marketing, and directs the bulk of foreign exchange earnings to the military.

In Sudan, an estimated 9 to 11 million people are at risk of starvation due to the failure of traditional agriculture, which has been chronically unsupported, and of the massive mechanized agricultural schemes favored by both donors and successive governments. The central government of General Omer Hassan al-Bashir, which came to power in a military coup in mid-1989, denied that there was a famine until the early spring of 1991, and continues to dispute food needs in the southern regions of the country held by the Sudan People's Liberation Army. The regime was accused of bombing relief centers in southern Sudan on several occasions during 1990 and of selling grain reserves to finance the war effort, which is costing Sudan in excess of $1.5 million a day.

The war in Chad, which ended with the overthrow of the government of Hissene Habre in December of 1990, is the main cause of the famine threatening half a million people in that country.

Similarly, the thirteen-year war between the government of Mozambique and the RENAMO movement continued to be the major cause of severe hunger for 5 million Mozambicans and tens of thousands of new refugees forced from their homes in 1990. The government of Mozambique claims that the country continues to suffer from an estimated $15 billion in direct and indirect war-related losses, and United Nations officials estimate that the conflict has displaced 4 million people. Human rights organizations have likened RENAMO to Cambodia's Khmer Rouge, and charged it with gross human rights violations and the intentional destruction of civilian property.

The United States-based human rights organization Africa Watch charges that UNITA, the armed movement opposing the government of Angola, has pursued an intentional strategy designed to impoverish and starve civilian populations. Coupled with a fourth year of drought, war in that country (which appears to have ended in the spring of 1991 following a peace agreement) has pushed 1.9 million people to the brink of survival.

Safe Passage

In these countries where war and famine converge, relief aid often becomes a weapon. While the parties to conflict in Africa continued to use hungry communities as pawns, there were some significant gains made in 1990 toward guaranteeing civilians the right to food in situations of conflict. Though it had run into serious obstacles by the close of 1990, "Operation Lifeline Sudan" – coordinated by UNICEF and involving numerous international and nongovernmental organizations, such as the International Committee of the Red Cross, Lutheran World Relief, Catholic Relief Services, Church World Service, World Vision, CARE, Mercy Corps, Air Serv, and the International Rescue Committee – delivered food from Kenya and Uganda into guerrilla-held areas of Southern Sudan with the agreement of both the central government and the SPLA. The United Nations was also able to negotiate "relief corridors" in Angola, although that operation was quickly hampered by government charges that UNITA was intentionally mounting attacks in the areas of free passage.

In Ethiopia, a consortium of Ethiopian churches and the anti-government Tigray People's Liberation Front agreed upon the "Southern Line" channel, which resulted in the successful delivery of emergency supplies from the government-held port of Assab to both government and opposition-held areas of northern Ethiopia. A significant aspect of the arrangement was that it was negotiated primarily between Ethiopians, with the donor community playing a supportive but not central role.

The capture by the Eritrean People's Liberation Front (EPLF) of the Red Sea port of Massawa provoked another significant agreement, but only after heavy civilian losses. The former Ethiopian government's Air Force bombed the port for several days after its capture, destroying most of the food aid in stock and killing and wounding hundreds of civilians. It took the U.N. World Food Programme almost a year to gain the agreement of the EPLF and the Ethiopian government to re-open the port, but in February 1991 Massawa began receiving monthly deliveries of aid divided equally between government and opposition-held areas.

Ethiopia

Despite these safe passage arrangements, the United Nations estimates that 5.6 million people are at risk in Ethiopia, the vast majority of them in the war-torn regions. The country reaped record harvests in the west and central regions in 1990, but war precluded the delivery of surplus grain to chronic deficit areas. Meanwhile, the conflicts escalated dramatically, with opposition movements doubling the size of the territory under their control by early 1991. In May, following U.S.-sponsored peace talks in London, the Ethiopian People's Revolutionary Democratic Front took power in Addis Ababa, officially bringing the wars in Ethiopia and Eritrea to an end. Former leader Mengistu Haile Mariam fled the county. The EPLF established a provisional government in Eritrea. The new government in Addis quickly announced that relief was one of its top priorities, but the legacy of three decades of war still poses a formidable challenge to emergency operations. The country faces the immediate problem of severe famine in the north and south.

Liberia

The plight of Africa's people was further exacerbated by the eruption of new violent conflicts. In December 1989, forces led by Charles Taylor invaded Liberia's Nimba County and launched a war that eventually involved four armies and led to the violent death of Samuel Doe, Liberia's unpopular president. By mid-1990, government forces, Taylor's rebels, fighters loyal to Prince

Johnson, and members of a West African peacekeeping force were engaged in brutal fighting that killed over 10,000 civilians. The conflict quickly took on an ethnic character. The opposition singled out members of Doe's Krahn nationality for attack and government loyalists targeted the Mano and Gio people for death.

By early 1991, Liberia had achieved a precarious peace, although some revenge killings continued. Well over half the population of 2.6 million people had either fled the country or been displaced internally. Relief officials estimated that over 120,000 children in the capital of Monrovia had no food, health care, or water. Only a tiny minority of Liberians were able to farm during 1990, with the main rice-producing areas in Nimba and Bong counties particularly hard-hit by the war.

Somalia

In late 1990, an already-devastating war in Somalia took a dramatic turn when troops of the United Somali Congress (USC) launched an attack on the capital of Mogadishu, forcing the ouster of Mohammed Siad Barre, Somalia's despotic ruler for over two decades. The fighting killed an estimated 1,500 civilians and unleashed a wave of revenge killings by civilians able to purchase weapons openly from the country's vast supply of armaments. Within weeks, fighting broke out between the USC and the Somali Patriotic Movement in the area surrounding Kismayu. At the same time, the Somali National Movement captured the port of Berbera and the rest of northern Somalia, declaring the territory's independence.

Though an interim government has been established, Somalia remains effectively divided among clan-based armed factions, and journalists continue to report on conditions of near-anarchy. Food and other emergency needs are assumed to be extensive, but most humanitarian organizations have refused to operate in the country until it is safe.

Refugees

The flow of refugees in Africa also contributed to growing hunger in 1990. As a result of the refugee movements triggered by civil strife in Liberia, for example, Guinea, Cote d'Ivoire, and Sierra Leone required emergency food assistance for the first time in several years. Mozambican refugees poured into neighboring Malawi at the rate of 10,000 per month for several months in 1990, while the population of Sudanese refugee camps in Ethiopia approached 400,000.

Altogether, according to the U.S. Committee for Refugees, there were 5.4 million refugees and asylum seekers in Africa at the end of 1990, including 783,000 from Sudan and Somalia in Ethiopia, 900,000 from Mozambique in Malawi, 371,000 (primarily from Angola) in Zaire, over 700,000 (mainly from Ethiopia) in Sudan, and over 350,000, mainly from Ethiopia, in Somalia.

Even greater in number, however, are Africa's internally displaced, who total over 13 million, according to the Refugee Policy Group. Uprooted within their own countries, the displaced cannot gain official refugee status, and so are cut off from many sources of international assistance.

Drought

While generally improved in much of Africa, weather adversely affected food production in several West African countries where farmers faced localized drought for the second year in a row. By 1990, many had expended traditional coping mechanisms – such as selling off their livestock and tools – while the lack of rain in the northern Sahel also deprived many herders of hay stocks during the dry season.

Over 2 million people in Burkina Faso faced their worst harvest since 1987, particularly in the densely-populated central plateau. The failure of the annual Senegal River flood caused severe food shortages for 120,000 people in Mauritania, where only one-third of the country's cereal consumption needs were met in 1990. Niger and Mali also recorded mediocre harvests and isolated crop failures.

Population Growth

Africa's population growth rate, put at 3.0 to 3.2 percent for 1990, continued to outpace economic growth. This meant that average income growth declined even with the increase in the overall economic growth rate. Population growth continues to be a consequence of sustained hunger in Africa. Rural African women usually have additional children to help ease the heavy burden of food production.

Role of Women

The spread of hunger in Africa continued to be exacerbated by the economic and political conditions afforded women, who comprise two-thirds of Africa's poverty-stricken population. The U.N.'s *World Survey on Women in Development* of 1989 reported that one-third of all rural households in Africa are headed by women, in large part because drought and debt have provoked a dramatic increase in male migration to urban centers. These women-headed households most often have more dependents and fewer breadwinners than households headed by men.

Nevertheless, women continue to face restricted access to productive resources such as credit and, according to *Africa Report*, still spend as much as sixteen hours per day growing, processing, and preparing food and gathering fuel and water. For the first time in years, maternal and infant mortality rates began to rise in 1990.

Debt and Structural Adjustment

The debt burden also continued to impede Africa's ability to increase food production in 1990. According to the U.N. Economic Commission for Africa, the external debt of sub-Saharan Africa grew by 6.8 percent in 1990. Debt-service obligations also continued to rise, with African countries dedicating an estimated 34 percent of the income generated by the export of goods and services to interest payments. Ten of Africa's poorest countries recorded debt-to-export ratios of over 1,000 percent in 1990.

A subject of some debate both within and outside of Africa, the structural adjustment programs (SAPs) promoted by the World Bank and other donors have also affected the spread of hunger in Africa. Central to adjustment programs, cuts in government food subsidies have triggered riots in many African capitals during the last several years and have meant that many families are unable to purchase sufficient amounts of bread, sugar, or other basic commodities. In Nigeria, where social service budgets were slashed, health care and food costs have risen by 400 to 600 percent. Throughout the continent, SAPs have called for the reduction of the often-bloated civil service sector, triggering widespread urban unemployment, and have also prescribed repeated currency devaluations, thus reducing the purchasing power of consumers.

While the donor community argues that it may take as long as twenty-five years for adjustment programs to be effective, there was by 1990 no indication that SAPs had yet had a significant impact in reversing

Africa's economic decline. According to Pauline Baker of the Carnegie Endowment for International Peace, even Ghana, a country considered an adjustment success story by many donors, is a dubious model for the rest of Africa. "Ghana's accomplishments, while impressive," writes Baker, "were made possible only by massive assistance" unavailable to most other African countries. International aid to the country doubled over the last four years to $850 million in 1990.

Though Africans concur that their economies are in need of reform, there is a growing consensus that the export-led growth model underpinning adjustment programs is perhaps ill-advised for the continent. As such, the African Alternative Framework for Structural Adjustment Programmes (AAF-SAP) designed and endorsed by Africa's finance ministers in 1989, calls for greater emphasis on food production for local consumption and increased regional cooperation to replace dependence upon the North.

Trade

The declining terms of trade for Africa's exports during 1990 seem to support this argument for greater self-sufficiency. While the prices of cocoa and coffee, two major African exports, increased slightly by the end of 1990, the year began with these commodities fetching lower prices than at any time since 1976. During 1989, cocoa prices had fallen by 17 percent and coffee by 12.5 percent. Overall, Africa's commodity dependency worsened during 1990, with its top three commercial crops accounting for over 80 percent of the continent's export earnings. Meanwhile, the terms of trade, which had already fallen by 11 percent during the 1980s, continued to decline.

The outcome of the multilateral General Agreement on Tariffs and Trade talks convened to liberalize international trade, in part by opening up the markets of developing countries, will also have an effect on hunger in Africa, and particularly on food production. Of key concern to African delegates to the GATT talks were whether or not the talks would halt the dumping of European and North American farm surpluses and whether the agreement would protect Africa's ability to pursue food self-security.

Although the outcome of the talks remains to be seen, preliminary indications do not bode well for Africa. The U.N. Conference on Trade and Development estimates that although current offers by participating governments to improve access to Northern markets for tropical products would increase developing country earnings by 3 percent, the loss in trade preferences would mean a net loss for sub-Saharan Africa. Meanwhile, the North would not reduce barriers for sugar, maize, cotton, and several other products exported by Africa.

At the same time, Africa is likely to see its own markets undercut. Botswana and Zimbabwe already face stiff competition from the European Community, which exports beef to African markets at prices lower than those offered by local producers, and a similar trend is expected in cereals. As a consequence of their inability to compete fairly, African farmers are increasingly disinclined to produce.

Impact of the Gulf Crisis

A major factor in Africa's continued economic decline during 1990 was the Persian Gulf crisis. The increase in world oil prices during the latter half of the year brought about an unexpected windfall for Africa's oil-producing countries, but spelled disaster for the majority of countries that are oil-dependent. Several countries are now allocating one-fifth of their import bills to oil; in Sudan, a gallon of gasoline now costs the consumer $20. The Economic Commission for Africa (ECA) estimates that the increase in oil import costs as a result of the Gulf crisis totalled $2.7 billion in 1990. At the same time, the doubling of the cost of oil had the collateral effect of dampening the demand for African exports and increasing the cost of nonoil imports to the continent.

For some African countries, however, the oil price hike generated much-needed capital. Seven African countries, according to ECA, earned an additional $10.5 billion. Northern Africa and Nigeria gained the most, but Angola, the Congo, and Gabon saw benefits as well. Worst-affected was southern Africa, where there is only one oil-producing country. Many observers fear that the entire continent will also be negatively affected by a shift in aid flows from Africa to the Middle East at a time when aid levels are already adversely affected by increased needs in Eastern Europe.

Arusha Charter

While poverty is still on the rise in Africa, there were several developments during 1990 that are likely to mitigate hunger in the future. Significant among them was the adoption of the "African Charter for Popular Participation in Development" at a major U.N.-nongovernment organization (NGO) conference held in Arusha, Tanzania. Later endorsed by African heads of government and the U.N. General Assembly, the Charter clearly sets forth the rights and obligations of the people of Africa, African governments, NGOs, and donor governments in the development process.

Central to the Charter is the theme of popular participation:

> We affirm that nations cannot be built without the popular support and full participation of the people, nor can the economic crisis be resolved and the human and economic conditions improved without the full and effective contribution, creativity, and popular enthusiasm of the vast majority of the people.

The document calls for the demilitarization of Africa, for freedom of political association, for the rule of law, and for social and economic justice, as well as for the equitable distribution of income. It is especially strong in advocating the elimination of biases "particularly with respect to the reduction of the burden on women" and calling for "positive action to ensure their full equality and effective participation in the development process."

Democratization

That the Arusha Charter represents popular sentiment on the continent was made clear by the dramatic upsurge of activity among grassroots populations demanding political change. During 1990, popular protests, demonstrations, and strikes brought about significant political changes in thirty-one African countries. In response to repressive political systems and the failure of economic development models imposed without their consent, women's organizations, trade unions, students, and community organizers took to the streets throughout the year. Consistent among popular demands were the calls for greater popular involvement in decision-making and increased local control over resources.

A February 1990 national conference in Benin dissolved the government, laid the groundwork for a new constitution, and established a transitional government that ruled until presidential elections were convened in March 1991.

March 1990 saw the adoption of a multiparty system in Gabon. In May 1990, the government of Cote d'Ivoire formally recognized opposition parties. In the face of widespread unrest, Malian president Moussa Traore agreed to place multi-party politics on the agenda of a March 1991 conference, but was arrested and ousted before the conference could be convened. Mozambique adopted a new constitution in November 1990 which calls for an independent judiciary, a free press, and the right of workers to strike. An elected constituent assembly adopted Namibia's first constitution just before independence from South Africa was declared in April 1990. Continued demonstrations and riots in Zambia provoked the legalization of opposition parties as well as a plan for parliamentary and presidential elections. ■

Asia and the Pacific Update

by Marc J. Cohen

Overview

The majority of the world's hungry people live in the Asia-Pacific region. There has been progress in increasing food production and reducing the proportion of the population which is hungry. Yet, there are still 300 million chronically hungry people in Asia and the Pacific, 60 percent of the hungry people in the developing world. The largest concentration of poor and hungry people is in rural South Asia. According to the World Bank, in 1985, 300 million people in this region lived on less than $275 per year, 250 million of them in India. Also, the Alan Shawn Feinstein World Hunger Program at Brown University has reported that in China in 1989, 70 million people (about 6 percent of the population) consumed insufficient calories to lead normal working lives.

Over half of the world's 800 million to 1 billion people at risk of iodine deficiency disorders live in Southeast Asia, and there is a high prevalence of vitamin A deficiency in South and Southeast Asia. The United Nations Children's Fund (UNICEF) reports that 80 percent of the world's underweight pre-school children are in Asia, 57 percent in South Asia and China, and 27 percent in India alone. According to the U.N. World Food Council, "projections show that food production growth will probably exceed demand [growth] over the next decade"[1] in Asia.

Economic growth in Asia (excluding Japan) was 5.8 percent in 1990, compared to 2 percent worldwide, but impressive growth figures may obscure serious hunger and poverty. For example, Thailand experienced 10 percent economic growth in 1990, but malnutrition, landlessness, and child labor persist, especially in the underdeveloped northeast.

Generally, Asia had good cereal harvests in 1990. The outlook for 1991 is favorable, assuming normal rains.

The Gulf crisis had a severe impact on several Asian countries in lost remittances and exports, higher oil prices, and the need to reintegrate returning migrant workers. Before August 1990, 517,000 contract workers in Iraq and Kuwait sent $900 million home annually to Bangladesh, India, Pakistan, the Philippines, Sri Lanka, and Thailand. These countries' oil import bills more than doubled in 1990. India estimates losses of $5.8 billion at a time when the country is facing a $70 billion debt burden. The state of Kerala was especially dependent on remittances. For Pakistan, losses totalled $2.1 billion. Korea and Thailand were also adversely affected; Vietnam claimed losses of $377 million.

Afghanistan

Civil war has raged since 1979, creating severe hunger problems. In some areas, opposition "mujahideen" commanders have negotiated de facto peace settlements with the government and have begun reconstruction efforts. However, widespread sowing of mines has made the resumption of farming and other economic activities difficult. Five million Afghan refugees remain in Pakistan, Iran, and the West.

The United States provided $250 million in aid to various opposition forces in fiscal 1990, along with a lesser level of food and other emergency aid to Afghan refugees in Pakistan. Members of the U.S. Congress are increasingly viewing the Afghan struggle as a Cold War anachronism, however.

Although the Soviet Union has encouraged President Mohammad Najibullah to negotiate a settlement, the Soviets continued to provide his government $300 million per month in economic and military aid in 1990. People in government-controlled areas depend heavily upon Soviet food aid.

In spring 1991, FAO forecast "deterioration of the already precarious food situation,"[2] due to slow delivery of Soviet food aid, extensive floods, an intense earthquake in the northeastern part of the country, and four years of drought in the northern and western regions. Many rural Afghans have abandoned farming because of the war. Natural disasters have caused additional internal displacement of people looking for food. The country's inability to earn much foreign exchange has led to shortages of agricultural inputs.

FAO estimates a 15 percent decline in wheat and barley crops in 1991, and that the Soviets will supply at best 80 percent of the 340,000 tons of food aid the country will require. India is likely to provide some of the balance; it shipped 500,000 tons in 1990. Additional foodstuffs are regularly smuggled to Kabul from Peshawar in Pakistan.

Bangladesh

In the second half of 1990, political turmoil, the devastating impact of the Persian Gulf war, government mismanagement of the economy, and austerity policies encouraged by foreign aid donors combined to make life even worse for the 51 million Bangladeshis who live below the poverty line and cannot afford an adequate diet. On April 30, 1991, a punishing cyclone hit the Bay of Bengal coast.

The storm killed over 100,000 people. An estimated 65 percent of those killed were children under the age of ten, because many parents had tied their children to sturdy trees, hoping they would not be blown away. Those hardest hit by the disaster were landless farm laborers who live and work on silt islands at the mouth of the Ganges river. The cyclone also killed 900,000 head of cattle, left 12 million people homeless, and put at least 4 million at risk of starvation, cholera, dysentery, and snakebite. A cholera outbreak had already taken some 900 lives before the cyclone arrived, but the government refused to acknowledge this, fearing bans on fish and shrimp exports. Damage estimates range from $600 million to $2 billion.

The destruction includes the loss of tens of thousands of acres of food, feed, and forestry crops, a million houses and thousands of schools and public buildings, as well as stored foodstuffs worth $100 million. Losses of mangrove plantations will likely cause coastal erosion. The disaster shut down the multi-million dollar shrimp export industry, clogged the main port of Chittagong with damaged ships and industrial plants, and wrecked most of the ship and cargo handling facilities.

Continued poor weather (which killed scores more people elsewhere in the country), communications breakdowns, a short-

Laos: Wrestling With Change

by Marc J. Cohen

In December 1975, communists who had been participating in a coalition government seized control of the country and established the Lao People's Democratic Republic, abolishing the monarchy. Although all land theoretically had belonged to the throne, small farmers effectively controlled the land they worked and its products. The Lao People's Revolutionary Party decreed the collectivization of agriculture, but peasant resistance made implementation ineffective. The authorities also attempted to establish central planning throughout the economy, with the first five-year plan begun in 1981.

Between 1963 and 1975, noncommunist and coalition governments had depended upon foreign aid, primarily from the United States, for virtually all government revenue. Urban areas relied upon imports from Thailand for their food. The United States maintained diplomatic and trade ties after 1975, but terminated all aid and encouraged other donors to follow suit.

The new government, lacking foreign exchange, embarked on a program of food self-sufficiency, including intensified rice production. Initially, the government sought to improve yields of traditional rice varieties through greater use of organic fertilizer and improved weeding techniques. As foreign aid has increased since the mid-1980s, the government has stepped up purchases of chemical inputs as well. In addition, since 1975, the authorities have encouraged every family and all government offices to grow vegetables. In light of the failure of collectivization, the government pursued "socialist agriculture" by encouraging the development of informal mutual aid groups to carry out irrigation and mechanization, purchase inputs, and receive extension services. By 1985, virtually all the food in markets of the capital, Vientiane, was locally produced, whereas ten years earlier, 85 percent came from Thailand.

The authorities encouraged farmers to abandon "slash-and-burn" cultivation of rain-fed rice for settled, irrigated rice farming. This will increase rice harvests and preserve dwindling forest resources, which provide a large share of exports. In 1990-1991, the government shifted 700 new families into wet rice farming. The United Nations Development Programme has supported efforts to resettle upland rice farmers, who come mainly from ethnic minority groups such as the Hmong.

The resettlement program seeks to offer increased economic opportunities to minority peoples, but some Hmong complain that resettlement schemes are a crude government attempt to increase social control and undermine their way of life. Many Hmong opposed the communists during Laos' 1963-1973 civil war.

Laos's second five-year plan, begun in 1986, launched the New

age of boats and aircraft, and bureaucratic inefficiency made relief efforts difficult. In many areas, the military had to drop food and water to displaced people from the air. Foreign aid donors responded with $250 million in food, supplies, equipment (including helicopters), and cash. In addition to $7.2 million in relief aid, the United States sent 12,600 marines and sailors to deliver disaster assistance. The government says that it will need an additional $1.5 billion in aid to carry out reconstruction, plus another 200,000 tons of food aid. On

the positive side, monsoon rains are expected to wash the salt out of the fields, and the country expects an average rice harvest despite the damage.

Even before the cyclone hit, the Gulf crisis had cost the financially strapped country about $1.5 billion in lost remittances from overseas workers, repatriating 100,000 workers, lost exports, higher oil prices, and foregone Kuwaiti aid. Remittances are the country's leading source of foreign exchange. Inflation rose, while the urban unemployment rate hit 20 percent.

Economic Mechanism, which increases reliance on market forces, enlarges the scope for private property, and welcomes foreign investment. In agriculture, all land remains nominally state property, but in effect, family farming is again the norm. Output has increased significantly, but agriculture remains highly vulnerable to the weather. Drought and flooding led to a Lao request for substantial food aid in 1977-1978, and drought in 1987 reduced the harvest by nearly 60 percent over the previous year. A localized drought had a similarly devastating impact on five southern provinces the following year. Fertilizer shortages, low prices, and a lack of credit also limit yields. Nevertheless, FAO estimated reduced food import requirements for 1991 – 40,000 tons as compared to 95,000 in 1990.

Another serious problem for agriculture is the presence of large quantities of unexploded bombs in rural Laos. The United States intensively bombed the country between 1965 and 1973 to destroy North

Vietnamese supply lines (the "Ho Chi Minh Trail") and keep the Lao communists from gaining territory. Farmers risk severe injury or death. The American Friends Service Committee and Mennonite Central Committee have worked to provide Lao farmers with lighter weight shovels for greater safety. U.S. bombing also heavily depleted the Lao water buffalo herd. More than fifteen years after the war ended, many households still must share draft animals.

Since 1975, Laos has had close political ties to Vietnam and the Soviet bloc, and has relied heavily on Eastern European aid, which was terminated in 1990. The Soviets have announced that they will convert their aid to trade. To replace these resources, Laos has eagerly sought investment and aid from China, Thailand, Japan, Australia, and the West. Japan is providing some rural development assistance, as are U.S. private voluntary organizations and some European governments. Since 1990, the United States has provided modest aid for drug eradication and school construction,

plus a Peace Corps program. Investors complain that the legal system remains unsupportive of a market economy, however.

Declining revenues due to cuts in Eastern European aid have reduced health services in recent years, and inflation surged to 60 percent in 1990 because of increased exports and money supply. Persistent trade deficits have led to mounting foreign debt.

Laos remains one of the world's poorest countries, with a per capita GNP of only $170. Nutrition surveys conducted in 1984 and 1986 found significant problems. Forty-nine percent of the children under five were underweight, 48 percent were stunted, and more than 8 percent were wasted. The incidence of underweight was even higher among children aged 12-24 months, 63 percent. Thirty to 40 percent of newborns had low birthweights. Goiter is common among the mountain-dwelling minorities. ■

For years, massive food imports (1.5 million tons in 1989-1990) have mostly benefited relatively well-off city dwellers and contributed to balance of payments deficits and a growing foreign debt.

Cambodia

The four sides in Cambodia's 20-year-old civil war agreed to a "permanent ceasefire" and transitional government at the end of June 1991. Previous efforts to achieve peace have, however, repeatedly broken down. Disagreement remains over the future role of the Khmer Rouge, the strongest armed opposition faction, which killed at least a million Cambodians when it ruled the country between 1975 and 1978.

The Khmer Rouge launched a major offensive in 1990. By mid-1991, the fighting had displaced almost 200,000 people within the country. Thin food stocks limited the pro-Vietnamese government's ability to feed these people. Another 350,000 Cambodians live in camps on the Thai-Cambodian border; some refugees have resided in these camps for twelve years. Another 20,000 refugees live in camps in the Thai interior.

The fighting disrupted rice planting, and the government removed 35,000 people – some of them against their will – from their villages in 1990 so as to deprive the Khmer Rouge of recruits, porters, and food. For their part, the Khmer Rouge reportedly forced civilians, in areas under their control, to act as laborers and human shields during battles. They denied food and medical care to those who refused to cooperate. Relief officials charge all parties to the conflict with indiscriminate attacks on towns.

Although the United States has reduced its hostility toward the government, Washington continues to maintain a trade embargo against the country. In 1990, the U.S. Congress voted to provide humanitarian assistance to Cambodia, with part of the funds allocated to government-controlled areas, but the Bush administration resisted providing aid to Phnom Penh. Soviet and East European aid, which had accounted for 80 percent of the regime's budget, declined drastically.

Inflation (about 200 percent in 1990, with food price inflation reaching 300 percent early that year), corruption, high levels of military spending, and an uncontrolled black market caused the economy to deteriorate. Rice, the staple food, cost ten times as much in 1991 as it did two years earlier. The government provided increased incentives to farmers to produce both food and export crops, but these did little to inspire consumer confidence, and widespread hoarding of food was reported prior to the main 1990 harvest.

A combination of drought and floods in various parts of the country, along with late delivery of Soviet fertilizer, led to a 5 percent decline in the 1990 rainy season rice crop. Production fell substantially in the traditional western "rice bowl" provinces. Food supplies in traditionally food deficit southern provinces were especially tight. Fighting has disrupted agriculture in the northwest, and unexploded land mines have made large areas nonproductive for years to come.

China

In July 1991, the heaviest rains of the 20th century flooded eighteen of China's thirty provinces, killing 1,700 people and leaving 4 million homeless. About 10 percent of the summer grain crop was lost, and expected additional floods, along with drought in southern China, threatened the crucial autumn harvest. The government estimates the damage at $7.5 billion. Transportation was severely disrupted in the affected areas, including Shanghai, China's largest city. Worst hit were Anhui and Jiangsu Provinces, where 60 percent and 20 percent, respectively, of the grain crops were destroyed. Anhui is one of the country's poorest areas. Outbreaks of cholera, diarrhea, and other diseases have been reported. Poorly maintained flood control infrastructure is partly to blame for the scope of the disaster.

Two years of bumper harvests and effective government relief efforts, including the mobilization of 600,000 soldiers, will minimize the immediate hunger impact. For the first time since the establishment of communist rule in 1949, the government appealed for emergency foreign assistance. Some donors said that the $200 million aid request exceeded actual needs.

Government austerity measures succeeded in lowering inflation from 40 percent in 1987-1988 to 3 percent in 1990, but at the expense of serious unemployment in both rural and urban areas. Favorable crops led to sizeable price declines, and in view of the recession, the government stepped up its procurement of rice to aid both farmers and consumers. Robust growth in 1991 has led to a resurgence of inflation, and reduced consumer subsidies have caused price increases of 160 percent and 75 percent, respectively, for cooking oil and rice. The prospects, therefore, are for significant short-term increases in hunger.

East Timor

Indonesia has illegally occupied the former Portuguese colony of East Timor since 1975, in defiance of the United Nations General Assembly. Continued armed resistance to the occupation and Indonesian restrictions on villagers' movements severely disrupt local agriculture. Poorly fed Indonesian soldiers regularly seize food from farmers who continue to work, and a third of the population is hungry. Occupation authorities divert food aid to Indonesian

investors. Medicine is also in short supply.

Mongolia

Like many communist countries, Mongolia is undergoing rapid political and economic change, having held its first free elections and taken steps toward a more market-oriented economy. In the face of declining Soviet aid and a debt to the Soviets in excess of $16 billion, the country has moved to diversify its sources of foreign assistance, trade, and investment. The economy is in serious trouble, with rising inflation and unemployment (which reached more than 20 percent in 1990), a mounting government budget deficit, and shortages of most goods, including food and medicine, which have increased infant mortality. In response, the authorities have rapidly expanded private ownership and free market sales in agriculture. The livestock herd increased to the highest level in fifty years, and 25 percent of the herd is now in private hands.

Since mid-1990, natural disasters have contributed to significant deterioration in the food situation. Fires destroyed large areas of forest and pasture land, killing substantial numbers of cattle and sheep, and damaging some telecommunications and food storage facilities. Late in the year, excessive rains reduced the grain harvest, and an extremely severe winter caused further problems. Continuing bad weather meant unfavorable crop prospects for 1991. By the beginning of 1991, food prices doubled, due to short supplies and further economic liberalization. The government has begun rationing meat, milk, and other food, and has reduced the size of wheat rations. Flour, bread, butter, fruit, vegetables, and rice are also in short supply, due in part to bottlenecks in the state distribution system. Much hoarding and black marketing have resulted. By July 1991, analysts predicted widespread starvation unless the country received $150-200 million in emergency aid.

Myanmar (Burma)

Though Myanmar (formerly Burma) was once a leading exporter of rice, and agriculture still employs 63 percent of the workforce, low mandatory procurement prices have caused declines in output and rampant smuggling and black marketing. Vio-

lent repression has further damaged the economic and social fabric. Thousands of refugees have fled to Thailand, which has forcibly repatriated some of them.

The Myanmar government reported economic growth of 7.4 percent in 1989-1990, after three years of decline, and grain output increased in 1990-1991. The government no longer forces farmers to sell it their entire crop, but retains monopoly control of fertilizer and credit, and compels the sale of

Hunger, Inequality, and Conflict in Sri Lanka

by Rapti Goonesekere

Sri Lanka, often referred to as the pearl in the Indian Ocean, was once considered a human development model in the developing world. A strong government commitment to social welfare has resulted in high social indicators over the years. Although this country has a per capita GNP of only $430, statistics for 1989 show an under-five mortality rate and infant mortality rate of thirty-six and twenty-seven, respectively, per 1,000 live births; a life expectancy at birth of seventy-one years and a total adult literacy rate of 87 percent. These social indicators are superior to those of middle-income countries like South Africa and Mexico and even of a high-income country like Saudi Arabia. Sri Lanka ranked second highest among Asian coun-

tries on the United Nations Development Programme's Human Development Index in 1990.

However, these impressive national statistics mask poor conditions among plantation workers, landless farmers, residents of conflict-ridden areas, and refugees, as well as regional disparities in well-being. Ongoing civil disturbances, the increasing refugee problem, and the recent Persian Gulf crisis have had a devastating impact on food production and the socioeconomic development of the country.

Over the past decade, Sri Lanka recorded average annual economic growth of 5 percent. With an agricultural growth rate of 4.5 percent in real terms in 1990, the country is almost self-sufficient in rice production. Cereal output increased by 11 percent in 1990, due to favorable weather. Sri Lanka's production of fruits and vegetables, livestock, fish, and forestry products grew by 3.5 percent in 1989-1990.

Yet, malnutrition is still a serious problem. Morbidity due to diarrheal diseases and malnutrition among both women and children is unusu-

ally high. UNICEF surveys have shown that 60 to 70 percent of pregnant mothers suffer from anemia. Maternal malnutrition and poor weight gain during pregnancy contribute to a high incidence of low birthweight. Almost half the children under age five suffer from stunting and about 25 percent from wasting.

On the positive side, Sri Lanka is among the leading developing countries in immunization coverage. The Universal Child Immunization scheme begun by UNICEF and the World Health Organization in 1978 achieved universal coverage against tuberculosis, polio, tetanus, diphtheria, and whooping cough a year before the 1990 target. However, rates are not as high in certain urban slums and conflict regions.

On state-owned plantations, children under five years of age account for 15 percent of the total population, while women account for more than 50 percent. Conditions on the plantations improved during the past decade, but 1989 figures show an infant mortality rate of 43 per 1,000 live births and

about 20 percent of the rice crop in exchange for these inputs.

The country has serious nutritional problems, despite widespread availability of cheap food. Malnutrition, diarrhea, and respiratory infections are prevalent among children under five. Surveys from the mid-1980s found one-third to one-half of the rural children under five to be stunted and one-half to two-thirds to be underweight. Surveys from the early 1980s found even higher rates of malnutrition among urban children. Independent surveys have found low birthweight rates of 16-30 percent, due to poor maternal health and nutrition, but the government's statistic is 6 percent for rural areas. FAO characterizes the average Burmese diet as "of poor nutritional quality."[3] In most households, men and working children consume the choice portions, while women and small children get leftovers. Anemia is widespread, affecting over

a maternal mortality rate of 300 per 100,000 live births, far higher than the national averages. Similarly, nutrition levels and literacy rates are much lower on plantations. Because of attention given to these conditions, the government invested $212 million in development of the plantation sector between 1985 and 1989. However, the armed conflict between the government and the separatist Liberation Tigers of Tamil Eelam has caused a loss of plantation income and other economic problems, making it increasingly difficult for plantations to finance social development programs.

Sri Lanka's 16.8 million population is extremely heterogenous, comprised of Sinhalese (74 percent), Tamils (18 percent), Muslims (7 percent) and Dutch-Burghers (1 percent). The ethnic conflict, which began in 1983 in the northern and eastern provinces, has caused tremendous misery and misfortune for farmers from the Sinhalese majority and Tamil and Muslim minority groups alike. More recently, a Sinhalese uprising against the government has destabilized the situation in the south as well. Total civilian and military casualties between 1984 and 1990 are estimated at 30,000. The fighting has displaced nearly 800,000 people, who are seeking refugee status. The government, meanwhile, has increased the share of the budget devoted to the military.

Civil unrest has reduced food production in the northern region. The region's orientation toward growing commercial crops (e.g. chili peppers and onions) has exacerbated food problems. Relief agencies such as CARE are trying to increase production of food crops, (e.g. legumes, other vegetables, and cereal crops). In spite of favorable weather in 1990-1991, only a small proportion of land could be cultivated in the northwestern Mannar District due to the armed conflict and migration of many farmers to other parts of the country and India.

In addition to food production difficulties, health services have deteriorated in the conflict zones. The intermittent breakdown in regular disease control programs has caused wide outbreaks of communicable diseases. Malaria has increased; polio cases have been reported among unimmunized refugee children; and malnutrition is worse than in other regions.

Children suffer the most from the violence, and the psycho-social impact on children from regions of civil unrest in both the north and the south is devastating. The fighting has continually disrupted schooling, and many children have been orphaned or lost a parent. The government and private relief agencies have tried to provide affected districts with immunizations, oral rehydration therapy, and nutritional services.

The Persian Gulf crisis caused 100,000 Sri Lankan migrant workers to return from Kuwait to a tight job market. Their remittances had given families back home vital funds to buy food, build houses, and improve land. The U.N. trade embargo against Iraq and Kuwait cost Sri Lanka 12.5 percent of its critical tea exports at the same time that oil prices increased. It is hardly surprising that Sri Lanka ranked as the country fourth worst affected by the Gulf crisis. ∎

70 percent of pregnant women, 36 percent of nonpregnant women, and 48 percent of the children between five and fourteen years of age. Goiter is endemic in the highlands, as the government has failed to pursue salt iodination vigorously.

In recent years, malnutrition has worsened among poor urban dwellers. Years of negative economic growth, inflation (100 percent in 1990), pervasive corruption, and continued military dominance of the economy have buffeted urban incomes. A hospital in a working-class suburb of the capital of Yangon (formerly Rangoon) reported a 300 percent increase in malnutrition-related cases between 1988 and 1990. Similar trends are apparent in other large cities.

Papua New Guinea

Since the mid-1980s, the influx of more than 10,000 refugees from the Indonesian-controlled western part of New Guinea and a violent secessionist movement on the offshore island of Bougainville have had an enormous impact on Papua New Guinea's (PNG) economy and politics.

The Bougainville rebellion ended with a ceasefire in early 1991 after it had closed the country's main copper and gold mine, which had produced 40 percent of export earnings and 17 percent of government revenues, and dried up the island's cocoa exports (half PNG's total). In an attempt to crush the rebellion, the government had blockaded shipments of food and medicine.

As the economy deteriorated in 1990, the government devalued the currency, slashed spending, tightened credit, sold off public enterprises, laid off civil servants, and partially froze wages, as aid donors insisted on structural adjustment as a condition for new aid. The authorities resisted calls for an end to export crop price supports, however, fearing political unrest.

Tribal conflicts in key coffee growing areas helped reduce coffee output 20 percent, and production of other export crops also declined, due to soft world markets. Plantations laid off several thousand workers.

Philippines

Natural disasters, rising oil prices and other effects of the Gulf War, $26 billion in foreign debt, and government economic policies converged to worsen the lot of the 70 percent of Filipinos who are poor and hungry in 1990 and 1991. The twenty-two-year-old communist insurgency, continued military rebellions, and a growing climate of lawlessness claimed the lives of poor people caught in the crossfire. Average per capita food consumption supplied less than recommended minimum levels of calories. The most serious economic crisis since 1983-1984 hit poor urban dwellers – including metro Manila's 3 million squatters – especially hard. Unemployment climbed to 15 percent, underemployment higher.

In 1990, a major earthquake, floods, and typhoons left more than 150,000 Filipinos homeless and caused nearly a billion dollars in damage. The earthquake and floods in northern Luzon added to the severe ecological stress of indiscriminate mining and logging that ruin 2,500 lowland rice acres annually. Typhoons significantly reduced sugar output on the central islands of Cebu and Negros.

These disasters paled by comparison to the June 1991 eruption of Mount Pinatubo, which left 250,000 people homeless and deprived over 650,000 people of their livelihoods. Ash and acidic lava damaged 200,000 acres of crops, some for years to come, and killed 700,000 head of livestock. The flooding of choked waterways during the rainy season will likely cause further agricultural losses. The government, which was slow in getting food and water to displaced people, has allocated $500 million to immediate rehabilitation efforts. Long-term costs include U.S. abandonment of Clark Air Force Base, which employed 42,000 Filipinos and pumped $200 million a year into the economy.

The Gulf War added enormously to what *Far Eastern Economic Review* called the country's "cocktail of woe."[4] Half a million Filipinos working abroad had been expected to send $2 billion back home in 1990, but remittances fell to $1.2 billion (still the Philippines single largest source of foreign exchange), as 23,000 Filipinos left Kuwait and another 30,000 remained stranded with no work. The country expects $1 billion in remittances in 1991, as Gulf reconstruction has created some new jobs.

Iraq and Kuwait had supplied nearly half of the Philippines' oil imports. Rising prices due to the Gulf conflict added nearly half a billion to the $4 billion 1990 trade deficit and contributed to currency depreciation.

Under pressure from the International Monetary Fund (IMF), the government raised petroleum prices by over 60 percent in late 1990 and cut back on fuel subsidies for urban dwellers. These subsidies, along with debt service, accounted for much of the budget deficit, which equaled 5 percent of GNP in 1990. Inflation soared to more than 18 percent, and in metro Manila it exceeded 21 percent. Interest rates hit 32 percent. Investors sent $145 million out of the country, twice the 1989 withdrawal rate.

President Corazon C. Aquino in early 1991 imposed a 9 percent surcharge on all imports to generate revenue and contain the trade deficit, again at the insistence of the IMF. This regressive tax was politically easier to carry out than progressive taxes on wealthy Filipinos. It led to an influx of $1 billion in new foreign aid between November 1990 and March 1991. The economy began showing signs of recovery.

Poor and hungry Filipinos will not receive much benefit, however. The import levy undercut some of the post-Gulf war decline in oil prices, contributed to inflationary pressures, and reduced the output of food crops by raising fertilizer prices.

A second year of drought led to agricultural stagnation in 1990, and falling world prices for coconut products reduced the incomes of a third of the country's farmers. Secondary harvests of rice and corn were expected to be average in mid-1991. Aquino has all but abandoned her promises of land reform.

In response to IMF demands for spending controls, the government has reduced outlays for health and nutrition programs. According to one study, the plan would eliminate nearly 400,000 poor children from nutrition programs, increasing their susceptibility to diseases for which they will be unlikely to receive care. This will further lower living standards and add to the increased poverty rate created by the 1990 downturn.

The country's Roman Catholic prelate, Cardinal Jaime Sin, has joined members of the Philippine Congress in calling for selective repudiation of the foreign debt. Debt service consumes one-third of export earnings, and Sin called these payments "morally wrong" given "such widespread lack of basic necessities among our people."[5] However, Aquino prefers to negotiate with creditors, and has threatened to veto any unilateral debt repudiation measures. ∎

Notes

1. World Food Council, p. 6.
2. *Foodcrops and Shortages* No. 4, p. 19.
3. Qureshi, p. 10.
4. *Asia 1991,* p. 197.
5. Timberman, pp. 158-159.

Latin America and the Caribbean Update

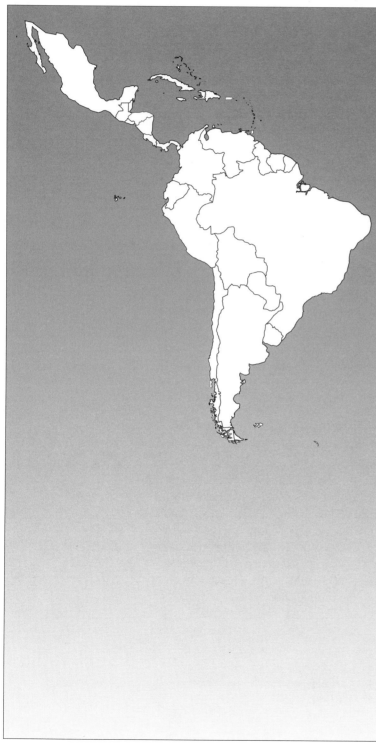

by Ana E. Avilés and Maria Simon

Overview

In 1990 and 1991, Brazil, Nicaragua, and Haiti elected new governments. These new administrations, like most in Latin America and the Caribbean, continue to struggle with extraordinary economic problems. The debt crisis of the early 1980s drastically reduced real wages and increased poverty. The region still has not regained the level of average income it had reached before the crisis. Not much progress has been made in reducing Latin America's excessive debt, and some countries are plagued by rampant inflation.

Bolivia and Venezuela introduced structural adjustment programs which included measures to alleviate poverty and continue basic services for poor people. However, these measures have not been sufficient to protect poor people from the effects of the crisis. While some social indicators, such as life expectancy and literacy rates, continued to improve around the region during the 1980s, the quality of health services and education declined considerably.

Peru faced a serious cholera epidemic in 1991. The disease spread rapidly, reaching Colombia, Guatemala, and Mexico.

Millions of people in the region are still hungry. As another world recession began to take hold in the early 1990s, some countries, e.g. Bolivia, again experienced negative economic growth.

Caribbean

Cuba

While Cuba continues to provide basic nutritional needs and free health services to its population, the economy is unstable, due mainly to the collapse of communism in Eastern Europe, Cuba's major trading partners, along with internal inefficiencies, and a drastic drop in Soviet aid, including food aid.

Cuba's ration system ensures that basic nutritional needs can be met; however, food supplies and imports declined after the disruption in trade with Eastern Europe. In 1991, the level of grain output, particularly of rice, is expected to increase following bad weather in 1990. One of the priorities of the government's austerity plan is food production, as well as improvements in food marketing and use of new agricultural technologies.

The significant change in the economy has led to much discontent among Cubans. While the majority of people still seem to support socialism, they oppose the internal inefficiencies of the bureaucracy which the socialist system has generated. For example, one commonly expressed concern is that people must wait in long lines to buy food. Cubans also express displeasure with the government's plan to relocate people to the countryside for food production and the employment of energy saving measures such as bicycles and oxcarts for transportation.

Cuba's austerity plan seeks to cut down on oil use, boost food production, and shift resources into activities such as tourism. The food production component of the plan consists of having urban Cubans, about 20,000 of whom were laid off during 1991, participate in planting crops. Cuba also expects to expand trade with new partners, such as China.

Health services remain among the best in Latin America. Services are free and accessible to all people, but the health sector is beginning to suffer shortages. Cuba's future remains cloudy given the state of the economy and the government's struggle to maintain popular support.

Dominican Republic

Despite an increase in social expenditures per capita, the living standard for many Dominicans did not improve in 1990. The drastic decline in GDP figures in 1988 had a major impact on the provision of basic services such as water, electricity, and waste management. Poverty and serious health problems are areas of major concern in urban areas; these are caused by overcrowding, environmental deterioration, and malnutrition.

The food supply and production outlook for the Dominican Republic is well below average, as in 1990. This resulted mainly from dry weather and lack of agricultural credit. In 1991, despite better weather, reduced rice crops and other agricultural shortages are expected. The total production of cereals in 1990 was 16 percent below the previous year.

A major economic decline distinguished the Dominican Republic among the Caribbean countries during 1990. Inflation declined from 58 percent in 1988 to 42 percent in 1989, but jumped to 70 percent in 1990, due primarily to the increase in oil prices.

Haiti

Following Haiti's 1991 democratic presidential election, donors increased their aid. The United States alone boosted its 1991 assistance to $83 million from $54 million the previous year. The infusions of aid are welcome, given the precarious state of the economy. In mid-April 1991, food shortages were reported, resulting from the looting of warehouses in the northern port of Cap-Haitien.

In 1990, Haiti suffered a severe drought during its main cereal season; this hit the corn crop particularly hard. However, the 1991 harvest is expected to recover, if the weather remains favorable. The domestically produced food supply is expected to be limited, especially for small farmers in the northern parts of the country, where crops nearly failed last year. To alleviate this food crisis, Haiti will have to rely heavily on international food aid throughout 1991.

In spite of all these obstacles, the new government of populist President Jean-Bertrand Aristide seems hopeful that it can carry out social, political, and economic changes which will begin to benefit the long neglected population of the poorest country in the Western Hemisphere.

Central America

Nicaragua

Nicaragua's economy is on the verge of collapse. Social programs instituted under the Sandinista government have suffered serious deterioration. Within weeks after the 1990 presidential election, food prices soared, the value of the currency declined drastically, and the black market re-emerged.

The economic crisis has increased poverty and unemployment levels. Like most Central American countries during the past decade, Nicaragua is attempting to

Hunger and Poverty in Mexico and the North American Free Trade Agreement

by Barbara Segal

Faced with a massive debt burden and plummeting oil revenues in the early 1980s, the Mexican government embarked on an extensive liberalization and adjustment of the economy. This has included reduction of import barriers, promotion of foreign investment, support of export production, privatization of state enterprises, and introduction of austerity measures. Currently, the Mexican government is negotiating a Free Trade Agreement with the United States and Canada which would accelerate the ongoing integration of the U.S. and Mexican economies. The agreement would likely result in the elimination of most of the remaining economic barriers among the three countries by outlawing quotas, tariffs, and investment laws that still protect each nation's industries.

Recent Trends in Hunger and Poverty in Mexico

Mexico's structural adjustment programs have helped to reduce inflation and the government's budget deficit, but have contributed to the concentration of wealth, poverty, and hunger since 1980. Business owners and investors' share of the nation's privately held wealth increased from 55 percent in 1980 to 72 percent in 1989. More than 50 percent of the population is now unemployed or underemployed, and the real purchasing power of the minimum wage in 1989 was about two-thirds that of 1970.

The country is also plagued by a profound agricultural crisis. According to *The Economist,* between 1980 and 1989, public investment in agriculture declined by 90 percent. Rural credit fell by more than half.[1] By 1989, Mexico imported 10 million metric tons of grain, more than 40 percent of national consumption, and grain production continues to fall. In 1990, the country experienced an agricultural trade deficit of $1.4 billion, due primarily to imports of corn, milk, sugar, sorghum, beans, and soybeans. The staple crops, corn and beans, occupy a decreasing proportion of the country's arable land, as farmers plant more profitable crops. Corn and beans are now produced chiefly by many small farmers who cultivate rainfed plots using relatively labor-intensive techniques. Given the low returns,

recover from political and economic strife. Land ownership remains a contentious issue: soon after the election, some previous landowners took over land which peasants had managed cooperatively since the 1979 revolution. The new government of President Violeta Chamorro has also given former "contra" rebels farmland.

There are about 300,000 landless peasants, many are farmers displaced by the civil war. Many Nicaraguans have expressed discontent over unfulfilled promises of land and jobs. The government also needs to revitalize agriculture to strengthen the economy.

Economic indicators are abysmal: the official unemployment rate is 46 percent, up from 30 percent in 1990. Many families can afford to eat only one meal a day. The inflation rate has reached five digits. Many Nicaraguans believe that the government's inability to resuscitate the economy will have major political repercussions.

The government also has a plan to improve the infrastructure, including the building of health, education, and housing facilities. However, a growing movement headed by the pro-Sandinista National Workers' Front, the largest labor organization, has called on the government to mod-

lack of credit, expense of fertilizers and pesticides, ecological problems, and competition from low-cost imports, many farmers have stopped producing marketable surpluses or abandoned cultivation. Commercial production of wheat, sorghum, oilseeds, and other crops is found chiefly on large, irrigated farms in northern Mexico.

For Mexican consumers, the government has reduced or eliminated subsidies on basic foods. Recently, the government cut subsidies on tortillas. The price immediately increased 137 percent for most Mexicans, although some poor families receive a free kilo of tortillas every three days.

Malnutrition is widespread. In 1979, the National Institute of Nutrition reported that 28 percent of Mexicans suffered from malnutrition; two-thirds lived in rural areas. Between 1982 and 1990, milk consumption fell by 21 percent, beans by 29 percent, and corn by 10 percent. By 1990, more than 40 per-

cent of the population suffered from malnutrition.[2]

Potential Impacts of the Free Trade Agreement

Further integration into the world economy, and particularly with the U.S. economy, has been a central component of Mexican policy. The United States is Mexico's main trading partner, and takes 70 percent of Mexico's agricultural exports. In 1987, Mexico and the United States signed an agreement to increase their economic cooperation.

The goal of the North American Free Trade Agreement (NAFTA) negotiations is to create a continental market that would eliminate tariffs and other barriers to the free flow of goods, services, and investment in an area stretching from the Canadian Yukon to Mexico's Yucatán Peninsula. The details of an agreement are still to be negotiated, but it is possible to analyze the views of proponents and critics.

Proponents believe that free trade will promote economic growth in both the United States and Mexico. They argue that an agreement would allow each country to specialize in goods and services suited to their respective economic structures, natural resources, and labor forces. U.S. business and government proponents argue that combined North American ventures would make the United States more competitive in the world market (particularly against Asia and Europe), generating new jobs for U.S. workers. They argue that the jobs likely to move to Mexico would be low-paying by U.S. standards, but a boon to poor, unemployed Mexicans.

Mexican government officials believe that an agreement will attract additional foreign investment, open up U.S. markets to Mexican goods, and create employment. According to Mexican President Carlos Salinas de Gortari:

ify its austerity plan and initiate programs to benefit poor people by providing food and medical aid. The Front has led a wave of strikes.

Food supplies continue to be limited due to the reduced cereal harvest of 1990, as well as the effects of newly implemented structural adjustment programs, which have reduced access to food for a large part of the population. The 1991 cereal crops are expected to be limited, due to adverse weather, falling demand, scarce credit, and increased input costs.

Preliminary information on the U.S. food aid program in Nicaragua, which totalled $17 million in 1990, indicates some negative impacts on domestic grain production. Nicaraguan farmers have bitterly criticized U.S. food aid, like the now defunct Soviet import program, because it has lowered the prices of local agricultural products.

The political and economic outlook for Nicaragua remains uncertain. The Chamorro government faces the daunting challenge of making an orderly transition, respecting vested rights, securing employment, and implementing effective efforts to revive the economy.

One of the best ways to strengthen our sovereignty is to improve the standard of living through an influx of investment in Mexico. . . . Either you have access to the huge trading blocs or you are left out of the dynamics of development and growth. . . . So I decided that it was time for Mexico to recognize this reality and belong to this future by building on the already strong trade relations we have with the U.S.[3]

He points to the large amount of private investment already entering the country and the reduction in inflation from 159.7 percent in 1987 to 29.9 percent in 1990 as evidence of the relative success of the current economic liberalization.[4]

Critics argue that Mexico is dominated by a one-party system, and some Mexican groups who have come out against NAFTA have faced reprisals. Critics also charge that an agreement could depress wages in the United States without significantly raising wages in Mexico. They say that NAFTA would jeopardize the livelihood of some Mexican farmers and employees of small businesses, make Mexico more dependent on the United States, and increase environmental degradation in the United States and Mexico. Mexican opposition leader Cuauhtemoc Cardenas sums up the views of many Mexican critics:

Mexico will sell off its cheap labor to attract foreign capital, which in turn will guarantee the survival of one of the last remaining authoritarian political regimes in Latin America. Low wages, antidemocratic union practices, the disgraceful lack of environmental regulations, dangerous working conditions, and unprotected consumers are proudly presented by the Mexican government as assets in the struggle for international competitiveness.[5]

Growth or Underdevelopment?

Most proponents and critics agree that the explosive growth of the "maquiladora" industry, foreign-owned assembly plants operating on the Mexican border, is a key indicator of NAFTA's potential for economic growth and abuses alike. Mexico has established a special free trade zone along the border, where 1,850 U.S.-owned factories import raw materials from the United States and export finished products. NAFTA proponents point out that "maquiladoras" have generated half a million jobs and provided desperately needed hard currency for servicing Mexico's debt.

Critics, like Jorge Castaneda, retort that after more than twenty-five years, "maquiladoras" make little use of Mexican raw materials and technology and have not stimulated development beyond the border region. The industry has drawn tens of thousands of people to the border areas. Yet wages

Panama

Panama has been attempting to recover from the economic crisis left behind by former dictator Manuel Antonio Noriega's mismanagement, the 1988 U.S. economic sanctions, and the 1989 U.S. invasion. During 1988 and 1989, real gross domestic product declined by 17 percent. This economic crisis caused significant levels of poverty in Panama. From 1983 to the first part of 1987, Panama executed a series of stabilization and structural adjustment programs under the supervision of the International Monetary Fund and the World Bank. However, in 1989, 85 percent of Panama's savings and deposits were frozen. Its access to international credit was shut off and the external debt continued to grow.

Control of the Canal Zone, locally called the Colon Free Zone, has been a long-debated issue between the United States and Panama, and its oil pipeline and export activities have been affected by the world recession and the economic crisis in Latin America. Recently, in addition to plans for complete Panamanian operation of the Canal by 1999, there are plans to gradually close all ten U.S. air bases and transfer their management and operations to Panama. The estimated value of proper-

remain low, turnover is high, independent labor unions are suppressed, and child labor is common. Safety standards are extremely poor; housing and other services are scarce or nonexistent. Prices for basic commodities are sometimes higher than across the border in the United States.[6]

NAFTA proponents argue that the economic growth generated by increased foreign investment and new jobs will raise wage rates in Mexico. Critics argue that Mexico has an enormous pool of unemployed and underemployed workers, and that despite rapid growth, wages have remained extremely low in the "maquiladora" industry.

According to Jesus Sílva-Herzog, former Mexican finance minister, trade liberalization efforts have already wiped out many Mexican textile manufacturers, and many small- and medium-sized industries have become importers of products or components they once produced.[7] Pointing out that U.S. and Japanese industry developed with the aid of protectionist laws, Herzog argues that Mexico should be allowed to nurture its industrial base in the same manner. While President Salinas and other Mexican free trade advocates concede that some small businesses have closed, they insist that NAFTA would force Mexican industries to become more efficient, and in the long-run strengthen them.

Agricultural Growth for Whom?

Proponents argue that NAFTA would eliminate further agricultural trade restrictions to the overall benefit of farmers and consumers in both countries. A U.S. General Accounting Office survey reveals that some agricultural producers, such as tomato and broccoli growers, believe that they may be hurt by the agreement, while others, such as poultry and grain producers, believe they will benefit.

Mexican proponents believe that NAFTA would benefit Mexico by opening the U.S. market to more Mexican agricultural products. The Mexican government, in agreement with large-scale producers, will likely ask the United States to eliminate or relax tariff and nontariff barriers. However, according to *The Economist,* the elimination of trade barriers would wipe out Mexican peasants who grow corn and other grains and could increase the dependence of Mexican consumers on imported grains.[8] Proponents respond that freer competition will oblige Mexican producers to become more competitive to the benefit of the Mexican economy.

Environmental Protection for Mexico or Lower U.S. Standards?

Environmental problems have emerged as one of the main concerns about NAFTA. Runaway pollution and accompanying public health threats exist in virtually every Mexican city along the U.S.-

ties and land of the air bases is over $100 million.

While the United States provided considerable aid per capita to the Central American region during the 1980s, the level is expected to decline in the 1990s. Panama received a total of $420 million in U.S. aid after the invasion in 1989; however, by 1992, Panama is expected to receive just $27 million.

Some studies estimate that between 36.9 and 44.6 percent of the population lives below the poverty line. The nutrition of the vast majority of Panamanians is inadequate. More than a year after the U.S. invasion, thousands of civilians were still displaced and 18,000 people became refugees. Some are living in areas "occupied" and patrolled by the U.S. military. At Albrook Air Force Base, 3,000 people live in cardboard cubicles surrounded by barbed wire fences. They receive only two meals a day, provided through the U.S. Agency for International Development and served by the Red Cross. Most of these refugees live under inadequate conditions and rely on U.S. assistance for their subsistence.

Among the pressing health concerns in Panama are: the AIDS epidemic; the spread of dengue and yellow fevers; and the results of Hurricane Joan, which destroyed part of the health facilities in two provinces. The health infrastructure has yet to develop adequate services and safeguard the health of the population, as mandated by the current constitution. In

Mexican border, partially because of the explosive growth of the "maquiladora" industry, which operates with inadequate or unenforced environmental regulations. Critics argue that the current pollution and public health problems on the border offer a preview of what NAFTA would bring to the rest of Mexico. The pollution from these industries affects both sides of the border. Likewise, hepatitis and other epidemics have swept communities on both sides of the border because untreated sewage seeps into underground wells which provide water for washing, cooking, and drinking. Many NAFTA advocates say that economic growth, as a result of free trade, is necessary to generate the resources for the Mexican government to address these environmental problems.

Conclusion

The completion of a North American Free Trade Agreement would accelerate a decade-long integration of the U.S. and Mexican economies. Such integration may bring economic benefits to both nations, but the equitable distribution of those benefits is questionable. Economic integration will also increase Mexico's dependence on the United States. Reconciling divergent environmental standards and enforcement will be difficult.

However, an agreement on trade needs to be part of a broader continental development strategy that includes measures to assist vulnerable groups, protect the environment, and promote democratic participation. Unless such investments are made, liberalized trade could widen the gaps between low- and high-income earners in both nations.

Several critics of NAFTA have recommended that a trade agreement include a "Social Charter," similar to that adopted by the European Community. Such a charter would guarantee both Mexican and U.S. workers basic health and safety standards and collective bargaining rights. It would also provide for a gradual increase in Mexico's minimum wage, harmonization of environmental standards, and debt relief. A trade agreement responding to these concerns could help promote sustainable development for the long-term benefit of people in both countries. ■

Notes

1. "Mexico: Not So Sweet Corn."
2. B. Suarez, D. Barkin, and B. DeWalt.
3. Salinas de Gotiari, pp. 5-6.
4. *Ibid.,* p. 8.
5. Cardenas.
6. Davidson.
7. Silva-Herzog.
8. "Mexico...."

1985, the population covered by health insurance/services was 59.8 percent, and by 1987 it had reached 64.5 percent. President Guillermo Endara's government has promoted a government/community approach to health care. This strategy aims at the population's participation in the eleven regions of Panama, where the integrated health systems are broken into sectors and the residents from each region set up health committees.

Sanitation and water supply continue to be serious problems. Sanitary conditions, especially in the rural areas, where it is necessary to build latrines, are poor. The Ministry of Health and the National Institute of Water Supply and Sewerage Systems are the responsible entities for ensuring basic sanitation operations. Reports indicate that the Ministry of Health provides drinking water to 500 or fewer citizens.

The unemployment rate in Panama has been high for the last decade. The Endara government has proposed an emergency employment program.

Panama's economic situation is terrible and its political situation uncertain. But the government – relying heavily on its people – has made some impressive social gains against those odds.

South America

Bolivia

Bolivia is the poorest country in South America, and has great income inequality. The poorest 40 percent of the population receives 12 percent of household income, while the wealthiest 20 percent enjoys a 58 percent share.

During the early 1980s, Bolivia experienced the worst economic crisis of the century. With its economy based on the production of raw materials (the country suffered negative growth rates), GNP declined by 20 percent, as international commodity prices dropped, per capita income fell 30 percent from 1980 to 1984, and legal exports shrunk by 25 percent between 1984 and 1986. The final blow to the Bolivian economy came in 1985, when the tin market collapsed. Tin was Bolivia's leading export and, as a result of the crash, some 20,000 miners lost their jobs. Unemployment climbed steadily in the mid-eighties, reaching 21.5 percent in 1987. This recession was accompanied by rampant inflation, reported to be around 24,000 percent in 1985.

In 1985, President Victor Paz Estensorro instituted an austerity plan with the approval of the International Monetary Fund. This stabilized inflation, which dropped to double digits in 1986-1987, but economic and social deterioration continued. However, the government also established a three-year Emergency Social Fund (ESF) in late 1985. ESF was set up primarily to provide short-term employment and social services to the most affected poor population until a permanent economic solution could be attained. It operated in several program areas: economic infrastructure, social infrastructure, social assistance (such as school feeding programs), and group credit plans.

In spite of these efforts, poverty and malnutrition remain widespread in Bolivia. According to a United Nations estimate, 85 percent of rural Bolivians lived below the poverty line (1977-1986).[1] Malnutrition is the main cause of 57 percent of the deaths of children under six years old.

Women of reproductive age account for close to one-fourth of the total population. The classification "pregnancy, birth and postpartum complications" is among the five primary causes of death.[2] In a 1986 study, the Bolivian Gynecological Society discovered that high levels of unsafe abortion account for 26 percent of total maternal mortality.[3]

The population continues to grow at an annual rate of 2.8 percent, the fastest growth rate in the region. The population under fifteen years of age accounts for approximately 43.8 percent of the total.

The population boom, combined with a trend toward urbanization, will exert increasing pressure on an inadequate health infrastructure and sanitation services. PAHO reports that "the health conditions in Bolivia are the most precarious in the hemisphere."[4] In 1988, the coverage of sewage and sanitation services extended to only 22 percent of the urban population and did not reach the rural population. The lack of such facilities has lead to the contamination of several major rivers. These waters are used to irrigate vegetables.

The provision of health services is further constrained by budget cuts: the percentage of total expenditure on health fell two-thirds from 1972 to 1988. These findings are alarming in light of the recent outbreak of cholera in neighboring Peru, although as this report went to press, the epidemic had not spread to Bolivia.

Brazil

While there have been some economic and political changes, poverty remains widespread in Brazil. Urban poor people in Brazil have been the most vulnerable to hunger and health problems during 1991. Brazil's economy and its rate of population growth have affected the living standards of this sector of the population, particularly in the area of health. A recent study reports that inadequate water systems are causing serious health problems in some urban areas of the country. Among the priorities for national preventive health measures are surveys of maternal and child health.

The declining economy has affected many urban areas, where families barely earn enough money to pay high utility bills; these families are unable to afford adequate food. The money used to pay for utility bills could instead buy fifty-five pounds of beans. Poverty rates are increasing, and the weak economy leads to water shortages and deteriorating schools and hospitals.

There are no current official statistics available on urban poverty, since last year's census was cancelled due to lack of funds. However, unpublished findings show that the numbers of people in the "poor" and "super poor" categories, a sector of the population that President Fernando Collor de Mello calls the "shirtless," increased by 20 percent during the 1980s. This means that in 1980, there were approximately 3.6 million poor and 1.7 million super-poor people in metropolitan São Paulo. By the end of the decade, the number of poor and super poor people had increased to 4.7 million and 3 million, respectively.

A recent World Bank study indicates that during the period 1974-1989, government programs have been effective in combating malnutrition among children under five.[5] The report indicates a 62 percent reduction in malnutrition among infants who participated in government programs such as the National Milk Program and the Supplementary Food Program. Other improved factors were basic sanitary conditions, immunization programs, and lower birth rates. In spite of these indicators, 5 percent of the surveyed population remains malnourished and 10 percent remains undernourished. These numbers are undoubtedly higher in the general population.

In the areas of crops and food supply, Brazil seems to have an uncertain but improved outlook for 1991, following reduced 1990 grain crops due to poor weather. Corn output is expected to increase due to diversion of land from soybeans, but localized drought may reduce actual production levels. The supplies of meat, milk, and cooking oil in Brazil's main cities are reported to be limited after the announcement of a price freeze in the early part of 1991. The government increased its food imports.

Recent policy changes may improve the lot of poor people. President Collor has proposed a 50 percent tax reduction on essential agricultural products, in order to ease food prices and encourage production. Another government sponsored plan, funded by the Inter-American Development Bank, seeks to improve sanitation facilities and create jobs. The health problems of urban poor people, coupled with continuing economic decline and the constricted food supply, mean that the immediate future does not look bright for hungry Brazilians.

Colombia

Unlike most of its Latin neighbors, Colombia has maintained slow but steady economic growth over the last decade and has experienced manageable inflation. This generally positive picture is clouded by a burgeoning drug trade. Annual cocaine export earnings of $1.5 to 3 billion exceed those of coffee, the country's principal legal export.

Peru '*Hambre*'

by Maria Simon

"Peru, 'Hambre.'" Peru is hungry, is the most common graffiti one sees in Peru. In the shanty towns around Lima, between 23 and 40 percent of the children aged one to six are malnourished, according to Catholic Relief Services. Also in Lima, the number of households with an inadequate calorie intake increased 22 percent between 1986 and 1989, and the share of household income required for food in the poorest individual households increased from less than 40 percent in 1972 to around 75 percent in 1989.

Peru entered the 1990s struggling to resuscitate a collapsing economy, to stop guerilla insurgency, and to control its growing drug trade. The recent outbreak of cholera, termed an "emergency situation" by the World Health Organization (WHO), further strained the ability of poor people to survive and of the government to meet the basic needs of the population. One hundred and seventy-seven thousand cases of cholera had been reported with 1,300 deaths as of May 1991. This nearly equals the entire number of cases reported in 1971, the peak year of the last cholera epidemic.[1] Transmitted through contaminated water and foodstuffs, cholera is spreading rapidly through Peru's urban and costal regions due to overpopulation combined with poor sanitation and poor drinking water supplies.

Cholera, characterized by severe diarrhea, can be successfully treated with simple therapeutic measures, including oral rehydration therapy. However, Peru's health infrastructure is inadequate to meet the present emergency situation, and the ratio of doctors to patients actually decreased from the 1960s through the 1980s. The lack of health care is more pronounced in rural areas and the death toll from cholera has been up to 10 to 40 percent higher in some rural areas.

In a recent report, the Pan American Health Organization estimated that it would cost $3.2 billion over the next decade to provide decent water and sewage to all 22 million Peruvians.[2] Sewage disposal in the capital city of Lima, where 97 percent of the raw sewage is dumped directly into the Pacific, is an example of the extent of the lack of basic services. Lima is now home to 9 million people, although it was built for only 500,000. As a result, overcrowding, make-shift housing and inadequate services characterize the living situation of a large percent of the residents.

Colombia's population will increase from 33 million to 54 million by the year 2025 at its present growth rate. Income distribution is heavily skewed, with the most affluent 20 percent enjoying 53 percent of overall income while the lowest 40 percent manage with only a 12.7 percent share. UNICEF reports that 32 percent of the urban population and 70 percent of the rural population lived below the absolute poverty line during the 1980s.[6]

The urban population of Colombia has grown rapidly, reaching 69 percent in 1989. The infrastructure and provision of basic services has not kept pace with the urban explosion. PAHO reports that only 79 percent of urban and 17 percent of rural peo-ple have access to water. The majority of those without service are concentrated on the outskirts or margins of urban areas, where 84 percent are not connected to a water supply system, or in scattered rural areas, where this percentage reaches 90 percent.[7] Fifty-three percent of the population does not have access to sewage ser-vices. Again, this is concentrated in marginal urban areas, where 72 percent do not have excreta disposal, and in the scat-tered rural population, where 84 percent are without services. Twenty percent of waste is dumped into surface water ways, 50 percent goes to open-cut spillways, and only 30 percent to sanitary landfills.

This lack of basic services is alarming in

The government is squeezed by a $22 billion foreign debt and a steadily declining national econo-my; hence, Peru is in a poor posi-tion to confront these problems. However, the damage caused by ignoring problems is equally devas-tating. Peru has spent more than 1 billion dollars to fight cholera at the same time it has lost more than 1 billion in tourism and exports, mostly of canned fish. The impact of this loss is immense, as it ac-counts for almost half of Peru's total export earnings, which reached $2.6 billion in 1989.

Not surprisingly, it is poor peo-ple who suffer the most from the epidemic. Twenty-three percent of the population have no access to electricity, drinking water, or public sewage services; an additional 38.5 percent have incomplete services; and only 38.5 percent of the popu-lation enjoy complete services, according to PAHO.[3] This leaves at least 500,000 Peruvians without vital services.

Fish is believed to be a principal carrier of the cholera, and the pop-ulace has been advised not to eat it. For most poor Peruvians crowd-ed into shanty towns along the coast, it is a choice to eat fish or to go hungry. Health experts also advise boiling water for ten min-utes before drinking, and cooking fish before eating, because heat kills the bacteria that causes cholera. The implementation of this sound advice causes further finan-cial hardship for poor people who can scarcely afford fuel.

President Alberto Fujimori, elect-ed in the fall of 1990, attempted to counter recession and hyperinfla-tion by implementing an austerity program. Called "Fuji-shock," the program includes reducing govern-ment expenditures to slow infla-tion, ending food and petroleum subsidies, and a tight monetary policy. While this economic pro-gram has won praise from the IMF and the international banking com-munity, who promise future loans, it has had a devastating short-term effect on many Peruvians.

Before implementation of the reforms, one-third of the popula-tion lived in extreme poverty; now, 52 percent, or 12 million Peruvians, fall into that category. More than 35 percent of the population living in extreme poverty are children less that 14 years old, and 20 percent are less than five years old. Infla-tion remains high at 10 percent or more per month. With the removal of government price controls, basic consumer goods prices rose be-tween 400 percent and 3,000 per-cent. For example, gasoline prices rose 3,000 percent after govern-ment de-regulation, and staple food prices increased by up to 700 per-cent. Food prices in general in-creased 500 to 1,000 percent.

light of the appearance of cholera in the country in 1991. The Health Ministry has proclaimed the Pacific coast of the country, where most people are poor and black, an "emergency zone," and has advised residents to take precautions to prevent infection. Forty percent of food processing plants have no sanitary license, thus increasing the risk of infections and other health problems.

Colombia is carrying a $17 billion foreign debt. In 1988, debt servicing consumed 38 percent of export income while health and education received only 3.6 percent of GNP. The United States has more than quintupled its military aid to Colombia to $40.3 million in 1990 in connection with the "war on drugs."

Venezuela

Venezuela, a country known for its abundant natural resources, particularly oil, has the highest per capita income in Latin America. In 1989, the administration of President Carlos Andres Perez began efforts to address the critical state of the economy and widespread poverty. However, the country experienced a major economic downturn at the end of the decade, with a growth level 20 percent lower than the previous ten years. The decade of the 1980s was financially unstable. The Perez government introduced an economic reform program in early 1989 in an effort to

These price increases coincided with a reduction in purchasing power and an increase in unemployment. In one month, the earnings of public sector employees fell 59.8 percent and that of the private sector, 39.7 percent. The legal minimum wage covers only one-third of the cost of the government's minimum family food basket. One million Peruvians have lost their jobs, and only 9 percent of Lima's economically active population are now fully employed.

In addition to the cholera epidemic, poverty, malnutrition, and the lack of government investment in primary health care underlie the other major causes of death in Peru: gastrointestinal disease (up 781 percent in ten years), respiratory infections, influenza (up 1,218 percent), malaria (up 194 percent), whooping cough, and typhoid. Curt Schaeffer, regional manager of Latin America for CARE, recently

reported that 40,000 children under five die each year in Peru from dehydration due to diarrhea, which is frequently related to malnutrition.

In general, the incidence of malnourishment is higher in rural areas, particularly in the highlands, than in coastal, urban areas. Rural areas were hit by a severe drought, which lowered food production in 1991. This compounds a general decline in food production over the last two decades; the level of food production per capita in 1991 was only half its 1970 level. Food imports increased 260 percent in volume and 360 percent in value between 1970 and 1987. Peru's present production levels and import capabilities do not meet food needs. An estimated million tons of food aid in 1990-1991 is needed to meet status quo needs and a significantly higher amount, 1.2 to 1.3 million tons, would be required to assure all Peruvians an adequate

diet.

Peru's informal economy is burgeoning in response to high unemployment and decreased purchasing power. The informal sector is characterized by unregistered, unlicensed activity, which ranges from street vendors and petty traders to drug traffickers. By 1989, it was estimated that the informal sector would include 60 percent of the Peruvian economy.[4] Mario Vargas Llosa, a presidential candidate in 1990, described the informal economy as "the people's creative response to the state's incapacity to satisfy the basic needs of the impoverished masses." It affords poor people some means of survival, albeit at a subsistence level.

While the informal sector consists of poor people creating alternatives to starvation, it also exposes the harsh conditions of poverty. The Peruvian National Institute of Statistics reports that 5.2 million

transform the country's economy from one based on oil revenues to one based on development activities.

Around this period, the term "extreme poverty" became commonly used among Venezuelans. A recent World Bank study estimates that 22 percent of the population could not afford to meet daily food requirements.[8] Other studies indicate that general economic and social indicators declined over the last decade, especially those related to the nutritional status of infants, pregnant women, nursing mothers, and children under six years old.

While poverty is more acute in rural areas, it has reached many sectors of the urban population. The Perez government's poverty reduction plan (PEP) has been effective in shifting resources from generalized food subsidies benefiting mainly affluent Venezuelans to targeted programs benefiting the poorest sectors of the society.

PEP emphasizes three principles: increased targeting to the poor, decentralized programs, and increased private sector participation in delivering services to the poor. PEP includes a nutritional grant program, which gives direct financial assistance to low-income families with school age children; a maternal-child health feed-

children aged five to fourteen were participating in the informal sector in 1987; that is one-fourth of Peru's overall population and more than one-half of the approximately 9 million Peruvians under fourteen years old.[5] The Institute estimates that the number will reach 6.5 million by the year 2000, or 23.3 percent of the country's population. "Poverty is forcing more children aged 5-14 to work, almost always in exploitive conditions."[6]

One of the largest and most lucrative areas of the informal sector is narcotics production. Peru's 150-square-mile Upper Huallaga Valley is the world's largest coca-growing region. There, a peasant can earn an average of twelve times more per month cultivating coca than he or she can on any legal export crop. On the national level, cocaine provides Peru with $800 million to $1.2 billion each year in foreign exchange income, accounting for around 30 percent

of export earnings, more than any other crop.

The collapsing Peruvian economy and successive governments' inability to control the economic crisis have created space for the growth of an indigenous Maoist movement, called the *Sendero Luminoso,* or Shinning Path. *Sendero* directs its energies to armed struggle against the present order, which includes both the government and the peasants themselves. This open campaign of terrorism has had high costs for Peru. Political violence took 20,000 lives over the last ten years, 1,600 in 1989 alone. During an eight-month period in 1989, 76 percent of Sendero's victims were peasants or poor city dwellers. The economic damage caused by terrorism is estimated at $18 billion over the past eleven years.

Already bowed by poor economic conditions, a harsh economic adjustment program, widespread poverty, and unemployment, Peru

is scarcely braced for the present onslaught of cholera. While the epidemic will eventually subside, until the population has potable water and improved sanitation conditions, cholera and other preventable diseases will continue to plague the nation. The solution of larger national problems of terrorism and drug trafficking cannot be separated from the eradication of extreme poverty and hunger in Peru, which leave poor Peruvians with few alternatives for survival. ■

Notes

1. World Health Organization, "Statement of," p. 1.
2. Lane, p. 44.
3. Pan American Health Organization, *Health Conditions,* p. 241. *State of World's Population* puts access to safe water (1985-88) at 55 percent, p. 46.
4. World Council of Churches.
5. World Bank, *World Development Indicators,* 1990. In 1988, 39.1 percent of the population was under 14 years old.
6. PAHO, *Health Conditions,* p. 243.

ing program; and a community-based day care program for children of working mothers living in low-income neighborhoods.

Between 1981 and 1989, there was a drastic jump in food costs, making it harder for poor people to cope with the already high cost of living. Therefore, the government has implemented another program aimed at providing monthly cash grants to low-income families with children up to age 12, enabling them to meet urgent nutritional needs.

PEP does not address health and education, however. Although Venezuela spends more per capita on health than any other Latin American country, the health status of the population is deteriorating and the quality of health services has declined. There has been an increase in endemic diseases in recent years, particularly malar-

ia. Funding for the reduction of these epidemics has declined by almost half.

The economic crisis has had a negative impact on income distribution. Some survey data show a shift from the poorest 10 percent of households to the highest 10 percent. It is estimated that among poor people, the amount of money used to buy food ranges from 50 to 80 percent of household incomes. The unemployment rate remained at high levels during the decade of the 1980s.

Currently, some modifications in poverty reduction initiatives are being proposed to the government, based on improving the efficiency of these efforts with existing resources. It is hoped that through such measures, the level of poverty will be effectively reduced and the economy could return to positive growth. ■

Notes

1. UNDP, *Human Development Report 1990*, p. 132.
2. PAHO/WHO offprint, pp. 19, 27.
3. *Ibid.*, p. 19.
4. PAHO, *Report*, p. 122.
5. Findings of World Bank study were summarized in an article in the *Jornal do Brazil*, March 17, 1991, p. 15.
6. UNICEF, *The State of the World's Children 1991*, p. 113.
7. PAHO, *Health Conditions*, p. 99.
8. World Bank, *Venezuela*.

Middle East Update

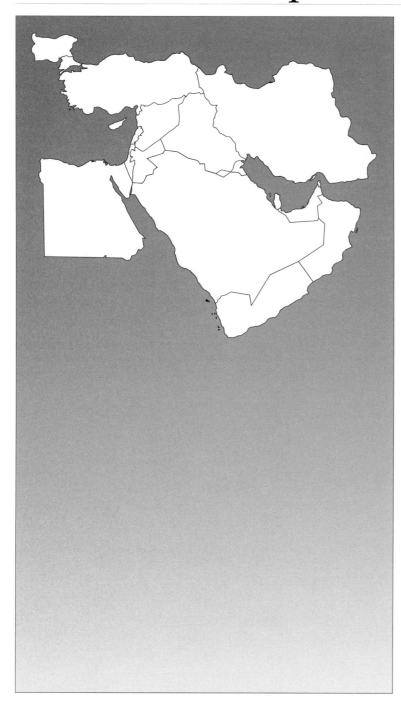

by Rapti Goonesekere

The crisis which followed Iraq's invasion of Kuwait on August 2, 1990, led to increased hunger in much of the Middle East, as well as in other countries dependent on the remittances of migrant workers. Economic sanctions on Iraq and Kuwait cost Turkey and Jordan important markets. Massive numbers of refugees and transiting migrant workers placed heavy economic burdens on Jordan, Turkey, and Iran. Sanctions, war, and civil strife had tremendous human costs in Iraq itself. The donor community – particularly the United States and Saudi Arabia – put political conditions on humanitarian and development aid. Thus, governments which sympathized with Iraq during the crisis, such as Yemen and Jordan, have received little compensation for their substantial losses, while those which supported the Allied cause, e.g. Egypt and Turkey, have obtained considerable financial support. Western and conservative Gulf governments continue to distrust Iran, so it has received little assistance in coping with over a million Iraqi refugees.

The Allies sought to uphold the right to food of Kurds along the Iraqi-Turkish border (see sidebar, page 144). Similarly, private voluntary organizations, United Nations agencies, and the International Committee of the Red Cross struggled to maintain impartial relief efforts throughout the region. According to the United Nations World Food Council, the Middle East will need substantial emergency aid for some time; this will likely divert resources from long-term development aid to poor countries.

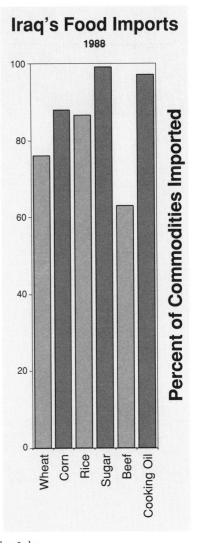

Iraq's Food Imports
1988

Percent of Commodities Imported

Wheat · Corn · Rice · Sugar · Beef · Cooking Oil

Iraq

Iraq's invasion of Kuwait and the response of the United States and its allies, led to the "most momentous and destructive war" since 1945.[1] The impact of the Persian Gulf war ("Operation Desert Storm") was devastating to the whole region and created history in more ways than one – it was the most effective killing campaign led by any military force. The war resulted in one of the largest movements of civilians in the shortest periods of time; it caused one of the biggest oil spills and worst oil fires in history, leading to unprecedented environmental ruin. This new model of war, referred to as "hyper war," lasted only forty-three days and killed more Iraqis than the eight-year long Iran-Iraq war[2] – 100,000 to 120,000 Iraqi military personnel were killed. By the beginning of May 1991, 49,000 to 76,000 Iraqi civilians had died due to the war. Over 6 million people were directly affected during the initial embargo period (August 1990 to January 1991), the war (January and February), and its aftermath (February to July). Iraq's social and economic fabric has been crippled for a long time.

Referring to the post-war conditions in Iraq, Under-Secretary-General Martti Ahtisaari, who led a United Nations mission to Iraq in March 1991, reported:

> . . .[N]othing that we had seen or read had quite prepared us for the particular form of devastation which has now befallen the country. The recent conflict has wrought near apocalyptic results upon the economic infrastructure of what had been, until January 1991, a rather highly urbanized and mechanized society. Iraq has, for some time to come, been relegated to a pre-industrial age, but with all the

disabilities of post-industrial dependency on an intensive use of energy and technology.[3]

The destruction of power plants, oil refineries, and energy resources has been the cause of much devastation in post-war Iraq. Prior to the Gulf crisis, water from the Tigris river was purified and supplied by seven treatment stations, and Baghdad received approximately 450 litres per person per day. Central water treatment stations and many smaller water projects supplied purified water to the rest of the country. All stations operated on electric power, and the destruction of power plants led to grave problems of sanitation and public health. The supply of water in Baghdad dropped to less than ten litres per day, but by July 1991 increased to thirty to forty litres in 70 percent of the area. Sewage contamination is high, as untreated sewage is dumped directly into the river, which is the main source of water supply.

A nationwide shortage of clean drinking water has led to the quadrupling of intestinal infections among children, and the World Health Organization (WHO) has warned that the country is facing a threat of typhoid and cholera epidemics. The restoration of basic health care and the resumption of water and electrical services to medical facilities, as well as the international relief effort by private organizations, such as the International Committee of the Red Cross (ICRC) and Catholic Relief Services (CRS), averted outbreaks of such infectious diseases during the summer of

1991. However, an acute shortage of infant formula, problems of water sanitation, and a temporary breakdown in immunization have increased infant mortality tremendously. A Harvard University medical team has estimated that unless the situation improves, more than 100,000 children under the age of one will die by fall 1991. "The children are melting," said an Iraqi doctor.[4] According to recent reports, 55,000 children died during the first half of 1991 due to severe shortages of food and medicine.[5] Health conditions are worst in southern Iraq, where, according to CRS, typhoid has reached epidemic levels.[6]

The projected doubling of child mortality rates is catastrophic for Iraq, which before the war had one of the most modern health care delivery systems in the developing world. According to UNICEF reports, 95 percent of Iraq's population had easy access to medical facilities.

Malnutrition was rare, due to government subsidized formula sales and low food prices; immunization coverage was excellent and access to safe drinking water was almost universal. According to a July 1990 United Nations study, Iraq reduced its infant mortality rate to forty per 1,000 births.[7] Of Iraq's total population of 18.8 million, 20 percent are young children. UNICEF stated in March 1991 that three

Upholding the Right to Food in a "New World Order"

by Marc J. Cohen

The 1990-1991 Persian Gulf crisis which followed Iraq's invasion of Kuwait has raised profound questions about the universal right to food. On the one hand, the United States insisted on enforcing the narrowest possible interpretation of United Nations economic sanctions against Iraq, including the seizure of ships carrying food. Although the U.N. resolutions imposing the sanctions allowed food shipments "in humanitarian circumstances," the embargo caused a substantial increase in Iraqi infant mortality even before the outbreak of war,

according to International Physicians for the Prevention of Nuclear War.[10] There is also evidence that the Iraqi government diverted food aid intended for needy mothers and children to the ordinary food rationing system.

On the other hand, the United States took the lead in an allied effort to create a safe zone within Iraq where Kurds displaced by post-war conflict with the Iraqi government could safely receive food and other humanitarian assistance. In April 1991, U.S. President George Bush sent 10,000 troops to protect a zone within Iraqi territory near the Turkish border. Twelve other allied nations sent an additional 10,000 troops to provide security in the 2,300 square-mile zone. After three months, allied forces withdrew from their direct role in providing humanitarian aid and security in favor of U.N. and voluntary agencies, along with U.N. peace-keeping forces. The allies

have based 3,000 troops in Turkey for "rapid return" to the safety zone if needed.

The Kurds in northern Iraq face enormous problems in achieving repatriation, resuming normal life, and establishing a just and secure relationship with the Iraqi government. Nevertheless, allied intervention into Iraq had important features. With the endorsement of the United Nations, the allies upheld the principle that the right to food and other humanitarian assistance outweighs the claims of national sovereignty. Also, the creation of the safety zone facilitated the opening of negotiations between the Kurds and the Baghdad authorities.

In these two respects, creation of the safety zone mirrored Operation Lifeline Sudan. In April 1989, United Nations officials obtained agreement from the government of Sudan and the armed opposition, the Sudan People's Liberation Movement, to permit the safe pas-

million children under the age of five were "at risk" of disease and starvation due to prevailing health conditions of the country.[8]

Before the war, Iraq imported 70 percent of its food, including seeds and livestock feed, mostly from the United States and the United Kingdom (see graph, page 143). Thus the economic sanctions, sponsored by the United States and adopted by the United Nations, caused severe food shortages within the country. The looting and theft of animals and stored supplies during the occupation of Kuwait initially eased food shortages somewhat. Although the United Nations has permitted the delivery of medicine and "humanitarian" food, Iraq lacks the money to purchase supplies on the world market. The estimated cost to feed Iraq's population is $2.6 billion a year, or $216 million a month. Prince Sadruddin Aga Khan, the U.N. secretary-general's special representative for humanitarian affairs in the region, completed a two-week assessment mission in Iraq in July 1991. The U.N. team strongly recommended the easing of sanctions against Iraq, to enable the country to obtain cash to buy food, medicine, and spare parts that are urgently needed. Sadruddin's delegation recommended that Iraq be allowed to sell oil or unfreeze its assets abroad. "The bottom

sage of food and other humanitarian assistance through "corridors of tranquillity." This allowed safe passage of relief supplies to people in need in both government- and opposition-controlled territory. Ultimately, Operation Lifeline collapsed, but it did facilitate the flow of aid for six months, and created what UNICEF Executive Director James Grant has called "an environment for peace."[11] The relief corridors, like the security zone in Iraq, were an important confidence-building measure that furthered, though did not guarantee, the process of negotiating peace in a conflict zone.

Elsewhere in Africa and in Central America, warring parties have similarly agreed to create "space" in which all citizens can receive food and other basic necessities of life. Again, these agreements have helped foster an atmosphere in which broader peace negotiations can take place. In September 1990, the parties to Angola's civil war agreed to establish "relief corridors" when two years of drought and fifteen years of civil conflict combined to put 2 million people at risk of starvation. The U.S. government played a key role in establishing these "peace corridors," as well as the subsequent negotiated settlement of Angola's civil war. And, since the mid-1980s, the two sides in El Salvador's civil war have agreed to regular ceasefires on designated days to permit children to be vaccinated against five readily preventable diseases.

While these efforts are encouraging, they fall short of coordinated and consistent international action to uphold the right to food and humanitarian assistance. Since 1990, for example, both sides of the conflict in Sudan have interfered with deliveries of food and other emergency assistance. In numerous recent instances – Cambodia, Ethiopia, Liberia, and Somalia – the assertion of national sovereignty has prevented the delivery of needed assistance.

In the United States, Congressmen Tony Hall and Bill Emerson, chairman and ranking minority member, respectively, of the Select Committee on Hunger, have proposed legislation elevating the right to food within U.S. foreign policy. Their bill also calls on the U.S. administration to take the lead in creating a U.N. Convention on the Right to Food, which would institutionalize the U.N.'s ability to assure assistance to people in need, even when their governments object. And, the legislation calls for the creation of a permanent U.N. under-secretary-general for humanitarian affairs, a call echoed at the 1991 economic summit of the seven leading industrial powers. ∎

line is that sanctions were never designed to make the people of Iraq suffer in the way that we noted they are suffering," said Sadruddin.[12] The pressure from the U.N. mission caused the Bush administration to draw up a plan in July 1991 to allow the U.N. Security Council to ease the sanctions.

Supply shortages and breakdowns in transportation have caused the prices of most basic commodities to increase more than ten-fold since the imposition of sanctions in August 1990. Prices of many items have risen by 2,000 to 3,000 percent. Hyperinflation has caused many incomes to collapse. At the official rate of exchange, the average salary in Iraq is equivalent to $450 to $600 a month. Employees cannot withdraw deposited funds, as the banking system barely functions.

A food rationing system was initiated by the government in September 1990 to provide families with some of their basic needs at prices comparable to those existing before August 1990. Food continued to be rationed through July 1991, and the government's daily allocation per person was set at a thousand calories (one-third of the nutritional requirement of an individual). Government rations provide three loaves of bread per person per month, and milk powder is available only for sick children with a doctor's prescription.

Agricultural production in Iraq is highly mechanized and dependent on pumped-water irrigation. Despite favorable weather conditions, in July 1991, the U.N. mission in Iraq estimated the June 1991 cereal harvest at about one-third of the previous year's,[13] due to the failure of irrigation and drainage systems and the lack of fuel, pesticides, fertilizers, and seeds. However, high yields of wheat and barley are expected in northern Iraq. In addition, livestock farming has been adversely affected by sanctions, as many feed products are im-

ported. Widespread starvation may be imminent, and ICRC has warned that without a substantial response by aid donors, the situation in Iraq will become "a long-term disaster."[14]

President Saddam Hussein's attack on Shiite and Kurdish rebels in the south and north of Iraq, respectively, resulted in a mass exodus of Iraqis. More than 800,000 Kurds fled to the Turkish border and another 1.2 million fled to the Iranian border. Refugee camps have been established in Jordan, Iran, Syria, and Turkey. Earlier attacks in 1988 led thousands of Kurds to flee to Turkey, and 28,000 Kurdish refugees were reported to be living in camps prior to the recent civil war. In May 1991, between 25 and 50 percent of the refugees in these camps were reported to be suffering from malnutrition, and it was estimated that there was only one doctor per 100,000 refugees. In addition, the destruction of homes during the war left at least 72,000 persons homeless throughout Iraq.

Kuwait

Before August 1990, Kuwait was ranked by UNDP as the most "comfortable" country in the Gulf region. With a per capita GNP of $16,150 and a very low infant mortality rate, Kuwait ranked high on UNDP's Human Development Index (HDI).

The Iraqi invasion of Kuwait and the resulting Gulf war changed this dramatically. The occupation and war severely damaged power and water desalination plants, and destroyed much of Kuwait's physical infrastructure. Hospitals, medical equipment, schools, and water and sewage systems were affected, leading to a rapid decline in socio-economic conditions within the country. Pollution occurring due to the burning of 600 oil wells since late February 1991 has created an environmental crisis and health hazard.

Prior to the war, two-thirds of Kuwait's 2.2 million population were foreigners. Most of the migrant workers came from developing countries in the region (Egypt, Jordan, the West Bank, and Gaza) and Asia (India, Sri Lanka, Pakistan, Bangladesh, Korea, and the Philippines). The war has displaced many of these workers and created a significant vacuum in Kuwait's labor force. A majority of the doctors and nurses in the country were foreigners, and the exodus of such skilled personnel has crippled Kuwait's medical services, which before the Gulf crisis were among the best in the world.

Due to water scarcity, there is little arable land in Kuwait. Thus, only 1 percent of the land is cultivated, and prior to the Gulf crisis, Kuwait imported approximately 95 percent of its food. The country has also undertaken hydroponic agriculture. Although food shortages occurred during the crisis, the United Nations reported that by March 1991, the Kuwaiti government had established an effective food system aimed at providing necessary food for the entire population. Thus, no external food aid to Kuwait was required.[15]

By June 1991, Kuwait City showed signs of recovery. Business and commercial sectors, as well as the more prosperous residential areas, were returning to normal. Water, electricity, telephones, and emergency services were restored by March 1991. Drinking water is once again available to most Kuwaiti households, as 60 percent of the water mains and most of the desalination plants have resumed operation. However, restoration of services has been slower in poor and working class neighborhoods where many Palestinians and other foreigners live. For example, in Abdili, a tent city where stateless "Bedoons" (undocumented persons who had previously been working in Kuwait and wish to regain Kuwaiti citizenship or residence) are refugees, Red Cross volunteers tried to prevent increasing rates of infant mortality, malnutrition, and diarrheal diseases. Situated in northern Kuwait, this camp accommodated approximately 1,000 persons in March 1991, with the Kuwaiti Red Crescent providing food and medical assistance to the occupants.

Egypt

The Persian Gulf war has caused many socio-economic problems within Egypt, adding to poverty, unemployment, and political discontent. The total cost to the economy is estimated to be $1 billion (3 percent of the country's GNP). Before August 1990 there were 1.8 million Egyptian workers in Iraq and Kuwait – the largest number of foreign workers in these two countries. According to the International Labor Organization (ILO), migrant workers in the two Gulf nations accounted for 7.1 percent of Egypt's economically active population. Their remittances dramatically reduced poverty among Egypt's landless laborers.

An ILO survey found that 75 percent of the poorest 30 percent of villagers received remittances; remittances constituted more than 75 percent of the meager incomes of the absolutely poorest people. Thus, the return of over 450,000 migrant workers has left Egypt's poor people a lot poorer. Unemployment is expected to rise from the recent level of 25 percent, and the Egyptian government estimates the cost of providing new jobs at nearly $5 billion. The Libyan leader, Colonel Qadhafi, has invited 150,000 Egyptian peasant farmers and their families to settle in Libya to work on a public works project; this may ease unemployment somewhat.

The UNDP reports that Egypt's food import dependency between 1984 and

Human Effects of the Gulf Crisis: Jordan

	Before the crisis	After the crisis
Population (millions)	3.25	3.45
Unemployment (%)	15	20
Families below poverty line (%)	20	24
Inflation (%)	14.0	16.1
Drinking water (million cubic mt)	170	182

Source: UNDP,"Direct and Indirect Impact of the Gulf Crisis on Jordan," April 1991.

1986 was 47 percent; however, the country's wheat consumption is among the highest in the world, and two-thirds of the grain that is consumed is imported at the cost of $1.2 billion a year. Due to the 1990 record wheat harvest of 4.2 million tons, the Food and Agriculture Organization (FAO) estimates imports of wheat and wheat flour in 1990-1991 to be lower. However, Egypt's total agricultural imports in 1991 are expected to rise.

The UNDP characterizes Egypt as "miserable" in terms of economic and social conditions. The economy is stagnant. Child labor is increasing as families struggle to survive amidst rising costs of living. Price increases for meat and other basic foods have caused the quality of diets to deteriorate. In addition, the lack of public services has resulted in widespread health problems, especially among women and children.

Iran

It is ironic that after fighting an eight-year war with Iraq, Iran should be the largest provider of asylum to Kurdish and Shiite refugees fleeing Iraq. Since the beginning of the Gulf crisis, Iran maintained an "open door" policy towards Iraqis; 1.2 million Kurdish and Shiite refugees are reported to have found asylum in Iran. By June 1991, the total refugee population (consisting mostly of Afghans and Iraqis) was nearly 4 million.

Despite its weakened economy, Iran committed $60 million as aid for the arriving refugees in spring 1991; but the flow of refugees overwhelmed the country. In July 1991, 500,000 additional refugees were waiting to enter Iran and up to 1,000 daily deaths were reported among them.

Iran established fourteen camps in the northwestern province of Bakhtaran for approximately 450,000 Iraqi refugees. Most refugees have been provided blankets, high protein food, and other relief items; however, only one-third of the refugee population in some camps have access to shelter. To alleviate this situation, 50,000 tents were set up.

Jigran camp, located a short distance inside Iran, consists of makeshift tents that shelter 150,000 people. Sanitation is poor, since the only available water is from polluted streams. The incidence of diarrheal disease was increasing among children in June 1991, with long lines forming outside the camp's small tent hospital. "The situation here is a time-bomb, and it will explode very soon if nothing is done," said Daniel Mora-Castro, the water and sanitation specialist of the United Nations High Commissioner for Refugees (UNHCR).[16] Epidemics of cholera and typhoid were predicted if a solution to the water crisis was not found during the hot summer of 1991, which caused the narrow streams in the region to dry up. "If we stay here long, we will all die," observed a new arrival to the camp.[17]

By June 1991, efficient and equitable distribution of relief supplies was urgently required, as some camps in Bakhtaran had not received any assistance for forty days. Iranians provided the occupants with bread and potatoes to prevent starvation. The U.N. World Food Program (WFP) calculated that approximately 27,500 metric tons of food, such as wheat flour, rice, and pulses were needed through August 1991. Iran's refugee burden has created major shortages of food, baby formula, and other commodities within the country.

The Iranian government and its citizens, along with UNHCR and the Iranian Red Crescent Society, have borne most of the burden of the refugee crisis. Although Iran appealed to the international community for aid, the response was minimal, and the U.S. response almost nonexistent.

Germany, France, Italy, Japan, the United Arab Emirates, and many other countries gave some aid to Iran. The U.S. Committee for Refugees (USCR) stated in spring 1991, "Iran is the only one of the countries bordering Iraq that has – to date – acted in consistent, admirable, humanitarian fashion."[18]

Jordan

Apart from Iraq and Kuwait, the Gulf crisis has affected Jordan the worst. Prior to the Gulf crisis, Jordan was referred to by UNDP as one of the "comfortable" states in the region. However, Jordan's economy is heavily dependent on the prosperity of its oil-rich neighbors.

The cost of the Gulf war is estimated at $2 billion, 32 percent of Jordan's GNP. In addition, rising inflation rates, unemployment, shortages in housing and water, and an overburdening of the infrastructure have resulted. UNDP reports that 24 percent of families now live below the poverty line, compared to 20 percent before August 1990 (see table, page 148).

In spite of limited resources, the Jordanian government spent $55 million to provide food, shelter, and water for 800,000 refugees transiting through Jordan. The refugee camps near Amman were reported as being clean and well-run during this period. However, the government has thus far been compensated for only 1 percent of the $55 million it spent. Many members of the U.S. Congress want to reduce aid to

Jordan significantly because this long-time U.S. ally leaned toward Iraq, its key trading partner, before and during the Gulf war.

According to ILO, 11.6 percent of the economically active population of Jordan were migrant workers in Iraq and Kuwait, and the loss of remittances from these workers dealt a heavy blow to the economy. The return of 220,000 workers has led to a 10 percent increase in the labor force. UNDP projects that by the end of 1991, almost one-quarter of the working population will be unemployed.[19]

Iraq was a leading importer of Jordanian products. Thus, the U.N.-imposed trade embargo, as well as severed trade links with Saudi Arabia, have devastated the economy. Before the crisis, Jordan's primary market for fruits and vegetables (10 percent of its $1.2 billion in exports in 1989) was the Gulf region. Sanctions caused the loss of 80 percent of this trade. In addition, Jordan's sympathetic stance toward Iraq caused Saudi Arabia to stop importing Jordanian products and to block Jordan's access to the United Arab Emirates and Bahrain. However, the loss of trade was partially offset due to Jordan's tacit agreement to export fresh produce to occupied Kuwait and Iraq. The war further deprived the country of $200 million in aid from Iraq, Kuwait, and Saudi Arabia in the second half of 1990.

Lacking in natural resources, particularly water, energy, and indigenous food, Jordan's food import dependency between 1984 and 1986 was 97 percent, the second highest in the world after the United Arab Emirates.[20] Government austerity measures in connection with an International Monetary Fund (IMF) structural adjustment program have resulted in price increases in basic foods, gasoline, transportation, and other items. Persistent budget deficits have increased pressure to cut food subsidies. A ration consumption card system, started by the Ministry of Supply in 1990, entitled an individual to 1.5 kilos of sugar and 1.5 kilos of rice a month at subsidized prices.

Turkey

Along with Egypt and Jordan, Turkey is one of the "frontline" countries affected by the Gulf war. Although it emerged from the conflict with strengthened links to the western powers, the massive influx of 800,000 Kurdish refugees in the beginning of April 1991 created great economic problems. By May 1991, 415,000 refugees were reported to be living in nine different sites along the Iraq/Turkey border. The Turkish Red Crescent and Turkey's own Kurdish villagers did their best to carry out relief efforts, but could not cope with such a large flood of people. In April 1991, about 1,000 refugees were reported to be dying daily from hunger, disease, and exposure in squalid camps. However, UNHCR-supported voluntary repatriation to the valleys, cities, and villages of northern Iraq gained momentum by the middle of May 1991. The population in camps on the Turkish border declined to a range of 20,000 to 50,000 by the end of June 1991.

Loss of revenue due to the closing of two Iraqi-Turkish pipelines, termination of trade with Iraq, reduced transport revenues, and loss of remittances cost Turkey approximately $5 billion.[21] The United States has provided Turkey with $82 million in aid to help offset the $800 million it incurred in defense costs. The Bush administration has also recommended $700 million in economic and military assistance to Turkey for fiscal year 1992.[22] In addition, because of their active participation in the anti-Iraq coalition, Egypt and Turkey are expected to receive $10 billion between them from the Gulf Crisis Financial Coordination Group, a group of twenty-four countries, including some Gulf States, and the European Community.

Extreme poverty and famine are highly unusual in Turkey. However, poverty exists among farming families with inadequate access to public services, urban unemployed groups, and disabled persons. It is most severe in rural areas and worst in southeastern Anatolia, due to a less favorable agricultural environment and extremely low incomes of sharecroppers and agricultural workers.

Gulf war disruptions, added to rapid growth and the pressure of debt servicing, have exacerbated high rates of inflation, which hit 60 percent in 1990. Popular discontent was expressed over inflation, which averaged 39 percent between 1980 and 1988.

Yemen

In May 1990, the People's Democratic Republic of Yemen (PDRY, or South Yemen) and the Yemen Arab Republic (YAR, or North Yemen) united to form the Republic of Yemen. With the most fertile lands in the Arabian peninsula, North Yemen was once referred to as "Happy Arabia."[23] Unfortunately, today, the vast majority of the population of this country is far from happy, and the Gulf crisis had a punishing impact. Yemen is one of the poorest states in the Gulf region; PDRY and YAR both ranked "low" on UNDP's 1990 Human Development Index (HDI).

The increasing emigration of agricultural workers and farmers to oil-rich Arab countries during the past few years caused a severe labor shortage in the agricultural sector. This led to a rise in production costs, a decline in grain production, a change in the structure of agricultural production, and the abandonment of cultivated land. Recent surveys also indicate that more male workers are leaving poorer subsistence farming areas than wealthier cash crop areas. However, there is no doubt that remittances from emigrant workers alleviated rural poverty in Yemen to some degree. Housing, as well as food consumption and nutrition, have improved among families receiving remittances.

Until August 1990, almost 1 million Yemeni workers enjoyed a privileged status in Saudi Arabia, where they were exempt from two laws that require foreigners to have a Saudi sponsor for a work permit and to have a Saudi partner in any business venture. However, Yemen's neutral stand in the Persian Gulf war caused the Saudi government to revoke these privileges, and approximately 800,000 Yemeni workers were reported to have left Saudi Arabia by November 1990.[24] These return migrants equal approximately 15 percent of Yemen's total labor force. Their return also caused the loss of 1 to 2 billion dollars a year in remittances (20 percent of the country's foreign currency receipts). Yemen is the second most severely affected country after Jordan, and the Gulf war has cost it almost $1 billion, or 10 percent of its GNP.

In response to Yemen's stance in the war, the United States cut aid by over 90 percent, from $41 million in fiscal year 1990 to $2.9 million in fiscal year 1991. This sudden cutback will significantly affect the supply of food and the country's socio-economic development.

According to the Swedish Save the Children Fund (SSCF), prior to the war, 70,000 to 80,000 Yemeni children under the age of five died each year from preventable diseases as a result of low standards of public sanitation and domestic hygiene.[25] Urban projects to increase clean water supplies and allow hygienic disposal of waste, as well as small-scale initiatives in rural areas, have slightly improved conditions in recent years. However, unofficial evidence shows that Yemen's maternal mortality rates are as bad as those of Ethiopia and Bangladesh. "The increase in the number of modern health facilities and physicians serving the country appears to have made little difference to the health status of the population," observes SSCF.[26] The deterioration of the economy due to the Gulf crisis is certain to make conditions worse. ∎

Notes

1. Arkin.
2. *Ibid.*
3. United Nations, Report to the Secretary General on Humanitarian Needs in Kuwait and Iraq.
4. *Washington Post,* June 20, 1991, p. A27.
5. Penny.
6. Pezzullo testimony.
7. *Washington Post,* June 20, 1991, p. A27.
8. Arkin.
9. Reid testimony.
10. Associated Press, "Embargo Has Gone Too Far."
11. Larry Minear, Humanitarianism Under Siege, p. 132.
12. *Washington Post,* July 13, 1991, p. A14.
13. U.N. Mission Report, July 1991.
14. *Washington Post,* April 15, 1991, p. A9.
15. FAO, *Food Crops and Shortages,* June 1991.
16. Marwan.
17. *Ibid.*
18. USCR testimony.
19. UNDP, *Impact of the Gulf Crisis.*
20. UNDP, *Human Development Report 1990.*
21. The Turkish government's preliminary estimate. Source: UNDP, *Impact of the Gulf Crisis.*
22. *The Christian Science Monitor,* March 14, 1991, p. 7.
23. *The Third World Guide,*1991-92.
24. *ODC Policy Focus,* May 1991.
25. *Middle East Economic Digest,* 25 August 1989.
26. *Ibid.*

North America Update

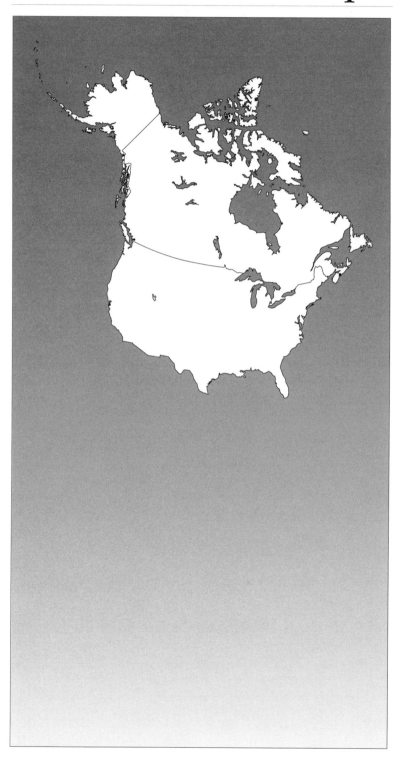

Canada
by Jennifer Kennedy

The United Nations *Human Development Report 1991* ranks Canada as the second best country in the world to live in, based on life expectancy, literacy rates, educational attainment, and other quality of life indicators. The current constitutional debate over the extent of federal responsibility for social programs may result in a decline in this rating. Whatever the outcome, and in spite of a generally excellent system of social services, the rising rate of participation in food banks signals the existence of serious unmet needs.

Politically, Canada is a confederation with a parliamentary system. Historically, there has been an uneasy political truce between the federal government and strong provincial governments. Responsibility for the administration of Canada's extensive network of social programs is divided between federal and provincial governments, with the provinces accepting the primary duties. Many social programs exist, but the Canada Assistance Program (CAP) is the keystone of anti-poverty programs and "the safety net of last resort." Under CAP's cost-sharing agreement, the federal government pays half of all expenditures for setting up and operating provincial programs providing direct financial assistance and subsidized social services for the country's neediest people.

On February 1, 1991, a law scaled back federal transfers of tax revenues for CAP programs in the "wealthier" provinces – British Columbia, Ontario, and Alberta, which have nearly 50 percent of all welfare recipients. The law limited CAP increases to 5 percent per year for the next two years, despite an estimated 14 percent annual rise in social spending. Provincial estimates predict losses of at least C$865 million for the two fiscal years (C$1.11 Canadian = U.S.$1). The cut is supposed to reduce the nation's C$30 billion budget deficit, but is seen by some as whittling away the federal commitment to social well-being. Critics say the real reason for the cuts is not the deficit, but the administration's policy of decreasing federal involvement in social programs. The British Columbia Court of Appeals overturned the law, delaying its implementation, but the federal government has appealed the decision to the Supreme Court of Canada.

This federal withdrawal could have negative effects on public services nationwide. Canada's much lauded health and welfare system has been based on the concept of "cooperative federalism," with federal, provincial, and sometimes municipal governments working in concert to provide vital services. The federal government sets standards of reasonable accessibility and quality of services, but provinces determine program particulars according to widely varying regional needs. The 1990-1991 estimate of CAP's total cost for all levels of government is C$12 billion, of which C$5.9 billion is federal – less than 4 percent of the total C$153 billion federal budget. Canada's social programs delivered C$54 billion in direct financial benefits to Canadians in 1986-1987. Without the efforts of the three levels of government, poverty and hunger would be more widespread and severe.

Canada has no official poverty line, although various government and non-governmental agencies have set poverty indicators. Statistics Canada, the government demographic agency, publishes annual Low Income Cut-offs – income levels by family size and differing degrees of urbanization that function as poverty lines.

In general, these lines are much higher than the official U.S. poverty line, making Canadian poverty estimates relatively higher. However, when Statistics Canada gathers the data, it excludes residents of the Yukon and Northwest Territories, native peoples living on reserves, and inmates of correctional and mental institutions. This omission is important because these groups are among those most vulnerable to poverty and hunger.

The Canadian Council on Social Development calculates that in 1975, a minimum wage worker with two dependents living in a large unspecified city would have needed to work fifty hours a week year-round to earn the applicable low income cut-off. By 1986, the real value of the minimum wage declined so that the same worker would have had to work eighty-seven hours a week to maintain the same living standard. Even if two parents had worked forty hours a week at minimum wage, their combined yearly income would fall C$1,370 short of the low-income cut-off.

With government cutbacks and the 1982-1983 and 1990-1991 recessions, demands on private charities have increased. Organizations such as the Salvation Army have a long history of charitable work, but the first official food bank was founded in Edmonton, Alberta, only in 1981. The Canadian Association of Food Banks began an annual survey of its member banks, *HungerCount,* in 1989. Though not comprehensive, *HungerCount* surveyed food banks in sixty-five cities and towns, and determined that 1.85 million people used food banks an average of 3.5 times during 1990. This was higher than the 1989 figure, 1.4 million people. *HungerCount* 1990 also estimates that 2.1 million of the total population of 26 million people will need food

Education Levels of Toronto Food Bank Recipients

	1987	1991
Eighth grade or less	33%	16%
Some high school	54%	44%
High school graduates	5%	22%
Some vocational school/university	4%	9%
Graduate vocational school/university	4%	9%

assistance in 1991. The association states:

"Hunger and food bank use are not synonymous. Most people who use food programs would otherwise have gone hungry, but not all hungry people can or choose to go to food banks."

These and other limitations of the survey, says the association, emphasize the conservative nature of its figures.

Statistics for 1991 from a Toronto food bank describe the demography of hunger in Canada's largest city. Sixty-five percent of the recipients lived in Toronto five years or more; a majority, more than ten years. Only 14 percent had arrived within the year. Eighty-five percent were Canadian citizens or permanent immigrants (see table, above).

These statistics suggest that the recession is affecting groups once thought invulnerable to poverty and hunger. Education and long-term residence are no longer guarantees against economic difficulty, debunking myths about food bank recipients. As the Daily Bread Food Bank reports, "while set apart by their immediate circumstances, food bank clients have become markedly [closer] in backgrounds to those of the public at large."

In comparison with most countries, hunger is minimal in Canada. However, the recent proliferation of food banks and the changing faces of those who use their services are disturbing. Food banks can provide only immediate relief, not lasting policy solutions. In the current atmosphere of diminished government spending, food banks may be unwittingly incorporated into the public safety net. If this happened, federal and provincial responsibility for hungry people might be reduced further, and deeper issues of policy direction ignored. Such a scenario could result in increased economic vulnerability and lengthening breadlines.

Canada has shown a greater commitment to public policy, rather than private solutions to hunger, poverty, and health care than the United States. Canada's military expenditures are almost 70 percent less per person than the United States. These two factors alone reflect a basic difference in the way each nation sees itself and thus in quality of life indicators (table, page 155). ■

Native Peoples in the United States and Canada

by Jennifer Kennedy

"Native American" and "Native Canadian" describe a diverse group of people. They are discussed together in this section because tribal areas and histories do not recognize borders set by French, English, and Spanish speaking colonists, and because Native peoples share a common history of broken treaties and government neglect.

The United States has three main ethnic groups of Native people – America Indian, Eskimo, and Aleut – comprising 505 tribes. The 1990 census counts 1,959,234 Native persons (0.8 percent of the U.S. population).

The federal agency for Native programs in Canada, the Department of Indian Affairs and Northern Development (DIAND), recognizes 596 tribes, ten linguistic groupings, and six major cultural types. In the 1986 census, 711,725 (3 percent) of Canadians reported at least one Native ancestor. The Indian population in 1990 was 466,337, of whom 260,337 lived on reserves.

Considerable underreporting of native-related statistics is likely in both countries because of uncertainty about racial classification among public and private agencies (social workers, medical doctors, coroners, et al.) and among Natives themselves. "Indianness" is difficult to define due to the complex interaction of racial, ethnic, and cultural factors.

In Canada, "tribes" are sometimes called "bands," and Native peoples are sometimes referred to as aboriginal peoples. However, native Canadians prefer the title "First Nations citizens." "Registered" or "status" tribal members, i.e., persons recognized by the government because they are members of

Public Policy vs. Private Voluntary Solutions to Hunger

	Canada	United States
1990 Life expectancy (yrs.)	77	75.9
1989 Infant mortality rate*	7	10
1980-1988 Maternal mortality rate**	3	8
1980-1988 Infants with low birthweight	6%	7%
1984-1986 Per capita calorie supply as % of daily requirements	129	138
1990 Adult literacy rate	99%	99%
1989 Education expend. % of cent. gov. exp.	2.9	1.8
1989 Health expend. as % of cent. gov. exp.	5.5	12.9
1989 Mil. expend. as % of cent. gov. exp.	7.3	24.6
Gross national product (US$) per capita	$19,030	20,910
1988 Military expend., as % of GNP	2.1	6.3
1988 Mil. expend., US$ per capita	$384	1,250

* per 1.000 live births

** per 100,000 live births

tribes with established treaties with the Canadian government, are eligible for federal programs for Native people. The Métis, of mixed aboriginal and French ancestry, and Inuit, formerly called Eskimos, do not qualify for such programs because they are not "registered." The designation of status is arbitrary, as some tribes without treaties have been recognized under the powerful Indian Act, the broad legislative mandate defining federal powers and responsibilities. However, all groups qualify for national health care and other government benefits available to the general populace of Canada.

The federal governments of both countries determine which groups qualify for assistance, as well as the limits upon sovereignty of the tribes/bands. Tribes in the United States "are acknowledged to possess certain governmental powers, but are neither States nor foreign powers – rather they lie somewhere between the two." The nature of sovereignty has been a major political problem in Canada as well, e.g, the armed standoff between Mohawks and the Canadian government in Oka, Québec in September 1990. The ambiguities of sovereignty confuse questions about who is responsible for collecting information and responding to poverty and hunger.

In 1988, the United States Bureau of Indian Affairs (BIA) estimated that 864,500 Native persons lived on or adjacent to reservations. Neither the BIA nor the DIAND have accurate records of the number and condition of Native persons living in urban areas, now one of the fastest growing Native groups. The U.S. Indian Health Service only records data about Native persons on or adjacent to reservations. DIAND's reports focus primarily on status Indians.

There are few statistics on Native hunger per se in either country, and the official data about poverty, welfare assistance, and health care are mainly based on census findings and hospital admissions. Oftentimes these data are dependent on government definitions and timetables, not accounting for situations unique to Natives. Some records exist only at the tribal level, with no standardized systems for data collection. However, enough information exists to paint a picture of desperation.

Some inferences can be made from health and quality of life indicators. In 1981, life expectancy at birth for Native Americans was 71.1 years, 3.3 years less than for U.S. whites. In 1991, life expectancy for status Indians in Canada was approximately eight years less than the national average. In the United States, the infant mortality rate for American Indians and Native Alaskans was 9.8 per 1,000 live births in 1985-1987, compared to the rate of 10.4 per 1,000 for all races in 1986. In Canada in 1986, status Indians had an infant mortality rate of 17.2 per 1,000 live births; the Inuit rate was 28.2 in the Northwest Territory; this compares to the overall figure of 7.9. In the United States in 1987, 2.5 per 100,000 Native Americans died of tuberculosis, five times the rate of all races. Diabetes mellitus was the cause of death for 23.4 per 100,000 Indians, as compared to the overall 9.8 rate.

According to the 1986 Canadian census, 37.2 percent of status Indians fifteen years of age and over had less than a ninth grade education, over twice the overall rate. The proportion is even higher for Inuits, 53 percent. Forty-five percent of First Nations citizens living on reserves were functionally illiterate. First Nations citizens living off-reserve had a 17 percent unemployment rate ("not working and looking for a job"), two-and-a-half times the Canadian national average of 7 percent. Incomes of First Nations citizens average half those of the general population. In the United States, 55.8 percent of Native Americans graduated from high school and 7.7 percent graduated from college in 1980. Thirteen percent of the civilian labor force sixteen years and older was unemployed. And 27.5 percent of all Native Americans had incomes below the 1979 poverty line.

Although fragmentary, data released at a U.S. congressional committee hearing, "Standing Rock Reservation: A Case Study of Food Security Among Native Americans," illustrates the conditions leading to Native hunger. The Standing Rock Sioux Reservation, located in both North and South Dakota, is home to 10,300 Lakota (see table, page 157).

Two U.S. federal food programs most commonly used by Native Americans are the Food Stamp Program and the Food

Distribution Program on Indian Reservations (FDPIR). FDPIR is administered by state agencies or tribal governments to eligible Indian and non-Indian reservation households and Indian households near reservations. An alternative and predecessor to food stamps, FDPIR provides foods like canned meats and fruits in a monthly package weighing about fifty to seventy-five pounds. In 1988, FDPIR distributed 100 million pounds of food valued at $49 million to 135,000 participants per month, with an average monthly value of $29 per person. In 1990, the average monthly participation was 143,000, with the monthly food package valued at $38.17.

A 1989 U.S. General Accounting Office study of federal food assistance programs on four reservations found widespread poor nutrition and diet-related health problems – obesity, diabetes, heart disease, and hypertension – despite a 30 to 90 percent participation rate in the programs. The report concluded that the government programs were not designed for the specific dietary needs of Native Americans. Ironically, dependence on federal programs has robbed Native Americans of their richest source of nutrition – their traditional foods

Food Security Among Native Americans	U.S.	Standing Rock
Percentage living in poverty	13.1	90.0*
Percentage unemployment	5.5	87.0*
Percentage low birth weight	6.9 ('87)	6.3
Percentage graduate from high school	66.5	50.8
Infant mortality per 1,000	9.8	19.7

*estimated
Figures are from 1988-1989 unless otherwise noted.

and food preparation methods.

In the midst of the confusion introduced by differing government and tribal institutions, social programs, and statistical categories, poverty, hunger, and malnutrition remain major problems for Native peoples in the United States and Canada. Insufficient official data, extensive government bureaucracy, and the weak political voice allowed Native peoples to contribute to the lack of full knowledge about hunger. Five hundred years after their ancestors greeted Columbus, much about the conditions of Native peoples remains to be known, let alone addressed. ■

United States
by Richard A. Hoehn

Hunger Increases

Poverty and hunger increased in the United States in 1990 and 1991. The U.S. Conference of Mayors reported that 1990 emergency food requests were up 22 percent and shelter requests up 24 percent over 1989. The Salvation Army said that donations increased 8 percent, while requests for aid increased 20 percent in 1990.[1]

A New Orleans study of the nutritional status of homeless people concluded, "77.4 percent of the adult homeless in New Orleans are suffering from [protein-energy] malnutrition." When asked why they missed meals, 54 percent of the homeless people answered, "no money."[2] A federal survey concluded that the median monthly cash income of single homeless people was $64, and that 18 percent went without eating for two-day stretches once a week.[3]

A Food Research and Action Center (FRAC) survey found that 92 percent of families who experience hunger reported running out of food money an average of six days out of the previous thirty.[4] FRAC also reported that those households which go to food pantries for help average $186 gross income per person per month.

In July 1991, the American Public Welfare Association reported an 18 percent increase in Aid to Families with Dependent Children (AFDC) recipients over the previous twelve months. An additional 3,000 children per day were added to the AFDC program over the previous six months. "More than three million persons have been added to the Food Stamp Program in just the last year." More than 23 million Americans were on food stamps in April 1991.[5]

Food and shelter assistance are particularly helpful since, by FRAC's estimate, the poorest households spent three times as much of their income on shelter as the average American family. And, "families with incomes below the poverty level spent, on average, 60 percent of their post-shelter income on food." Expressed in real dollars, their food expenditure was $277 per month, or 68 cents per person per meal.

The poverty rate for individuals in the United States was 22 percent in the 1950s, 12.1 percent in 1969, a low of 11.1 percent in 1973, and 12.8 percent (31.5 million people) in 1989. Eleven percent of the aged were poor in 1989, and 20 percent of children. The disparity between relatively high federal funding for the aged and relatively low for children invited comparisons which cast one deserving group in the society against the other.

The 1989 poverty rate for whites was 10 percent, for blacks 30.7 percent, and for persons of Hispanic origin 26.2 percent. FRAC's study indicated that 76 percent of hungry households are nonwhite.

Kids Can't Wait While Adults Debate[6]

A divorced 24-year-old mother couldn't find day care for her 5-year-old daughter while she worked a second job as a department store sales clerk. The mother drove to the shopping mall and left the girl in her car, clad in pajamas and comforted by a stuffed animal, a flashlight and a doughnut.[7]

Children are the largest single group (12.6 million in 1989) of poor people in the nation. Descriptions of hunger are first and foremost descriptions of the situation of children. FRAC reported in early 1991 that an estimated 5.5 million children under age twelve (one out of every eight) are hungry in the United States, and an additional six million children are at risk of hunger due to family food shortages.

About one in five children under age eighteen lives in poverty. Under age six the rate is almost one in four. Roughly 15 percent of white, 36 percent of Hispanic, and 44 percent of African-American children live in poverty. Fifty-five percent of all children in female-headed households live in poverty. For black female-headed households the figure is 67 percent.[8] Estimates of the number of homeless children in the late 1980s ranged from 35,000 to 500,000. (See table, page 159.)

Children who live in poverty are likely to suffer from health problems, with the danger that some conditions will become chronic. The National Center for Children in Poverty says:

Poor children are more likely than nonpoor children to be born too soon or too small; to die in the first year of life or during early childhood; to experience acute illnesses, injuries, lead poisoning, or child abuse or neglect;

and to suffer from nutrition-related problems, chronic illnesses, and handicapping conditions.[10]

Sixteen percent of all children, and 34 percent of poor children under age six had no health insurance coverage in 1986. This figure included 13 percent of white, 21 percent of black, and 30 percent of Hispanic children.

A federal study found that 22 percent of all children and 72 percent of black children born between 1967 to 1969 had been participants in the AFDC program.[11] In the past ten years the average monthly AFDC stipend per recipient dropped from $148 to $131 (in 1990 dollars), less than the $137 received in 1965 or $168 in 1970.[12] If AFDC had kept up with inflation from 1972 to 1990, a mother with two children and no outside income would now receive $7,836 rather than the present $4,801. "The sharp decline in AFDC benefits has contributed to the rise in the child poverty rate from 15.1 percent in 1972 to 19.6 percent in 1989," the study said.[13] Whereas "in 1979 government cash benefits lifted 20 percent of all poor children out of poverty," because of cuts and the declining value of benefits, those programs now lift out 10 percent.[14]

The actual number of poor people and those eligible for public programs is higher than is reflected in the number receiving Food Stamps or AFDC. FRAC's study found that 37 percent of the eligible families surveyed were not receiving food stamps. The reasons the families most often gave were that they did not know they were eligible or were embarrassed to use food stamps. Many of the eligible families surveyed were found to be hungry or at risk of hunger.

One program that has removed 239,000 families from AFDC because of increased income (though the effect on total benefit income is unclear) is the Child Support

America's Children[9]	
Percent of poor children who in 1989 were	
White, non-Hispanic	41%
Black, non-Hispanic	35%
Hispanic	21%
Asian or Pacific Islander	3%
Rural	26%
Suburban	29%
Central city	46%

Enforcement program. Every $1 spent ($1.6 billion in 1990) led to the collection of $3.76 ($6.0 billion). The program helped locate more than 2 million absent parents and establish almost 400,000 paternities. When parental income is increased, families are able to provide better nutrition.

Of the 9.4 million women under age 21 who had children from an absent father in 1987,[15] "3.2 million (34 percent) had incomes below the poverty level. Of these women only 39 percent (1,231,000) had agreements to receive child support and were due payments in 1987," and within that group 28 percent did not receive payments even though they were supposed to. White mothers (69 percent) were more likely to be awarded child support payments than black (36 percent) or Hispanic mothers (42 percent). Women with some college background, and women over thirty were more likely to be awarded support than women who had not completed high school. Child support arrangements mirror other race and status distinctions in society.

The early 1990s are likely to see a rising wave of concern for children and families, providing a popular base for policy changes. In the fall of 1990, more than seventy heads of state and representatives of 150 countries met at the United Nations World Summit for Children. They set goals

U.S. Median Income, 1989

	Males	Females	Families
Black	$12,609	$7,875	$20,209
White	$20,863	$9,812	$35,975
Ratio B/W	.604	.803	.562

to reduce the world-wide infant mortality rate substantially, and to provide access to education and safe drinking water for every child.

The following spring, members of Congress sent a letter to President Bush urging him to sign the 1989 U.N. Convention on the Rights of the Child. They pointed out that the United States is among a small group of nonsigners that includes Ethiopia, Iran, Iraq, Libya, and South Africa. One hundred thirty-five heads of state have signed the Convention, which took a decade to draft.

In the United States, one sign of increased concern is the proposed federal consolidation of $27 billion in children's programs into a single agency, the Administration for Children and Families, which would link the AFDC program with many social services, including child abuse prevention and early childhood learning.

Another sign is the numerous bills with significant child-related provisions introduced into the 102nd Congress, e.g., The Working Family Tax Relief Act of 1991 to reduce taxes for families with children, the Freedom from Want Act, and the World Summit for Children Implementation Act. Proposals include expanding employment opportunities, full funding for the Special Supplemental Food Program for Women, Infants, and Children (WIC), reforms in the Food Stamp Program, and funding increases for food stamps and school nutrition programs.

As FRAC says, "Hunger hurts everybody. As a society we cannot afford millions of hungry kids, their illness or their illiteracy."

Unemployment and Poverty

The 1990-1991 recession contributed to increases in hunger through rising unemployment and declining incomes. Fifty-five thousand businesses went bankrupt in 1990. Productivity declined 0.7 percent in 1989 and 0.8 percent in 1990. Unemployment rose from 5.3 percent in January to 6.1 in December, and averaged 5.5 percent (white 4.7 percent; black 11.3 percent) for the year. It hovered around 7 percent in the summer of 1991, with some analysts predicting a high of eight percent before making a turnaround.

A federal study of unemployed persons determined that approximately 48 percent were "job losers," 15 percent were "job leavers," 27 percent were re-entering the job market, and 10 percent were new entrants to the job market. The lowest unemployment rates were in Nebraska (2.2 percent), Hawaii (2.8 percent), and South Dakota (3.7 percent). The highest rates were in Puerto Rico (14.2 percent), West Virginia (8.3 percent), and both Michigan and Mississippi at 7.5 percent.

Thirty seven percent of unemployed persons received unemployment insurance benefits in 1990, compared with 81 percent in April 1975. The reasons for this surprisingly small percent are multiple. Roughly 12 percent of employed persons are not covered by unemployment insurance. To qualify, a person must have worked for a specific period of time for a state-specified amount of wages. In Hawaii, a person could qualify for the minimum weekly unemployment benefit of $5 if he/she had earned $150 in a recent "base year," whereas to qualify for the minimum benefit of $16 per week in Oklahoma required a base year income of $3,640. Twenty-two percent of the 17.3 million "monetarily eligible" (people who had earned enough to qualify for unemployment insurance) in 1990 were disqualified for other reasons, e.g. for voluntarily leaving a job without a good cause. Some people were counted as non-recipients because between the time they applied and the benefits began, they found another job.

The maximum weekly benefit ranged from $96 in Indiana to $423 in Massachusetts. Payments extend for a maximum of twenty-six weeks in all states except Washington and Massachusetts (30

weeks). In 1990, 2.3 million individuals exhausted their unemployment benefits. One million Americans lost their jobs between June 1990 and February 1991.[16] More than one and a half million persons used up their unemployment benefits in the first half of 1991. Congress hastily passed legislation to extend benefits beyond the normal cutoff, but President Bush vowed to veto the bill. Though the recession gave some signs of bottoming out in the summer of 1991, large numbers of people continued to be laid off and to use up their benefits. High unemployment is predicted for another year or two even in the event of an economic upturn.

Most workers eventually find new jobs. Seventy-eight percent of the people who reported job losses in 1988 were employed in January 1990. Twelve percent had dropped out of the workforce. Women and workers of both genders who had held long-tenure jobs were less likely than others to find work. Workers over age fifty-five and those who had not completed high school were much less likely than others to find work. However, 29 percent of those displaced in 1988 but working in January 1990 were earning one-fifth less in their new jobs. This drop is partly attributable to people losing long-held, higher paying jobs and then starting over in lower wage jobs.

> *The worst off among the unemployment insurance recipients who had not returned to work were the approximately 40 percent who had no other earners in their families. Two of every three families were poor. Overall, this group had an average family income of about $500 per month – only about one-third of its previous level. Social Security benefits and pensions accounted for one-half this group's average income.*[17]

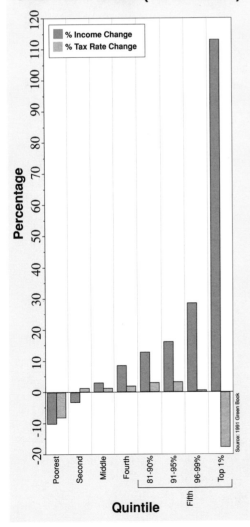

Changes in Family Income and Tax Rates (1977-1992)

Legend:
- % Income Change
- % Tax Rate Change

Y-axis: Percentage (-20 to 120)

X-axis (Quintile): Poorest, Second, Middle, Fourth, 81-90%, 91-95%, 96-99%, Top 1% (Fifth)

Source: 1991 Green Book

National wage averages tend to obscure differences among sub-groups within a society. While the percent of males in prime earning years who earned near-poverty level wages rose between 1973 and 1987, the rise for white males was from 8 to 13 percent, for black males 25 to 30 percent, and for Hispanic males from 20 to 34 percent. The percent of low-earners ($12,000 a year, roughly the poverty level for a family of four) was higher not only among persons who had not completed high school, but also among blacks and Hispanics who were college graduates.

Though the recession enlarged the ranks of hungry people, other long-term factors account for the depth and distribution of hunger and poverty in America. In 1989, the serious gaps in income between males and females, and between blacks and whites, reflected long-term patterns of employment discrimination.[18] (See table, page 160.)

Interracial conflicts provided further evidence of the remaining prejudices and divisions among people in American society.

Tensions also rose, however slightly, between rich, near-rich, and poor people. Between 1977 and 1992, the rich did become richer and the poor poorer. The U.S. House Committee on Ways and Means says that "on an after-tax money income basis, the United States is the most unequal of the 10 modern nations studied . . . [and] has the highest level of poverty."[19]

Tax policies, instead of redressing the imbalance, contribute to it. The Congressional Budget Office estimates that federal taxes will have increased $13 billion per year for middle-income families between 1977 and 1992, while being lowered $65

Hunger Bytes

by Richard A. Hoehn

Information about conditions which contribute to or help alleviate hunger:

- The Head Start Program, widely accepted as being one of the success stories of the "War on Poverty," costs $3,000 per child per year.

- Every day 100,000 American children are homeless. "Every day, 1,512 children drop out of school."[27]

- U.S. high school dropout rates have declined significantly among blacks and are approximately comparable to those of whites.

- The United States imprisons more black males per capita than South Africa. In Washington, D.C., "nearly four times as many black men were jailed . . . as graduated from its public schools."[28]

- Prison costs more than Harvard. "The average cost for incarcerating a juvenile in America is $29,500 a year.. . . Annual costs for room, board, and tuition at Harvard come to just over $18,000."[29]

- "The 1990 [income tax] exemption of $2,150 [per child] would have to have been $7,781 in order to have the same value it had in 1948."[30]

- Over 90 percent of all food stamp participants are children under eighteen, adults sixty or older, women, and disabled people. The average award is fifty-eight cents per person per meal. Seven out of every ten recipient households have income under $300 a month.

- Forty-seven percent of households receiving food stamps are white, 36 percent are black, and 12 percent are Hispanic.[31]

- The U.S. Senate Committee on the Budget says, "At the start of the 1980s, a CEO made about 29 times as much as the average worker. Today that multiple is close to 100 times."[32]

billion on the richest 1 percent.[20] A person who makes $350,000 contributes 1 percent of income to payroll taxes while the person who earns $20,000 pays 7 percent.[21] (See graph, page 161.)

Some Americans believe that it is inappropriate for the government to play a role in reducing income inequalities. Within that group a smaller segment believe that government, especially at the national level, should also withdraw from providing social services. Many Americans who otherwise believe that government should provide basic services for poor and hungry people are reluctant to pay the taxes that might meet temporary needs and reduce long-term dependency. The distribution of the GNP suggests they had other priorities.

In 1988 the U.S. GNP was $4.9 trillion. Of that amount, $969 billion, approximately 20 percent, went for federal, state, and local purchase of goods and services, including $298 billion for national defense, while $3 trillion or 60 percent went for personal consumption expenditures. "Personal consumption" included $177 billion for meals and beverages consumed outside the home, $433 billion for medical care, $101 billion for new cars, $247 billion for recreation, and $76 billion for religious and welfare activities.

Budget Crunch

Federal and state governments share the costs for the AFDC and Medicaid programs. Escalating human needs (and in the case of Medicaid, the rapidly rising cost of medical care) put heavy pressure on states and localities, which were hit by falling revenues and 1980s federal decisions to turn many federal programs over to states. States received 25 percent of their income

- The Center on Budget and Policy Priorities reported that in 1990, the richest 1 percent of the population had nearly as much income after taxes as the bottom 100 million (40 percent) of Americans.[33]

- Top profits earned among the Fortune 500 in 1990 were: IBM ($6 billion), Exxon ($5 billion), General Electric ($4.3 billion), Philip Morris ($3.5 billion), and DuPont ($2 billion)[34]

- The Employee Benefit Research Institute estimates that 34.4 million people under age 65 are not covered by private or public health insurance. More than half are employed adults. Twenty-nine percent, 10 million, are children.

Thirty percent live below the poverty line. Minority groups are disproportionately represented.

- GAO estimates that the United States would save $67 billion annually if it shifted to a Canadian-style health insurance system. Other analysts estimate savings might be as much as $100 billion.

- In 1990, Americans spent $12 billion at McDonald's and almost $12 billion on 393 million pairs of brand-name athletic shoes.[35]

- The General Accounting Office estimates that in 1988 about 166,000 15-year-olds were working either more hours than legally allowed, or were under the minimum age for their occupation.[36]

- Maryland is depositing welfare payments, child support, and food stamps into a "bank account" that enables participants to use an ATM card for withdrawals or show at grocery stores. The card is expected to cut down on theft, fraud, the stigma attached to welfare, and save $1.2 million annually in administrative costs.[37]

- According to Wendell Berry, "The real work of planet-saving will be small, humble, and humbling, and (insofar as it involves love) pleasing and rewarding. Its jobs will be too many to count, too many to report, too many to be publicly noticed or rewarded, too small to make anyone rich or famous." [38] ■

from federal government sources in the late 1970s. That share dropped to 17 percent by 1990.[22] State spending doubled during the 1980s.[23]

In 1991, states raised $10.3 billion in taxes above 1990, but projected another $6.7 billion would likely be needed for fiscal year (FY) 1992.[24] New York state alone predicted a $6 billion shortfall in FY 1991-1992. Budgets were so tight states could only come up with 65 percent of the money needed to qualify for $800 million in federal matching funds available for welfare reforms. When Bridgeport, Connecticut, became the first city since the Great Depression to file for bankruptcy, officials received a spate of inquiries from other cities looking for a way out of their financial crunch. Their fiscal bind was likely to get worse and made increased state and local taxes a virtual certainty.

The recession also cut into federal tax receipts. In mid-1991, the Bush administration raised the federal budget deficit estimate for FY 1992 (Oct. 1, 1991 to Sept. 30, 1992) an additional $70,000,000,000 to $348,300,000,000, the largest ever. Other causes of the shortfall were failed savings and loans (estimated cost, $76,000,000,000) and the Persian Gulf War. A low estimate of the cost of the war to the United States is $20 billion, not including post-war occupation costs or allies' defaults on burden-sharing pledges; a high estimate, including veterans benefits and interest, is $480 billion, which after burden-sharing would still cost $2,000 per adult American.[25]

There was increasing evidence that the savings and loan crisis might very quickly be followed by a similarly expensive series of bank failures. The war and the savings and loan crisis were considered "off budget," thus exempt from the rules that normally limit federal spending. Whether on or off budget, the bills have to be paid and social programs and services are likely to suffer.

A *New York Times* headline commenting on the source of the recession said: "It Isn't Just a Downturn, It's the Bill for the 1980s."[26] Programs that could have alleviated social problems and built a stronger economy were cut in the early 1980s, resulting in preventable suffering and sometimes higher costs later. For example, little help was provided to the half-million people released from mental hospitals as part of deinstitutionalization. Instead of becoming self-supporting, many are worse off now than when they were released.

During the 1980s, the national debt rose from $1 trillion to $2.5 trillion, much of it for a massive military build-up. The U.S. Senate Committee on the Budget estimates that net interest paid on the deficit from 1991 to 1996 will be more than $1,000,000,000,000 ($1 trillion), which puts pressure on legislators to neglect human service programs.

Meanwhile, costs are not likely to decline. The General Accounting Office estimated that while health care costs consumed one sixteenth of the GNP in 1965, by the year 2000 they will consume one sixth, or $1.6 trillion. As private insurance plans become more and more costly, there is likely to be a wave of public sentiment urging the federal government to assume a greater role in paying for health care. In 1991, it appeared that the major domestic issues for the next few years would be demilitarization, health care, and the well-being of children and families.

Gains in Nutrition

Hunger 1990 emphasized the need for a system of nutrition monitoring in the United States. After ten years of persistent lobbying by hunger activists and nutritionists, the 101st Congress (1990) passed a nutrition monitoring bill. The bill establishes a National Nutrition Monitoring Advisory Council and provides for the development of a ten-year nutrition monitoring research program and publication of a report, "Dietary Guidelines for Americans," which should begin to clarify expected national standards for good nutrition.

Consumers already notice the results of a nutrition labeling law. The Food and Drug Administration is developing and enforcing guidelines for food product labeling: disclosure of fat, salt, and caloric content of foods; and defining terms like "light" and "low-fat." While nutritional issues are matters of concern to all income levels in society, Congress and the administration are likely to be more responsive to the voices of middle- and upper-class Americans, who will push for further legislation regulating nutritional content and labeling. ∎

Notes

1. Community Nutrition Institute, p. 1.
2. Bread for the World, pp. 5, 11.
3. U.S. House, *1991 Green Book*, p. 1071.
4. FRAC, p. 15.
5. APWA, p. 1.
6. Williams, p. C5.
7. FRAC, p. xv.
8. Williams, p. C5.
9. Taylor, "Children" p. A7.
10. Klerman, p. 3.
11. Rich, "The Many."
12. Broder, p. D7.
13. Rich, "Inflation's Bite," quoting Issac Shapiro of the Center on Budget and Policy Priorities, p. A17.
14. Taylor, "Children," citing CDF, "Child Poverty in America," and "Youth Indicators" published by the U.S. Department of Education, p. A7.
15. *Green Book 1991*, p. 668.
16. Pianin, p. A6.
17. *Green Book 1991*, p. 516.
18. Dewart, pp. 32, 35.
19. *Green Book 1991*, p. 1152.
20. Citizen's Budget Campaign.
21. U.S. Congress, "President Bush's," p. 16.
22. Hinds and Eckhholm, p. 1.
23. Postrel, p. C3.
24. Dionne, p. A8.
25. Estes, p. 2.
26. Silk, p. E5.
27. U.S. Congress, Senate, "President Bush's," pp. 26, 29.
28. "America's Blacks," p. 17.
29. Raspberry, p. A11.
30. Taylor, "Saving," pp. D1-2.
31. FRAC, 1990 cited in "Food Stamp Fraud," p. 13.
32. U.S. Senate, "President Bush's," p. 15.
33. Shapiro and Greenstein, p. 5.
34. *Fortune*, p. 286.
35. McDonald's, p. 1 and Brubaker, p. 1.
36. Frazier, "Summary."
37. Spayd, p. A1.
38. Berry, p. 63.

Soviet Union and Eastern Europe Update

by Remy Jurenas

While the Soviet Union struggles with its political and economic future, the Eastern European countries have started to introduce free market principles and practices into their deep-rooted, centrally planned economies. This difficult transition will most affect poor people, especially retirees and large families with children. With limited resources, governments are trying to cushion the impact of substantial price increases, especially of food, on these more vulnerable groups by expanding or creating new social programs.

Overview

The gradual and uncertain pace of economic reform in the Soviet Union, combined with continued tension between the central Soviet government and the republics, is expected to contribute to a dramatic fall in economic output and living standards in 1991. The deteriorating economy will hit poor people – estimated at 80 million in early 1991 (more than one quarter of the population) – the hardest. Both the central government and the republic governments plan to cushion some of the impact of substantial food price increases which went into effect in April 1991. However, the prospect of accompanying inflation, combined with continued shortages, is expected to result in a decline in living standards, which would weigh most heavily upon poor people.

The momentous political changes in Eastern Europe since late 1989 have enabled most popularly elected governments to dismantle state control over the economy and introduce some market-oriented policies intended to spur economic growth. The pace of these changes has varied from country to country, depending upon the political skills of newly elected leaders to introduce radical new policies and the ability of the entrenched old guard to oppose and subvert policy changes that directly challenge their power base. The pace has also been affected by people's concerns about the effects these reforms could have on their living standards, and by the success these new governments have in securing foreign aid and investment to assist the economic transition.

The Communist-controlled governments installed in Eastern Europe after World War II succeeded in collectivizing agriculture in all countries but Poland and Yugoslavia, where private farms remained important to total production. Collectivization followed the Soviet experience of the 1930s, where private farmers and their land were forced into larger production units.

Communist ideology, which emphasized that all productive assets belong to all people, viewed the large state and collective or cooperative farms as a way to grant a stake to landless peasants, boost agricultural output, and generate profits to help develop each country's industrial base. In theory, all the members of a collective or cooperative own its land, animals, buildings, and equipment and are responsible for its maintenance and development. By contrast, state farm workers are paid a set wage but have no ownership stake in its operation.

Centrally planned agriculture initially required each farm to sell all of its agricultural output at state-set prices to designated purchasing agents. These "procurement" agencies distributed purchased commodities to food processing plants. Then, government-owned and -operated enterprises distributed and sold food products to consumers at set prices. Private farms, where allowed, were permitted to sell to purchasing agencies at set prices or directly to consumers for whatever price they could get. Later, in Hungary, Yugoslavia, and the Soviet Union, collective and state farms were also permitted to sell a portion of their output in private markets.

Over time, agricultural output on these farms began to lag behind population growth, prompting planners to allocate more funds for new machinery and other inputs to boost productivity. As governments increased farm subsidies to cover rising production costs, they also raised consumer subsidies to keep state store food prices at levels people were used to paying.

In some countries, farm and food subsidies began to represent a large portion of the national budget. Even with subsidies, consumers in the mid-1980s spent, on average, from almost one-third to one-half of their income on food and beverages. With food costs accounting for such a sizable portion of household expenses – even more for poorer households – most Communist governments kept consumer prices low to stave off political unrest. They feared a repeat of past protests sparked by food price increases. For this reason, public reaction to price increases in Eastern Europe and the Soviet Union will be an indicator of their governments' success in introducing broad but painful economic reforms.

For the most part, the Eastern European countries and the Soviet Union have increased food production to meet their populations' needs. The quantity of food available usually has been sufficient to meet most consumer demand. Per capita food production levels increased so that, by the late 1980s, food supplies per person (measured in terms of calorie intake) in all countries in this region (except Albania) were comparable to those found in developed nations. To boost protein availability, these countries imported feed grains and oilseeds

. . . [P]ublic reaction to price increases in Eastern Europe and the Soviet Union will be an indicator of their governments' success in introducing broad but painful economic reforms.

Food shortages in state retail stores occurred because of a breakdown in trading between Soviet farms and input suppliers, and the inability of other firms in the food chain to transport, process, distribute, and market food products in an efficient and timely manner.

to help increase the output of meat and dairy products.

Agriculture and food are important components in the economies of all these countries. These sectors employ a sizable portion of the labor force – levels much higher than those found in many Western countries. Because of their productivity, three Eastern European countries (Bulgaria, Hungary, Romania) have also been net exporters of agricultural products.

The recent disintegration of centrally administered food production, processing, and marketing contributed to serious food shortages during the winter of 1990-1991 in the Soviet Union, Albania, Bulgaria, and Romania. Another year of drought contributed to the short food supplies reported in the latter three countries. Ironically, the USSR experienced food shortages even with its 1990 bumper grain crop. All four countries were forced to introduce rationing of selected foods. To improve food supplies, these countries, with limited hard currency, have sought to increase food imports by securing credits from Western exporting countries and/or have received food and feed aid.

Implementation of further economic reforms in this region will depend much upon the willingness of people to put up with falling incomes in the interim. Critical to keeping workers and farmers employed, and to generating the financial resources to rebuild these economies, will be whether the Eastern European countries succeed in opening up markets primarily in Western Europe for some competitively priced products. For the Soviet Union, resolution of political differences between the center and the republics will dictate the direction of reforms and their impact. While the populace, particularly poor people, will experience difficulties during the transition to more market-oriented economies, their

patience could wear thin if promises made do not result in an improvement in their living standards within a few years.

Soviet Union

The food shortages that appeared in the Soviet Union in late 1990 were not due to any dramatic shortfall in production or collapse of the agricultural infrastructure, but rather reflected evidence of the disintegrating Soviet economy. Food shortages in state retail stores occurred because of a breakdown in trading between Soviet farms and input suppliers, and the inability of other firms in the food chain to transport, process, distribute, and market food products in an efficient and timely manner. Differences between the central Soviet government and the republics over the country's political and economic future also affected the flow of food across internal borders. Lack of progress in addressing these fundamental issues could lead to a food supply situation that gets worse before improving.

Soviet agriculture (24 percent of GNP and employing just over one-fifth of the labor force) is organized into state and collective farms. Since the 1930s, central planners have subjected these farms to meeting output targets. This socialized sector held almost 99 percent of the farmland, and accounted for 75 percent of agricultural production from 1986 to 1990. Private plots, tended by state farm workers and members of collectives, took 1.5 percent of the land, but accounted for 24 percent of output during the same period. In 1989, these small plots accounted for at least half the country's production of fruits, berries, and potatoes, and more than a quarter of its vegetables, meat products, and milk.

Despite substantial investments over the years to improve productivity on socialized farms, Soviet agriculture faces numerous problems. These include the virtual disappearance of personal initiative among farm workers, the lack of financial incentives, poor infrastructure (particularly in the road transportation network), limited access to quality inputs, and the continuing need to subsidize unprofitable farms.

Though the Soviet Union is one of the world's main producers of grain, meat, milk, potatoes, and fish, substantial losses occur as food is processed, distributed, and marketed. The Soviets estimate that 20 percent of each year's grain production is lost or spoiled as a result of poor harvesting, drying, transportation, and storage. Officials acknowledge that in order to meet the needs of its population, the USSR must import grains at a level roughly equivalent to these losses. Also, slow processing causes a considerable loss of protein before milk reaches Soviet consumers. Losses of up to 50 percent occur on potatoes and some fruits and vegetables before reaching retail outlets.

The Soviet government has offered various incentives to increase agricultural productivity. Recent changes include raising prices that the state pays farms for grain, offering farmers foreign currency for grain, granting more legitimacy to organizations that support private farmers, and allowing each republic to implement its own land reform and private property laws. Plans call for increased investment in projects that reduce post-harvest food losses, such as boosting the production of food processing equipment in some defense industry facilities converted for this purpose. In addition, the Soviet Union has relied on soybean and soymeal imports to meet protein requirements for livestock production.

Despite the near record grain crop, overall 1990 agricultural production fell 2.3 percent below 1989. Though not a significant drop, other factors explain why food shortages occurred. Farms were increasingly reluctant to sell the production they had pledged to state agencies at low prices and accept rubles that were quickly losing purchasing power. Farms often preferred to deal directly with other enterprises on a barter basis to obtain needed supplies and consumer goods. Food trade declined between republics. Consumers hoarded much of the limited food that appeared on state store shelves. Although scarce supplies (particularly meat and dairy products) sold at low, state-subsidized prices until April 1991, adequate stocks of many food products were usually available in the private markets at much higher prices. For example, by late 1990, the price of meat in private markets was four times higher than in the state shops. Poor people generally could not afford to shop in private markets.

To cope with food shortages, many cities and some republics resorted to rationing. To improve food availability, the central Soviet government increased food imports, assigned the Committee on State Security (KGB) to crack down on corrupt officials and black marketeers, ordered republics and regions to meet all food supply contracts, raised the prices that state agencies paid for commodities, and reinstituted mandatory deliveries by farms to the state. Some Western European countries have targeted food aid shipments toward children and elderly people living on low, fixed pensions, who are vulnerable to short supplies. The level of such aid has been quite small compared to the quantity of food the Soviet Union normally imports.

The near collapse of the Soviet economy (a 10 percent fall in GNP during the first half of 1991 over the previous year) has added to pressure on the central Soviet leadership to introduce economic reforms. The debate over whether to move quickly to introduce market-oriented reforms or to take gradual steps to revitalize the economy

. . . [B]y late 1990, the price of meat in private markets was four times higher than in the state shops.

In the first quarter of 1991 alone, living standards fell as retail prices in both the state stores and private markets increased 124 percent while wages only rose 19 to 26 percent.

using traditional central planning methods has become caught up in the ongoing negotiations between the central government and nine of the fifteen republics over the draft "Union" treaty. Settlement of the remaining political and economic differences will affect the introduction of economic reforms and in turn, the nature and degree of Western nations' response to Soviet requests for aid.

In the first quarter of 1991 alone, living standards fell as retail prices in both the state stores and private markets increased 124 percent while wages only rose 19 to 26 percent. The drop in purchasing power continued through mid-year following the government's decree raising prices, effective April 2, on most food products and consumer items sold by state retail stores. Food price hikes averaging 240 percent were a substantial jump over 1990s 8 percent increase. Even so, prices of food sold in private markets were higher. Some experts express concern that this partial move toward freeing state retail prices and granting wage increases to disaffected workers will not solve fundamental economic problems. They fear that this policy could lead to a spiral of price and wage increases that results in extremely high inflation.

Estimates of the extent of poverty in the Soviet Union in early 1991 range from one quarter of the population (80 million) to over one-half (145 million) of its population of 291 million. The latter estimate takes into account the impact of the April 1991 price increases. Of all groups, poor people are most likely to be alarmed about food price increases, even though the central and republic governments have provided some offsetting compensation.

The poverty rate varied greatly across the Soviet Union in 1989, ranging from 8 percent (130,000) of Estonia's population to 73 percent (3.8 million) of Tadzhikistan's.

More than half of the population in the four Central Asian republics and in Azerbaijan fell below the official poverty line, using the 1990 level of almost 100 rubles per person per month. These five republics alone accounted for more than one-third (25 million) of all poor people in the Soviet Union in 1989.

Infant mortality rates in the Central Asian republics are much higher than the 1989 national average of 22.6 deaths per 1,000 live births – 54.6 per 1,000 in Turkmenistan, 43.4 in Tajikistan, 37.8 in Uzbekistan, and 32.6 in Kirgizia. "Glasnost," or openness, has revealed the existence of hunger in Turkmenistan and nutritional deficiencies in children and mothers in neighboring republics.

Poor people, who have depended on ration coupons and state stores to purchase relatively cheap food, will face more difficulty than others in coping with food shortages and higher prices. Poor households spent a considerably larger portion of their income on food than did workers (28 percent) and collective farmers (32 percent) in 1986. Two years later, Soviet families at or below the poverty level (then 75 rubles per person per month) spent more than half of their income on food. Families with per person monthly incomes of 75 to 100 rubles spent 43 percent of their income on food. More than 10 percent of families, particularly in the Central Asian republics and those living on fixed pensions, spent more than 70 percent of their income on food.

On average, food consumption of those with incomes below the poverty line does not meet the minimum recommended consumption levels set by the Nutrition Institute of the USSR Academy of Sciences. Available data show that the 32 million people with per capita incomes below 75 rubles per month in 1989 consumed only half of the minimum amounts of meat, eggs, and potatoes, and two-thirds of those for milk and dairy products, vegetables, and melons. Those with monthly incomes between 75 and 100 rubles ate almost 80 percent of the minimum set for eggs and vegetables, 87 percent of the minimum for potatoes, and 96 percent of the minimums for milk and dairy products. Another survey shows that poor people's diets average only 75 to 80 percent of minimum physiological norms, and are extremely unbalanced, consisting mainly of bread, groats, and potatoes.

In response to the April 1991 price increases, poor people will cut back on food purchases and shift their consumption toward lower cost foods, as people in the Eastern European countries did following similar food price increases. There are differences of opinion about the impact these price hikes will have on living standards. The central government is providing some assistance to people earning minimum wages and pensions to ease the burden of higher prices. Though the Central Asian republics have moved to cushion the effects by retaining subsidies on some staple foods and granting allowances to those most affected, the Baltic republics moved to raise food prices even higher to hasten market reforms.

Widespread labor unrest, such as the coal miners' strike in the spring of 1991, has raised concern that the announced assistance will not offset price hikes and could lead to further social tension. To avert this, the central and nine republic governments agreed in April 1991 to an economic and political compromise – the "anti-crisis" plan – that includes some indexing of wages to inflation.

The 1991-1992 food outlook largely depends on whether the Soviet Union comes to grips with the root causes of its current food shortages. Estimates of the 1991 Soviet grain crop range up to 205 million metric tons (MMT), down considerably from 1990s near record 235 MMT. Fewer plantings resulted from economic disruptions and drought in some regions. Many farms reported problems in securing seeds, fuel, and other needed inputs from their normal suppliers. Insufficient feed supplies are forcing some state farms to cut back on their livestock herds. Some farms are also cutting back on milk and meat output because state procurement prices do not cover their rapidly increasing production costs.

Also, as farms have cut back on sales to the state, food production – farm output purchased and processed by state facilities – has also fallen. Production of butter, cheese, and meat fell 13 percent in the first half of 1991. To boost supplies, the central and republic governments have offered additional incentives to farms to encourage sales. They will continue to seek foreign credits to purchase foodstuffs, feed grains, and soybeans overseas to preserve livestock herds on state farms.

However, declining Soviet creditworthiness as its foreign debt reaches record levels and its foreign exchange earnings fall may lead Western governments to question whether they should extend additional credits unless fundamental Soviet economic reforms take place. Experts differ in their views on whether the "anti-crisis" economic plan and resolution of the terms of the "Union" treaty will be implemented and approved, respectively, in time to provide incentives which will encourage individuals and enterprises (including farms) to boost 1991 production of raw materials, consumer goods, and food.

Though the Central Asian republics have moved to cushion the effects by retaining subsidies on some staple foods and granting allowances to those most affected, the Baltic republics moved to raise food prices even higher to hasten market reforms.

Eastern Europe

Albania

Continuing political turmoil and falling living standards, though, led to the creation of a noncommunist dominated coalition government in June 1991.

Albania, the poorest country in Europe, has the lowest per capita calorie intake and the highest infant mortality rate – 52 per 1,000 live births – on the continent. Isolated under the political and economic policies pursued by dictator Enver Hoxha until his death in 1985, Albania in recent years has re-established diplomatic ties with many of its European neighbors.

Albania's agricultural sector, rigidly planned since World War II, is organized into collectives, and accounts for one-third of national income. Two-thirds of the people live on farms and in small villages. Pursuing a policy of strict self-reliance during the isolationist period (1968-1985), the country attained self-sufficiency in grain production by 1976 even though only 6 percent of its territory is suitable for agriculture. Because of the difficulty in providing Albanians an adequate level of food consumption, particularly of meat, government policies in the early 1980s stressed more intensive development of agriculture. They concentrated livestock production in large, specialized complexes (cattle, hogs, and poultry), raised prices to boost incomes of agricultural workers, and allotted small plots of land to collective members to grow their own food.

A net agricultural exporter until recently, Albania during much of the 1980s earned foreign exchange selling fruit, vegetables, and tobacco. The agricultural sector, though, has not increased output sufficiently to meet the needs of the rapidly growing population – currently 3.2 million, with half under age twenty-six.

The communist leadership's recognition of the need to introduce limited economic reforms to reverse the decline in living standards led to a few policy changes in 1990. The regime granted peasants the right to own private plots (one-half acre in size), to raise livestock privately, and to sell their output in private markets. The government also raised procurement prices on a number of commodities. These initiatives failed to overcome the impact of the severe summer 1990 drought, which reduced agricultural output more than 5 percent. Lower production contributed to food shortages, which, combined with a deteriorating economy, falling living standards, and rising unemployment, fueled a refugee exodus in 1990-1991. Accompanying political discontent forced the communist government to hold in March 1991 the first free competitive elections since 1921. Continuing political turmoil and falling living standards led to the creation of a noncommunist-dominated coalition government in June 1991.

In early 1991, the authorities introduced widespread rationing of meat, cooking oil, sugar, and flour to cope with food shortages. Some villagers refused to vote in the elections unless they got food, and many rural residents subsisted only on bread and milk. Ironically, the government has had to increase imports of wheat, other raw commodities, and processed foods like margarine, which Albania previously exported. Italy and other Western European nations have shipped some food aid in response to Albanian requests.

Bulgaria

A serious economic crisis in 1990, during which economic output fell 11 percent and inflation soared more than 60 percent, brought about a serious fall in living standards for Bulgarians. Contributing factors included: uncertainty over the pace of economic reforms, a serious drought that cut grain output in half, the 1989 "forced" departure of Turks who cultivated personal plots of land critical to the country's agricultural production, and the withholding by communist provincial officials of food destined for cities where the noncommunist opposition had won political victories. As a result, serious food shortages broke out. One top health expert expressed concern that these shortages would lead to malnutrition and related health problems. The shortages continued into 1991, particularly in the cities. These occurred in a nation that traditionally has exported a large share of its agricultural bounty to the USSR and other East European countries.

To stretch limited food supplies, authorities in fall 1990 began rationing basic food items (rice, sugar, vegetable oil, meat, and dairy products) for the first time since World War II. They also imposed temporary bans on the export of rationed foods, feed grains, and milk powder. With practically no foreign exchange reserves for import purchases, Bulgaria has received some food aid from the United States and the European Community. Feed grain donations will go to maintain the livestock sector, which accounts for half of Bulgaria's agricultural output.

In recent years, agriculture contributed significantly to export earnings, even though Bulgarian economic policy for decades emphasized rapid industrial development at the expense of agriculture. The post-World War II communist regime collectivized farming, and during the 1970s combined state and collective farms into large "agricultural-industrial complexes." Socialized agriculture produced about half of Bulgaria's output, with the remainder coming from private plots allotted to collective members.

Measures introduced during the 1980s to boost agricultural productivity cut costs and gave farms more of a stake in their own performance, resulting in continued financial losses and slow agricultural growth.

Central authorities continued to fix prices for both agricultural producers and retail consumers. As a result, government farm and food subsidies represented an ever larger portion of the national budget.

At the urging of the International Monetary Fund (IMF), the new coalition government introduced "shock therapy" reforms in early 1991. The authorities deregulated producer and retail food prices, eliminated most subsidies, compensated workers for about 70 percent of the price increases for essential items, and strengthened the social safety net for retirees, the unemployed, and others living close to the minimum wage level. Since food accounted for at least 40 percent of average household expenses in 1986, the ending of food price controls is expected initially to increase inflation dramatically. The Bulgarian parliament has passed a land reform bill and other measures to reduce the state role in the food system. Economists predict that the reforms will lead to increased sales of food at relatively lower prices by 1992.

Czechoslovakia

Relatively prosperous by Eastern European standards, the people of Czechoslovakia enjoy the region's highest per capita food consumption, particularly of meat and dairy products. Agricultural policies adopted during the 1980s sought to encourage state and cooperative farms (which account for almost all the farmland) to boost output at less cost. These policies also enabled the more efficient private farms to produce a quarter of the milk, pork, and eggs. During the 1980s, the government sought to hold down retail food prices while centrally setting the prices of farm output and inputs. One result was that consumer food subsidies accounted for 13 percent of government expenditures by the late 1980s.

The government, democratically elected

after the December 1990 "Velvet Revolution," has introduced market-oriented economic reforms slowly, for fear of unleashing social unrest. Authorities have reduced food, housing, and energy subsidies in order to balance the budget. As a result, overall consumer prices increased 11 percent in 1990 and are projected to rise another 35 percent in 1991. A substantial reduction in farm price and consumer subsidies in July 1990 led to a 25 percent jump in retail food prices, which the government partially offset with a wage increase.

On January 1, 1991, the government abolished remaining food subsidies, allowing the marketplace to set the price for many food products, but left grains, potatoes, flour, sugar, pork, chicken, eggs, and milk subject to price ceilings. From January to mid-year 1991, food prices rose 40 percent. Also, real wages declined by 15 percent in the first quarter of 1991, compared to a fall of 6 percent for 1990. As a result, the government abandoned an early 1991 agreement to index minimum wages to price increases. Authorities proposed a comprehensive safety net for those adversely affected by the reforms, such as income support for the elderly, disabled, nonworking parents, children, and the unemployed. The parliament in April 1991 rejected the government's proposal to transform cooperative farms into privately owned voluntary associations.

East Germany

The states of the former East Germany adopted the free market policies and currency of West Germany upon agreeing to the economic union, effective July 1, 1990. This ended retail price controls and subsidies that had ensured low food prices to consumers in the former centrally planned economy. For East German agriculture (organized into large cooperatives and state

farms), union has meant access to some of the benefits available under the European Community's agricultural price support and market intervention programs. This is not expected, though, to stave off a substantial contraction in the agricultural sector, as farms adjust to operating in a much different economic environment.

The normally high crop yields (the best in Eastern Europe, but below levels found in Western Europe) and East German consumers' strong preference for West German food products resulted in mounting East German agricultural surpluses by late 1990. Food exports to the USSR have not eased the financial problems facing East German farms and food processors.

With union, East Germans (whose incomes were 60 percent of those in the Western part of the union) experienced substantial food price increases, although they can now buy any food they desire. Plans to transfer the ownership of overstaffed and inefficient state-operated East German enterprises into private hands are expected to cause social and economic dislocations. One expert estimates that as many as 400,000 farm workers (nearly half of those working in agriculture) could lose their jobs as a result of the break-up of large farms. Though the increasing numbers of unemployed and part-time workers are protected for a designated period under the social safety net programs established for eastern Germany, the economic impact of reunification could still lead to rising discontent and political unrest.

Hungary

In 1968, Hungary became the first country in Eastern Europe to introduce limited economic reforms by decentralizing some features of its centrally planned economy. These changes helped its agricultural sector (primarily organized into large state farms and cooperatives) increase output throughout the 1970s before it leveled off during the 1980s. With the most technically developed agricultural system in the region, rich land resources, and a long farming tradition, Hungary is self-sufficient in food production and a net agricultural exporter. The private sector, accounting for 15 percent of farm output, is vital to livestock production and important in fruit and vegetable production. Wheat, meat, and processed food exports generate one quarter of Hungary's foreign exchange earnings and are crucial to the new government's efforts to service its foreign debt (the highest per capita in Eastern Europe).

Hungary has eased controls on both producer and consumer retail food prices to help lower its budget deficit and gain access to IMF financial assistance. The democratically elected government reduced the price subsidies that farms received and ended fixed retail food prices in two stages (January 1990 and August 1990). As a result, consumer prices for all items (including food) rose 30 percent during 1990, and are projected to rise 25 to 35 percent in 1991. With food expenses accounting for more than 40 percent of household disposable income among industrial and collective farm workers, these price increases are viewed with alarm. To cushion the impact of higher prices on the poorest people, the government initiated a special compensation package. Others will see a drop in their purchasing power, as incomes are expected to increase more slowly than prices.

One study estimated that 1.3 to 1.5 million Hungarians (13 to 14 percent of the population) in 1987 lived below the official "subsistence level." Many were urban working families; children accounted for 40 percent of those in poverty. Another survey found that 3 million people lived below the "social minimum," a slightly higher poverty level. As living standards have fallen, urban homelessness has increased and soup kitchens have opened to feed and assist poor people.

Poland

Poland was the first East European country to adopt radical free market reforms in early 1990. "Shock therapy" lowered inflation but at the cost of declining output and mounting unemployment. Food shortages that were common a few years back, though, have disappeared. Food is plentiful but more costly.

More than two million private farms dominate Poland's agriculture and contribute 75 percent of the country's agricultural output. Because most private farms are small, averaging seventeen acres in size, productivity is low. Large state farms and smaller cooperatives account for the remaining one-quarter of total farm production.

In 1989, chronic food shortages prompted the last communist government to ease controls on the prices of farm output, inputs, and retail food. To make the agricultural and food sectors more market oriented, the Solidarity governments since then have substantially reduced the subsidies to state and cooperative farms, ended price controls, and broken up the state cooperatives' food marketing monopoly. Future plans are to continue turning the state-owned food processing industry over to the private sector.

With relatively good farm production in 1990 and a drop off in consumer demand because of higher prices, Poland's agricultural surpluses have hurt farmers. Their viability is jeopardized by low farm prices, higher production costs, an underdeveloped food processing industry and weak marketing, and distribution systems that cannot compete with the cheaper, subsi-

One expert estimates that as many as 400,000 farm workers (nearly half of those working in agriculture) could lose their jobs as a result of the break-up of the large farms.

dized food imports entering from Western Europe. To cope, farmers have agitated for higher minimum guaranteed commodity prices and restrictions on food imports. In response, the government is working to conclude export sales of food surpluses to the USSR. They have also decided to subsidize farm credit and to raise tariffs on imported food in 1991.

Due to the sluggish economy of the early 1980s, the number of poor people in Poland more than doubled from 1978 to 1987 – from 3.3 million (9 percent of the population) to 8.6 million (23 percent). Poverty, particularly in urban areas, may well have increased since then.

To help reduce the substantial budget deficit, the government has ended retail food price controls and subsidies. As a result, food prices rose 320 percent in 1989 and another 575 percent during 1990. In 1990 alone, real incomes fell an average of 31 percent, while inflation soared 249 percent. Food expenditures as a share of household income also rose, because incomes fell. In 1986, working-class families spent 38 percent of their income on food; by 1990, food expenditures took half the family budget. A 1990 IMF adjustment loan to Poland was designed in part to help the government develop a safety net with minimum social assistance and unemployment benefits for people most vulnerable to falling living standards.

Romania

Romanians had limited access to food supplies prior to the December 1989 violent revolution that overthrew dictator Nicolae Ceausescu. His regime's policies channeled agricultural production toward export markets to reduce the large foreign debt incurred during the 1970s and restricted farmers' sale of food from private plots (9 percent of the farmland). Poor weather in some years frequently required the government to ration food in spite of Romania's standing as a major agricultural producer in Eastern Europe.

During the 1980s, Romania's agricultural sector (primarily organized into state farms and cooperatives) suffered from economic mismanagement, input shortages, and unpopular policies that forced rural villagers and farm workers to live in large towns. To revitalize the farm sector and increase domestic food supplies, the reform-minded government since 1990 has introduced some agricultural policy changes to increase the role of the private sector in the farm economy. Reforms have redistributed cooperative land to private farmers, established free market prices, doubled state procurement prices, allowed imports of farm inputs and food, and introduced land reform. One result is that the 1990 output of private farms increased to 30 percent of total agricultural production, compared to 8 percent in 1989.

During the winter of 1990-1991, Romania experienced shortages of meat, eggs, potatoes, and baked goods. This resulted from an increase in consumer demand (due to continued retail price subsidies), a reluctance by farmers to sell their grain even at higher procurement prices, a decrease in feed grain production due to drought conditions, and a lack of foreign exchange to import feed. To boost supplies, the government imposed a temporary ban on food exports and received food and feed aid from the European Community and the United States.

Falling living standards (in 1990, inflation hit 38 percent) and mounting unrest prompted the government at first to move slowly to de-control prices on most foods and services. However, to attract IMF assistance, in early 1991, the government agreed to broad price reforms. The end of long-standing food subsidies on April 1, 1991, led to the doubling of prices of staples such as bread, eggs, and meat in state stores. To cushion the impact, the government offered cash handouts to the unemployed, children, and retirees; partially indexed wages to prices; and placed temporary ceilings on price increases.

Yugoslavia

The political, ethnic, and military crisis engulfing Yugoslavia and its republics in mid-1991 will likely intensify the country's serious economic problems. Though the federal government's economic reform package succeeded in dramatically reducing inflation from 2,655 percent in 1989 to 120 percent in 1990, continued tensions between republics contributed to a 40 percent fall in national output from early 1990 through mid-1991. As a result, living standards fell, as earlier policies to freeze prices and wages unraveled and as enterprises were unable to pay their workers. Many farmers went unpaid for months for crops delivered to food processors. In early 1991, some republics, such as Serbia, took steps to undermine the federal government's efforts to keep inflation and spending in check, and thus called into question the future of a unified Yugoslavian state.

Eighty percent of Yugoslavia's diverse agriculture is in private hands. Productivity is low because each private farmer faces difficulty in working small scattered land parcels and lacks access to inputs and credit. The socialized sector is organized into "kombinats," large agricultural enterprises involved mainly in the production and processing of grains, oilseeds, sugar beets, hogs, and poultry. The "kombinats" are self-managed, not state-owned, but must show a profit.

Agricultural reforms adopted in 1989-1990 sought to promote price competition, free wholesale and retail prices of agricultural commodities, and support private farmers. The government replaced the agricultural input subsidy program with a program paying farmers price premiums for major commodities. Some land confiscated from farmers after World War II and during the 1953 agrarian reform will also be returned to their original owners.

The number of poor people in Yugoslavia rose from 3.4 million (17 percent of the population) in 1978 to 5.1 million (25 percent) in 1987, as the economy faltered and prices rose faster than wages. While most people living below the "subsistence level" at the beginning of this period were tied to agriculture, urban poverty became more prevalent in the late 1980s, as rural residents moved to cities to try to improve their living standards. By 1987, close to half of the poor people lived in urban areas.

In 1986, food expenditures took 40 percent of household disposable income. Therefore, the public viewed the 1,100 percent increase in food prices during 1989 with alarm. Though prices fell by almost 20 percent in 1990, concern over high prices led the government to adopt a policy that releases federal commodity reserves when necessary to bring market prices down to targeted levels. The possibility of civil war, though, has led to increased hoarding of available food and reports that the country may face acute food shortages. ■

The end of long-standing Romanian food subsidies on April 1, 1991 led to the doubling of prices of staples such as bread, eggs, and meat in state stores.

Table 1: Demographic Indicators

	Population in millions 1990	Growth rate (%) 1990-1995	Infant mortality rate per thousand live births 1990	Under five mortality rate per thousand live births 1960/1989	Annual infant deaths in thousands 1990	Maternal mortality rate per 100,000 live births 1980-88	Percent of population urbanized 1990	Percent under 16 years 1989	Life expectancy 1991
ASIA AND MIDDLE EAST									
Afghanistan	16.6	6.7	162	381/296	132	690	18	43	na
Bangladesh	115.6	2.7	108	262/184	512	600	16	45	51
Bhutan	1.5	2.3	118	298/193	7	1710	5	40	48
Cambodia	8.2	2.2	116	218/200	38	na	12	35	na
China	1139.1	1.4	27	203/43	677	44	33	29	70
Fiji	0.8	1.5	26	98/32	0.5	41	39	48	64
India	853.1	2.1	88	282/145	2327	340	27	38	58
Indonesia	184.3	1.8	65	225/100	335	450	31	38	61
Iran	54.6	2.0	40	254/64	72	120	57	45	63
Iraq	18.9	3.4	56	222/89	44	na	71	47	64
Jordan	4.0	3.3	36	217/55	6	na	68	45	66
Korea, North	21.8	1.9	24	120/36	13	41	60	31	na
Korea, South	42.8	0.9	21	120/31	13	26	72	28	na
Kuwait	2.0	2.8	15	128/20	1	6	96	35	73
Laos	4.1	2.9	97	233/156	18	na	19	44	49
Lebanon	2.7	2.2	40	91/57	3	na	84	37	na
Malaysia	17.9	2.3	20	105/30	11	59	43	39	70
Mongolia	2.2	2.7	60	185/87	5	100	52	41	na
Myanmar	41.7	2.1	59	230/91	74	140	25	39	60
Nepal	19.1	2.3	118	298/193	88	830	10	44	51
Oman	1.5	3.7	34	378/53	2	na	11	47	64
Pakistan	122.6	2.9	98	276/162	553	500	32	46	55
Papau N.G.	4.0	2.3	53	248/83	7	900	16	41	54
Philippines	62.4	2.3	40	134/72	82	93	43	42	64
Saudi Arabia	14.1	3.8	58	292/95	34	na	77	46	64
Singapore	2.7	1.1	8	49/12	0.4	5	100	26	74
Sri Lanka	17.2	1.3	24	114/36	8.9	60	21	34	71
Syria	12.5	3.6	39	217/62	21	280	50	49	65
Thailand	55.7	1.4	24	149/35	28	50	23	35	65
Turkey	55.9	1.9	62	258/90	101	210	61	36	64
United Arab E.	1.6	2.2	22	239/31	1	na	78	31	71
Vietnam	66.7	2.2	54	232/84	112	140	22	41	66
Yemen	9.2	3.7	107	378/192	51	na	25	63	51
AFRICA									
Algeria	25.0	2.8	61	270/102	52	130	52	45	64
Angola	10.0	2.8	127	345/292	60	na	28	46	45
Benin	4.6	3.2	85	310/150	19	na	38	48	51
Botswana	1.3	3.5	58	173/87	4	250	28	46	67
Burkina Faso	9.0	2.9	127	363/232	57	810	9	44	47
Burundi	5.5	3.0	110	260/196	29	na	6	46	49
Cameroon	11.8	3.4	86	276/150	49	300	41	48	56
Cent. Afr. Rep.	3.0	2.9	95	308/219	13	600	47	47	50
Chad	5.7	2.5	122	325/220	31	960	30	44	46
Congo	2.3	3.3	65	241/112	7	900	40	48	53
Cote D'Ivoire	12.0	3.8	88	264/139	53	na	40	48	53
Egypt	52.4	2.2	57	301/94	102	320	47	41	63
Ethiopia	49.2	3.0	122	294/226	300	na	13	47	47
Gabon	1.2	3.3	94	287/167	5	na	46	33	53
Gambia	0.9	2.7	132	375/241	6	na	23	43	44
Ghana	15.0	3.2	81	224/143	53	1000	33	46	54
Guinea	5.8	3.0	134	336/241	40	na	26	47	43
Guinea-Bissau	1.0	2.1	140	336/250	6	400	20	41	42

Table 1: Demographic Indicators (continued)

	Population in millions 1990	Growth rate (%) 1990-1995	Infant mortality rate per thousand live births 1990	Under five mortality rate per thousand live births 1960/1989	Annual infant deaths in thousands 1990	Maternal mortality rate per 100,000 live births 1980-88	Percent of population urbanized 1990	Percent under 16 years 1989	Life expectancy 1991
AFRICA (CONTINUED)									
Kenya	24.0	3.7	64	208/111	71	170	24	51	59
Lesotho	1.8	2.9	89	208/132	7	na	20	44	56
Liberia	2.6	3.3	126	310/209	15	na	46	46	50
Libya	4.5	3.6	68	269/116	13	80	70	47	61
Madagascar	12.0	3.2	110	364/179	61	240	24	46	50
Malawi	8.8	3.6	138	336/258	68	100	12	49	47
Mali	9.2	3.2	159	369/287	75	na	19	48	47
Mauritania	2.0	2.9	117	321/217	11	na	47	45	46
Mauritius	1.1	1.1	20	104/29	0.4	100	40	27	67
Morocco	25.1	2.4	68	265/116	60	300	48	42	61
Mozambique	15.7	2.7	130	331/297	92	300	27	45	48
Namibia	1.8	3.1	97	263/171	8	na	28	44	na
Niger	7.7	3.3	124	321/225	50	420	19	48	45
Nigeria	108.5	3.2	96	317/170	500	800	35	48	51
Rwanda	7.2	3.5	112	248/201	41	210	8	50	49
Senegal	7.3	2.8	80	299/189	26	600	38	47	48
Sierra Leone	4.2	2.7	143	385/261	29	450	32	45	42
Somalia	7.5	2.4	122	294/218	45	1100	36	47	47
South Africa	35.3	2.2	62	192/80	70	na	83	59	61
Sudan	25.2	2.9	99	292/175	110	660	22	46	50
Swaziland	0.8	3.6	107	226/155	44	na	33	46	56
Tanzania	27.3	3.8	97	249/173	135	340	26	50	53
Togo	3.5	3.2	85	305/150	13	na	25	46	53
Tunisia	8.2	2.1	44	254/66	12	310	54	39	66
Uganda	18.8	3.7	94	223/167	81	300	10	51	48
Zaire	35.6	3.2	75	269/132	123	800	39	47	52
Zambia	8.5	3.8	72	228/125	31	150	50	49	53
Zimbabwe	9.7	3.1	55	181/90	22	480	28	46	59
LATIN AMERICA									
Argentina	32.3	1.2	29	75/36	20	69	86	32	71
Bolivia	7.3	2.8	93	282/165	10	480	51	45	53
Brazil	150.4	1.9	57	159/85	69	120	75	37	65
Chile	13.2	1.6	19	143/27	6	47	86	32	72
Colombia	33.0	1.9	37	157/50	33	110	70	38	68
Costa Rica	3.0	2.3	17	121/22	1	36	47	37	75
Cuba	10.6	0.9	13	87/14	2	29	75	26	76
Dominican Rep.	7.2	2.0	57	199/80	13	74	60	39	66
Ecuador	10.6	2.4	57	184/85	19	190	56	42	66
El Salvador	5.3	2.5	53	207/90	10	70	44	45	63
Guatemala	9.2	2.9	48	230/98	18	110	39	47	62
Guyana	0.8	0.8	48	126/73	0.5	na	35	32	64
Haiti	6.5	2.0	86	270/133	20	230	28	42	55
Honduras	5.1	3.0	57	232/103	11	50	44	47	64
Jamaica	2.5	1.2	14	89/21	2	110	52	36	73
Mexico	88.6	2.0	36	140/51	89	82	73	40	69
Nicaragua	3.9	3.2	50	209/92	8	47	60	46	64
Panama	2.4	1.9	21	105/33	1	57	53	38	72
Paraguay	4.3	2.7	39	134/61	6	380	47	42	67
Peru	21.6	2.0	76	233/119	49	88	70	39	62
Trinidad/Tobago	1.3	1.4	14	67/18	0.5	54	69	39	71
Uruguay	3.1	0.6	20	57/27	1	38	85	29	72
Venezuela	19.7	2.4	33	114/44	20	59	90	40	70

Table 2: Health and Nutrition 1980-89

	% Children underweight 0-48 months	% Children stunted 24-59 months	% Children wasted 12-23 months	% Infants fully immunized 1988-1989	% Infants with low birthweight 1980-1988
ASIA AND MIDDLE EAST					
Afghanistan	na	na	na	22	20
Bangladesh	71	70	28	49	28
Bhutan	38	56	4	36	na
Cambodia	20	na	na	20	na
China	21	41	8	95	9
Fiji	na	na	na	na	14
India	41	na	na	69	30
Indonesia	51	46	11	68	14
Iran	43	55	23	88	5
Iraq	na	na	na	82	9
Jordan	na	na	na	84	5
Korea, North	na	na	na	94	na
Korea, South	na	na	na	86	9
Kuwait	6	14	2	92	7
Laos	37	44	20	20	39
Lebanon	3	4	6	na	10
Malaysia	na	na	na	50	10
Mongolia	na	na	na	84	10
Myanmar	38	75	17	45	16
Nepal	na	na	na	54	na
Oman	na	na	na	92	7
Pakistan	52	42	17	64	25
Papau N.G.	35	na	na	52	25
Philippines	33	42	7	78	18
Saudi Arabia	na	na	na	86	6
Singapore	14	11	4	87	7
Sri Lanka	38	34	19	81	28
Syria	25	na	na	86	11
Thailand	26	28	10	66	12
Turkey	12	na	na	16	7
United Arab E.	na	na	na	66	7
Vietnam	42	60	12	68	18
Yemen	53	61	15	45	na
AFRICA					
Algeria	10	14	4	73	9
Angola	na	na	na	18	17
Benin	na	na	na	41	8
Botswana	15	51	19	80	8
Burkina Faso	46	na	na	49	18
Burundi	38	60	10	73	9
Cameroon	17	43	2	48	13
Cent. Afr. Rep.	na	na	na	56	15
Chad	na	na	na	20	na
Congo	17	23	10	75	16
Cote D'Ivoire	12	20	17	41	14
Egypt	13	32	2	75	5
Ethiopia	38	43	19	23	na
Gabon	na	na	na	65	na
Gambia	18	24	7	na	35
Ghana	27	39	15	51	17
Guinea	na	na	na	16	na
Guinea-Bissau	18	na	na	47	na

Table 2: Health and Nutrition 1980-89 (continued)

	% Children underweight 0-48 months	% Children stunted 24-59 months	% Children wasted 12-23 months	% Infants fully immunized 1988-1989	% Infants with low birthweight 1980-1988
AFRICA (CONTINUED)					
Kenya	na	42	10	65	15
Lesotho	16	23	7	75	11
Liberia	na	na	na	28	na
Libya	na	na	na	70	5
Madagascar	33	56	17	40	10
Malawi	24	61	8	84	20
Mali	31	34	16	26	17
Mauritania	31	37	24	28	11
Mauritius	24	22	16	82	9
Morocco	16	34	6	79	na
Mozambique	57	na	na	39	20
Namibia	na	na	na	na	na
Niger	49	38	23	11	15
Nigeria	na	na	21	57	20
Rwanda	na	na	na	83	17
Senegal	22	28	8	47	11
Sierra Leone	23	na	14	34	17
Somalia	na	na	na	18	na
South Africa	na	na	na	na	na
Sudan	41	68	13	43	na
Swaziland	na	na	na	na	na
Tanzania	48	na	17	82	14
Togo	24	37	10	55	20
Tunisia	10	23	4	82	8
Uganda	23	25	4	40	na
Zaire	na	na	na	38	13
Zambia	28	na	na	80	14
Zimbabwe	12	31	2	70	15
LATIN AMERICA					
Argentina	na	na	na	74	na
Bolivia	13	51	2	40	12
Brazil	5	31	2	54	8
Chile	3	10	1	91	7
Colombia	12	27	1	73	8
Costa Rica	6	8	3	87	10
Cuba	na	na	1	94	8
Dominican Republic	13	26	3	40	16
Ecuador	17	39	4	54	11
El Salvador	15	na	na	62	15
Guatemala	34	68	3	38	14
Guyana	na	na	na	55	11
Haiti	37	51	17	31	17
Honduras	21	34	2	75	20
Jamaica	7	7	6	71	8
Mexico	na	na	na	65	15
Nicaragua	11	22	1	61	15
Panama	16	24	7	71	8
Paraguay	32	na	na	58	7
Peru	13	43	3	52	9
Trinidad/Tobago	7	4	5	59	na
Uruguay	7	16	na	75	8
Venezuela	6	7	4	49	9

Table 3: Human Welfare Indicators – Urban/Rural

	% without access to health facilities 1985-88	% without access to safe water 1985-88	% below absolute poverty level 1980-88	Adult literacy male/female 1985
ASIA AND MIDDLE EAST				
Afghanistan	20/83	62/83	18/36	38/9
Bangladesh	55	96/51	86/86	45/19
Bhutan	35	na/81	na	45/19
Cambodia	20/50	90/98	na	41/17
China	na	15/na	na/10	80/55
Fiji	0	na	na/30	90/80
India	20	24/50	28/40	58/29
Indonesia	20	57/64	26/44	80/64
Iran	5/35	5/45	na	59/36
Iraq	3/12	0/46	na	64/41
Jordan	3	0/12	14/17	86/62
Korea, North	na	na	na	98/91
Korea, South	3/14	10/52	18/11	na
Kuwait	0	3/na	na	75/63
Laos	33	72/80	na	na
Lebanon	na	5/15	na	86/69
Malaysia	na	4/24	13/38	83/65
Mongolia	na	na	na	na
Myanmar	0/89	64/76	40/40	88/69
Nepal	na	30/75	55/61	34/11
Oman	0/10	10/51	na	na
Pakistan	1/65	17/73	32/29	43/18
Papau N.G.	4	5/85	10/75	60/32
Philippines	na	51/46	50/64	88/87
Saudi Arabia	0/12	0/12	na	69/43
Singapore	0	0	na	na
Sri Lanka	7	18/71	na	92/81
Syria	8/40	2/46	na	74/44
Thailand	15/20	44/34	15/34	95/87
Turkey	na	5/37	na	88/64
United Arab E.	10	na	na	na
Vietnam	0/25	30/61	na	90/80
Yemen	62	3/74	na	47/21
AFRICA				
Algeria	0/20	15/45	20/na	65/35
Angola	70	13/85	na	50/23
Benin	82	20/66	na/65	26/12
Botswana	0/15	16/54	40/55	82/60
Burkina Faso	49/52	57/31	na	23/6
Burundi	39	2/79	55/85	53/32
Cameroon	56/61	57/76	15/40	61/36
Centr. Afr. Rep.	55	87/na	na/91	45/19
Chad	70	na	30/56	34/13
Congo	3/30	58/93	na	66/38
Cote D'Ivoire	39/89	70/90	30/26	63/34
Egypt	na	8/44	21/25	60/30
Ethiopia	54	31/91	60/65	na
Gabon	10	8	na	70/43
Gambia	na	na	na/40	36/15
Ghana	8/51	7/61	59/37	64/42
Guinea	0/60	59/88	na	26/8
Guinea-Bissau	na	na	na	na

Table 3: Human Welfare Indicators – Urban/Rural (continued)

	% without access to health facilities 1985-88	% without access to safe water 1985-88	% below absolute poverty level 1980-88	Adult literacy male/female 1985
AFRICA (CONTINUED)				
Kenya	na	39/79	10/55	77/53
Lesotho	20	35/70	50/55	na
Liberia	50/70	0/77	na/23	43/21
Libya	na	0/10	na	70/40
Madagascar	44	19/83	50/50	86/68
Malawi	20	3/50	25/85	na
Mali	85	54/90	27/48	31/15
Mauritania	70	27/na	na	40/16
Mauritius	0	0	12/12	na
Morocco	0/50	0/75	28/45	54/30
Mozambique	0/70	62/91	na	39/16
Namibia	na	na	na	na
Niger	1/70	65/51	na/35	32/11
Nigeria	25/70	0/80	na	55/31
Rwanda	40/75	21/52	30/90	59/32
Senegal	60	21/62	na	45/19
Sierra Leone	na	32/93	na/65	21/6
Somalia	50/85	42/78	40/70	27/9
South Africa	na	na	na	na
Sudan	10/60	40/90	na/85	39/10
Swaziland	na	na	45/50	70/66
Tanzania	1/28	10/58	na	93/88
Togo	39	1/59	42/na	51/25
Tunisia	0/20	0/69	20/15	68/47
Uganda	10/43	63/82	na	57/29
Zaire	60/83	48/79	na/80	79/53
Zambia	0/50	24/59	25/na	77/59
Zimbabwe	0/38	na/68	na	70/55
LATIN AMERICA				
Argentina	20/79	37/83	na	95/94
Bolivia	10/64	25/87	na/85	81/65
Brazil	na	15/44	na	80/77
Chile	3	2/29	na	93/92
Colombia	4	0/24	32/70	86/84
Costa Rica	0/37	0/17	na	92/92
Cuba	na	na	na	94/91
Dominican Republic	20	15/67	45/43	82/79
Ecuador	8/60	19/69	40/65	86/81
El Salvador	20/60	32/60	20/32	73/65
Guatemala	53/75	28/86	66/74	60/44
Guyana	na	na	na	86
Haiti	50	41/70	65/80	54/42
Honduras	15/35	44/55	14/55	71/65
Jamaica	10	1/7	na/80	98/98
Mexico	55	11/53	na	88/82
Nicaragua	0/40	24/89	21/19	na
Panama	5/36	0/36	21/30	87/86
Paraguay	10/62	47/92	19/50	91/86
Peru	40	27/83	49/na	90/75
Trinidad/Tobago	1	0/5	na/39	97/95
Uruguay	18	5/73	22/na	96/95
Venezuela	na	7/35	na	84/88

Table 4: Economic Indicators

	per capita GNP 1989	average GNP growth (%) 1965-88	% of 1989 central gov. expend. health	% of 1989 central gov. expend. education	% of 1989 central gov. expend. defense	Total debt in billions of US $ 1989	Debt servicing as % of export earnings 1988	Food as % of exports 1980-89	Food as % of imports 1980-89
ASIA AND MIDDLE EAST									
Afghanistan	na	na	na	na	na	na	na	31	20
Bangladesh	180	0.4	10	11	10	10.7	14	17	30
Bhutan	180	na	6	13	0	0.1	na	na	na
Cambodia	na	na	na	na	na	na	na	na	na
China	350	5.7	na	na	na	45	7	15	4
Fiji	1520	na	na	na	na	na	10	63	19
India	340	1.8	2	3	17	62.5	19	22	8
Indonesia	500	4.4	2	10	8	53.1	34	12	7
Iran	3200	0.5	7	19	12	na	na	1	13
Iraq	na	na	5	na	na	na	13	5	13
Jordan	1640	na	4	15	26	7.4	24	15	19
Korea, North	na	na	na	na	na	na	na	na	na
Korea, South	4400	7.0	2	19	25	33.1	28	31	6
Kuwait	16150	4.0	7	14	20	na	na	1	17
Laos	180	na	na	na	na	0.1	129	na	na
Lebanon	na	na	na	na	na	0.5	na	21	na
Malaysia	2160	4.0	na	na	na	18.6	18	15	12
Mongolia	na	na	na	na	na	na	na	na	na
Myanmar	na	na	5	14	19	4.2	22	42	na
Nepal	180	0.6	5	10	5	1.4	9	30	14
Oman	5220	6.4	5	10	42	2.9	na	2	16
Pakistan	370	2.5	1	3	30	18.5	17	14	14
Papau N.G.	890	0.2	9	15	5	2.5	16	27	20
Philippines	710	1.6	4	17	13	28.9	25	22	11
Saudi Arabia	6020	2.6	na	na	na	na	4	0.4	16
Singapore	10450	7.0	5	19	21	na	na	6	7
Sri Lanka	430	3.0	6	11	5	5.1	14	37	18
Syria	980	3.1	2	10	40	5.2	19	7	19
Thailand	1220	4.2	6	19	18	23.5	11	37	5
Turkey	1370	2.6	3	16	12	41.6	31	25	5
United Arab E.	18430	na	7	15	44	na	na	2	10
Vietnam	na	na	na	na	na	na	na	15	22
Yemen	650	na	na	na	na	5.7	12	50	26
AFRICA									
Algeria	2320	2.5	6	25	9	26.1	71	0.4	28
Angola	610	na	na	na	na	na	13	16	31
Benin	380	-0.1	6	18	9	1.2	4	36	25
Botswana	1600	8.5	6	20	12	0.5	4	17	9
Burkina Faso	320	1.4	5	14	18	0.8	7	25	26
Burundi	220	3.6	na	na	na	0.9	25	90	16
Cameroon	1000	3.2	3	12	7	4.7	12	40	15
Cent. Afr. Rep.	390	-0.5	na	na	na	0.7	6	20	21
Chad	190	-1.2	na	na	na	0.4	3	44	15
Congo	940	3.3	na	na	na	4.3	29	1	19
Cote D'Ivoire	790	0.8	4	21	4	15.4	na	61	17
Egypt	640	4.2	3	12	14	48.8	10	9	27
Ethiopia	120	-0.1	4	11	50	3.0	37	79	30
Gabon	2960	0.9	na	na	na	3.2	na	2	18
Gambia	200	na	7	12	0	na	14	83	na
Ghana	390	-1.5	9	26	3	3.1	20	70	11
Guinea	430	na	na	2.6	22	na	na	na	na
Guinea-Bissau	190	na	5	5	4	na	130	85	20

Table 4: Economic Indicators (continued)

	per capita GNP 1989	average GNP growth (%) 1965-88	% of 1989 central gov. expend. health	% of 1989 central gov. expend. education	% of 1989 central gov. expend. defense	Total debt in billions of US $ 1989	Debt servicing as % of export earnings 1988	Food as % of exports 1980-89	Food as % of imports 1980-89
AFRICA (CONTINUED)									
Kenya	360	2.0	6	22	12	5.7	19	67	9
Lesotho	470	5.0	7	16	10	0.3	5	3	21
Liberia	na	na	7	16	9	1.8	na	9	25
Libya	5310	-3.0	na	na	na	na	6	na	16
Madagascar	230	-1.9	na	na	na	3.6	39	81	15
Malawi	180	1.0	7	12	5	1.4	18	91	8
Mali	270	1.7	2	9	8	2.2	11	23	21
Mauritania	500	-0.5	3	10	29	2.0	22	64	30
Mauritius	1990	3.0	9	15	1	0.8	10	44	25
Morocco	880	2.3	3	17	15	20.9	20	26	13
Mozambique	80	na	na	na	na	4.7	8	69	na
Namibia	1030	na	na	na	na	na	na	na	na
Niger	290	-2.4	4	18	4	1.6	21	16	24
Nigeria	250	0.9	1	3	3	32.8	24	5	16
Rwanda	320	1.2	5	19	13	0.7	10	88	12
Senegal	650	-0.7	na	na	na	4.1	17	41	28
Sierra Leone	220	0.2	6	13	3	1.1	6	31	21
Somalia	170	0.3	36	2	1	2.1	5	98	20
South Africa	2470	0.8	na	na	na	na	na	9	4
Sudan	480	0	1	10	13	13.0	7	24	19
Swaziland	810	na	9	25	5	na	11	na	na
Tanzania	130	-0.1	6	18	16	4.9	17	63	7
Togo	390	0	5	20	11	1.2	12	38	26
Tunisia	1260	3.3	6	15	6	7.0	22	12	17
Uganda	250	-2.8	2	15	26	1.8	14	90	na
Zaire	260	-2.0	4	6	14	8.8	7	18	na
Zambia	390	-2.0	7	9	0	6.9	14	2	7
Zimbabwe	650	1.2	8	23	17	3.1	25	44	3
LATIN AMERICA									
Argentina	2160	-0.1	2	9	9	64.7	33	60	4
Bolivia	620	-0.8	7	20	12	4.4	33	10	18
Brazil	2540	3.5	6	4	4	111.3	36	32	8
Chile	1770	0.3	6	10	8	18.2	15	30	5
Colombia	1200	2.3	na	na	na	17.0	38	42	8
Costa Rica	1780	1.4	27	17	2	4.5	17	66	8
Cuba	1170	na	na	na	na	na	6	82	12
Dominican Rep.	790	2.5	12	13	8	4.3	11	40	12
Ecuador	1020	3.0	10	23	15	11.3	21	55	5
El Salvador	1070	-0.4	7	18	28	1.9	17	68	16
Guatemala	910	0.9	na	na	na	2.6	27	68	8
Guyana	340	na	2	3	na	na	12	59	18
Haiti	360	0.3	na	na	na	0.8	6	21	24
Honduras	900	0.6	2	5	30	3.4	25	85	9
Jamaica	1260	-1.3	7	11	8	4.3	12	30	19
Mexico	2010	3.0	2	12	2	95.6	30	14	13
Nicaragua	na	-2.5	na	na	na	9.2	47	57	10
Panama	1760	1.6	20	19	8	5.8	na	68	12
Paraguay	1030	3.0	3	11	10	2.5	25	57	10
Peru	1010	-0.2	6	16	20	20.0	8	20	23
Trinidad/Tobago	3230	0.4	na	na	na	2.0	9	6	20
Uruguay	2620	1.2	5	8	8	3.8	27	32	8
Venezuela	2450	-1.0	10	20	6	33.1	26	2	13

Table 5: Demographic Indicators – Small Countries

	Population in thousands 1989	Average growth rate 1990-95	Infant mortality rate per thousand live births 1989	Under five mortality rate per thousand live births mid-1980s	Annual infant deaths in thousands mid-1980s	Maternal mortality rate per 100,000 live births mid-1980s	Percent of population urbanized mid-1980s	Percent of population under 16 yrs. mid-1980s
Antigua	76	1.4	na	26	28	na	31	32
Bahamas	249	2.1	na	32	166	19	58	38
Bahrain	498	3.1	15	27	34	19	27	32
Barbados	254	0.3	11	12	60	143	45	28
Belize	183	3.0	na	32	975	na	51	46
Brunei	258	3.3	12	13	70	46	59	38
Cape Verde	359	3.4	42	70	874	107	63	31
Comoros	531	3.6	96	113	1775	na	64	46
Cook Islands	18	-0.7	22	7	100	30	50	na
Djibouti	397	2.9	119	169	2087	61	81	na
Dominica	82	1.2	18	21	94	47	na	na
Eq. Guinea	345	2.6	124	195	1966	30	29	na
Grenada	85	1.8	34	34	36	47	na	na
Kiribati	65	1.8	62	84	250	38	41	na
Maldives	208	3.5	87	91	585	22	45	na
New Caledonia	155	1.3	36	44	90	160	58	36
Niue	4	-1.5	21	na	na	na	na	na
Qatar	354	3.4	30	32	335	84	34	na
Samoa	167	33.0	50	40	29	48	na	na
São Tome & Principe	118	2.9	49	91	244	40	38	na
Seychelles	68	0.9	68	21	46	56	38	na
Solomon Islands	310	3.7	43	55	589	10	10	48
St. Kitts/Nevis	44	-0.5	40	46	84	45	na	na
St. Lucia	148	1.9	21	25	60	40	50	na
St. Vincent	114	1.6	25	30	106	26	44	na
Suriname	414	1.8	32	31	260	50	43	na
Tonga	95	1.0	26	31	32	20	40	na
Tuvalu	8	1.7	46	10	33	na	na	na
Vanuatu	154	3.2	56	75	9	107	18	45

Table 6: Health and Nutrition – Small Countries

	% of children underweight	% of children stunted	% of children wasted	Age (months)	Survey year	% infants fully immunized mid-1980s	% infants with low birthweight mid-1980s
Antigua	10	7	10	0-59	1981	73 *	8
Bahamas	na	na	na	na	na	62 *	5
Bahrain	68	na	na	0-59	1980	63 *	7
Barbados	5	7	4	0-59	1981	77 *	na
Belize	18	29	3	0-59	1979	44	na
Brunei	15	na	na	0-59	1984	na	10
Cape Verde	19	26	3	12-72	1985	90 *	na
Comoros	16	na	na	0-59	1982	31	na
Cook Islands	na	na	na	na	na	75 *	2
Djibouti	na	na	na	na	na	na	na
Dominica	5	6	2	0-23	1985	82	11
Eq. Guinea	na	na	na	na	na	34	na
Grenada	na	na	na	na	na	31 *	na
Kiribati	13	na	na	0-59	1979	na	18
Maldives	56	48	29	0-59	1981	9 *	26
New Caledonia	na	na	na	na	na	98	7
Niue	na	na	na	na	na	8 *	4
Qatar	na	na	na	na	na	22	na
Samoa	1	5	1	0-59	1977	78	2
São Tome/Principe	17	26	5	0-59	1986	22	8
Seychelles	6	5	2	0-59	1988	99	14
Solomon Islands	17	34	2	0-59	1980	87	9
St. Kitts/Nevis	na	na	na	na	na	85 *	9
St. Lucia	14	11	6	0-59	1976	60	10
St. Vincent	na	na	na	na	na	32	10
Suriname	na	na	na	na	na	na	13
Tonga	20	na	na	0-59	1984	90	2
Tuvalu	na	na	na	na	na	65	3
Vanuatu	20	19	na	0-59	1983	18 *	5

* = TB, DPT, or measles information not available

Table 7: Economic Indicators – Small Countries

	Adult literacy 1985	% without access to health facilities urban/rural mid-1980s	% without access to safe water urban/rural mid-1980s	Total debt in millions of US $ 1987	Debt servicing as % of export earnings 1987	Food as % of exports 1980-89	Food as % of imports 1980-89
Antigua	95	0/0	5	198	5	0.1	na
Bahamas	na	0/0	41	721	15	2	6
Bahrain	73	0/0	0/0	958	4	3	6
Barbados	98	0/0	0/80	508	11	27	16
Belize	91	25	0/62	124	10	74	27
Brunei	na	4	10	27	1	na	21
Cape Verde	50	na	1/79	130	29	61	43
Comoros	48	18	1/48	190	3	65	na
Cook Islands	75	0/0	20	3	na	73	28
Djibouti	12	63	47/80	289	40	na	na
Dominica	94	0	23	85	8	69	50
Eq. Guinea	45	na	53	155	18	na	na
Grenada	96	20	15	76	12	84	56
Kiribati	96	5	7/75	12	6	15	17
Maldives	93	0/3	83	61	6	0.3	23
New Caledonia	na	0/0	0/0	359	3	5	23
Niue	na	na	na	na	na	na	na
Qatar	76	5	2/50	216	2	na	11
Samoa	98	0/0	20	72	14	95	24
São Tome/Principe	58	na	2/21	97	102	na	na
Seychelles	88	1	5	134	12	11	20
Solomon Islands	15	42	0/9	107	10	60	19
St. Kitts/Nevis	90	1	25	40	5	43	23
St. Lucia	82	0/0	30	49	2	84	24
St. Vincent	82	20	25	36	4	88	35
Suriname	93	0/0	7/13	45	1	20	12
Tonga	78	20	5	36	6	87	29
Tuvalu	95	0/0	0/0	na	na	na	27
Vanuatu	53	20	55	134	36	99	26

Table 8: Income Distribution (by quintiles in percentages)

	Lowest 20 percent	Second quintile	Third quintile	Fourth quintile	Highest 20 percent	Year
Bangladesh	10	14	17	22	37	1985-86
India	8	12	16	22	41	1983
Indonesia	9	12	16	22	41	1987
Korea, South	6	11	15	22	45	1976
Philippines	6	10	15	22	48	1985
Sri Lanka	5	9	12	18	56	1985-86
Thailand	6	10	14	21	50	1976
Cote D'Ivoire	5	8	13	21	53	1986-87
Egypt	5	11	15	21	49	1976
Kenya	3	6	12	19	60	1976
Mauritius	5	8	11	17	55	1981
Zambia	4	7	11	17	63	1976
El Salvador	6	10	15	22	47	1977
Mexico	3	7	12	20	61	1977
Trinidad/Tobago	4	9	14	23	50	1976
Uruguay	6	10	15	23	46	1983
Venezuela	5	9	14	22	51	1987
Pakistan	8	11	15	21	46	1984-85
Morocco	10	13	16	21	39	1984-85
Guatemala	6	9	12	19	55	1979-81
Colombia	4	9	14	21	53	1988
Jamaica	5	10	14	21	49	1988
Botswana	3	7	12	21	59	1985-86
Costa Rica	3	8	13	21	55	1986
Malaysia	5	9	14	21	51	1987

Table 9: Change in Real Minimum Wages

(Base Year 1980 = 100)	Index of real minimum wages	Last year of index	% change 1980-last year of index
Argentina	68	1989	-32
Bolivia[a]	37	1988	-63
Botswana[b]	119	1980	+19
Brazil	69	1989	-31
Burkina Faso	89	1986	-11
Chile	64	1989	-36
Colombia	105	1989	+5
Congo	62	1986	-38
Costa Rica	110	1989	+10
Cote D'Ivoire	79	1986	-21
Dominican Republic	78	1989	-22
Ecuador	44	1989	-56
El Salvador	36	1989	-63
Ghana	155	1986	+55
Guatemala	79	1988	-21
Guinea	64	1985	-36
Haiti	98	1989	-2
Honduras	74	1989	-26
Kenya	62	1986	-38
Mexico	47	1989	-53
Nicaragua	47	1985	-53
Nigeria	54	1985	-46
Panama	100	1989	0
Paraguay	137	1989	+37
Peru	23	1989	-77
Senegal	74	1986	-26
Tanzania	38	1986	-62
Togo	77	1986	-23
Uganda	26	1985	-74
Uruguay	79	1989	-21
Venezuela	77	1989	-23
Zambia	94	1985	-6

a = base year 1983   b = base year 1975

Table 10: United States – Trends in Poverty

	1970	1980	1982	1984	1985	1986	1987	1988	1989
Population in millions	205.1	227.8	232.5	237.0	239.3	241.6	243.9	246.3	248.3
Total poverty rate (%)	12.6	13.0	15.0	14.4	14.0	13.6	13.4	13.1	12.8
White poverty rate (%)	9.9	10.2	12.0	11.5	11.4	11.0	10.4	10.1	10.0
Black poverty rate (%)	33.5	32.5	35.6	33.8	31.3	31.1	32.6	31.6	30.7
Hispanic poverty rate (%)	na	25.7	29.9	28.4	29.0	27.3	28.1	26.8	26.2
Elderly poverty rate (%)	24.6	15.7	14.6	12.4	12.6	12.4	12.5	12.0	11.4
Total child poverty rate (%)	15.1	18.3	21.9	21.5	20.7	20.5	20.5	19.7	19.6
White child poverty rate (%)	na	13.9	17.0	16.7	16.2	16.1	15.4	14.6	14.8
Black child poverty rate (%)	na	42.3	47.6	46.6	43.6	43.1	45.6	44.2	43.7
Hispanic child poverty rate (%)	na	33.2	39.5	39.2	40.3	37.7	39.6	37.9	36.2
Poverty rate of people in female-headed households (%)	38.1	36.7	40.6	38.4	37.6	38.3	38.3	37.2	32.2
Percent of federal budget spent on food assistance	0.5	2.4	2.1	2.1	2.0	1.9	1.9	1.9	1.9
Total infant mortality rate *	20.0	12.6	11.5	10.8	10.6	10.4	10.1	10.0	10.0
White infant mortality rate *	17.8	11.0	10.1	9.4	9.3	8.9	8.6	8.5	8.5
Black infant mortality rate *	32.6	21.4	19.6	18.4	18.2	18.0	17.9	17.6	17.6
Unemployment rate (%)	4.9	7.1	9.7	7.5	7.2	7.0	6.2	5.5	5.3
Income distribution (per quintile in percentages)+									
Lowest	na	5.0	4.5	4.4	4.4	4.3	4.3r	4.4r	3.8
Second	na	11.6	11.0	10.7	10.8	10.8	10.6r	10.7r	9.5
Middle	na	17.3	16.9	16.7	16.7	16.7	16.6r	16.7r	15.8
Fourth	na	24.5	24.2	24.1	24.1	24.2	24.1r	24.2r	24.0
Highest	na	41.5	43.5	44.2	44.1	44.2	44.4r	44.1r	46.8

+ = might not add up to 100.0 due to rounding
* = per 1,000 live births
r = indicates a revised methodology

Table 11: United States – Conditions of Poverty

	Population in millions July 1988	% of population living below poverty level late 1980s	AFDC benefits as % of poverty level - 3 person family 1989	% of poverty population receiving AFDC 1990
Alabama	4.1	21.6	14	18
Alaska	0.5	11.0	82	35
Arizona	3.5	13.6	36	26
Arkansas	2.4	21.8	25	14
California	28.3	12.7	84	52
Colorado	3.3	12.7	43	24
Connecticut	3.2	6.3	83	60
Delaware	0.7	9.8	40	32
District of Columbia	0.6	13.2	50	61
Florida	12.3	12.5	36	23
Georgia	6.3	14.4	33	32
Hawaii	1.1	9.7	67	41
Idaho	1.0	15.4	39	11
Illinois	11.6	13.0	45	42
Indiana	5.6	11.2	35	24
Iowa	2.8	12.8	52	26
Kansas	2.5	9.7	50	32
Kentucky	3.7	17.8	28	27
Louisiana	4.4	22.5	23	28
Maine	1.2	11.6	55	40
Maryland	4.6	8.3	49	48
Massachusetts	5.9	8.9	65	49
Michigan	9.3	12.9	57	55
Minnesota	4.3	11.4	65	34
Mississippi	2.6	25.8	15	26
Missouri	5.1	14.5	35	28
Montana	0.8	16.8	45	21
Nebraska	1.6	12.5	44	21
Nevada	1.1	9.1	40	23
New Hampshire	1.1	4.6	61	32
New Jersey	7.7	8.1	52	50
New Mexico	1.5	20.6	38	20
New York	18.0	13.6	85	40
North Carolina	6.5	13.7	33	25
North Dakota	0.7	12.3	49	19
Ohio	11.0	12.9	41	45
Oklahoma	3.2	16.6	39	21
Oregon	2.8	11.8	54	27
Pennsylvania	12.0	10.2	51	43
Rhode Island	1.0	8.8	66	52
South Carolina	3.5	16.0	25	23
South Dakota	0.7	15.9	47	17
Tennessee	4.9	18.4	24	23
Texas	17.0	17.7	22	20
Utah	1.7	10.8	47	25
Vermont	0.6	10.2	80	38
Virginia	6.0	10.4	43	24
Washington	4.6	11.3	61	43
West Virginia	1.9	21.6	30	27
Wisconsin	4.9	8.6	63	56
Wyoming	0.5	11.8	44	25
UNITED STATES	245.8	13.4		

Infant mortality rate per 1,000 live births – all races 1988	Infant mortality rate per 1,000 live births – whites 1985-87	Infant mortality rate per 1,000 live births – blacks 1988	% of white infants with low birthweight 1988	% of black infants with low birthweight 1988	% of eligible people receiving WIC in Feb. 1991
12.1	10	17	6	12	57
11.6	9	na	5	9	56
9.7	9	18	6	12	65
10.7	10	17	7	13	50
8.6	9	16	5	13	53
9.6	9	12	8	13	58
8.9	8	16	6	13	79
11.8	10	21	6	13	55
23.2	12	26	5	17	88
10.6	9	17	6	13	63
12.6	10	19	6	13	67
7.2	8	na	6	9	35
8.8	11	na	5	na	40
11.3	9	21	6	14	61
11.0	10	20	6	12	63
8.7	9	na	5	12	51
8.0	9	17	6	12	50
10.7	10	17	6	12	55
11.0	8	14	6	13	66
7.9	9	na	5	na	53
11.3	9	18	6	13	60
7.9	8	15	5	11	53
11.1	9	22	5	14	71
7.8	9	20	6	12	66
12.3	9	16	6	12	69
10.1	9	16	6	13	46
8.7	9	na	6	14	49
9.0	9	22	5	13	50
8.4	9	19	7	15	70
8.3	9	na	5	na	63
9.9	8	19	5	13	55
10.0	9	na	7	11	48
10.8	9	18	6	14	60
12.5	9	20	6	12	58
10.5	8	na	5	na	59
9.7	9	16	6	13	57
9.0	10	13	6	12	41
8.6	10	na	5	12	54
9.9	9	20	6	14	68
8.2	8	na	6	9	65
12.3	10	17	6	13	71
10.1	9	na	6	na	54
10.8	9	19	6	13	62
9.0	9	14	6	12	58
8.0	9	na	6	12	39
6.8	9	na	5	na	83
10.4	9	18	5	12	56
9.0	10	16	5	11	47
9.0	10	na	5	11	51
8.4	8	16	5	13	59
8.9	11	na	7	na	64
10.0	9	18	6	13	57

Sources for Tables

Sources for International Data

The data cited in the tables are indicative, rather than absolute; they are largely derived from government and United Nations sources whose methods may disguise and underestimate conditions of hungry people. For many indicators, data were available for different years across countries; a range is specified where appropriate.

Population and Population Growth Rate:

Population refers to estimated population in millions in 1990, and growth rates are estimates for the period 1990-1995. Source: *The State of World Population 1991*. For most countries with fewer than one million, entries for population refer to 1989 and population growth rates refer to the period 1990-1995. Sources: *The State of the World's Children 1991* and *The State of World Population 1991*.

Infant Mortality Rate:

For most countries the latest infant mortality rate estimates refer to 1990. Source: *The State of World Population 1991*. For countries at war, the infant mortality rate is likely to be appreciably higher than the U.N. estimates. Where the 1990 estimates were not available, particularly for countries with populations under one million, 1989 or circa 1989 data are given. Sources: *The State of the World's Children 1991*, and *Evaluation of the Strategy for Health for All by the Year 2000*, Geneva, World Health Organization (WHO), 1987.

Under Five Mortality Rate:

All entries are from 1989. Source: *The State of the World's Children 1991*.

Total Infant Deaths:

The number of infant deaths in thousands was calculated by multiplying the total population by the birth rate per thousand and by the infant mortality rate.

Maternal Mortality Rate:

The entries refer to the period 1980-88. Sources: *The State of the World's Children 1991*; for smaller countries, *Compendium of Statistics and Indicators on the Situation of Women, 1986*, United Nations Department of International Economic and Social Affairs, 1989, and *Evaluation of the Strategy for Health for All by the Year 2000*.

Percent Urban 1990:

For most countries this entry indicates the percent of the total population which is urbanized in 1990. Source: *The State of World Population 1991*.

Percent Below 16 Years:

The State of the World's Children 1991 provides 1988 data. In cases where UNICEF did not furnish data, the figures refer to the percent below 16 years circa 1985. Source: *Evaluation of the Strategy for Health for All by the Year 2000*.

Nutritional Information:

Source: *The State of the World's Children 1991*.

Percent of Infants Fully Immunized:

The numbers indicate the greatest possible percentage of children under the age of one who have been immunized against TB (tuberculosis), DPT (diphtheria, pertussis, and tetanus), Poliomyelitis, and Measles in the period 1988-89. Source: *The State of the World's Children 1991*. For smaller countries, mid-1980 data were obtained from *Evaluation of the Strategy for Health for All by the Year 2000*. In some cases, either TB, DPT, or Measles information was not available; such estimates are followed by a *.

Percent of Infants with Low Birthweight:

Incidence of low birthweight for a year in the period 1980-88. Sources: *The State of the World's Children, 1991*, and for smaller countries, *Evaluation of the Strategy for Health for All by the Year 2000*.

Percent of Population without Access to Health Facilities (Urban/Rural):

Access to health facilities means ability to reach appropiate health care services by local transportation in no more than one hour. Figures refer to the period 1985-1988. Where no breakdown of urban and rural populations is available, a single number appears. Sources: *The State of the World's Children 1991*, and for smaller countries, *Evaluation of the Strategy for Health for All in the Year 2000*.

Percent of Population without Access to Adequate and Safe Water (Urban/Rural):

Figures refer to the period 1985-1988. Where no breakdown of urban and rural populations is available, a single number appears. Sources: *The State of the World's Children 1991*, and for smaller countries, *Evaluation of the Strategy for Health for All by the Year 2000*.

Percent of Population Below Absolute Poverty Level (Urban/Rural):

Estimates of population in poverty in any year within the period 1980-88. Where no breakdown of urban and rural populations is available, a single number appears. Source: *The State of the World's Children 1991*.

Adult Literacy (Male/Female):

Adult literacy rates are for the year 1985. Sources: *The State of World Population 1991*, and for smaller countries, *Evaluation of the Strategy for Health for All by the Year 2000*. Where only a single figure is listed the estimate refers to total literacy, male and female.

GNP Per Capita and GNP Growth:

Figures for GNP per capita refer to 1989; figures for GNP growth refer to the period 1965-1988. Source: *World Development Report 1991*.

Percent of Central Government Expenditures Spent on Health, Education, Defense:

Refers to the period 1989. Source: *World Development Report 1991.*

Total Debt and Debt Servicing as a Percent of Export Earnings:

Total debt refers to figures in $US 1989. Source: *World Development Report 1991.* For smaller countries, total debt is expressed in $US 1989. Source: *Handbook of International Trade and Development Statistics, 1989 Supplement*, Geneva, UNCTAD, 1990.

Food as Percent of Exports and Food as Percent of Imports:

The figures listed refer to the period 1980-1988. Source: *Handbook of International Trade and Development Statistics, 1989 Supplement.*

Income Distribution by Quintiles:

The latest available distributions are reported. Source: *World Development Report 1991.*

Change in Real Minimum Wages:

The index numbers listed are base year 1980. Sources: *Economic and Social Progress in Latin America, 1990 Report*, Washington, Inter-American Development Bank, 1990, and *Africa Misunderstood, or Whatever Happened to the Rural-Urban Gap*, V. Jamal and J. Wecks, Geneva, ILO, 1989.

Sources for the United States Data

Population:

Source: *1991 Green Book.*

Poverty Rates:

Source: *Money Income and Poverty Status in the United States: 1989*, Current Population Reports, Consumer Income, Series P-60, No. 168, Bureau of the Census, Department of Commerce.

Share of Federal Budget Spent on Food and Nutrition Assistance:

Includes the Food Stamp Program, Supplemental Feeding Programs (WIC and CSFP), Food Donations Program, and Child Nutrition Programs, found by dividing the total 1991 outlay estimate spent of food assistance by the total estimated 1991 budget outlay. Source: *Historical Tables: Budget of the United States Government, FY 1992*, Washington, Executive Office of the President, Office of Management and Budget, 1991.

Infant Mortality Rate:

Sources: *S.O.S America! A Children's Defense Budget* and *The State of America's Children 1991*, Washington, Children's Defense Fund, 1991.

Unemployment Rate:

The average annual official unemployment rate. Source: *1991 Green Book.*

Income Distribution:

Share of adjusted family income (weighted by persons) by income quintile. Source: *Money and Income and Poverty Status in the United States, 1989.*

Population:

Population estimates as of July 1988 in thousands. Source: *1991 Green Book.*

Poverty Rate:

Rate of poverty refers to the average annual poverty rate for the late 1980s. Source: *1991 Green Book.*

AFDC Benefits as Percent of Poverty Level:

AFDC benefits in 1989 as a percent of the 1988 federal poverty level for a three person family. Source: *The State of America's Children 1991.*

Percent of Poverty Population Receiving AFDC:

Calculated by determining the number of people represented by the poverty rate in each state and then dividing this number into the average AFDC caseload for that state. Sources: *The State of America's Children 1991*, and *1991 Green Book.*

Infant Mortality Rate:

Annual average infant mortality rates in 1985-1987 for Whites and 1988 for Blacks. Sources: *1991 Green Book* and *The State of America's Children 1991.*

Percent of Infants with Low Birthweight:

Percent of infants with low birthweight in 1988, by race. Source: Children's Defense Fund.

Percent of Eligible People Receiving WIC:

Percentage of those eligible for WIC being served in February 1991. Source: Center on Budget and Policy Priorities.

Abbreviations and Glossary

Abbreviations

AAF ....African Alternative Framework
ACC/SCN .......U.N. Administrative Committee on Coordination/Subcommittee on Nutrition
AFDC ....Aid to Families with Dependent Children
AID ....Agency for International Development
BFW ....Bread for the World
CARE.............Cooperative for Assistance and Relief Everywhere
CDF ....Children's Defense Fund
CRS................Catholic Relief Services
CWS ....Church World Service
CSFP.............Commodity Supplemental Food Program
ECA...............U.N. Economic Commission for Africa
FAO ....Food and Agriculture Organization of the United Nations
FDPIR ....Food Distribution Program on Indian Reservations
FRAC.............Food Research and Action Center
FY ....Fiscal Year
GAO...............General Accounting Office
GPO ....Government Printing Office
HDI ....Human Development Index
IAF ....Industrial Areas Foundation
ICDS...............Integrated Child Development Services
ICRC..............International Committee of the Red Cross
IFAD .............U.N. International Fund for Agricultural Development
ILO ................U.N. International Labor Organization
IMF................International Monetary Fund
MCC ....Mennonite Central Committee
NAFTA...........North American Free Trade Agreement
NGO ....Nongovernmental organization
PAHO ....Pan American Health Organization
PVO ....Private Voluntary Organization
SAP................Structural Adjustment Program
TEFAP............The Emergency Food Assistance Program
U.N.................United Nations
UNCTAD ....United Nations Conference on Trade and Development
UNDP ....United Nations Development Programme
UNHCR.........United Nations High Commissioner for Refugees
UNICEF..........United Nations Children's Fund
USCR..............U.S. Committee for Refugees
USDA ....United States Department of Agriculture
WFC...............U.N. World Food Council
WFP ..............U.N. World Food Programme
WHO ....World Health Organization
WIC...............Special Supplemental Food Program for Women, Infants, and Children

Glossary

Absolute poverty - The income level below which a minimally nutritionally adequate diet plus essential non-food requirements are not affordable.

Adult literacy rate - Percentage of persons aged 15 and over who can read and write.

Anemia - A condition in which the hemoglobin concentration (the number of red blood cells) is lower than normal as a result of a deficiency of one or more essential nutrients, such as iron.

Birth rate (crude) - The annual number of births per 1,000 population.

Child mortality rate - The annual number of deaths of children between one and five years of age per 1,000 live births.

Daily calorie requirement - The number of calories of dietary energy needed to sustain normal levels of activity and health, taking into account age, sex, body weight, and climate.

Death rate (crude) - The annual number of deaths per 1,000 population.

Debt service - The sum of repayments of principle and interest on debt.

Desertification - The change of arable land into a desert, either from natural causes or human activity.

Fallow - To leave land uncultivated for one or more seasons.

Famine - A situation of extreme scarcity of food, potentially leading to widespread starvation.

Food security - Assured access for every person, primarily by production or purchase, to enough nutritious food to sustain productive human life.

Goiter - Enlargement of the thyroid gland (causing a swelling in the front of the neck) from iodine deficiency.

Green revolution - A term used to describe technological changes in agricultural production methods since World War II. The technologies rely on the use of improved seeds, known as high-yielding varieties, chemical fertilizers, and pesticides.

Gross domestic product (GDP) - The total value of goods and services produced by an economy.

Gross national product (GNP) - The total domestic and foreign value added claimed by residents of a country, calculated without making deductions for depreciation. It includes GDP plus income residents receive from abroad for labor and capital, less similar payments made to nonresidents who contribute to the economy.

Hunger - A condition in which people lack the basic food intake to provide them with the energy and nutrients for fully productive, active, and healthy lives.

Infant mortality rate - The annual number of deaths of infants under one year of age per 1,000 live births.

Low birth weight infants - Babies born weighing 2,500 grams (five and one half pounds) or less. They are especially vulnerable to illness and death in the first month of life.

Malnutrition - Impairment to physical and/or mental health resulting from a failure to achieve nutrient requirements. Malnutrition may result from consuming too little food, a shortage or imbalance of key nutrients, or overconsumption of certain nutrients, e.g., refined sugar and fat.

Marginal farmers - Farmers who control and work the barest minimum of land, and have so few assets that they usually manage to subsist with difficulty.

Maternal mortality rate - The annual number of deaths of women from pregnancy-related causes per 100,000 live births.

Monocropping or Monoculture - Repeated cultivation of a single type of crop, as opposed to mixed cropping (growing several types of crops during a single season) or crop rotation (growing different crops in successive seasons).

Morbidity - The proportion of sickness or of a specific disease in a geographic locality.

Poverty line - An official measure of poverty defined by national governments. In the U.S., for example, it is based on ability to afford the USDA "Thrifty Food Plan," which provides a less-than-adequate diet.

Structural adjustment - Economic policy changes, often imposed upon an indebted country by its lenders as a condition for future loans, intended to stimulate economic growth. These generally involve reducing the role of government in the economy and measures to increase exports.

Stunting - Failure to grow to normal height caused by chronic undernutrition during the formative years of childhood. Some anthropologists and nutritionists have criticized the definitions used for "normal height" as culturally biased.

Sustainability - Society's ability to shape its economic and social systems so as to maintain both natural resources and human life.

Underemployment - The situation of not being fully employed year round.

Under five mortality rate - The annual number of deaths of children under five years of age per 1,000 live births.

Undernutrition - A form of mild, moderate, or acute malnutrition which is characterized by inadequate intake of food energy (measured by calories), usually due to eating too little. Stunting, wasting, and being underweight are terms for common outcomes of undernutrition.

Underweight - A condition in which a person is seriously below normal weight for his/her age. The term can apply to any age group, but is most often used as the standard measurement of undernutrition in children under five.

Vitamin A deficiency - A nutritional deficiency that can lead to eye disorders and ranks as the leading cause of childhood blindness in many developing countries.

Vulnerability to hunger - A term used to describe individuals, households, communities, or nations who have enough to eat most of the time, but whose poverty makes them especially susceptible to hunger due changes in the economy, climate, or political conditions.

Wasting - A condition in which a person is seriously below the normal weight for his or her height due to acute undernutrition.

Sources and Bibliography

General

Abdalla, Nazem. *Impact of the Gulf Crisis on Developing Countries*. Report prepared for the U.N. Development Program's Gulf Task Force, June 1991.

Avery, Dennis T. *Global Food Progress, 1991*. Indianapolis, In.: Hudson Institute, 1991.

Berer, Marge, ed. *Maternal Mortality & Morbidity: A Call to Women for Action*. International Day of Action for Women's Health, May 28, 1990. Amsterdam: Women's Global Network for Reproductive Rights, 1990.

Bread for the World Institute on Hunger & Development. *Hunger 1990: A Report on the State of World Hunger*. Washington, D.C.: BFWI, 1990.

——————. *Food as a Weapon Study Kit*. Washington, D.C.: BFWI, 1991.

Brown, Robert McAfee, ed. *Kairos: Three Prophetic Challenges to the Church*. Includes The Kairos Document (South Africa), Kairos Central America, and the Road to Damascus (Africa, Central America & Asia). Grand Rapids, Mich.: Eerdmans, 1990.

Cornell University Program in International Nutrition. *Hunger and Society*. Vol. I: Understanding the Causes; Vol. II: Examination of Country Cases; Vol. III: Causes and Strategies in Tanzania, 1988. Ithaca: Cornell University, 1988.

Cornia, Giovanni Andrea, Richard Jolly, and Frances Stewart, eds. *Adjustment with a Human Face, Volume I: Protecting the Vulnerable and Promoting Growth, A Study by UNICEF*. Oxford: Clarendon, 1987.

"Development that Works: Lessons from the Grassroots." *Food Monitor* No. 36 (Spring 1986).

Drèze, Jean and Amartya Sen. *Hunger and Public Action*. Oxford: Clarendon, 1990.

Durning, Alan B. *Action at the Grassroots: Fighting Poverty and Environmental Decline*. Worldwatch Paper No. 88. Washington, D.C.: Worldwatch Institute, January 1989.

Evangelical Lutheran Church in America. Hunger Program. *Hope for a Hungry World: 1991-92 Hunger Resources Packet*. Chicago: ELCA, 1991.

Feinberg, Richard E., et al. *Economic Reform in Three Giants: U.S. Foreign Policy and the USSR, China, and India*. New Brunswick: Transaction, 1990.

Food and Agriculture Organization of the United Nations. *FAO at Work* No. 1/91, Rome: FAO, February 1991.

——————. *Foodcrops and Shortages*, Special Report Nos. 2-6. Rome: FAO, April-June 1991.

——————. *Food Outlook* Nos. 3-6. Rome: FAO, March-June 1991.

Garst, Rachel and Tom Barry. *Feeding the Crisis: U.S. Food Aid and Farm Policy in Central America*. Lincoln, Neb.: University of Nebraska, 1990.

Hamilton, John M. *Entangling Alliances: How the Third World Shapes Our Lives*. Cabin John, Md: Seven Locks, 1990.

Harrison, Paul. *The Greening of Africa: Breaking Through in the Battle for Land and Food*. London: Paladin Grafton for International Institute for Environment and Development, 1987.

Hirschoff, Paula M. "Development that Works: Fresh Look at an Age-Old Endeavor." *Hunger Notes* 13, Nos. 11-12, (April-May 1988).

Institute of the Third World. *Third World Guide 91/92*. London: Oxfam, 1991.

International Conference on Popular Participation in the Recovery and Development Process in Africa. *African Charter for Popular Participation in Development and Transformation (Arusha 1990)*. Addis Ababa: U.N. Economic Commission on Africa, 1990.

International Food Policy Research Institute. *Report 1990*. Washington, D.C.: IFPRI, 1991.

Joint Consultative Group on Policy. *Poverty Alleviation - A Global Challenge*. IFAD. Report of the September 1990 meeting.

Kutzner, Patricia L. *World Hunger*. Contemporary World Issues Series. Santa Barbara, Calif: ABC-CLIO, 1991.

Lake, Anthony. *After the Wars: Reconstruction in Afghanistan, Indochina, Central America, Southern Africa, and the Horn of Africa*. New Brunswick: Transaction, 1990.

Lewis, John P., et al. *Strengthening the Poor: What Have We Learned?* New Brunswick: Transaction Books, 1988.

Millman, Sara R. *The Hunger Report: Update 1991*. Providence, R.I.: Alan Shawn Feinstein World Hunger Program, Brown University, 1991.

Minear, Larry. *Helping People in an Age of Conflict: Toward a New Professionalism in U.S. Voluntary Humanitarian Assistance*. New York: InterAction, 1988.

——————, et al. *Humanitarianism Under Siege: A Critical Review of Operation Lifeline Sudan*. Trenton, N.J.: Red Sea and Washington, D.C.: BFWI, 1991.

Mitchell, Tim. "America's Egypt: Discourse of the Development Industry." *Middle East Report* (March-April 1991), 18-34, 36.

Pan American Health Organization. *Health Conditions in the Americas. 1990 Edition*. Vol. 2. PAHO Scientific Publication No. 524. Washington, D.C.: PAHO, 1990.

Rau, Bill. *From Feast to Famine: Official Cures and Grassroots Remedies to Africa's Food Crisis*. Atlantic Heights, N.J.: Zed, 1991.

Sivard, Ruth Leger, et al. *World Military and Social Expenditures 1991*. Washington, D.C.: World Priorities, 1991.

Starving in Silence: A Report on Famine and Censorship. London: Article 19, 1990.

Steinberg, David, ed. *In Search of Southeast Asia: A Modern History*. Honolulu: University of Hawaii Press, 1987.

Streeten, Paul. P. *Hunger*. Boston: Institute for Economic Development, Boston University, Discussion Paper Series, December 1989.

United Nations. Administrative Committee on Coordination, Subcommittee on Nutrition. *Recent Trends in Nutrition in 33 Countries*. New York: ACC/SCN, Jan./Feb. 1989.

United Nations Children's Fund. *The State of the World's Children 1991*. New York: Oxford, 1991.

——————. *Statistics on Children in UNICEF Assisted Countries*. New York: Oxford, 1990.

United Nations Development Programme. *Human Development Report 1990*. New York: Oxford, 1990.

——————. *Human Development Report 1991*. New York: Oxford, 1991.

U.N. Economic Commission for Africa. *African Alternative Framework to Structural Adjustment Programs for Socio-Economic Recovery and Transformation (AAF-SAP)*. Addis Ababa: ECA, 1989.

United Nations Population Fund. *The State of World Population 1991*. New York: UNFPA, 1991.

United Nations World Food Council. *Ending Hunger: The Cyprus Initiative*. Summary of the Council's report "The Cyprus Initiative Against Hunger in the World." *Hunger Project Occasional Paper*. San Francisco: The Hunger Project, 1990.

——————. *Hunger and Malnutrition in the World: Situation and Outlook*. Rome: WFC, 1991.

——————. *Meeting the Developing Countries' Food Production Challenges of the 1990s and Beyond*. Summary report of the WFC/UNDP Interregional Consultation, April 1991.

United States Committee for Refugees. *World Refugee Survey 1991*. Washington, D.C.: USCR, 1991.

United States Department of Agriculture. *Global Food Assessment: Situation and Outlook Report*. Washington, D.C.: GPO, November 1990.

————. *World Agriculture, Trends and Indicators, 1970-89*. USDA Statistical Bulletin No. 815.

Wisner, Ben. *Power and Need in Africa*. Trenton, N.J.: Africa World, 1989.

World Bank. *Social Indicators of Development 1990*. Baltimore, Md.: Johns Hopkins University, 1991.

————. *Sub-Saharan Africa: From Crisis to Sustainable Growth*. Washington, D.C.: World Bank, 1989.

————. *World Debt Tables 1990-91, Vol. 1*. Washington, D.C.: World Bank, 1990.

————. *World Development Report 1990*. New York: Oxford, 1990.

————. *World Development Report 1991*. New York: Oxford, 1991.

World Hunger Program, Brown University. *Hunger in History: Food Shortage, Poverty, and Deprivation*. New York: Basil Blackwell, 1990.

Worldwatch Institute. *State of the World 1990. Report on Progress Toward a Sustainable Society*. New York: W.W. Norton, 1990.

————. *State of the World 1991. Report on Progress Toward a Sustainable Society*. New York: W.W. Norton, 1991.

Ideas that Work

Food Bank Networks

Christian Science Monitor, October 27, 1987.

Food and Poverty, September/October 1990.

Second Harvest, Maryland Food Committee. Personal interviews.

Maryland Food Committee. *Annual Report, 1990*. Baltimore, Md.: MFC, 1990.

————. *Not by Bread Alone*. Baltimore, Md.: MFC, 1990.

St. Petersburg Times, March 13, 1990.

WHY, Fall 1990/Winter 1991.

Food Aid

Agarwal, Mamta and Shobha A. Udipi. "The Impact of Nutrition Education on Child Feeding Practices among Low-Income Urban Indian Mothers." *Food and Nutrition Bulletin* 11, No. 1 (March 1989), 32-36.

Bajaj, Satinder. "The Nutritional Security System at the Household Level: Policy Implications." *Food and Nutrition Bulletin* 11, No. 4 (December 1989), 6-11.

Berg, Alan. *Malnutrition: What Can Be Done?* Baltimore, Md.: Johns Hopkins, 1987.

Bremer-Fox, Jennifer and Laura Bailey. *The Development Impact of U.S. Program Food Assistance: Evidence from the A.I.D. Evaluation Literature*. Washington, D.C.: Agency for International Development, August 1989.

Brown, Lowell H. Director, Office of Community Outreach, Church World Service. Personal interview.

Brown University Faculty. "Overcoming Hunger: Promising Programs and Policies." *Food Policy* 15, No. 4 (August 1990), 286-298.

Cooperative for American Relief Everywhere (CARE). "Facts at a Glance – 1990."

Cassen, Robert and Associates. *Does Aid Work?* Oxford: Clarendon, 1986.

Cathie, J. "Some Contrasts Between European and U.S. Food Aid Policies." *Food Policy* 15, No. 6 (December 1990), 458-460.

Catholic Relief Services/CARITAS. *Growth Monitoring and Nutrition Education: Impact Evaluation of an Effective Applied Nutrition Program in the Dominican Republic, 1983-1986*. Report prepared for AID, February 1988.

Clay, E.J. and H.W. Singer. "Food Aid and Development: Issues and Evidence, A Survey of the Literature Since 1977 on the Role and Impact of Food Aid in Developing Countries." *World Food Programme Occasional Papers* No. 3, 1985.

Cohen, Marc J. "Food as a Weapon." *Bread for the World Institute Issue Brief*. Washington, D.C.: BFWI, May 1991.

————. "Food for War in Southeast Asia: U.S. Food Aid Policy, 1973-1987." *Wisconsin Papers on Southeast Asia* No. 16, 1988.

————. "U.S. Food Aid to Indonesia: The Carter Administration and Beyond." *Prisma* No. 22 (September 1981), 77-93.

————. "U.S. Food Aid to Southeast Asia, 1975-1983." *Food Policy* 9, No. 2 (May 1984), 139-155.

Food Aid Monitor No. 6. Rome: WFP, March 1991.

Food and Agriculture Organization of the United Nations. Committee on World Food Security. *Prospects for Food Aid and Its Role in the 1990s*. 16th Session. Rome: FAO, 1991.

————. *Meeting the Nutrition Challenge: A Joint FAO/WHO Framework Paper*, October 1990.

Franke, Richard W. and Barbara H. Chasin. "Kerala: Radical Reform as Development in an Indian State." *Food First Development Report* No. 6, October 1989.

Gopaldas, Tara. "Nutrition in India's Eighth Plan." Lecture sponsored by CARE Washington Liaison Office, November 15, 1990.

Guhan, S. "Aid for the Poor: Performance and Possibilities in India." In Lewis, *Strengthening the Poor*, pp. 189-208.

Hay, R.W. and E.J. Clay. "Food Aid and the Development of Human Resources." *World Food Programme Occasional Papers* No. 7, 1986.

Hopkins, Raymond F. Testimony presented to before the Subcommittee on International Economic Policy and Trade, Committee on Foreign Affairs, U.S. House of Representatives, Washington, D.C., April 18, 1990.

———— and Donald Puchala. *Global Food Interdependence*. New York: Columbia University Press, 1980.

Jackson, Tony and Deborah Eade. *Against the Grain: The Dilemma of Project Food Aid*. Oxford: Oxfam, 1982.

Kennedy, Eileen T. "Alternatives to Consumer-Oriented Food Subsidies for Achieving Nutritional Objectives." In *Food Subsidies in Developing Countries: Costs, Benefits, and Policy Options*. Ed. Per Pinstrup-Andersen. Baltimore, Md.: Johns Hopkins University, 1988, pp. 147-158.

———— and Harold H. Alderman. *Comparative Analyses of Nutritional Effectiveness of Food Subsidies and Other Food- Related Interventions*. Washington, D.C.: IFPRI/Joint WHO-UNICEF Nutrition Support Program, 1987.

———— and Per Pinstrup-Andersen. *Nutrition-Related Policies and Programs: Past Performances and Research Needs*. Washington, D.C.: IFPRI, 1983.

King, Joyce, et al. "Program Review of CARE MCH (ICDS and SNP) Title II Program in India." New Delhi: USAID, October 1986.

Lappe, Frances Moore, Rachel Schurman, and Kevin Danaher. *Betraying the National Interest*. New York: Grove, 1987.

Library of Congress. Foreign Affairs and National Defense Division, Congressional Research Service. *Feeding the World's Population: Developments in the Decade Following the World Food Conference of 1974. Report Prepared for the Committee on Foreign Affairs, United States House of Representatives.* Washington, D.C.: GPO, 1984.

Mahajan, R.C. Administrator, CARE-Karnataka. Personal interview.

Minear, Larry. "Development Through Food: Some Nongovernmental Reflections." In *Report of the World Food Programme-Government of the Netherlands Seminar on Food Aid*, pp. 55-66.

Mora, José, Joyce M. King, and Charles H. Teller. "The Effectiveness of Maternal and Child Health Supplementary Feeding Programs." Washington, D.C.: AID, September 1990.

National Institute of Public Cooperation and Child Development, *Perspective Plan on Child Development (1980-2000).* New Delhi: NIPCCD, 1984.

Pinstrup-Andersen, Per. "Nutrition Interventions." In Cornia, Jolly, and Stewart, *Adjustment*, pp. 241-256.

Relief and Development Institute, London. "A Study of Triangular Transactions and Local Purchases in Food Aid." *World Food Programme Occasional Papers* No. 11, July 1987.

Ruttan, Vernon W. "International Food Aid: Interest Groups and Clients." *Choices*, Third Quarter 1990, pp. 12-16.

——————. "International Food Aid: Changed, but Contradictions Continue." *Choices*, First Quarter 1991, pp. 3-7.

Sadasivan, T.R. Administrator, CARE-Rajasthan. Personal interview.

Schomer, Mark. "Food Aid: Beyond Deploring." *Bread for the World Background Paper* No. 30. Washington, D.C.: BFW, December 1978.

Shaw, D.J. Economist, United Nations World Food Programme. Personal interview.

Singer, Hans, John Wood, and Tony Jennings. *Food Aid: The Challenge and the Opportunity.* Oxford: Clarendon, 1987.

Singh, Tarlok. "Food, Food Aid, and Development." In *Report of the World Food Programme-Government of the Netherlands Seminar on Food Aid.* Rome: WFP, 1983, pp. 47-54.

Stevens, Christopher. *Food Aid and the Developing World.* London: Croon Helm and Overseas Development Institute, 1979.

"A Survey of India." *Economist*, May 4, 1991.

Sykes, Charles. Vice President for Public Policy, CARE. Personal interview.

Teller, Charles H. and Lucas Owuor-Omondi. *Summary Report: A Systems Analysis and Baseline Study of the Maternal and Child Health and Nutrition Program.* Nairobi: Catholic Relief Services, February 1991.

Turnipseed, R. Lawrence. Director for Southern Asia, Church World Service. Personal interview.

United Nations Children's Fund. *ICDS – Integrated Child Development Services in India.* New Delhi: UNICEF, 1984.

United Nations World Food Programme. *1991 Food Aid Review.* Rome: WFP, 1991.

——————. *Report of the World Food Programme-Government of the Netherlands Seminar on Food Aid.* Rome: WFP, 1983.

United States Agency for International Development. *Congressional Presentation, Main Volume, FYs 1990-1991.*

United States Department of Agriculture. *Food for Peace: Annual Reports on Public Law 480, FYs 1984-1987.*

Vanderslice, Lane. "Malnutrition, Children, and the P.L.-480 Program, A Report by the National Council for International Health." Washington, D.C.: NCIH, March 30, 1990.

Weinbaum, Marvin. *Egypt and the Politics of U.S. Economic Aid.* Boulder, Colo. and London: Westview, 1986.

Weiner, Myron. *The Child and the State in India.* Princeton: Princeton University, 1991.

Saving Trees

Aaronson, Terri. "World Priorities." *Environment* 14, No. 6 (July/August 1972), 4-13.

Abrol, I.P. "Salt-Affected Soils: Problems and Prospects in Developing Countries." In *Global Aspects of Food Production.* Eds. M.S. Swaminathan and S.K. Sinha. London: Tycooly, 1986.

Agarwal, Anil. *Beyond Pretty Trees and Tigers: The Role of Ecological Destruction in the Emerging Patterns of Poverty and People's Protests. Fifth Vikram Sarabhai Memorial Lecture.* New Delhi: Indian Council of Social Science Research, August 13, 1984.

—————— and Sunita Narain. *Towards Green Villages: A Strategy for Environmentally-Sound and Participatory Rural Development.* New Delhi: Centre for Science and Environment, 1989.

Agarwal, Bina. *Cold Hearths and Barren Slopes: The Woodfuel Crisis in the Third World.* Riverdale, Md.: Riverdale Co., 1986.

Ahmad, Yusuf, Salah E. Serafy, and Ernst Lutz. *Environmental Accounting for Sustainable Development.* Washington, D.C.: World Bank, 1990.

Bandyopadhyay, Jayanta and Bandana Shiva. "Chipko: Rekindling India's Forest Culture." *Ecologist* (January/February 1987).

Barghouti, Shawki and Dominique Lallement. "Water Management: Problems and Potentials in the Sahelian and Sudanian Zones." In *Desertification Control and Renewable Resource Management in the Sahelian and Sudanian Zones of West Africa.* Eds. François Falloux and Aleki Mukendi. *World Bank Technical Paper* No. 70. Washington, D.C.: World Bank, 1988.

Bonfiglioli, Angelo M. "Management of Pastoral Production in the Sahel – Constraints and Options." In *World Bank Technical Paper* No. 70.

Brown, Janet Welsh. "Poverty and Environmental Degradation: Basic Concerns for U.S. Cooperation with Developing Countries," in Janet Welsh Brown, ed. *In the U.S. Interest: Resources, Growth, and Security in the Developing World.* Boulder, Colo.: Westview, 1990.

Brown, Lester. "The New World Order." In Worldwatch, *State of the World 1991.*

—————— and John E. Young. "Feeding the World in the Nineties." In Worldwatch, *State of the World 1990.*

Burand, Deborah K. *The Debt-for-Nature Exchange: A Tool for International Conservation, 1991 Update.* Washington, D.C.: Conservation International, 1991.

Center for International Development and Environment, World Resources Institute. *From the Ground Up* Series. Washington, D.C., 1990.

Chew, Siew Tuan. *Agroforestry Projects for Small Farmers: A Project Manager's Reference.* Washington, D.C.: AID, 1989.

Clarke, Robin and Lloyd Timberlake. *Stockholm Plus Ten.* London: International Institute for Environment and Development, an Earthscan Paperback, 1982.

Cook, Cynthia C. and Mikael Grut. *Agroforestry in Sub-Saharan Africa: A Farmer's Perspective.* Washington, D.C.: World Bank, 1989.

Dankelmann, Irene and Joan Davidson. *Women and Environment in the Third World: Alliance for the Future.* London: Earthscan, 1988.

Durning, Alan B. *Poverty and the Environment: Reversing the Downward Spiral. Worldwatch Paper* No. 92. Washington, D.C.: Worldwatch Institute, November 1989.

Falloux, François and Alain Rochegude. "Land Tenure as a Tool for Rational Resource Management." In *World Bank Technical Paper* No. 70.

Fearnside, Phillip M. "A Prescription for Slowing Deforestation in Amazonia." *Environment* 31, No. 4 (May 1989).

Floor, Willem and Jean Gorse. "Household Energy Issues in West Africa." In *World Bank Technical Paper* No. 70.

Food and Agriculture Organization of the U.N. *Agriculture: Toward 2000*. Rome: FAO, 1980.

Global Tomorrow Coalition. *Sustainable Development: A Guide to "Our Common Future"*. Washington, D.C.: GTC, 1989.

Gómez, Manel I. "A Resource Inventory of Indigenous and Traditional Foods in Zimbabwe." *Zambezia: Journal of the University of Zimbabwe* 15 (1988).

Harley, Richard M. *Breakthroughs on Hunger: A Journalist's Encounter with Global Change*. Washington, D.C.: Smithsonian, 1990.

Henry, Neil. "Arid Botswana Keeps Its Democracy Afloat – Government Bows to Public's Wish and Postpones River Dredging, Irrigation Scheme." *Washington Post*, March 21, 1991, p. A31.

International Institute of Tropical Agriculture. *Annual Report 1989/1990*. Ibadan, Nigeria: IITA, 1990.

Jackson, Ben. *Poverty and the Planet: A Question of Survival*. London: Penguin, 1990.

Jacobson, Jodi L. *Environmental Refugees: A Yardstick of Habitability*. Worldwatch Paper No. 86. Washington, D.C.: Worldwatch Institute, November 1988.

Jain, Shobhita. "Women and People's Ecological Movement: A Case Study of Women's Role in the Chipko Movement in Uttar Pradesh." *Economic and Political Weekly*, October 13, 1984, pp. 1788-1794.

Joshi, P.K. and Dayanatha Jha. "Environmental Externalities in Surface Irrigation Systems in India." In *Environmental Aspects of Agricultural Development*. IFPRI Policy Briefs No. 6. Washington, D.C.: IFPRI, 1989.

Kerkhof, Paul. *Agroforestry in Africa: A Survey of Project Experience*. London: Panos Institute, 1990.

Kumar, Shubh K. and David Hotchkiss. *Consequences of Deforestation for Women's Time Allocation, Agricultural Production, and Nutrition in Hill Areas of Nepal*. Research Report No. 69. Washington, D.C.: IFPRI, 1988.

Lutz, Ernst and Mohan Munasinghe. "Accounting for the Environment: An Improved Way of Preparing National Accounts Could Help Achieve More Sustainable Development." *Finance and Development* (March 1991).

Mearns, Robin. "Environmental Implications of Structural Adjustment: Reflections on Scientific Method." *IDS Discussion Paper* No. 284, February 1991.

Mellor, John. "The Intertwining of Environmental Problems and Poverty." *Environment* 30, No. 9 (November 1988).

Munasinghe, Mohan and Ernst Lutz. *Environmental-Economic Evaluation of Projects and Policies for Sustainable Development. Environment Department Working Paper* No. 42. Washington, D.C.: World Bank, January 1991.

National Research Council. Committee on the Role of Alternative Farming Methods in Modern Production Agriculture. *Alternative Agriculture*. Washington, D.C.: National Academy, 1989.

Oxfam and the Environment. Boston: Oxfam, 1991.

"Partnership in West Africa: The Road to Freedom From Hunger." *Hunger Notes* 16, No. 3 (Winter 1991).

Pimentel, D. et al. "World Agriculture & Soil Erosion." *Bioscience* 37 (1981), 277-283.

Poole, Peter. *Developing a Partnership of Indigenous Peoples, Conservationists, and Land Use Planners in Latin America. World Bank Policy, Planning, and Research Working Papers*. WPS 245. Washington, D.C.: World Bank, Latin America and the Caribbean Technical Department, August 1989.

Postel, Sandra. "Saving Water for Agriculture." In Worldwatch, *State of the World 1990*.

——— and Christopher Flavin. "Reshaping the Global Economy." In Worldwatch, *State of the World 1991*.

——— and John C. Ryan. "Reforming Forestry." In Worldwatch, *State of the World 1991*.

Reardon, Thomas. "Sustainability Issues in Sahelian Agricultural Development and Research." In *Environmental Aspects of Agricultural Development. IFPRI Policy Brief* No. 6. Washington, D.C.: IFPRI, 1990.

Reid, Walter V.C. "Sustainable Development. Lessons from Success." *Environment* 31, No. 4 (May 1989).

———, James N. Barnes, and Brent Blackwelder. *Bankrolling Successes: A Portfolio of Sustainable Development Projects*. Washington, D.C.: Environmental Policy Institute and National Wildlife Federation, 1988.

Repetto, R. *The Forest for the Trees*. Washington, D.C.: World Resources Institute, 1988.

Sands, Michael. "Community Land Use Management Project in Ecuador." In *Experiences in Success*. Eds. Kenneth Tull and Michael Sands. Emmaus, Pa.: Rodale International, 1987.

"Senegal's Small Farmers Speak Out." *Hunger Notes* 16, No. 3 (Winter 1991).

Singh, R. P. "Dryland/Rainfed Agriculture and Water Resources Management Research and Development in India." In *Sharing Innovation: Global Perspectives on Food, Agriculture, and Rural Development*. Ed. Neil G. Kotler. Washington, D.C.: Smithsonian, 1990.

Task Force on International Development & Environmental Security, Environmental & Energy Study Institute. "Partnership for Sustainable Development: A New U.S. Agenda for International Development and Environmental Security." Washington, D.C.: EESI, May 1991.

Timberlake, Lloyd. *Africa in Crisis: The Causes, the Cures of Environmental Bankruptcy*. London and Washington, D.C.: International Institute for Environment and Development, an Earthscan Paperback, 1988.

Towards Sustainable Development: Fourteen Case-Study Reports Prepared by African and Asian Journalists for the Nordic Conference on Environment and Development (May 8-10, 1987, Stockholm, Sweden). London: Panos Institute, 1987.

Tull, Kenneth and Michael Sands, eds. *Experiences in Success: Case Studies in Growing Food through Regenerative Agriculture*. Emmaus, Pa: Rodale, 1987.

United Nations Environment Programme. *General Assessment of Progress in the Implementation of the Plan of Action to Combat Desertification*. New York: U.N., 1984.

United Nations World Food Council. *The Global State of Hunger and Malnutrition*. Rome: WFC, 1990.

United States Agency for International Development. *Highlights* 7, No. 3 (Winter 1990).

World Commission on Environment and Development. *Our Common Future*. New York: Oxford, 1987.

World Resources Institute. Unpublished proposals to the Michigan State University Conference on Cooperation for International Development. East Lansing, Mich: MSU, May 15-18, 1988.

Wright, Eleanor. "Banking on Environmental Protection: The World Bank and NGO Initiatives." *Hunger Notes* 13, Nos. 9 & 10 (Feb./March 1988).

Green Revolution

Bernsten, Rick. Personal communication.

Global Tomorrow Coalition. *The Global Ecology Handbook*. Boston: Beacon, 1990.

Mellor, John W. and Ginvant M. Desai, eds. *Agricultural Change and Rural Poverty*. Baltimore: Johns Hopkins, 1985.

Wolf, Edward C. *Beyond the Green Revolution: New Approaches for Third World Agriculture*. Worldwatch Paper No. 73. Washington, D.C.: Worldwatch Institute, 1986.

Costa Rica

Ameringer, Charles D. *Don Pepe: A Political Biography of José Figueres of Costa Rica*. Albuquerque, N.M.: University of New Mexico, 1979.

Anderson, Leslie. "Alternative Action in Costa Rica: Peasants as Positive Participants." *Journal of Latin American Studies* 22 (February 1990), 89-113.

Barry, Tom and Deb Preusch. *The Central American Fact Book*. New York: Grove, 1986.

Bell, John Patrick. *Crisis in Costa Rica: The Revolution of 1948*. Austin, Tex.: University of Texas, 1971.

Biesanz, John and Mavis. *Costa Rican Life*. New York: Columbia, 1944.

Bird, Leonard. *Costa Rica: The Unarmed Democracy*. London: Shepard, 1984.

Booth, John A. "Representative Constitutional Democracy in Costa Rica: Adaptation to Crisis in the Turbulent 1980s." In *Central America: Crisis and Adaptation*. Eds. Steve C. Ropp and James A. Morris. Albuquerque, N.M.: University of New Mexico, 1984.

————— and Mitchell A. Seligson, eds. *Elections and Democracy in Central America*. Chapel Hill, N.C.: University of North Carolina, 1989.

"Building a Contra Air Base. A Memo from Robert Owen to Lieutenant Colonel Oliver North." Reprinted in Edelman and Kenan, pp. 349-354.

Edelman, Marc and Joanne Kenen, eds. *The Costa Rica Reader*. New York: Grove Weidenfeld, 1989.

Fallas, Carlos Luis. "The Great Atlantic Banana Plantation Strike of 1934." In *Mamita Yunai*. San José: Librería Lehmann, 1980. Quoted in Edelman and Kenen.

Fernández, Juan Mora. "Mensaje del Poder Ejecutivo a la Asamblea, 1828." In *Juan Mora Fernández*. Ed. Carmen Lila Gómez. San José: UNED, 1984. Quoted in Edelman and Kenen.

Food and Agriculture Organization of the United Nations. *Potentials for Agricultural and Rural Development in Latin America and the Caribbean: Annex I, Economic and Social Development*. LARC 88/3. Rome: FAO, 1988.

Jantzi, Vernon Eugene. *Structural Determinants of the Location of Rural Development Institutions in Costa Rica*. Diss. *Cornell University Latin American Studies Program Dissertation Series* No. 65, January 1976.

McNeil, Frank. *War and Peace in Central America*. New York: Charles Scribner's Sons, 1988.

Nelson, Harold D., ed. *Costa Rica: A Country Study*. Washington, D.C.: GPO, 1983.

"Nutrition and Health in the Americas." *Food and Nutrition Bulletin* 9, No. 3 (September, 1987).

Rolbein, Seth. *Nobel Costa Rica*. New York: St. Martin, 1989.

Sheahan, John. *Patterns of Development in Latin America: Poverty, Repression, and Economic Strategy*. Princeton: Princeton, 1987.

United Nations. *Disarmament Yearbook*. Vol. 14. New York: U.N., 1989.

Demilitarization

Beckmann, David. "Sober Prospects and Christian Hope." In Beckmann, et al. *Friday Morning Reflections at the World Bank: Essays on Values and Development*. Washington, D.C.: Seven Locks, 1991, pp. 17-35.

Deger, Saadet and Somnath Sen. "Defense Expenditures, Aid, and Economic Development." Paper presented at the World Bank's Annual Conference on Development Economics, Washington, D.C., April 25-26, 1991.

Kaldor, Mary. "Problems of Adjustment to Lower Levels of Military Spending in Developed and Developing Countries." Paper presented at the World Bank's Annual Conference on Development Economics, Washington, D.C., April 25-26, 1991.

McNamara, Robert S. "The Post-Cold War World and Its Implications for Military Expenditures in Developing Countries." Paper presented at the World Bank's Annual Conference on Development Economics, Washington, D.C., April 25-26, 1991.

Melman, Seymour. *The Demilitarized Society*. Montreal: Harvest House, 1988.

Oberdorfer, Don. "Strategy for Solo Superpower." *Washington Post*, May 19, 1991.

Pearlstein, Steven. "The Big Bucks in Dirty Weapons." *Washington Post*, May 19, 1991.

Sanders, Ralph. *Arms Industries: New Suppliers and Regional Security*. Washington, D.C.: National Defense University, 1990.

Simon, Arthur. *Harvesting Peace: The Arms Race and Human Need*. Kansas City, Mo.: Sheed & Ward, 1990.

United Nations Department for Disarmament Affairs. *Disarmament Publications*. Sixth Edition. New York: U.N., 1990.

United States Arms Control and Disarmament Agency. *World Military Expenditures and Arms Transfers 1989*. Washington, D.C.: GPO, October 1990.

Winter, Gibson. "Hope for the Earth: A Hermeneutic of Nuclearism in Ecumenical Perspective." *The 1983 William Henry Hoover Lecture on Christian Unity*. Chicago: The Disciples Divinity House of the University of Chicago, 1983.

Economic Policies

Abba, Alkasum. et al. *The Nigerian Economic Crisis, Causes, and Solutions*. Zaria, Nigeria: Ahmadu Bello University, 1985.

Abdullahi, Y.A. "The State and Agrarian Crisis: Rhetoric and Substance of Nigerian Agricultural Policy." Paper Read at Workshop on State of the Economy, Zaria, Nigeria, Ahmadu Bello University, 1983.

Adam, Mohammed. "Nigeria: The Busted Boom." *International Perspectives* (January-February 1987).

Agbroko, G. "Pains for Gains." *The African Guardian* 3, No. 25 (July 4, 1988), 14-25.

Bevan, David, Paul Collier, and Jan Gunning. *Indonesia and Nigeria*. Unpublished. September 1988.

Bonat, Zuwaghu and Yahaya A. Abdullahi. "The World Bank, IMF, and the Nigerian Agricultural and Rural Economy." In *The IMF, the World Bank, and the African Debt: The Social and Political Impact*. Ed. Bade Onimode. London: Zed, 1989.

Bonner, Raymond. "The New Order." *The New Yorker* (June 6 and 13, 1988).

Business Concord. Lagos, Nigeria, May 21, 1986.

Central Bank of Nigeria. *1987 Budget* and *1988 Budget*. Lagos: Central Bank of Nigeria.

Elabor-Idemudia, P. *A Study of Factors Affecting Extension in Nigeria with Particular Emphasis on Rubber Farming in Bendel State*. Master's Thesis. University of Guelph, Canada, 1984.

—————. "The Impact of Structural Adjustment Programs on Women and their Households in Bendel and Ogun States, Nigeria." In *Structural Adjustment and African Women Farmers*. Ed. Christina Gladwin. Gainesville, Fla.: University of Florida, 1990.

—————. "The Impact of Structural Adjustment Programmes on Rural Women's Production Resources and Quality of Life in Nigeria." New York: U.N., forthcoming.

Elson, Dianne. "The Impact of Structural Adjustment on Women: Concepts and Issues." Paper No. 2 for the Institute for African Alternatives Conference on the Impact of IMF/World Bank Policies on the People of Africa, London, September 7-10, 1987.

Emmerson, Donald K. "Indonesia in 1990." *Asian Survey* 31, No. 2 (Feb., 1991) 179-187.

Food and Agriculture Organization of the United Nations. *Indonesia: ESN – Nutrition Country Profile.* Rome: FAO, 1989.

—————. *The Fifth World Food Survey, 1985.* Rome: FAO, 1987.

Government of Indonesia and UNICEF. *Situation Analysis of Children and Women in Indonesia.* Jakarta, 1988.

Helleiner, K. *Peasant Agriculture, Government and Economic Growth in Nigeria.* Homewood, Ill.: Richard D. Irwin, 1966, pp. 152- 159.

Human Rights Watch. *Human Rights in Indonesia and East Timor: An Asia Watch Report.* New York, 1989.

International Fund for Agricultural Development. *Rural Indonesia: Socio-Economic Development in a Changing Environment.* Rome: IFAD, 1988.

Lancaster, Carol. "Economic Restructuring in Sub-Saharan Africa." *Current History* 88 (May 1989), 538.

Loxley, John. "The Berg Report and the Model of Accumulation in Sub-Saharan Africa." *Review of African Political Economy* Nos. 27/28.

Mohammed, Abdul. "Issues Paper for Subregional Workshop on Grassroots Perspectives on Africa's Crisis." Unpublished. February, 1990.

National Concord. Lagos, Nigeria, August 16, 1990.

Ojo, M.O. "An Appraisal of the Socio-Economic Impact of Structural Adjustment Policies." *Central Bank of Nigeria: Economic and Financial Review* 27, No. 1 (1989), 2.

Toyo, Eskor. *The Working Class and the Nigerian Crisis.* Ibadan: Mimeo, 1986.

World Bank. *Accelerated Development in Sub-Saharan Africa: An Agenda for Action* (The "Berg Report"). Washington, D.C.: World Bank, 1981.

—————. "Development in a Javanese Village." *World Development Report 1990*, p. 41.

—————. *Indonesia: Strategy for a Sustained Reduction in Poverty.* Washington, D.C.: World Bank, 1990. David Beckmann contributed to this report.

—————. *Toward Sustained Development in Sub-Saharan Africa: A Joint Program of Action.* Washington: World Bank, 1984.

—————. *World Development Report 1989.* Washington, D.C.: World Bank, 1989.

Refugees in El Salvador

Barry, Tom. *El Salvador: A Country Guide.* Albuquerque, N.M.: Inter-Hemispheric Education Resource Center, 1990.

————— and Deb Preusch. *The Soft War.* New York: Grove, 1990.

Catholic Relief Services. "Human Rights and Humanitarian Aid in European Economic Community-Supported Populations in El Salvador." Paper prepared for Resident European Economic Community Ambassadors in El Salvador.

Church World Service. "Humanitarian Concerns in El Salvador: An Update." Statement before the Subcommittee on Western Hemisphere Affairs, Committee on Foreign Affairs, U.S. House of Representatives, April 11, 1991.

Compher, Vic. and Betsy Morgan. *Going Home: Building Peace in El Salvador, the Story of Repatriation.* New York: Apex, 1991.

CRIPDES News Bulletin. San Salvador. March 1991.

Edwards, Beatrice and Gretta Tovar-Siebentritt. *Places of Origin: The Repopulation of Rural El Salvador.* Boulder, Colo.: Lynne Reinner, 1991.

Foundation CORDES. San Salvador. February 1991.

Popkin, Eric. "The Impact of the Repopulation Movement on the U.S. Counterinsurgency Project in El Salvador, 1986-1990." Draft manuscript, January 1991.

"Salvadoran Refugees Under Fire." *Honduras Update* 6 (June/July 1988), 9-10.

Schrading, Ron. "The Repopulation Movement of El Salvador." The Project Counselling Service for Latin American Refugees. Mimeographed, October 1990.

Segal, Barbara. "U.S. Aid and the Crisis of Hunger and Poverty in El Salvador." *Bread for the World Background Paper* No. 121. Washington, D.C.: BFW, May 1991.

United States General Accounting Office. *El Salvador: Flow of U.S. Military Aid,* March 1991.

Tanzania

African Development Foundation (ADF) Field Staff in Tanzania. Fax. May 16, 1991.

—————. "*Project Appraisal Memorandum, August 9, 1988.*" Mimeographed. Washington, D.C.: ADF.

Brown University. *The Associates Report.* Vol.6, No. 1, Winter 1991. Providence, R.I.

Broad, Robin, John Cavanagh, and Walden Bello. "Development: The Market Is not Enough." *Foreign Policy*, No. 81 (Winter 1990-1991).

Budget Summary. Appendix A-1 of ADF Memorandum of August 15, 1988. Mimeographed. Washington, D.C.: ADF.

Cheru, Fantu. *The Silent Revolution in Africa: Debt, Development and Democracy.* London: Zed, 1989.

Durning, Alan B. "Life on the Brink." *Worldwatch* 3, No. 2 (March-April 1990).

"Grant Application, Water Supply Project of Usseri and Takakea Divisions, September 24, 1987." Mimeographed. Washington, D.C.: ADF.

Helen Keller International. "Primary Eye Health Programme, September 1990." Field Report from Dodoma, Tanzania. New York: HKI.

Jacobson, Jodi. "The Forgotten Resource." *Worldwatch* 1, No. 3 (May-June 1988).

Korten, David. *Getting to the 21st Century: Voluntary Action & Global Agenda.* W. Hartford, Conn.: Kumarian, 1990.

—————. *People-centered Development: Contributions Toward Theory and Planning Frameworks.* W. Hartford, Conn.: Kumarian, 1984.

Maskini, As. Chairman of Shauritanga Memorial Fund. "Address on the Occasion of ADF President L. Robinson's Visit, Dar Es Salaam, March 2, 1990." Mimeographed. Washington: ADF, 1990.

Pauling, Sharon. "Ending War and Famine in the Horn of Africa through Grassroots Initiatives." *Bread for the World Background Paper* No. 119. Washington, D.C.: BFW, March 1991.

Pearce, David W. *Sustainable Development: Economics and Environment in the Third World.* Great Britain: Billing & Sons, 1990.

Pradervand, Pierre. *Listening to Africa: Developing Africa from the Grassroots.* New York: Praeger, 1989.

A Proposed Programme for Child Survival and Development in Rombo District. Mimeographed. Dar Es Salaam: District Executive Directors Office, Rombo and the Tanzania Food and Nutrition Program, July 1986.

Uphoff, Norman. *Local Institutional Development: An Analytical Sourcebook with Cases.* W. Hartford, Conn: Kumarian, 1986.

United States Geological Survey. *Water Supply Study Paper 2350.* Washington, D.C.: GPO, 1990.

United States. Congress. Office of Technology Assessment. *OTA Report Brief: Grassroots Development, the African*

Development Foundation. Washington, D.C.: GPO, June 1988.

──────. *Grassroots Development: the African Development Foundation*. OTA-F-378. Washington, D.C.: GPO, June 1988.

"Women Show the Way to Better Health." *Oxfam News*, Spring 1991.

St. Louis

Missouri Association for Social Welfare, Taskforce on Hunger. *Hunger in Missouri*. Jefferson City, Mo.: MASW, 1986.

IAF

Alinsky, Saul. *Reveille for Radicals*. New York: Random House, Vintage, 1969.

──────. *Rules for Radicals: A Pragmatic Primer for Realistic Radicals*. New York: Random House, Vintage, 1971.

Bobo, Kim, Jackie Kendall, and Steve Max. *Organizing for Social Change: A Manual for Activists in the 1990s*. Washington, D.C.: Seven Locks, 1991.

Cortes, Ernesto. "The 'organizer's organizer' on organizing: remarks by." *Texas Observer* 78, No. 14 (July 11, 1986); reprinted in *Christianity and Crisis* 47, No. 1 (February 2, 1987), 20-22.

Finks, P. David. *The Radical Vision of Saul Alinsky*. New York: Paulist, 1984.

Hoehn, Richard. *Up From Apathy: A Study of Moral Awareness and Social Involvement*. Nashville, Tenn: Abingdon, 1983.

Horwitt, Sanford D. *Let Them Call Me Rebel: Saul Alinsky – His Life and Legacy*. New York: Knopf, 1989.

Richards, Cecile. Fax, June 10, 1991.

Rocawich, Linda. "Interview: Ernesto Cortes, Jr." *Texas Observer* 82, No. 23 (November 1990), 9-11.

Rogers, Mary Beth. *Cold Anger: A Story of Faith and Power Politics*. Denton, Tex: University of North Texas, 1990.

Sanders, Marion K. *The Professional Radical: Conversations with Saul Alinsky*. New York: Harper & Row, 1970.

Citizen Advocacy

Food Research and Action Center. *WIC: A Success Story, Third Edition*. Washington, D.C.: FRAC, 1991.

Harris, Sam. "Mobilizing Opinion: Achieving Results." *Food Policy* 15, No. 4 (August 1990).

Hertzke, Allen D. *Representing God in Washington: The Role of Religious Lobbies in the American Polity*. Knoxville: University of Tennessee, 1988.

Simon, Arthur. *Christian Faith and Public Policy: No Grounds for Divorce*. Grand Rapids, Mich.: Eerdmans, 1987.

Updates

Africa

Adedeji, Adebayo. "A Preliminary Assessment of the Performance of the African Economy in 1990 and Prospects for 1991." Addis Ababa: ECA, January 14, 1991.

Africa News, October 22, 1990 and January 29, 1990.

Africa Recovery 4, No. 2 (July-September 1990) and 4, Nos. 3-4 (October-December 1990).

Africa Watch Committee. *Somalia: A Government at War with Its Own People*. New York: Human Rights Watch, 1990.

Bailey, Jane, et al. "Famine in Sudan: The Proceedings of a One Day Symposium." *Institute of Development Studies Discussion Paper* No. 283, December 1990.

Baker, Pauline H. "Africa in the New World Order." *SAIS Review* 10 (Summer-Fall 1990).

"Can Africa Feed Itself?" *World Development*, November 1990.

Catholic Relief Service. "Somalia: Current Conditions and U.S. Policy." *Report for Congress*, May 12, 1990.

Clark, Andrew and Ann Weston. "Africa's Commodity Problems: The Fraser Report and the OAU Response." Ottawa: North-South Institute, n.d.

Copson, Raymond W. "Sudan: Foreign Assistance Facts." *Catholic Relief Service Issue Brief*, updated January 10, 1991.

Dagne, Theodore S. "Ethiopia: War and Famine." *Catholic Relief Service Issue Brief*, updated March 14, 1991.

Dejene, Alemneh. *Environment, Famine and Politics in Ethiopia: A View from the Village*. Boulder, Colo.: Lynne Rienner, 1990.

"Ethiopia: 200 Days in the Death of Asmara." *News from Africa Watch*, September 20, 1990.

Horn of Africa Bulletin, December 1990 and January-February 1991.

"Mengistu has Decided to Burn Us Like Wood."*News From Africa Watch*, July 24, 1990.

Middle East Journal 14, No. 4 (Autumn 1990).

Prendergast, John. "The Crisis of Survival." *Africa Report*, January-February 1991.

──────. *The Struggle for Sudan's Soul: Political and Agrarian Roots of War and Famine*. Washington, D.C.: Center of Concern, September 1990.

────── and Sharon Pauling. *Peace, Development and People of the Horn of Africa. Hunger Policy Occasional Paper* No. 1. Washington, D.C.: Bread for the World Institute on Hunger and Development, forthcoming.

"Somalia: Evading Reality." *News From Africa Watch*, September 12, 1990.

"Sudan: Nationwide Famine." *News From Africa Watch*, November 7, 1990.

Topouzis, Daphne. "The Feminization of Poverty." *Africa Report*, July-August 1990.

United Nations Non-Governmental Liaison Service. *Impact of Armed Conflict on Africa's Development. Voices from Africa* No. 3, March 1991.

United States Agency for International Development. Famine Early Warning System. *Bulletin* No. 1/91, March 8, 1991.

──────. *Bulletin* No. 13/90, January 30, 1991.

──────. "Harvest Assessment of Cereal Production," January 1991.

United States Congress. House. Select Committee on Hunger. *Crisis of the Third World Refugees*. Hearing Report, February 8, 1990.

Von Braun, Joachim and Leonardo Paulino. "Food in Sub-Saharan Africa: Trends and Policy Changes for the 1990s." *Food Policy* 15, No. 6 (December 1990).

Westlake, Melvyn. "Why a Continent Suffers in Silence." *Guardian*, February 5, 1991.

Asia and the Pacific

General

Asian Development Bank Quarterly Review, May 1991.

──────. *Asian Development Outlook 1991*. Manila: ADB, 1991.

Cohen, Marc J. and Jenny Jones. "Changes in Asian Agriculture: 1970-1990." *AMPO Japan-Asia Quarterly Review* 22, Nos. 2-3 (1991), 46-55.

Far Eastern Economic Review, July 18, 1991, pp. 47-48. (Thailand)

Far Eastern Economic Review Asia 1991 Yearbook.

Gopalan, C. *Nutrition Problems and Programmes in South-East Asia*. SEARO, 1987, pp. 39-42.

Qureshi, Rahmat U. *Food Consumption, Nutritional Situation and Nutritional Concerns in Selected Countries of the Asia-Pacific Region*. Bangkok: FAO, 1987.

Singh, Inderjit. *The Great Ascent: The Rural Poor in South Asia*. Washington, D.C.: Johns Hopkins, 1990.

Afghanistan

Elliot, Theodore F., Jr. "Afghanistan in 1990: Groping Toward Peace?" *Asian Survey* 31, No. 2 (February 1991), 125-133.

Far Eastern Economic Review, March 7, 1991.

Bangladesh

Baxter, Craig. "Bangladesh 1990: Another New Beginning?" *Asian Survey* 31, No. 2 (February 1991), 146-152.

Far Eastern Economic Review. March 14 and 28, May 16, 1991.

Washington Post, News coverage of the cyclone and relief efforts. May 1-8 and 10-13, 1991.

Cambodia

"Coming Back from the Border." *Refugees* (April 1991), 30.

Far Eastern Economic Review, April 25, May 30, and July 4, 1991.

"Still on the Critical List." *Refugees*, (December 1989), 21.

Van der Kroef, Justus M. "Cambodia in 1990: The Elusive Peace." *Asian Survey* 31, No. 1 (January 1991), 94-102.

China

"Chinese Floods." *Washington Post*, July 18, 1991.

Far Eastern Economic Review, June 27, July 25, and August 1, 1991.

Leung, Julia. "Floods Destroy 10% of Summer Crop in China & Threaten Autumn Grain." *Wall Street Journal*, July 17, 1991.

Sun, Lena H. "Floods Spur China to Ask World for Aid." *Washington Post*, July 12, 1991.

East Timor

Dos Reis, Joao. "East Timor: Emerging from Silence." *AMPO Japan-Asia Quarterly Review* 22, No. 1 (1990), 30-34.

Laos

Far Eastern Economic Review, April 18 and July 11, 1991.

Gunn, Geoffrey C. "Laos in 1990: Winds of Change." *Asian Survey* 31, No. 1 (January 1991), 87-93.

Wilson, T. Hunter. "The Work of Peace: Changes in Laos Under the Lao People's Democratic Republic." *Indochina Newsletter* No. 48 (November-December 1987).

"Laos – The Year There Was No Rice." *WFP Journal* No. 15 (July-September 1990), 28-30.

Refugees (December 1989), 21.

Stuart-Fox, Martin. "Laos at the Crossroads." *Indochina Issues*, No. 92 (March 1991).

Vijayaraghavan, K. "Assignment Report: Analysis of Nutrition Survey Data, Lao People's Democratic Republic." (WP)NUT/LAO/NUT/001-E. Geneva: World Health Organization, February 22, 1988.

Myanmar (Burma)

Far Eastern Economic Review, April 18, 1991.

Guyot, James F. "Myanmar in 1990: The Unconsummated Election." *Asian Survey* 31, No. 2 (February 1991), 205-211.

Khaw, Moe, exiled Burmese student leader. Personal interview. Food and Agriculture Organzation of the United Nations. "Myanmar, Union of." *ESN-Nutrition Country Profile*. Rome: FAO, 1990.

Papua New Guinea

Far Eastern Economic Review, February 7, 1991.

Wesley-Smith, Terence. "Papua New Guinea in 1990." *Asian Survey* 31, No. 2 (February 1991), 188-195.

Philippines

Far Eastern Economic Review, January 10, February 7, 14, and 21, March 21, April 11, June 13 and 27, July 4, 18, and 25, 1991.

Manila Chronicle, December 24, 1990, January 9 and 14, March 7, 1991.

New Chronicle, n.d., April 26, and July 2, 1991.

Philippine Daily Inquirer, December 1 and 24, 1990, March 25, 1991.

Philippine Star, December 21, 1990.

Timberman, David G. "The Philippines in 1990: On Shaky Ground." *Asian Survey* 31, No. 2 (February 1991), 153-163.

Sri Lanka

Economist, May 25, 1991.

Oxfam News, Summer 1991.

United Nations Children's Fund. *Sri Lanka: Country Programme Recommendation*. New York: UNICEF, February 22, 1988.

—————. *Programme Development in South Central Asian Region*. New York: UNICEF, February 11, 1991.

—————. *Recommendation for Supplementary Funding for Programme in the Asia Region without Recommendation for Funding from General Resources*. New York: UNICEF, 15 February 1991.

Refugees (April 1989).

Latin America and the Caribbean

General

Andreas, Peter and Coletta Youngers. " 'Busting' the Andean Cocaine Industry." *World Policy Journal* 6, No. 3 (Summer 1989), 541-42.

Bowen, Sally. "Bowed by Debt, Economic Woes, Peru Struggles to Lift Itself." *The Christian Science Monitor*, April 25, 1991, p. 6.

Catholic Relief Services. *CRS Update: Cholera and the Social Diseases of Poverty in Peru*. Baltimore, Md.: CRS, May 1991.

Central American Historical Institute. "Preliminary Information on the PL-80 Food Aid Program in Nicaragua," May 2, 1991.

The Christian Science Monitor, March 6, p. 8, April 7, p. 11, and April 17, 1991, p. 10.

De Soto, Hernando. *El Otro Sendero: La Revolution Informal*. Lima: Editorial El Barranco, 1986.

"Export and Die." *Economist*, March 2, 1991, p. 42.

Foreign Broadcast Information Service. Daily Report. "Pesquisa Nacional Sobre Saude e Nutricao." Instituto Nacional de Alimentacao e Nutricao, Ministerio da Saude, Brazil, March 1990.

—————. "Brazil." *Latin America*, April 26, 1991, p. 23.

Global Exchange. *Global Exchanges* No. 6, Spring 1991, pp. 1, 7-8.

Graham, Carol. "Peru's Blighted Path." *The Christian Science Monitor*, April 30, 1991, p. 19.

Inter-American Development Bank. *Economic and Social Progress in Latin America 1990 Report*. Washington, D.C.: IADB, October 1990.

Kawell, Jo Ann. "The Addict Economies." *NACLA's Report on the Americas* 22, No. 6 (March 1989), 33.

"Killer Virus." *Economist*, February 23, 1991, p. 43.

Lane, Charles. "Cholera Stalks a Continent." *Newsweek*, May 6, 1991, p. 44.

Michaels, Julia. "Latin America's Sanitation Crisis." *The Christian Science Monitor*, May 2, 1991, p. 4.

New Peace Times, April 1991, p. 6.

Pan American Health Organization. *Report of the Director*, Quadrennial 1986-89, Annual 1989. Washington, D.C.: PAHO, 1990.

—————/WHO offprint "Health Conditions in the Americas, 1981-84."

"Peru Situation." Catholic Relief Services Electronic
    Communication. Baltimore, Md.: CRS, April 24, 1991.
Sanchez-Grinan, Maria Ines, and Victor Galarreta. *Analysis and
    Transfer of Information Needed for Effective Decision-
    Making in Improving Childhood Nutrition, Final Report.*
    Lima, Peru: Instituto de Investigación Nutricional.
    Unpublished. January 4, 1991.
Schaeffer, Curt. *Preliminary Overview of the Economy of Latin
    America and the Caribbean.* New York: CARE, 1990.
————. Statement before the Subcommittee on Western
    Hemispheric Affairs, Committee on Foreign Affairs, U.S.
    House of Representatives. Washington, D.C.: CARE
    Washington Liaison Office, May 1, 1991.
United States Congress. House. Committee on Government Oper-
    ations. *United States Anti-Narcotics Activities in the
    Andean Region,* November 30, 1990.
Washington Post, March 28, 1991, p. A27.
World Bank. *Venezuela Poverty Study: From Generalized
    Subsidies to Targeted Programs.* Washington, D.C.:
    World Bank, 1991. Cited with permission.
World Council of Churches. *Report on October 1990 Delegation to
    Peru.* Geneva: WCC, forthcoming.
World Health Organization. "Statement of Dr. Hiroshi Nakajima,
    Director-General of the World Health Organization on
    Cholera." Palais de Nations, Geneva: WHO,
    Mimeographed, April 1991.
Woy-Hazelton, Sandra and William A. Hazelton. "'Sendero
    Luminoso' and the Future of Peruvian Democracy." *Third
    World Quarterly* 12, No. 2 (April 1990), 29.

North American Free Trade Agreement
Barkin, David. *Distorted Development: Mexico in the World
    Economy.* Boulder, Colo.: Westview, 1990.
"Brave New World." *Euromoney,* March 1991.
Cardenas, Cuauhtemoc. "A Continental Treaty for Development."
    The Other Side of Mexico, January-February 1991.
Davidson, Miriam. "Organizing in the 'Maquilas.'" *NACLA's Report
    on the Americas: The New Gospel North American Free
    Trade Agreement* 24, No. 6 (May 1991).
De Gotiari, Carlos Salinas. "North American Free Trade: Mexico's
    Route to Upward Mobility." *New Perspectives Quarterly*
    8, No. 1 (Winter 1991).
Dornbusch, Rudiger. "U.S. Mexico Free Trade." Testimony before
    the Finance Committee, U.S. Senate, February 20, 1991.
Faux, Jeff and Richard Rothstein. "Fast Track, Fast Shuffle: The
    Economic Consequences of the Administration's
    Proposed Trade Agreement with Mexico." *Economic
    Policy Institute Briefing Paper.* Washington, D.C.: EPI,
    1991
Inter-Hemispheric Education Resource Center. "Mexico Opens Up
    – The United States Moves In." *Resource Center Bulletin*
    No. 23 (Spring 1991).
LaBotz, Dan. *A Strangling Embrace: State Suppression of Labor
    Rights in Mexico.* Washington, D.C.: International Labor
    Rights Education and Research Fund, 1991.
"Mexico: Not So Sweet Corn." *Economist,* March 2, 1991, p. 44.
    Morici, Peter. *Trade Talks with Mexico: A Time for Real-
    ism.* Washington, D.C.: National Planning Association,
    1991.
Rothstein, Richard. "Exporting Jobs and Pollution to Mexico." *New
    Perspectives Quarterly* 8, No. 1 (Winter 1991).
Sílva-Herzog, Jesus. "Why Rush to Free Trade?" *New
    Perspectives Quarterly* 8, No. 1 (Winter 1991).
Suarez, B., D. Barkin, and B. DeWalt. "The Nutritional Impact of
    Rural Modernization: Strategies for Smallholder Survival
    in Mexico," n.d.
Suro, Roberto. "Border Boom's Dirty Residue Imperils U.S. Mexico
    Trade." *New York Times National,* March 31, 1991.
United States General Accounting Office. *U.S. and Mexico Trade:
    Impact of Liberalization in the Agricultural Sector,* March
    1991.
————. *U.S.-Mexico Trade: Trends and Impediments in
    Agricultural Trade,* January 1990.

Middle East

General
Arkin, William M., et al. *On Impact: Modern Warfare and the
    Environment, A Case Study of the Gulf War.*
    Washington, D.C.: Greenpeace, May 1991.
Church, George J. "Mission of Mercy." *Time,* April 29, 1991,
    pp. 40-41.
Elkhoury, Marwan. "A Million Lives in the Balance." *Refugees,*
    (June 1991).
Institute for Policy Studies. *Crisis in the Gulf.* Washington, D.C.:
    IPS, October 1990.
"Landmark Hunger Bill Introduced." Select Committee on Hunger,
    U.S. House of Representatives, Press Release, May 8,
    1991.
Minear, Larry. "The Military's Mission." Letter to the Editor.
    Washington Post, June 13, 1991.
———— and Thomas G. Weiss. "Humanitarianism Across Bor-
    ders." *Christian Science Monitor,* May 16, 1991, p. 18.
Overseas Development Council. *ODC Policy Focus.* Washington,
    D.C.: ODC, May 1991.
Ottaway, David B. "U.S., Angola Agree on Famine Relief."
    Washington Post, September 25, 1990.
Palmer, Ingrid. *The Impact of Male Out-Migration on Women in
    Farming.* West Hartford, Conn.: Kumarian, 1985.
Refugees, (June 1991).
Richard, Alan and John Waterbury. *A Political Economy of the
    Middle East.* Boulder, Colo.: Westview, 1990.
Sadowski, Yahya. "Power, Poverty and Petrodollars." *Middle East
    Report,* May-June 1991.
United Nations. "Summary of Report by Prince Sadruddin Aga
    Khan, the U.N. Secretary-General's Special Humanitari-
    an Envoy to the Region." Week of July 15, 1991.
————. "Report to the Secretary General on Humanitarian
    Needs in Kuwait and Iraq in the Immediate Post-Crisis
    Environment by a Mission to the Area Led by Mr. Martti
    Ahtissari, Under-Secretary-General for Administration
    and Management." March 28, 1991.
United States Agency for International Development. *Congression-
    al Presentation Fiscal Year 1991,* Annex II. Washington,
    D.C.: AID, 1991.
United States Department of Agriculture. *Agricultural Outlook.*
    Washington, D.C.: USDA, September 1990.
————. *World Agriculture.* Washington, D.C.: USDA, Septem-
    ber 1990.

Egypt
Christian Science Monitor, April 14, 1991.
Economist Intelligence Unit. *Egypt Country Report* No. 1, 1991.
Middle East Report, March-April 1991.
————, May-June 1991.
World Vision, February-March 1991.

Iran
Roger P. Winter. *Iraqi Refugees and Displaced People.* Washing-
    ton, D.C.: USCR, April 23 1991.

Iraq
Brown, John Murray. "Allies Finish N. Iraq Withdrawal."
    Washington Post, July 16, 1991.
Economist, April 20, 1991, p. 12.
New York Times, July 17, 1991, p. A1.
————. July 23, 1991, p. A3.
Pezzullo, Lawrence. "Testimony before the International Task

Force, Select Committee on Hunger, U.S. House of Representatives, on the Situation in Iraq." Washington, D.C., August 1, 1991.

Reid, Richard. "Testimony before the International Task Force of the Select Committee on Hunger, U.S. House of Representatives, on the Situation in Iraq." Washington, D.C., 1 August 1991.

"U.S. Says Iraq Diverts Donated Food Supply." *Washington Post*, June 6, 1991.

Washington Post, February 26, 1991, p. A10; April 15, 1991, p. A9; June 20, 1991, p. A27; July 12, 1991, p. A25; July 13, 1991, p. A14.

Yang, John E. and Barton Gellman. "U.S. Forces to Set Up Refugee Camps in Iraq." *Washington Post*, April 17, 1991.

Jordan

Christian Science Monitor, November 7, 1990.

Clark, David. "Jordan Copes with Recession and Austerity." *Israel Economist*, February 1989.

Khades, Bichara, et al., eds. *The Economic Development of Jordan*. London: Croon Helm, 1987.

Middle East Economic Digest, June 16, 1989.

Middle East Executive Reports, December 1990.

Oxfam News, Summer 1991.

Kuwait

New York Times, July 16, 1991, p. A3.

Washington Post, June 25, 1991, p. A13.

Turkey

The Christian Science Monitor, March 14, 1991.

Economist, April 20, 1991, p.12.

Economist Intelligence Unit. *Turkey Country Report* No. 2, 1991.

Middle East Economic Digest, April 27, 1990.

Oxfam News, Summer 1991.

Yemen

Al-Kasir, Ahmed. "The Impact of Emigration on Social Structure in the Yemen Arab Republic." In *Economy, Society and Culture in Contemporary Yemen*. B.R. Pridham, ed. London: Croon Helm, 1985.

Middle East Economic Digest, August 25, 1989.

North America

Canada

Anderson, Doris. "No Good Reason to Envy America." *Toronto Star*, January 25, 1991.

Canadian HungerCount 1989, Summary. Toronto, Ontario: Canadian Association of Food Banks, November 1989.

Canadian HungerCount 1990. Toronto, Ontario: Canadian Association of Food Banks, 1990.

Canadian Council on Social Development. "Family Income Adequacy," Fact Sheet 2 from *A Choice of Futures: Canada's Commitment to Its Children*. Ottawa: CCSD, no date.

Claiborne, William. "No Quick Fix." *Washington Post Health*, July 23, 1991.

Daily Bread Food Bank. "The Toronto Hunger Experience. Fax, June 4, 1991.

Ferguson, Jonathan. "Tory Cutbacks Called Blow to Health Care." *Toronto Star*, January 23, 1991.

Harris, Jennifer. "Cap on CAP: BC legal action saves provinces from federal social services cuts." *Catalyst, Citizens for Public Justice Newsletter,* July 1990.

National Council of Welfare. *The Canada Assistance Plan: No Time for Cuts*. Ottawa: Minister of Supply & Services Canada, 1991.

Riches, Graham. *Food Banks and the Welfare Crisis*. Ottawa: Canadian Council on Social Development, 1986.

Ross, David P. and Richard Shillington. *The Canadian Fact Book on Poverty 1989*. Ottawa: Canadian Council on Social Development, 1990.

Statistics Canada. *Canada Yearbook 1990*. Ottawa: Minister of Supply & Services Canada, 1989.

————. "Low Income Cut-offs of Family Units, 1988." Appendix Table 1. *Income Distribution by Size in Canada 1988*. Ottawa: Minister of Supply & Services Canada, 1989.

"Will the Supreme Court of Canada Stop the Injustice?" *Provision, Newsletter of the Canadian Association of Food Banks*, April 1991, pp. 1-2.

Native Peoples

Basic Departmental Data 1990. Ottawa: Indian and Northern Affairs Canada, 1990.

Brascoupé, Pat and Georges Erasmus. "Index on Native Canadians." *Canadian Forum* 32 (April 1990).

Cumming, Peter A. and Neil H. Mickenberg. *Native Rights in Canada*. 2nd ed. Toronto: Indian-Eskimo Association of Canada with General Publishing, 1972.

Frideres, J.S. *Canada's Indians: Contemporary Conflicts*. Scarborough, Ontario: Prentice-Hall of Canada, 1974.

Hagey, N. Janet, Gilles Larocque, and Catherine McBride. *Highlights of Aboriginal Conditions 1981-2001: Part II, Social Conditions*. Ottawa: Indian and Northern Affairs Canada, December 1989.

————. *Highlights of Aboriginal Conditions 1981-2001: Part III, Economic Conditions*. Ottawa: Indian and Northern Affairs Canada, December 1989.

Indian Health Service. *Trends in Indian Health 1990*. Washington, D.C.: U.S. Department of Health and Human Services, 1990.

Jones, Richard S. "American Indian Policy: Background, Nature, History, Current Issues, Future Trends." *CRS Report for Congress*. Washington, D.C.: GPO, March 12, 1987.

Larocque, Gilles Y. and R. Pierre Gauvin. *1986 Census Highlights on Registered Indians: Annotated Tables*. Ottawa: Indian and Northern Affairs Canada, 1989.

————. *Resident Population Distribution for the United States by Race and Hispanic Origin: 1990*. Washington, D.C.: GPO, June 12, 1991.

United States Congress. House. Select Committee on Hunger. "Standing Rock Sioux Reservation: A Case Study of Food Security among Native Americans." *Hearing*. 101 Cong., 2nd sess. Serial No. 101-15. Washington, D.C.: GPO, 1990.

United States Department of Agriculture, Food and Nutrition Service. *The Food Distribution Program on Indian Reservations (FDPIR)*, June 1991.

United States Department of Health & Human Services. Public Health Service. *Healthy People 2000*. Washington, D.C.: GPO, 1990.

United States Department of the Interior, Bureau of Indian Affairs. *American Indians Today: Answers to Your Questions*. Washington, D.C.: GPO, 1988.

United States General Accounting Office. *Food Assistance Programs: Nutritional Adequacy of Primary Food Programs on Four Indian Reservations*, September 1989.

————. *Food Assistance Programs: Recipient and Expert Views on Food Assistance at Four Indian Reservations*, June 1990.

United States

"America's Blacks." *Economist* March 30, 1991, pp. 17-21.

American Public Welfare Association. "Managing Need: Strategies for Serving Poor Families." Washington, D.C.: APWA, July 1991.

Berry, Wendell. "Out of Your Car, Off Your Horse." *Atlantic Monthly*, February 1991, pp. 61-63.

Bread for the World, New Orleans. "The Nutritional Status of the Adult Homeless in New Orleans." New Orleans: Loyola University Institute of Human Relations, October 1990.

Broder, David S. "Activist Government Works, Mr. President." *Washington Post*, May 19, 1991, p. D7.

Brown, J. Larry and H. F. Pizer. *Living Hungry in America*. New York: Macmillan, 1987.

Brubaker, Bill. "Athletic Shoes: Beyond Big Business." *Washington Post*, March 10, 1991, pp. A1, A18, A19.

Center for the Study of Social Policy. *Kids Count Data Book: State Profiles of Child Well-Being*, 1991.

Children's Defense Fund. *Children's Defense Fund 1990 State Fact Sheets*. Washington, D.C.: CDF, 1990.

————. *Children in 1990: A Report Card, Briefing Book and Action Primer*. Washington, D.C.: CDF, 1990.

————. *S.O.S. America: A Children's Defense Budget*. Washington, D.C.: CDF, 1990.

Citizens Budget Campaign. "The Working Family Tax Relief Act of 1991: Fact Sheet," photocopied.

Community Nutrition Institute. *Nutrition Week* 20, No. 50 (December 21, 1990).

Dewart, Janet, ed. *The State of Black America: 1991*. Citing U.S. Bureau of the Census. *Current Population Reports*, March 1990. New York: National Urban League, 1991.

Dionne, E.J., Jr. "Recession Cutting Deeply Into State Revenues." Citing Ray Scheppach, executive director of the National Governors' Association. *Washington Post*, May 12, 1991, p. A8.

Down and Out in North America: Recent Trends in Poverty Rates in the U.S. and Canada. NBER Working Paper No. 3462. Washington, D.C.: NBER, October 1990.

Edsall, Thomas Byrne with Edsall, Mary D. "Race." *The Atlantic*, May 1991.

Estes, Ralph. "What Did the War Really Cost?" *The Real Costs of the War. IPS Policy Watch Reports*. Washington, D.C.: Institute for Policy Studies, May 1991.

Food Research and Action Center. *Community Childhood Hunger Identification Project: A Survey of Childhood Hunger in the United States*. Washington, D.C.: FRAC, 1991.

"Food Stamp Fraud: The Cycle of Drugs, Poverty and Hunger." *Washington Post: Health*, January 8, 1991.

Fortune, April 22, 1991.

Frazier, Franklin. "Child Labor: The Characteristics of Working Children in the United States." Testimony. Washington, D.C.: GAO, March 19, 1991.

Guy, Kathleen. *Welcome the Child: A Child Advocacy Guide for Churches*. Washington, D.C.: CDF, 1991.

Heise, Lori. "Killing the Children of the Third World." *Washington Post*, April 21, 1991, pp. B1-B2.

Hinds, Michael deCourcy with Eric Eckholm. "80's Leave States and Cities in Need." *New York Times*, December 30, 1990, pp. 1, 16, 17.

Hughes, Dana, et al. *The Health of America's Children: Maternal and Child Health Data Book*. Washington, D.C.: CDF, 1987.

Kamarck, Elaine C. & William Galston. *Putting Children First: A Progressive Family Policy for the 1990s*. Washington, D.C.: Progressive Policy Institute, September 1990.

Klerman, Lorraine V. *Alive and Well? A Research and Policy Review of Health Programs for Poor Young Children*. New York: National Center for Children in Poverty, Columbia University School of Public Health, 1991.

Mann, Judy. "The Abandoned U.S. Child." *Washington Post*, July 12, 1991.

McDonalds 1990 Annual Report. Oak Brook, Ill.: McDonald's, 1991.

National Center for Children in Poverty. *Five Million Children: A Statistical Profile of Our Poorest Young Citizens*. New York: Columbia University, 1990.

Pianin, Eric. "Congress Rushes Added Jobless Benefits." *Washington Post*, July 30, 1991, p. A6.

Postrel, Virginia I. "The States Are Becoming the New 'Big Government'." *Washington Post*, July 14, 1991, C3.

Raspberry, William. "Prison Costs More than Harvard." *Washington Post*, May 13, 1991, p. A11.

Rich, Spencer. "GAO: Canadian-Style Health Insurance Would Save $67 Billion." *Washington Post*, June 4, 1991, p. A21.

————. "Inflation's Bite on Benefits." *Washington Post*, May 14, 1991, p. A17.

————. "The Many Unknowns of Child Poverty." Quoting Assistant Secretaries of Health and Human Services Jo Anne Barnhart and Martin Gerry. *Washington Post*, March 5, 1990.

Shapiro, Isaac and Marion E. Nichols. *Unemployed and Uninsured*. Washington, D.C.: Center on Budget and Policy Priorities, March 1991.

Shapiro, Isaac and Robert Greenstein. *Selective Prosperity: Increasing Income Disparities Since 1977*. Washington, D.C.:Center on Budget and Policy Priorities, July 1991.

Silk, Leonard, "It Isn't Just a Downturn, It's the Bill for the 1980's." *New York Times*, December 30, 1990, p. E5.

Spayd, Liz. "Maryland Brings Welfare Benefits Into ATM Age." *Washington Post*, May 14, 1991, pp. A1, A14.

Taylor, Paul. "Children in Poverty: Who Are They?" Citing CDF. *Washington Post*, June 3, 1991, p. A7.

————. "Saving Our Children – By Cutting Our Taxes." *Washington Post*, June 9, 1991, pp. D1-2.

"Two Governors Face the Facts of Life in a Lean Time." *New York Times*, February 3, 1991, p. E20.

United States Congress. House. Committee on Agriculture, Subcommittee on Domestic Marketing. *Hunger in America, Its Effects on Children and Families, and Implications for the Future*. Hearing. May 8, 1991.

————. House Committee on Ways & Means. *1991 Green Book*. 102nd Cong., 1st sess. Washington, D.C.: GPO, May 1991.

————. Senate. Committee on the Budget. *President Bush's 1992 Budget: Review & Analysis*. February 6, 1991.

United States General Accounting Office. *Mother-Only Families: Low Earnings Will Keep Many Children in Poverty*, April 1991. Williams, Juan. "The Real Tragedy of Crack Babies." *Washington Post*, December 30, 1990, p. C5.

Soviet Union and Eastern Europe

General

Central Intelligence Agency. *The World Factbook 1990*. Washington, D.C.: GPO, 1990.

"Eastern Europe in Transition." *Financial Times*, 4 February 1991.

Korb, Penni and Nancy Cochrane. "World Food Expenditures." In United States Department of Agriculture. *National Food Review* 12, No. 4 (October-December 1989).

United States Department of Agriculture. "Agricultural Privatization and Land Reform in Central Europe." *World Agriculture*, April 1991.

————. "East European Reform Accelerates." *Agricultural Outlook*, May 1991.

————. "Inflation and Recent Price Reforms in Romania, Hungary, and Czechoslovakia." *Agriculture Report* 4, No. 1 (January/February 1991).

————. "Agricultural Trade Policy and Trade for Eastern Europe and the Soviet Union," September 1990.

————. *Foreign Agriculture 1989*, October 1989.

Soviet Union

Boulton, Leyla. "Private Agriculture Amid Collective Confusion." *Financial Times*, June 27, 1991.

Foreign Broadcast Information Service (FBIS). *Daily Report Soviet*

Union FBIS-SOV-91-064, April 3, 1991. "Numerous Price
Violations Reported." Moscow TASS in English, April 2,
1991.

—————. *Science and Technology/USSR: Life Sciences* JPRS-
ULS-91-005, February 19, 1991. Translation of "Child
Mortality Statistics, Medical Mission to Central Asia."
Moscow Semya, May 28-June 3, 1990.

—————. *Soviet Union/Economic Affairs* JPRS-UEA-90-040,
November 30, 1990. Translation of "Social and Economic
Policy: About Poverty – Not for the Last Time." *Novosi-
birsk Ekonomika i Organizatsiya Promyshlennogo
Proizvodstva (EKO)*, 7 (July 1990).

Gray, Kenneth. "The Soviet Food Complex in a Time of Change."
In United States Department of Agriculture. *National
Food Review* 12, No. 4 (October-December 1989).

International Monetary Fund, the World Bank, the Organization for
Economic Cooperation and Development, and the European Bank for Reconstruction and Development. *A Study
of the Soviet Economy*. Vol. 2, February 1991.

Moscow News, No. 14, 1990. "Social Portrait of a Phenomenon:...."

Komsomolskaya Pravda, April 25, 1990.

Reuters. "Amid Soviet Fears of Famine, 'Hunger' Replaces
'Perestroika'." May 6, 1991.

—————. "Soviet Butter, Cheese, and Meat Production Slump in
1991." July 11, 1991.

"Soviet Food Short for Many; Others Find Ways to Cope." *New
York Times*, December 5, 1990.

"Soviet Price Rise Estimates Attacked." *Financial Times*, May 1,
1991.

United States Department of Agriculture. "Agricultural Situation
Annual" for the Soviet Union. Unpublished Report Filed
by Agricultural Attaché, March 1, 1991.

Wegren, Stephen K. "Food Prices in the USSR." *Report on the
USSR* (March 23, 1990).

Albania

Cochrane, Nancy. "Albania." In United States Department of Agriculture. Global Review of Agricultural Policies, May 1988.

Dempsey, Judy. "Albanian General Strike Brings Down Elected
Government." *Financial Times*, June 5, 1991.

Graff, James L. "Campaigning, Albanian-Style." *Time,* April 8,
1991.

Economist Intelligence Unit. *Romania, Bulgaria, Albania: Country
Report* No. 4, 1990.

Harden, Blaine. "Albanian Communists Win Despite Losing Urban
Vote." *Washington Post*, April 2, 1991.

—————. "Struggling Albania: Failed Economy Puts Families
Under Stress." *Washington Post*, April 11, 1991.

Zanga, Louis. "A Watershed Year." *Report on Eastern Europe*
(February 8, 1991).

Bulgaria

Cochrane, Nancy. "Bulgaria." In United States Department of
Agriculture. *Global Review of Agricultural Policies*, May
1988.

International Monetary Fund. "Bulgaria: Tough Transition to a
Market-Oriented Economy." *IMF Survey* (March 18,
1991).

Nikolaev, Rada. "Between Hope and Hunger." *Report on Eastern
Europe* (January 4, 1991).

Perry, Duncan M. "Deteriorating Health Care." *Report on Eastern
Europe* (November 2, 1990).

Czechoslovakia

Hermann, A.H. "Czechs Set the Pace on Reform." *Financial Times*,
June 13, 1991.

Horstmeyer, Harold. "Economic Downturn Less Severe for Czechs
Shifting to Market Controls." *Journal of Commerce,* June
18, 1991.

Pehe, Jiri. "Czechoslovakia: The First Weeks of 1991: Problems
Solved, Difficulties Ahead." *Report on Eastern Europe*
(March 8, 1991).

East Germany

Goodhart, David. "East Germany Faces Big Rise in
Unemployment." *Financial Times*, April 25, 1991.

United States Department of Agriculture. "Germany's Agriculture
Making Difficult Adjustments." *Farmline* (March 1991).

Hungary

Oltay, Edith. "Hungary: Poverty on the Rise." *Report on Eastern
Europe* (January 25, 1991).

Szalai, Julia. "Poverty in Hungary During the Period of Economic
Crisis." Unpublished Background Paper Prepared for the
World Bank *World Development Report 1990*, November
1989.

Poland

"Poland." *Financial Times*, May 3, 1991.

"Poles Boost Food Offer to Soviets." *Journal of Commerce,* April
15, 1991.

Schweitzer, Julian. "Transition in Eastern Europe – The Social
Dimension." *Finance & Development* 27, No. 4 (December 1990).

United States Department of Agriculture. "Agricultural Situation
Annual" for Poland. Unpublished Report Filed by Agricultural Attaché, March 3, 1991.

Romania

"Romanians Face Big Price Rises." *Financial Times*, April 2, 1991.

Shafir, Michael. "Promises and Reality." *Report on Eastern Europe*
(January 4, 1991).

Yugoslavia

Posarec, Aleksandra. "Poverty in Yugoslavia 1978-87."
Unpublished Background Paper Prepared for the World
Bank *World Development Report 1990*, November 1989.

Robinson, Anthony. "Separatist Upheavals Expose the Myth of
Yugoslavia's Self-Management Socialism." *Financial
Times*, July 5, 1991.

United States Department of Agriculture. "Agricultural Situation
Annual" for Yugoslavia. Unpublished Report Filed by
Agricultural Attaché, March 8, 1991.

"Yugoslav Army to Pull Out of Rebel Slovenia." *Financial Times*,
July 19, 1991.

Index

Hunger 1990 - numbers in italics
Hunger 1992 - non-italicized

Adventist Development and Relief Agency International (ADRA) 91, 215

Afghanistan *7, 13, 14, 35-36, 100, tables, bib.;* 7, 60, 119, tables, bib.

African Alternative Framework 68-69, 115, 196

African-American *88, 90, 91, 93;* 84, 85, 92, 105, 158-160, 162

Aid to Families with Dependent Children (AFDC) *5, 92, 98, tables;* 158-160, 163, 196

Albania 167, 168, 172, bib.

Algeria *tables;* tables

Anemia *10, 14, 16, 19, 22, 27, 28, 30, 42, 48, 49, 51, 52, 54, 56, 64, 71, 92, 98, 106;* 7, 29, 65, 101, 124, 125, 196

Angola *7, 10, 41, 57, 59, 61-62, tables;* 5, 7, 111-113, 116, 145, tables

Antigua *tables;* tables

Apartheid 41, 57-59, 61, 106

Argentina *56, tables;* tables

Austerity *15, 38, 44, 50, 56, 57, 74, 76, 80, 83, 86;* 54-56, 70, 90, 105, 119, 123, 129, 130, 132, 135, 138, 149

Bahamas *tables;* tables

Bahrain *tables;* 149, tables

Bangladesh *9-10, 13-14, 24-28, 100-101, 103, tables, bib.;* 7, 33, 43, 44, 119-122, 147, 151, tables

Barbados *tables;* tables

Belize *tables;* tables

Benin *tables;* 116, tables

Bhutan *tables;* tables

Bolivia *69, 78, tables;* 128, 135-136, tables

Botswana *57, tables;* 70, 115, tables

Brazil *66-67, 72-74, 100-102, tables, bib.;* 34, 38, 128, 136-137, tables

Bread for the World/BFW Institute on Hunger & Development *4;* 5, 9-11, 20, 31, 100-109, 196, 215

Brunei *tables;* tables

Bulgaria 168, 172-173, tables, bib.

Burkina Faso *51-52, tables, bib.;* 33, 35-37, 41, 61, 114, tables

Burma, see Myanmar

Burundi *tables;* tables

Bush, George 105, 106, 122, 144, 146, 150, 160, 161, 164

Calorie intake/requirement *28, 32, 50, 106;* 137, 167, 172, 196

Cambodia *7, 13, 14, 16-19, 22, 24, 100, tables, bib.;* 5, 7, 65, 111, 122, 145, tables, bib.

Cameroon *tables;* tables

Canada *91;* 7, 11, 103, 130, 152-157

Cape Verde *tables;* tables

CARE 8, 23-27, 31, 40, 91, 112, 125, 139, 196, 215, 216

Cash crops *21, 30, 38, 52, 58, 63-64, 69, 72;* 70

Catholic Relief Services (CRS) *4;* 27, 78, 91, 112, 137, 143, 144, 196, 215

Center on Budget and Policy Priorities 104

Central African Republic *tables;* tables

Chad *51, tables;* 60, 61, 111, tables

Child mortality *24, 25, 32, 51, 70, 106, tables;* 83, 90, 110, 144, 196

Child nutrition *49, 67;* 100, 104

Childhood Hunger Identification Project (CCHIP) 89

Children's Defense Fund (CDF) *90;* 105

Chile *67-68, 100, tables, bib.;* tables

China *8-9, 12-16, 100, 102, tables, bib.;* 44, 118, 121, 122-123, 129, tables, bib.

Cholera 7, 120, 123, 128, 136-140, 143, 148

Christian Children's Fund *4;* 215

Church World Service (CWS) *4;* 27, 28, 31, 91, 112, 196, 215

Civil war *7, 16, 25, 26, 35, 42, 45;* 51, 74, 75, 78, 81, 91, 119, 120, 122, 131, 145, 146, 177

Cold War *6-8;* 31, 61, 63, 119

Collectivization *14, 15, 17, 18, 55;* 120, 167

Colombia *7, 66, 69, tables;* 59, 128, 137-139, tables

Comoros *tables;* tables

Congo *tables;* 116, tables

Cook Islands *tables;* tables

Coordination in Development (CODEL) 215

Costa Rica *8, 66, tables;* 8, 50-58, 61, 63, 70, 81, tables, bib.

Cote D'Ivorie *tables;* tables

Cuba *4, 8, 26, 66, 84-85, 100, 102, tables;* 60, 128-129, tables

Czechoslovakia 173-174, bib.

Debt *12, 21, 26-28, 36-37, 40, 43-45, 57, 66-68, 70, 72-74, 76, 78, 81, 83,* *86, 100, 102-106, tables;* 8, 10, 29, 41, 44, 55, 59-61, 68, 70, 72, 114-115, 119, 121, 122, 123, 126-127, 128, 130, 132-134, 138, 139, 150, 164, 171, 175, 176, 196, tables

Deforestation *20, 21, 42, 86, 102;* 32-41, 71

Dehydration *86;* 139

Demilitarization *8;* 8, 10, 50-58, 61-63, 116, 165, bib.

Desertification *45;* 32-36, 196

Diarrhea *11, 41, 86;* 83, 120, 123, 125, 137, 139

Djibouti *tables;* tables

Dominica *tables;* tables

Dominican Republic *85-87, 102, tables, bib.;* 129, tables

Drought *15-16, 36, 38, 41-42, 44-45, 49, 51-52, 56, 61-62, 71, 73, 77-78;* 7, 35, 61, 91, 111, 113, 114, 119, 121, 122, 127, 129, 137, 139, 145, 168, 171, 172, 176, 215

Earthquake *77;* 119, 126

East Timor *7, 22, 24;* 123, bib.

Eastern Europe *6, 8, 19, 85;* 11, 116, 128, 129, 166, 167, 172, 174-176, 215

Ecuador *71-75, tables. bib.;* 40, tables

Egypt *37, 45, 46-47, 102, tables, bib.;* 7, 8, 26, 28-29, 30, 142, 147-148, 150, tables, bib.

El Salvador *7, 68, 76-78, 102, tables, bib.;* 9, 30, 74-81, 92, 145, tables, bib.

Elderly *59, 88, 93, 97;* 19, 79, 169, 174

Environment *6, 12, 32-33, 37, 52, 102-103;* 5, 8, 9, 32-41, 42, 46-48, 69, 103, 134, 145, 150, 174, 215, 216, bib.

Equatorial Guinea *tables;* tables

Eritrea *7, 41-43;* 91, 112

Erosion *16, 20-21, 42, 74, 86, 102;* 32, 33, 37-40, 45, 47, 80, 120

Ethiopia *7, 8, 10, 41-44, 100, 102, tables, bib.;* 5, 35, 46, 61, 111-113, 145, 151, 160, tables

European Community 31, 115, 134, 150, 173, 174, 176

Famine *7, 9-10, 12-14, 17, 25-26, 28-29, 40-43, 45, 51-52, 56, 100, 106;* 7-9, 91, 107, 108, 110-112, 150, 196, 215

Female-headed households *28, 77, 83, 90;* 71, 114, 158

Fertilizer *15, 22, 25-27, 55, 81, 102;* 37, 43-47, 64, 67, 79, 120-122, 124,

127

Fiji *tables;* tables

Floods *25, 28;* 33, 39, 114, 123, 150

Food aid/assistance *7, 13, 17, 21, 26, 28, 42, 47-48, 52, 58, 60, 62-63, 70, 77, 83, 86, 100;* 5, 8, 12-21, 22-31, 85, 88, 106, 111, 112, 113, 119, 121, 123, 129, 130, 132, 139, 144, 147, 157, 169, 172, 173, 196, bib.

Food and Agriculture Organization (FAO) *5, 10-11, 41, 43, 48, 50, 62, 70, 84;* 5, 9, 10, 28, 65, 119, 121, 125, 148, 196

Food bank/pantry 5, 8, 12-21, 153, 154, 158

Food export/import *tables;* tables

Food for Peace (PL 480) 23, 24, 26-31

Food Research and Action Center (FRAC) *89;* 7, 20, 102-105, 157-160, 196

Food security *16, 24, 31, 40-44, 46, 48, 52-54, 57, 60, 61, 64, 67, 70, 71, 75, 79, 81, 83, 87, 89, 100;* 28, 30, 35, 37, 41, 61, 69, 156, 196, 216

Food Stamp Program *26, 29, 84, 92, 97, 98;* 12, 18, 84, 102, 105, 156, 158, 160

Gabon *tables;* 116, 117, tables

Gambia, The *51, tables;* tables

Germany 7, 60, 103, 149, 174, bib.

Ghana *48-50, tables, bib.;* 115, tables

Goiter *14, 16, 18, 22, 27, 28, 30, 32, 34, 42, 48, 49, 52, 54, 56, 64, 70, 106;* 7, 121, 126, 196

Grameen Bank *28, 101, 103*

Green Revolution *12, 13, 20, 22, 25, 26, 29, 30, 82, 103, 106;* 8, 42-49, 66, 196

Grenada *tables;* tables

Guatemala *79-81, tables, bib.;* 77, 81, 128, tables

Guinea *tables;* 113, 126, tables

Guinea-Bissau *tables;* tables

Guyana *tables;* 60, tables

Haiti *85-87, tables, bib.;* 28, 39, 40, 128-130, tables

Hartford Food System 16-17

Health care *24-26, 30, 31, 33, 35, 46, 50, 51, 55, 58, 62, 73, 84, 88, 89, 96, 99, tables;* 10, 12, 37, 53, 55, 61, 71, 78-81, 82, 87, 91, 93, 113, 114, 135, 137, 139, 143-144, 154-156, 164-165, 215, 216, tables

Heifer Project International *4;* 216

Hispanic *88, 90, 91;* 92, 158, 159, 162

Homeless *20, 62, 90, 92-93, 99, 104;* 7, 12-21, 120, 122, 126, 146, 157, 158

Honduras *78-79, tables, bib.;* tables

Hong Kong *12*

Horn of Africa *40, 105;* 7, 11, 91, 110

Human Development Index (HDI) 124, 146, 150, 196

Hungary 167, 168, 174-175, bib.

Immunization *31, 45, 55, 76, tables;* 23, 24, 124, 136, 144, tables

Income distribution *26, 47, 64, 65, 77, tables;* 138, 141, tables

India *7, 9, 10, 12-14, 29-31, 100-103, tables, bib.;* 7, 8, 11, 23-27, 29, 33, 39, 42-49, 118, 119, 125, 147, tables

Indonesia *12, 13, 22-24, 100-102, tables, bib.;* 8, 43, 44, 59, 64-69, 71, 72, 123, tables

Industrial Areas Foundation (IAF) 9, 92-99, 196

Infant mortality *9, 27, 106, tables;* 60, tables

Integrated Child Development Services (ICDS) 8, 23-9, 196

Interfaith Action for Economic Justice, Interfaith/Impact 31, 102

International Labor Organization (ILO) 147, 149, 196

International Monetary Fund (IMF) *5, 6, 27, 38, 44, 46, 48, 49, 57, 60, 74, 80, 81, 83, 84, 86, 103;* 55, 72, 90, 127, 133, 135, 138, 149, 173, 175, 176, 196

Iodine deficiency *18, 19, 22, 34, 54, 70, 106;* 7, 65, 118, 196

Iran *tables;* 60, 119, 142, 143, 146, 148-149, 160, tables, bib.

Iraq *8, tables;* 7, 11, 60, 119, 125, 127, 142-150, 160, tables, bib.

Israel 60

Jamaica *67, 83-84, tables, bib.;* 70, tables

Japan 44, 103, 118, 121, 149

Job assistance/training *57, 67, 91, 99, 101;* 5, 17-21, 84-89, 101, 125, 156, 158, 160, 161, 216

Jordan *38-39, 101, tables, bib.;* 59, 60, 142, 146, 147, 149-151, 215, tables, bib.

Kenya *53-54, tables, bib.;* 37-39, 112, tables

Khmer Rouge *18, 19;* 63, 111, 122

Kiribati *tables;* tables

Korea *9, 12, 14, 100, tables;* 60, 119,

147, tables

Kuwait *8, tables;* 119, 125, 127, 142-147, 149, tables, bib.

Land distribution/reform *13, 14, 21, 22, 23-26, 28, 29, 31, 33, 34, 38, 42, 43, 48, 64, 68, 72, 74, 75, 77, 78, 79, 80, 81, 83, 102, 103;* 45, 53, 54, 67, 69, 118, 127, 169, 173, 176

Laos *22, tables;* 65, 120-121, tables, bib.

Lebanon *7, tables;* tables

Lesotho *57, tables;* tables

Liberia *7, tables;* 7, 112-113, 145, tables

Libya *47, tables;* 60, 147, 160, tables

Life expectancy *14, 25, 30, 31, 86;* 11, 69, 124, 128, 152, 156

Literacy *tables;* tables

Low birthweight *10, 45, 83, 87, 92, 106, tables;* 101, 124, 125, tables

Lutheran World Relief *4;* 5, 31, 91, 112, 216

Madagascar *tables;* tables

Malaria *10, 42, 52, 54;* 125, 139, 141

Malawi *64-65, tables, bib.;* 113, tables

Malaysia *9, tables;* tables

Maldives *tables;* tables

Mali *51, 52, tables;* 114, tables

Malnutrition *8, 11, 24, 30, 44, 54, 55, 60, 62, 67, 72, 73, 76, 78, 80, 81, 83, 92, 106;* 13, 23-25, 31, 60, 71, 107, 118, 124-126, 129, 131, 135, 136, 139, 144, 146, 147, 157, 173, 197

Maritius *tables;* tables

Maternal mortality *84, 106, tables;* tables

Mauritania *51, tables;* 114, tables

Mennonite Central Committee (MCC) 27, 78, 91, 121, 196, 216

Mexico *66, 81-84, tables, bib.;* 11, 51, 75, 96, 124, 128, 130-134, tables

Migrant *15, 37, 92;* 96, 119, 125, 142, 147, 149

Militarization *6, 8, 58-60, 78, 79, 100, 105;* 5, 10, 50-63, 107, 111

Military aid *8, 42, 47, 57, 69, 78;* 119, 139

Military expenditures *27, 34, 61, 76, tables;* 7, 8, 58-62, 154, tables

Minimum wage *21, 31, 68, 75, 81-82, 94-95, tables;* 12, 52, 130, 134, 139, 153, 173, tables

Mongolia *14, tables;* 123-124, tables

Morbidity *14, 15;* 124, 197

Morocco *47-48, tables, bib.;* tables

Mortality *9, 10, 14-16, 18, 22, 24-28, 30-33, 35, 41, 43, 45, 46, 48, 51, 56, 58, 60, 67, 70, 72, 73, 76, 80, 84, 85, 86, 92, 106, 107, tables;* 11, 24, 29, 60, 65, 83, 85, 90, 101, 110, 114, 123, 124, 125, 136, 144, 146, 147, 151, 156, 159, 170, 172, 196, 197, tables

Mozambique *7, 10, 41, 57, 58-60, 64, 101, tables, bib.;* 5, 7, 30, 61, 111, 113, 117, tables

Myanmar (Burma) *13, tables;* 124-126, tables, bib.

Namibia *41, 61, tables;* 117, tables

Native American/Canadian *80, 88, 92;* 11, 19, 96, 155-157, 196, bib.

Nepal *10, 13, 28, 32-33, 100, tables, bib.;* tables

New Caledonia *tables;* tables

Nicaragua *67, 75-76, 78, tables, bib.;* 50, 51, 54-57, 60, 75, 128, 130-132, tables

Niger *51, 52, tables;* 114, tables

Nigeria *50-51, tables, bib.;* 35, 41, 70, 72, 114, 116, tables

Niue *tables;* tables

Nutrition *11, 12, 14, 16, 26, 28, 31, 33, 35, 36, 43, 46, 49, 55, 56, 58, 67, 74, 82, 84, 86, 88, 89, 92, 93, 98, 101, 106;* 7, 13, 17, 19, 20, 23-26, 31, 33, 66, 67, 81, 83, 89, 91, 96, 97, 100, 101, 104, 121, 125, 127, 131, 134, 151, 157-160, 165, 170, 196

Oman *tables;* 60, tables

Operation Lifeline Sudan 112, 144

Oxfam 36, 89, 90

Pakistan *7, 10, 13, 25, 26, 33-35, 100, 101, tables, bib.;* 7, 59, 119, 147, tables

Panama *85, tables;* 50, 54, 55, 75, 133-135, tables

Papua New Guinea *tables;* 126, tables, bib.

Paraguay *tables;* tables

Peace *8, 39, 41, 46, 47, 58, 61, 62, 90, 100, 105;* 50-58, 63, 75, 78, 81, 97, 109, 111-113, 115, 119, 121, 122, 144, 145, 216

Per capita income *21, 25-27, 31, 32, 72;* 43, 135, 139

Persian Gulf *7, 8;* 5, 7, 44, 60, 115-116, 119, 124-125, 143-147, 151, 164

Peru *67-71, 101, tables, bib.;* 11, 27, 28, 128, 136-140, tables

Philippines, The *7, 13, 14, 20-22, 102, 103, tables, bib.;* 7, 8, 24, 42-46, 59, 119, 126-127, 147, tables, bib.

Poland 60, 167, 175-176, 215, bib.

Pollution 44-49, 133-134

Population growth/density *6, 9, 13, 14, 15, 19, 23-26, 32, 47, 53, 85, 101, 102, 103, tables;* 8, 10, 33, 44, 45, 69, 114, 136, 167, tables

Poverty line/level *9, 15, 19, 23, 28, 31, 34, 39, 43, 49, 73, 82, 83, 88, 89-99, 106, tables;* 12, 13, 21, 32, 42-44, 65-66, 84, 101, 119, 134, 135, 138, 149, 153, 156-163, 170, 175, 197, tables

Private Voluntary Organization (PVO) 8, 23, 26, 89, 196

Protestant 85, 102, 103, 105, 215

Qatar *tables;* 60, tables

Rainforest *74, 102*

Recession *66-67, 71, 73-74, 90, 92;* 64, 73, 88, 123, 128, 133, 135, 138, 154, 160-164

Recommended Daily Allowance (RDA) *19, 85, 106;* 19

Red Crescent 147, 149, 150

Red Cross (ICRC) 112, 134, 142, 143, 146, 147, 196

Refugee *19, 44;* 7, 29, 74-81, 113, 124, 125, 143-151, 172, 215, 216

RESULTS 103-104

Rice production *12, 17, 18, 20, 28, 30;* 27-28, 42-46, 66, 79, 113, 120-127

Roman Catholic *21, 57, 68, 77, 78, 95;* 27, 28, 31, 52, 75, 78, 80, 81, 85, 91, 102, 103, 105, 112, 127, 137, 143, 196, 215

Romania 168, 176-177, 215, bib.

Rural development *12, 22, 102;* 26, 27, 29, 30, 44, 80, 81, 121

Rural population *22, 27, 39, 43, 45, 53, 56, 67, 72, 75, 77, 79, 82;* 29, 42, 43, 74, 80, 81, 136, 138

Rural poverty *23, 46, 58, 66, 86, 87, 91;* 35, 42-44, 151

Rwanda *tables;* tables

Sahel *51-53, 56, 103, bib.;* 35, 37, 114

Samoa *tables;* tables

Sanitation *31, 73, 96;* 27, 81, 83, 96, 135-137, 140, 143, 144, 148, 151

São Tome/Principe *tables;* tables

Saudi Arabia *tables;* 60, 124, 142, 149, 151, tables

School breakfast/lunch *31, 74, 97, 99;* 19, 20

Second Harvest 13-20

Senegal *51, 52, tables;* 35, 114, tables

Seychelles *tables;* tables

Sierra Leone *tables;* 113, tables

Simon, Arthur *4;* 5, 9, 102, 106-109

Singapore *12, tables;* tables

Solomon Island *tables;* tables

Somalia *7, 43-44, tables, bib.;* 61, 113, 145, tables

South Africa *41, 57-61, 64, 106, tables, bib.;* 117, 124, 160, tables

Soviet Union *7, 8, 19, 35, 42, 85, 97, 100;* 11, 59-63, 111, 119, 121-123, 129, 132, 166-171, bib.

Special Supplemental Food Program for Women, Infants, and Children (WIC) *98-99, 105, tables;* 9, 19, 100-106, 108, 160, 196

Sri Lanka *7, 12-14, 25-29, 102, tables, bib.;* 7, 24, 43, 119, 124-125, 147, tables, bib.

St. Kitts/Nevis *tables;* tables

St. Louis Association for Community Organizations (SLACO) 84-87

St. Lucia *tables;* tables

St. Vincent *tables;* tables

Structural adjustment *22, 74, 84, 107;* 38, 68-72, 114-115, 126, 128, 130, 132, 133, 149, 196, 197

Stunting *10, 14, 16, 24, 28, 30, 32, 34, 37, 38, 43, 48, 51, 53, 58, 59, 74, 78, 85, 107, tables;* 124, 197, tables

Sudan *7, 10, 45-46, tables, bib.;* 91, 111-113, 116, 144, 145, tables

Suriname *tables;* tables

Sustainable development *52, 67;* 8, 10, 22, 27, 29-32, 34-35, 41, 46-47, 69, 74, 78-81, 91, 134

Swaziland *57, tables;* tables

Syria *tables;* 60, 146, tables

Tanzania *54-56, 57, 100, tables, bib.;* 82-91, 116, tables, bib.

Technology *22, 30, 36;* 5, 8, 9, 34, 41-49, 63, 71, 83, 85, 88, 132, 143, bib.

Thailand *3, 9, 13, 14, 18-20, 22, 100, 102, tables, bib.;* 43, 45, 59, 118-122, 124, tables

Tibet *14, 15, 32*

Tigray *41, 43;* 112

Togo *tables;* tables

Tonga *tables;* tables

Trinidad/Tobago *tables;* tables

Trull Foundation, The 216

Tunisia *tables;* tables

Turkey *14, 36-37, tables, bib.;* 142, 144, 146, 150, tables, bib.

Tuvalu *tables;* tables

Uganda *7, tables;* 111, 112, tables

Under five mortality *22, 32, 33, 35, 41, 46, 107, tables;* 24, 197

Underemployment *15, 16, 20, 24, 33, 75, 77, 79, 107;* 126, 197

Undernutrition *10, 11, 14, 15, 18, 19, 22, 26, 27, 30, 32, 35, 37, 41, 45, 48, 50, 51, 53, 54, 56, 58, 61, 62, 64, 67, 70, 75, 81, 83, 84, 86, 91, 94, 107;* 22, 25, 29, 65, 66, 83, 197

Underweight *10, 11, 14, 16, 18-20, 22, 25, 26, 30, 32-34, 36, 37, 42, 43, 48, 49, 51, 53-56, 58, 59, 62, 63, 67, 70, 71, 76, 80, 83-85, 87, 107, tables;* 23, 65, 118, 121, 125, 197, tables

Unemployment *10, 15, 16, 20, 21, 24-27, 29, 31, 33, 36, 37, 46, 50, 61, 67, 68, 73-79, 82, 83, 85, 90, 92, 95, 96, 107;* 11, 55, 78, 84, 85, 96, 114, 121, 123, 126, 130, 131, 135, 139-141, 147, 149, 156, 160, 161, 172, 175, 176

Unions *61, 68, 77, 78, 80, 95;* 52, 54, 69, 85-87, 89, 116, 133

United Arab Emirates *tables;* 60, tables

United Nations Children's Fund (UNICEF) *5, 6, 8, 10, 22, 34, 35, 43, 45, 55, 56, 59, 61, 73, 76, 78, 80, 85;* 7, 24, 27, 69, 72, 83, 110, 112, 118, 124, 138, 144, 145, 196

United Nations Development Programme (UNDP) 120, 124, 146-150, 196

United Nations Economic Commission for Africa (ECA) 68, 69, 116, 196

United Nations High Commissioner for Refugees (UNHCR) 75, 148-150, 196

United Nations World Food Council (WFC) 118, 196

United States Agency for International Development (USAID) *5, 10, 42, 52, 57, 77, 80, 81, 87, 100, 103;* 23-24, 26-30, 39-40, 57, 76, 77, 196

United States Congress *97, 98, 105;* 30, 31, 83, 100-109, 119, 122, 149, 160, 161, 165

United States Congress, House Select Committee on Hunger *92;* 106

United States Department of Agriculture (USDA) *98;* 18-19, 30, 101, 196, 197

United States, States of the, *Table 11*

Urban population/urbanization *16, 22, 23, 28, 34, 35, 37, 38, 39, 42, 49, 78, 86, 87, tables;* 136, 138, 140, 153, tables

Uruguay *tables;* tables

Values 50-54, 57, 58, 62, 63, 93-95, 109

Vanuatu *tables;* tables

Venezuela *tables;* 70, 128, 139-141, tables

Vietnam *7, 13, 16-18, 102, tables, bib.;* 43, 60, 119, 121, tables

Vitamin A *16, 18, 19, 22, 30, 32, 34, 49, 64, 107;* 7, 65, 118, 197

War *6-8, 16, 18, 19, 21, 25, 26, 31, 35, 36, 39-42, 44-46, 48, 57-60, 62, 64, 67, 69, 71, 72, 76-78, 90, 100, 101, 105;* 7, 11, 13, 22, 29, 31, 43, 44, 50, 51, 56-58, 60-63, 65, 74, 75, 77-81, 91, 111-113, 119-122, 126, 127, 131, 142-151, 164, 167, 172, 173, 177, 196, 215, 216

Wasting *22, 26-28, 30, 32, 34, 37, 43, 50, 51, 53, 56, 58, 59, 106, 107, tables;* 124, 197, tables

Welfare *14, 25, 27, 29, 49, 57, 76, 84, 85, 91, 95, 97-99;* 19-21, 24, 25, 44, 53, 55, 84, 105, 124, 152, 153, 156, 158, 163, 164

Women *5, 10, 13-16, 18, 19, 22, 24, 27-31, 34, 35, 41-43, 45, 47, 48, 49, 52, 54-57, 59, 61-64, 67, 68, 71-73, 77, 79-83, 85-88, 90, 93, 98, 99, 101, 102, 106;* 9, 10, 19, 20, 23, 25, 27-29, 32-38, 40, 43, 53, 67, 69, 70, 71, 76, 80, 83, 84, 86-89, 91, 92, 94, 100, 101, 105, 114, 116, 124-126, 135, 140, 148, 159, 160, 161, 196, 197, 216

World Bank *6, 9, 10, 12, 27, 46, 48, 49, 52, 57, 60, 66, 103;* 5, 8, 38-39, 66, 68-70, 72, 103, 114, 118, 133, 136, 140

World Food Programme 23, 24, 26, 30, 31, 32, 148, 196

World Health Organization (WHO) *5, 10, 50, 55, 76;* 124, 137, 143, 196

World Hunger Program 7, 23, 118

World Hunger Year 20, 103, 105

World Summit for Children 103, 104, 110, 159, 160

World Vision *4;* 91, 112, 216

Yemen *37-38, tables;* 7, 60, 142, 150-151, tables, bib.

Yugoslavia 60, 61, 167, 177, bib.

Zaire *3, 56-57, 103, tables, bib.;* 111, 113, tables

Zambia *57, tables;* 117, tables

Zimbabwe *57, 59, 62-64, 102, tables, bib.;* 30, 59, 64, 70, 115, tables

About the Writers

Ana E. Avilés is Program and Administrative Associate at Bread for the World Institute on Hunger & Development. She is a native of El Salvador, and is presently studying in the Department of Foreign Languages at the University of the District of Columbia.

David Beckmann is President of Bread for the World and Bread for the World Institute. Previously he worked at the World Bank, most recently as Senior Advisor on Nongovernmental Organizations. A pastor and economist, he holds degrees from Yale University, Christ Seminary, and the London School of Economics.

Marc J. Cohen is Research Director of Bread for the World Institute. He received a Ph.D. in political science at the University of Wisconsin-Madison with a dissertation on the Carter Administration's food aid to Southeast Asia. Previously, he was Associate Director of the Asia Resource Center.

Kathleen Crowley, a Sister of St. Joseph of Carondelet, is considering working with her community in Peru. Previously, she worked as a Domestic Hunger Policy Analyst for Bread for the World, and worked on the resident job policy as a staff member of the Archdiocesan Human Rights Office in St. Louis.

Patience Elabor-Idemudia is a citizen of Nigeria and a Ph.D. candidate in sociology at the Ontario Institute for Studies in Education, University of Toronto, Canada. She has worked in agricultural education and extension in her country.

Rapti Goonesekere is studying economics and political science at Wellesley College in Massachusetts. A citizen of Sri Lanka, she was a research assistant at Bread for the World Institute during the summer of 1991.

Richard A. Hoehn, Senior Research Associate at Bread for the World Institute, received his Ph.D. in Social Ethics from the University of Chicago with a dissertation on citizen participation in the Model Cities program. He has been a seminary professor and a Bread for the World organizer, and is the author of *Up From Apathy: A Study of Moral Awareness and Social Involvement* and other works.

Remy Jurenas is a specialist in agricultural policy at the Congressional Research Service (CRS), Library of Congress, Washington, DC. The views expressed in his chapter are his own and do not represent those of CRS or the Library.

Jennifer Kennedy is studying sociology and political science at Queen's University, Kingston, Ontario, Canada. Holding dual U.S. and Canadian citizenship, she was a research assistant at Bread for the World Institute during summer 1991.

Patricia L. Kutzner is Executive Director of World Hunger Education Service and the editor of its publication, *Hunger Notes*. She received her Ph.D. from Stanford University, and is the author of *World Hunger: A Reference Handbook*, published in 1991 by ABC-Clio.

LaDonna Mason is a graduate student in social policy at the University of Maryland School of Public Affairs and a graduate of Spelman College. During the summer of 1991, she worked as a research intern at Bread for the World Institute under a grant from the Evangelical Lutheran Church of America's Hunger Program.

John W. Mellor is President of John Mellor and Associates. Previously, he served as Director of the International Food Policy Research Institute, Chief Economist of the U.S. Agency for International Development, and Professor of Agricultural Economics, Economics, and Asian Studies at Cornell University. He is the author of numerous books and articles on agricultural development and poverty alleviation.

Barbara Murock was formerly Director of Community Education for Church World Service and an educator at the Hunger Action Coalition in Pittsburgh. As a volunteer, she assists Bread for the World Institute in designing educational materials.

Don Reeves is Director of Bread for the World Institute. During interludes from his farming career in Nebraska, he has been a policy analyst for the Friends Committee on National Legislation, Interfaith Action for Economic Justice, and Bread for the World. Since 1989, he has directed the Trade and Development Program, sponsored by the Institute and eight other farm and church groups.

Barbara Segal was an International Hunger Policy Analyst at Bread for the World from 1989 to 1991. Previously, she was a Fulbright scholar in Mexico, and received master's degrees in urban planning and Latin American studies from the University of California-Los Angeles. She has worked on development projects in Mexico and Central America.

Maria Simon is a 1989 graduate of Harvard University, and is presently studying at Columbia University Law School. She worked for a year at a community nutrition center in a barrio of Barquisimeto, Venezuela. From February to May 1991, she was a research assistant at Bread for the World Institute.

Gayle Smith is an independent consultant on Africa. She worked with relief programs in the Horn of Africa for a number of years, and has written numerous articles about that region.

Sponsors

Adventist Development and Relief Agency International (ADRA) is the worldwide agency of the Seventh-day Adventist church with the specific purpose of alleviating poverty in developing countries and responding to disasters. ADRA works on behalf of the poor in more than seventy developing countries spanning Africa, Asia, the Middle East, and Central and South America. It does so without regard to ethnic, political, or religious association. ADRA's projects to help the poor include working to improve the health of mothers and children, developing clean water resources, teaching agricultural techniques, building and supplying clinics, hospitals, and schools, training people in vocational skills, and feeding people in countries where hunger is a long-term problem. When disasters strike, ADRA sends emergency supplies and stays in the disaster area to help rebuild.

Bread for the World Institute on Hunger & Development seeks to inform, educate, nurture, and motivate concerned citizens for action on policies which affect hungry people. Based on policy analysis and consultation with poor people, it develops educational resources and activities including its annual *Hunger* report, occasional papers, policy briefs, and study guides, together with workshops, seminars, and briefings. Contributions to the Institute are tax-deductible. It works closely with **Bread for the World**, a Christian citizens' movement of 45,000 members, who advocate specific policy changes to help overcome hunger in the United States and overseas.

CARE is the world's largest relief and development organization not affiliated with a government or religion. Each year, CARE reaches more than 25 million people in thirty-nine nations in Africa, Asia, and Latin America. The organization's work began in 1946, when its famous CARE packages helped Europe recover from World War II. Today, CARE improves health care and the environment, helps subsistence farmers and small-business owners produce more goods, addresses population concerns, and reaches disaster victims with emergency assistance. The scope of CARE's work is broad. But its vision focuses on a single concept: helping people help themselves.

Catholic Relief Services (CRS) is the official overseas relief and development agency of the United States Catholic Conference. Established in 1943 in order to help displaced people in war-torn Europe, CRS now works in seventy-four countries in Africa, Asia, Latin America, Europe, the Caribbean, and the Middle East. CRS exists to serve the poor and disadvantaged throughout the developing world achieve social justice and economic self-sufficiency. Working in partnership with the Catholic church in each country, and with other local partner organizations, CRS provides disaster relief and development assistance throughout the world strictly on the basis of need.

Christian Children's Fund, with international headquarters in Richmond, Virginia, is a worldwide child care agency, providing assistance through individual sponsors to 535,000 children and their families in thirty-five countries. Now in its fifty-third year, CCF has begun new programs in eastern Europe, including Poland, Romania, the USSR and the Baltic states, and the Middle East (Jordan), and has opened international offices in Geneva and Paris. Another new program – ChildAlert – focuses on children considered beyond the reach of traditional sponsorship – children in refugee camps, children victimized by war and AIDS, and children of the streets.

Church World Service (CWS) is a shared ministry of thirty-two Protestant and Orthodox communions working as the service arm of the National Council of the Churches of Christ in the U.S.A. Since its founding in 1946, CWS has responded to requests for relief and development asssistance in more than seventy countries. In partnership with local ecumenical colleague organizations, CWS works with those directly affected by famine, drought, natural or human-caused disasters, and assists in developing long-term solutions. CWS also resettles refugees in the United States.

Coordination in Development (CODEL) encourages collaboration in the development activities of member agencies in Africa, Asia, the Pacific, Latin America, and the Caribbean. Member-sponsored projects in more than forty countries work for community development, agriculture, health care, communication, economic, and development planning. Intrinsic to project planning is the preservation of the environment in developing countries. A seminar program and educational outreach at home focus on the needs of disadvantaged peoples overseas.

Heifer Project International is a nonprofit, ecumenical organization which works to alleviate hunger through providing animals and related assistance to families and communities in need to help them produce food and income on a long-term basis. HPI enables participants, both the donor and recipient, to share resources in ways that enhance the dignity of all and enable everyone to make a difference in the struggle to end hunger. HPI educates people about the reality and root causes of hunger and poverty and the opportunities for alleviating them in our interdependent world, based on experience in using animals in development.

Lutheran World Relief, founded in 1945, acts in behalf of Lutheran Churches in the U.S.A. to "support the poor and oppressed of less-developed countries in their effort to meet basic human needs and to participate with dignity and equity in the life of their communities; and to alleviate human suffering resulting from natural disaster, war, social conflict, or poverty." The agency, which is headquartered in New York City, is geared to respond quickly to requests for emergency assistance and supports more than 200 long-range development projects in countries throughout Africa, Asia, the Middle East, and Latin America.

Mennonite Central Committee (MCC), founded in 1920, is an agency of the Mennonite and Brethren in Christ churches in North America, and seeks to demonstrate God's love through committed women and men who work among people suffering from poverty, conflict, oppression, and natural disaster. MCC serves as a channel for interchange between churches and community groups where we work around the world and North American churches. MCC strives for peace, justice, and dignity of all people by sharing our experiences, resources, and faith. MCC's concerns include: disaster relief and refugee assistance; rural and agricultural development; job creation (SELFHELP Crafts); health; and education.

The Trull Foundation (and predecessor B.W. Trull Foundation) has been interested in educational, religious, cultural, and social programs since 1948. Current priorities: 1. Concern for the needs of the Palacios, Texas area, where the Foundation had its roots. 2. Concern for the pre-adolescent, to direct and channel lives away from child abuse, neglect, and hunger, into an adolescence of good mental and physical growth. 3.

Concern for the Mexican-Americans in South Texas, to help them "catch up," hurdle a language barrier, a poverty barrier, and a system which has consistently kept them poor, uneducated, and unrepresented.

World Vision is an international Christian relief and development organization. Founded in 1950, World Vision today is an international partnership working in over ninety countries. World Vision receives the majority of its support from individual donors, but also works extensively with government, foundation, corporate, and church partners. World Vision seeks to help the poor move toward self-sufficiency through programs in areas such as emergency relief, water development, food security, child survival, primary health care, microenterprise development, and natural resource management. Through these programs, World Vision impacted more than twenty-eight million people in 1990.

Bread for the World

INSTITUTE

On Hunger &
Development

Publications Order Form

Item	Quantity	Cost	Total

HUNGER REPORTS

Hunger 1992: Second Annual Report on the State of World Hunger

Ideas That Work

Hunger and: food assistance programs in the United States, international
food aid and child survival, environmental protection, technology,
demilitarization, grass-roots development and empowerment, creating
market economies without increasing hunger, and public policy advocacy

Regional updates
Africa, Asia and the Pacific, Middle East, Soviet Union and Eastern Europe,
Latin America and the Caribbean, North America

New tables and bibliography *HR92*.. _____ x $12.95 = _____

Hunger 1992 Study Aid by Gretchen T. Hall *HR92ST* .... _____ x $ 3.00 = _____

Hunger 1990: A Report on the State of World Hunger

Forty-two country profiles: Asia and the Middle East, Africa, Latin America
and the Caribbean, United States

Case studies: Bangladesh – Vulnerability to Famine, Militarization and Hunger
in Mozambique, Wealth and Poverty in Brazil, Midwestern U.S.
Farmworkers – Model for Change

Eleven tables of socio-economic statistics

Bibliography, 300 entries *HR90* .... _____ x $ 9.95 = _____

Hunger 1990 Study Aid *HR90ST*.. _____ x $ 1.50 = _____

BOOKS

Harvesting Peace: The Arms Race & Human Need by Arthur Simon
"A persuasive case for seizing the opportunity to reverse the arms race"
(and find common security through meeting human needs).
– Willie Brandt, former Chancellor of West Germany *BK24*......................... _____ x $ 7.95 = _____

Christian Faith and Public Policy: No Grounds for Divorce
by Arthur Simon *BK14*.. _____ x $ 6.95 = _____

Humanitarianism Under Siege: Operation Lifeline Sudan by Larry Minear
Study of a 1989 international effort to provide humanitarian aid to two million
people caught in a civil war in Southern Sudan. "Offers lessons and encouragement as we grope for the appropriate strategies to reach those in need."
– Rep. Tony Hall, Chairman, House Select Committee on Hunger *BK15* .... _____ x $ 9.95 = _____

Bread for the World (revised and updated) by Arthur Simon *BK2*............. _____ x $ 5.95 = _____

Item	Quantity	Cost	Total
Lives Matter: A Handbook for Christian Organizing by Kimberly Bobo BK13	_____	x $ 8.95 =	_____

OCCASIONAL PAPER
Peace, Development and People of the Horn of Africa by John Prendergast and Sharon Pauling BK27 .... _____ x $ 3.00 = _____

STUDY GUIDES/KITS
Food as a Weapon Study Guide: issue brief by Marc J. Cohen, discussion guide, article reprints BK28 .... _____ x $ 2.00 = _____

Exploring the Linkages: Trade Policies, Third World Development & U.S. Agriculture: leader's guide, study booklet, issue briefs, commodity and country profiles LINK .... _____ x $ 5.00 = _____

A Chance to Survive: A Study Course on Child Health (includes slides) BK26 .... _____ x $ 5.00 = _____

Agriculture & Rural Communities: Guidelines for U.S. Policy BK20 . _____ x $ 2.00 = _____

BACKGROUND PAPERS
	Quantity	Cost	Total
Fact Sheet on Hunger BP99	_____	x $ .25 =	_____
Foreign Aid: A Primer BP92	_____	x .25 =	_____
Foreign Aid: Challenges For the Future BP111	_____	x .25 =	_____
The Case for Citizen Action Against Hunger BP83	_____	x .25 =	_____
The Right to Food BP4	_____	x .25 =	_____

BROCHURES
	Quantity	Cost
Bread for the World Institute BROC8	_____	FREE
Hunger 1992 BROCH92	_____	FREE
Hunger 1990 BROCH90	_____	FREE
Humanitarianism Under Siege BROCHS	_____	FREE
Exploring the Linkages BROCLINK	_____	FREE

SUBTOTAL .... $_____
POSTAGE & HANDLING .... $_____
   (Add $3 for orders under $25; $5 for orders $25-$50; $7 for orders over $50; overseas add $2 surface, $5 air)

TOTAL .... $_____

Please make your check payable to **Bread for the World Institute.**
Items available while supply lasts. Prices assured through May 31, 1992.
Quantity discounts available.

NAME _____ DAYTIME PHONE _____

STREET ADDRESS _____

CITY _____ STATE _____ ZIP _____

❏ I would like a complete list of Bread for the World/BFW Institute publications – background papers, citizen action resources, worship aids, bulletin inserts, children's resources, videos and brochures.

Return form to: **Bread for the World Institute**
   Attn: Publications Order
   802 Rhode Island Avenue, N.E.
   Washington, DC 20018

Or call: **(202) 269-0200**
FAX: (202) 529-8546

7/91

Bread for the World
INSTITUTE
On Hunger & Development

Publications Order Form

Item	Quantity	Cost	Total

HUNGER REPORTS

Hunger 1992: Second Annual Report on the State of World Hunger

Ideas That Work

Hunger and: food assistance programs in the United States, international
   food aid and child survival, environmental protection, technology,
   demilitarization, grass-roots development and empowerment, creating
   market economies without increasing hunger, and public policy advocacy

Regional updates
   Africa, Asia and the Pacific, Middle East, Soviet Union and Eastern Europe,
   Latin America and the Caribbean, North America

New tables and bibliography *HR92*.. _____ x $12.95 = _____

Hunger 1992 Study Aid by Gretchen T. Hall *HR92ST* .... _____ x $ 3.00 = _____

Hunger 1990: A Report on the State of World Hunger

Forty-two country profiles: Asia and the Middle East, Africa, Latin America
   and the Caribbean, United States

Case studies: Bangladesh – Vulnerability to Famine, Militarization and Hunger
   in Mozambique, Wealth and Poverty in Brazil, Midwestern U.S.
   Farmworkers – Model for Change

Eleven tables of socio-economic statistics

Bibliography, 300 entries *HR90* .... _____ x $ 9.95 = _____

Hunger 1990 Study Aid *HR90ST*.. _____ x $ 1.50 = _____

BOOKS

Harvesting Peace: The Arms Race & Human Need by Arthur Simon
   "A persuasive case for seizing the opportunity to reverse the arms race"
   (and find common security through meeting human needs).
   – Willie Brandt, former Chancellor of West Germany *BK24*....................... _____ x $ 7.95 = _____

Christian Faith and Public Policy: No Grounds for Divorce
   by Arthur Simon *BK14*... _____ x $ 6.95 = _____

Humanitarianism Under Siege: Operation Lifeline Sudan by Larry Minear
   Study of a 1989 international effort to provide humanitarian aid to two million
   people caught in a civil war in Southern Sudan. "Offers lessons and encouragement as we grope for the appropriate strategies to reach those in need."
   – Rep. Tony Hall, Chairman, House Select Committee on Hunger *BK15*.... _____ x $ 9.95 = _____

Bread for the World (revised and updated) by Arthur Simon *BK2*............. _____ x $ 5.95 = _____

Item	Quantity	Cost	Total
Lives Matter: A Handbook for Christian Organizing by Kimberly Bobo *BK13*	_____	x $ 8.95 =	_____

OCCASIONAL PAPER

Item	Quantity	Cost	Total
Peace, Development and People of the Horn of Africa by John Prendergast and Sharon Pauling *BK27*	_____	x $ 3.00 =	_____

STUDY GUIDES/KITS

Item	Quantity	Cost	Total
Food as a Weapon Study Guide: issue brief by Marc J. Cohen, discussion guide, article reprints *BK28*	_____	x $ 2.00 =	_____
Exploring the Linkages: Trade Policies, Third World Development & U.S. Agriculture: leader's guide, study booklet, issue briefs, commodity and country profiles *LINK*	_____	x $ 5.00 =	_____
A Chance to Survive: A Study Course on Child Health (includes slides) *BK26*	_____	x $ 5.00 =	_____
Agriculture & Rural Communities: Guidelines for U.S. Policy *BK20*	_____	x $ 2.00 =	_____

BACKGROUND PAPERS

Item	Quantity	Cost	Total
Fact Sheet on Hunger *BP99*	_____	x $ .25 =	_____
Foreign Aid: A Primer *BP92*	_____	x .25 =	_____
Foreign Aid: Challenges For the Future *BP111*	_____	x .25 =	_____
The Case for Citizen Action Against Hunger *BP83*	_____	x .25 =	_____
The Right to Food *BP4*	_____	x .25 =	_____

BROCHURES

Item	Quantity	Cost
Bread for the World Institute *BROC8*	_____	FREE
Hunger 1992 *BROCH92*	_____	FREE
Hunger 1990 *BROCH90*	_____	FREE
Humanitarianism Under Siege *BROCHS*	_____	FREE
Exploring the Linkages *BROCLINK*	_____	FREE

SUBTOTAL..$_____

POSTAGE & HANDLING............................$_____
(Add $3 for orders under $25; $5 for orders $25-$50; $7 for orders over $50; overseas add $2 surface, $5 air)

TOTAL..$_____

Please make your check payable to **Bread for the World Institute**.
Items available while supply lasts. Prices assured through May 31, 1992.
Quantity discounts available.

NAME _____ DAYTIME PHONE _____

STREET ADDRESS_____

CITY_____ STATE _____ ZIP _____

❑ I would like a complete list of Bread for the World/BFW Institute publications – background papers, citizen action resources, worship aids, bulletin inserts, children's resources, videos and brochures.

Return form to: Bread for the World Institute
   Attn: Publications Order
   802 Rhode Island Avenue, N.E.
   Washington, DC 20018

Or call: (202) 269-0200
FAX: (202) 529-8546

7/91